# WRECKED LIVES
# AND LOST SOULS

# WRECKED LIVES AND LOST SOULS

## JOE LYNCH DAVIS AND THE LAST OF THE OKLAHOMA OUTLAWS

JERRY THOMPSON

UNIVERSITY OF OKLAHOMA PRESS : NORMAN

Also by Jerry Thompson

*Tejano Tiger: José de los Santos Benavides and the History of the Texas-Mexico Borderlands, 1823–1891* (Fort Worth, 2017)

*A Civil War History of the New Mexico Volunteers and Militia* (Albuquerque, 2015)

*Cortina: Defending the Mexican Name in Texas* (College Station, 2007)

*Civil War to the Bloody End: The Life and Times of Major General Samuel P. Heintzelman* (College Station, 2006)

*Vaqueros in Blue and Gray* (Austin, 1977)

This book is published with the generous assistance of the Wallace C. Thompson Endowment Fund, University of Oklahoma Foundation.

Library of Congress Cataloging-in-Publication Data

Names: Thompson, Jerry D., author.
Title: Wrecked lives and lost souls : Joe Lynch Davis and the last of the Oklahoma outlaws / Jerry Thompson.
Other titles: Joe Lynch Davis and the last of the Oklahoma outlaws
Description: Norman : University of Oklahoma Press, [2019] | Includes bibliographical references and index. | Summary: "Historian Jerry Thompson uncovers the lawless life and times of his grandfather Joe Lynch Davis, a man at the center of systematic cattle rustling, feuding, gun battles, a bloody range war, bank robberies, and train heists in early 1900s Indian Territory and Oklahoma"— Provided by publisher.
Identifiers: LCCN 2019018702 | ISBN 978-0-8061-6436-6 (paperback)
Subjects: LCSH: Davis, Joe Lynch, 1891–1979. | Thompson, Jerry D.—Family. | Outlaws—Oklahoma—Biography. | Oklahoma—History—20th century.
Classification: LCC F700 .T46 2019 | DDC 976.6/053092 [B]—dc23
LC record available at https://lccn.loc.gov/2019018702

The paper in this book meets the guidelines for permanence and durability of the Committee on Production Guidelines for Book Longevity of the Council on Library Resources, Inc. ∞

*In memory of my mother, Jo Lee Thompson*

If you can't get rid of the skeleton in your closet, you'd best teach it to dance.

—George Bernard Shaw

→ ←

# CONTENTS

→ ←

# ILLUSTRATIONS

### Figures

## Maps

# ☙ DAVIS FAMILY ❧

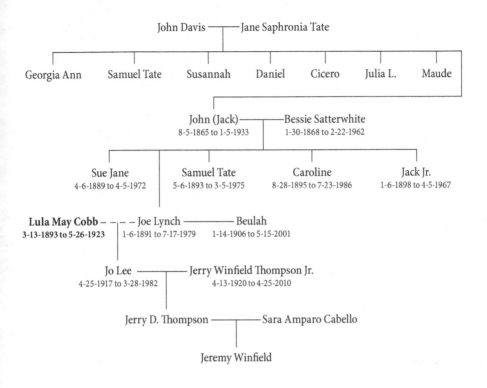

John Davis —— Jane Saphronia Tate

Georgia Ann    Samuel Tate    Susannah    Daniel    Cicero    Julia L.    Maude

John (Jack) ———— Bessie Satterwhite
8-5-1865 to 1-5-1933    1-30-1868 to 2-22-1962

Sue Jane    Samuel Tate    Caroline    Jack Jr.
4-6-1889 to 4-5-1972    5-6-1893 to 3-5-1975    8-28-1895 to 7-23-1986    1-6-1898 to 4-5-1967

**Lula May Cobb** – –│– – Joe Lynch ———— Beulah
**3-13-1893 to 5-26-1923**    1-6-1891 to 7-17-1979    1-14-1906 to 5-15-2001

Jo Lee ———— Jerry Winfield Thompson Jr.
4-25-1917 to 3-28-1982    4-13-1920 to 4-25-2010

Jerry D. Thompson ———— Sara Amparo Cabello

Jeremy Winfield

# ☙ COBB FAMILY ❧

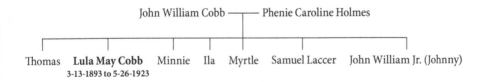

John William Cobb ——— Phenie Caroline Holmes

Thomas    **Lula May Cobb**    Minnie    Ila    Myrtle    Samuel Laccer    John William Jr. (Johnny)
**3-13-1893 to 5-26-1923**

# WRECKED LIVES
# AND LOST SOULS

→ ←

# PROLOGUE

## THAT'S JUST WHAT KIDS DID BACK THEN!

**W**hen my mother died in the winter of 1982, I found seventeen letters, a telegram, and five hand-colored greeting cards in a shoebox in the bottom drawer of an old dresser. Little did I know at the time that the letters would help unravel a long-lost family history of passion, violence, and despair. The letters exposed secrets of a Cherokee diaspora from Georgia to Indian Territory, a time of unimaginable lawlessness, and a grandfather I had never known—a mixed-blood Cherokee cowboy named Joe Lynch Davis. In the early twentieth century Davis was at the center of rampant cattle rustling, deadly gun battles, a bloody range war, daring bank robberies, equally audacious train heists, and prodigious court proceedings, which eventually resulted in fourteen years in Leavenworth Federal Penitentiary.

Coming of age in the mountains of western New Mexico in the 1940s and 1950s, I often wondered why my mother never mentioned her parents. They never came to visit during holidays and were seemingly invisible. As a child I was too young and immature to wonder why. My childhood was filled with more important things. In the old house where we lived there was neither electricity nor indoor plumbing, but the family did possess an old radio that my father plugged into a big battery, and at night the family gathered to listen to the Brooklyn Dodger games. Senator Joe McCarthy said that Communists were everywhere, not just behind the Iron Curtain, and my father seemed to agree. I once became convinced the school bus driver on the rocky route to Pie Town was a Communist. In 1952 Harry Truman declined to run for reelection, and Dwight D. Eisenhower, one of my father's heroes, promised to bring peace to Korea. Polio shots were a godsend at Pie Town Elementary School. I will never forget my mother watching with great anxiety as thirty-six nervous children lined up for vaccinations.

My father heard on the radio that Edmund Hillary and a Sherpa named Tenzing Norgay had reached the summit of Mount Everest, a feat I would re-create repeatedly on a nearby hill. To my great excitement, my father's father thought he had located the wreckage of a UFO that had crashed in some pine and juniper trees near the top of Baca Mesa—but it turned out to be a large silver-colored weather balloon with an attached parachute.

I vividly remember my father and mother driving through a blinding snow-storm to Pie Town, to a movie that featured the Battle of the Bulge, where my father had fought and almost died during the war. During one of the action scenes, with German soldiers dying right and left, a shell-shocked veteran in Pie Town hid helplessly behind a wooden bench in the tiny Farm Bureau building where the film was showing.

A classmate at Pie Town Elementary school gave me a mixed Cocker Spaniel dog that my mother named Rusty. The little brown canine became my constant companion on many an adventure in the woods and mountains. One of my father's cows died. My family life seemed an endless battle just to make ends meet. Life was hard. Many a day there was little more than cornbread and beans to eat.

### Osage Murders

In childhood I came to know my mother's grandmother Phenie Caroline Cobb, a bespectacled, no-nonsense, dictatorial little woman whom my mother adored. My mother was also close to an uncle, a jovial, skinny, delightful part-Cherokee little man named John William Cobb. He had married Mollie Burkhart, a full-blood Osage who had been at the center of the tragic "Reign of Terror" that swept over the Osage Nation in Oklahoma in the early 1920s. From 1921 to 1925, as many as fifty wealthy, full-blood Osage were shot, poisoned, even bombed, by ruthless, greedy white men who were determined to gain control of Osage headrights and lucrative oil royalties. As it turned out Mollie's previous husband, Ernest Burkhart, had even tried to poison her, but unlike her sisters and her first husband, she survived the terror.

After Mollie's divorce from her murderous second husband, Johnny Cobb became her personal chauffeur. Despite a twenty-year age difference, the two were married. There is little doubt that Cobb was attracted to Mollie's money, but she found safety and security in one of the first meaningful relationships of her life. By all accounts their marriage was a happy one, and it brought Mollie a degree of contentment she had never known before. Yet she took to her sickbed at the mere thought of her former husband's release from the life sentence he was serving at the state penitentiary at McAlester, Oklahoma.

Mollie Burkhart and the Osage were heirs to a wealth that was unimaginable to most Americans. Even during the depths of the Great Depression, when most people in the country were lucky to own even one car, every Osage could afford ten cars. In fact, the Osage were said to be the wealthiest people per capita in the world at the time.[1] Cobb told my father how he and Mollie would fill a suitcase with money, board the train at Pawhuska, and travel to distant places until the money ran out before returning home to the Osage settlement town of Gray Horse, on the prairie in southwest Osage County.

Just west of Gray Horse, in the boomtown of Fairfax, in the midst of the Osage Terror, my mother, Jo Lee Davis, came of age and graduated from high school in 1937. She was one of a class of just forty-seven. A month later, Mollie died unexpectedly at the age of fifty, and Cobb moved on, marrying a part-Choctaw widow, Lillian, he met while pheasant hunting in a corn field near Pawhuska. In the waning years of the Great Depression, Cobb headed west with his new wife, away from the tumult of the Osage Nation, and eventually settled in the remote high country of Catron County in western New Mexico, where he purchased a cattle ranch.[2]

### Grandma Cobb

Phenie Cobb (or Grandma Cobb, as she was known to everyone when I knew her), along with my mother, "followed along like bugs," as John Steinbeck wrote in his classic *Grapes of Wrath*. They were part of the seemingly never-ending, poverty-plagued Okie exodus to the West.[3] It was near the small adobe village of Mangas, nestled in the mountains of western New Mexico, that my father and mother met and married in 1941, only months before my father went off to fight in World War II.

Two years before the war my father and grandfather found employment with Johnny Cobb building a ranch house on a small plateau overlooking Mangas Creek. Nearby, they renovated a small two-room adobe cottage where Grandma Cobb lived and tended a small garden. The cottage was within easy walking distance of where I lived with my parents and paternal grandparents in an old log house. I still remember walking hand-in-hand with my mother in the late afternoons, sometimes in knee-deep snow, along a well-beaten path through a grove of piñon trees, across a dry arroyo, and up a small hill to Grandma Cobb's little house. The visits were always exciting, since Lillian and Johnny Cobb's young daughters, Anna and Boodie, were always there. In the winter we built snowmen and threw snowballs. In the summer we romped through the piñon trees playing hide-and-seek, pausing only to help Grandma Cobb harvest vegetables from her garden.

To escape the blistering Oklahoma heat in late summer, Mollie's children from her disastrous former marriage, Elizabeth Burkhart and James "Cowboy" Burkhart, frequently arrived at the Cobb Ranch. They would sometimes stay through the hunting season in early November. Both had witnessed the Osage Reign of Terror firsthand and were ostracized by many Osage because of their mixed blood and their father's hideous crimes. Despite declining oil revenues during the Depression, Elizabeth and James always had big shiny new cars, of which my father was always envious.

Much of the social life at the Cobb Ranch centered around fried chicken dinners, traveling to Pie Town for the movies, and cheering the veterans' baseball team. My father played second base and Johnny Cobb was the center fielder. There were also bone-rattling trips to the summit of Mangas Mountain, where my grandfather worked in the lookout tower during the fire season; two weeks of hunting mule deer and turkey in the fall; picnic excursions in the pine-shrouded mountains in the warming days of summer; and all-night, smoke-clouded poker games.

Not realizing that Johnny Cobb was related to Elizabeth and James by marriage and not by blood, I somehow thought that my mother—since she was a Cobb—had to be part Osage. There was little doubt that Oklahoma had been a large part of my mother's early life. To this day I can still hear her quietly humming an old Woody Guthrie ballad as we walked through the woods:

Many a month has come and gone
Since I wandered from my home
In those Oklahoma hills where I was born.[4]

Long before I found the shoebox letters, there were hints of my grandfather's outlaw past. I have a hazy memory of riding in the back of Johnny Cobb's car at the age of five or six in the late 1940s and hearing him tell my father about a fellow named Joe and his girlfriend, Lula. Everything would have been different, Cobb insisted, had "Joe not spent so much time in the pen at Leavenworth." Since my father and Cobb owned some livestock, I thought they were talking about a cattle pen somewhere. There was also confusion in my mind since my mother's name was "Jo," but I knew she had nothing to do with anyone's cows. Who was this guy named Joe and why had he spent time in a pen at Leavenworth? All I knew was that it had to be somewhere beyond the Continental Divide and the village of Pie Town, the edge of my world at the time.

### Letters in a Shoebox

After finding the shoebox in 1982, I carefully arranged the letters in chronological order and began reading. On September 19, 1952, my mother's aunt Ila Holley wrote to say that someone was desperately trying to contact my mother, and that the Davis family probably wanted to settle an estate. "It must be something concerning your father," she wrote. "May be he is dead & the estate can't be settled until they find you." There were other parts of the letter that were intriguing: "Sign your name Joe Lee instead of Jo," Ila insisted, "because that's the way your father knew your name when you were small."[5]

Grandma Cobb, who had moved with her son Johnny to California in 1948, wrote the same day in her spotty grammar, saying that she was compelled to "wright." She offered a bit of sobering reality: "Jo Lee, I have something to tell you," she said, "Your Father mite have past a Way," and it was likely she would get "some papers to sine." Don't "sine any thing," she warned. "Don't you do it. Til you get [a] lawyer to see to it. You know Jack Davis and Joe Davis did own a lot of land down there in the river bottoms, the other side of Texanna and you know they are getting oil down there and probely that is what she wants to know. Your Daddy might be dead." In fact, it was likely that "Joe has ben dead several years the reason you didn here from him when you rote to him."[6] It was obvious from the letters that my grandfather was named Joe Davis, but where was Texanna? and who was Jack Davis?

Three weeks after the letters arrived from Ila Holley and Grandma Cobb, a woman named Betty Ann Rushing wrote from Madill, Oklahoma, to introduce herself and say that she was the person looking for my mother.

"I hardly know how to begin this letter as we have never met, but I would like very much to know you," she wrote. "It was through some very good friends who helped me, that I was able to get your address," Rushing continued. As it turned out, my grandfather was not dead, as Grandma Cobb had speculated, but was living in Sand Springs, Oklahoma, on the Arkansas River, just west of Tulsa. "I am Joe Davis's niece, the only niece he has, my Mother is his younger sister Carrie," Rushing went on to say. Joe was in very bad health "with gall bladder trouble, and no cure seems to be able to help him." And there was news from Ardmore, Oklahoma, too: "Grandmother Davis is still living . . . and gradually going blind, she has cancer, and it is causing her blindness."[7]

From the correspondence that followed, it became evident that my mother had exchanged letters with her cousin Betty Ann who encouraged her to reach out to her long-lost outlaw father. Rushing had spent considerable effort, she said, "snooping around" to locate my mother. Her letters were full of information on my grandfather, his health, even the clothes he wore, his mannerisms, and the fact that he had recently married a woman named Beulah. But there was one line in a letter that proved tantalizing, yet another clue to the violent past of Joe Lynch Davis. Rushing said that, when she "found out about all of his troubles, we were never allowed to ask him any questions—it is something he never speaks of."[8] Rushing was hoping to see "Uncle Joe" in a few weeks, and she promised to give him my mother's address. But what exactly was the nature of his "troubles," and why was he so sensitive about anyone asking him any questions about his past?

In late November 1952 Rushing sent Davis's address, saying that despite his ill health he still worked for the Charles Page Foundation in Sand Springs. Rushing cautioned secrecy, not wanting Joe Davis to know how my mother had obtained his address. There were other fascinating clues to his violent and troubled past: "How old were you the last time you saw your daddy? Wasn't it just after he got out? I know he thought a lot of you when you were small."[9]

At the bottom of the shoebox were five neatly hand-colored Christmas and birthday cards tied in a bundle. They were all from Joe Lynch Davis to Jo Lee Davis, my mother, and they proved to be even more intriguing. One of the cards was in a small envelope with a 1923 postmark of Fort Leavenworth, Kansas. So Leavenworth was not a cattle pen the other side of Pie Town after all. Moreover, beneath the shoebox in the dresser was an old photo album of individuals I did not recognize, including several images of a cowboy on horseback twirling a lariat. It was obvious that many of the black-and-white photographs were of my mother when she was young, but who was the cowboy and who were all the other individuals?

### A Long-Lost Grandfather

The correspondence between Betty Rushing and my mother continued, off and on, for thirty years. Each time there was more information about my grandfather. The letters from Aunt Ila and Grandma Cobb also continued. "Jo Lee, you were 6 yrs. old when your mother died," Aunt Ila wrote:

> The trouble your father had happened just before you were born. He was accused of [a] train robbery in Arizona [in] 1916 and was sentenced to 25 yrs. But he was pardoned after 14 yrs. He served his term in Fort Leavenworth, Kansas. I never did know whether your dad was guilty of all that trouble or not or whether he was framed. It's too long a story to try to write it, about his ups & downs & notorious life. It goes way back to the wild & wooly cattle days of the west when there was cattle rustling, bank robberies & feuding & everything else, even before your dad was born. What I'm trying to say is—your dad was born & raised right into these feuds. . . .
>
> He seemed to grow right into it. It's a long story . . . everything that happened for miles & miles around the Davises were accused of it. Whether they were guilty or not they were always blamed for it. Cattle rustling, robberies, shootings & killings in those days were common. The feuds were in swing even when your dad was born. Soon as he was old enough to ride a horse he made a hand working with his dad's cattle. . . . I even can remember when they used to ride guard at night to keep people from cutting their fences & turning stock in on them so they would be accused of rustling, etc. . . . So as the feuds died down and your dad grew up & he was still looked on as belonging to the "Davis Gang" or so called "out laws." So he might have grown hard & bitter, with enemies double crossing & accusing them of everything that happened. He might have been guilty of some things but I'll never believe he did all that he was blamed of. I don't know if he did the train robbery in Ariz. or not, or if he ever had a part in it.[10]

Wow! A bank robbery in Arizona? Cattle rustling and feuding in Oklahoma? Any historian worth his salt would be thrilled to get to the bottom of all this. Why had my mother not lived with her father when he got out of Leavenworth, and what exactly happened to my grandmother Lula? This shocking family history was all vague and distant, but it was also part of the larger history of the American West that I had come to love. I placed the letters aside and walked away, but I came back several days later and reread them a second time, and then a third time, just to make sure I was not imagining it all.

A few days before Christmas 1952, Betty Rushing wrote to say that Uncle Joe was coming to Ardmore for the holidays to see his mother who was critically ill, and that she would try to take his photograph, despite the fact he was "very funny about anyone meddling in his affairs."[11] It was also evident from the letters that my mother had indeed written her father, but there had been no response. Rushing suspected that his overly possessive wife, Beulah, had thrown the letters away. Rushing also promised to ask Joe for his birthdate, so my mother could send him a card.

In March 1953 Rushing wrote that Bessie Satterwhite Davis, my great-grandmother, was dead at the age of eighty-five, after a series of strokes and a long bout with cancer. Then the letters abruptly stopped coming. Finally, in October 1963, Rushing wrote my mother again to say that she had not seen "Uncle Joe" in two years. She heard that he was retired and in bad health, even walking with a cane, but there was little other news. In July 1979, twenty-seven years after she had written my mother the first time, Rushing wrote to say that Joe Davis was dead at the age of eighty-eight, and that he was buried in Woodland Memorial Cemetery in Sand Springs.[12]

There was evidence that my grandfather finally communicated with my mother shortly before his death. She had sent him a Christmas card, the first one he received from her, and he responded with a Santa Claus greeting card of his own. On the back was a brief, half-literate note, signed simply, "Love Dad." Davis promised to "write a long letter soon," and he even inquired about the age of his grandson.[13]

The saddest letter in the shoebox was from my mother after she received the news of her father's passing. Although near death with emphysema herself, she wrote Rushing in her usual beautiful penmanship: "It is a shame that I never got to know him or any of his family," she stoically conceded. "But that is the way they were and there is nothing I can do about it now. A person is never ready to receive such news."[14]

### Family Tragedy

At the bottom of the shoebox were two letters from my elusive grandmother Lula, written from Colorado Springs, to her sister Ila Holley in 1923. "When I am gone, give this to Jo Lee, she wants it," Aunt Ila scribbled on the corner of one of the envelopes. While Joe Davis was confined at Leavenworth, Lula married a man named Tom Nelson, but the two had separated and she was seeking a divorce. Lula had been in a "battle royal" with Nelson, she wrote, and "I was cleaned upon proper," Lula concluded.[15]

In a second letter, written a month later, Lula complained that her estranged husband was stalking her in an effort to restore their failed marriage. "He is doing everything to get me back again," Lula wrote, "but I'll beg for something to eat before I'll live with him again." No one, she asserted, knew what she had been through. "I'm sorry for him," she continued, "but I'll never be his wife again. He said he was going to commit suicide. But I think he would take my life before he does his own."[16]

At the bottom of my mother's shoebox there was also a Western Union Telegram stamped 2:36 P.M., May 26, 1923, addressed to Ila Holley in Blackwell, Oklahoma, from Grandma Cobb at Colorado Springs: "Lula was killed today wire if you come."[17] Tom Nelson had walked into the laundry at Beth-El Hospital on Boulder Street where Lula was employed, brandishing a revolver. He shot Lula in the head before turning the gun on himself. As fate would have it, her life ended just as she had predicted. Perhaps few grieved as much as Joe Davis, who was in his sixth year at Leavenworth. After receiving a telegram from Grandma Cobb, he pleaded with the warden to allow him to attend his former lover's funeral. The answer was a resounding no. After all, this was Leavenworth.

All of this unfortunate family history was hard to fathom, even seventy years after the events described in the letters. I could only imagine what Lula's death must have been like for my mother. The last memory she had of her mother, she confessed to a sister-in-law many years later, was of Lula lying in a casket, cold and still in death, with a bullet hole between the eyes.[18] All of this dark and troubling bygone time—hidden for so many years now unfurling like a ribbon—would take years of historical sleuthing and a gleaning of innumerable sources to uncover.

With age and impending mortality comes a growing desire for a better understanding of who we are and where we came from. We yearn to learn more about our ancestors, and we spend hundreds of dollars on DNA tests that trace our bloodlines into the dark and distant past. Public libraries and archives are crowded with senior citizens huddled around computers and microfilm readers, struggling to make sense of their family history. Were those who came before us entrepreneurs, soldiers, farmers, homesteaders, or perhaps Dust Bowl refugees? Did they rob trains and banks, or were they law-abiding citizens like most decent Americans?

After rereading the letters I queried my father, but all he could offer was that my mother never wanted to talk about the Davises, but only of her mother's side of the family—the Cobbs—of whom she was very proud. If she chose not to share any of her family history, that was her business. My father loved her for who she was—a simple Oklahoma orphan who came west with her grandmother during the Great Depression, seeking a better life in the vastness of the American West, just like thousands of other Okies. She had struggled to make the most of her life and to raise her only child with the affection and tenderness that had been so cruelly absent in her own life.

## On the Trail of Joe Davis

I was distracted for over a decade by the toils of teaching and the seemingly never-ending academic pressure of publishing or perishing, but in the year 2000 I finally located Betty Rushing in Madill, Oklahoma, a small windswept farming community in the southern part of the state, not far from the banks of the Red River. After several friendly telephone conversations, we agreed to meet one scorching summer afternoon in the parking lot of the Muskogee Public Library.

Betty Rushing was in her seventies with short gray hair, and her mannerisms and looks reminded me a lot of my mother. She was far gentler than the figure I had conjured from reading the letters, the telephone conversations, and my imagination. In fact, she was bubbling over with energy and exuberance. Her eyes and infectious smile seemed to reflect some of her Uncle Joe's untamed yet tainted spirit. She brought family photographs and happily shared everything she knew about her family—and especially my grandfather who, she insisted, was her favorite uncle.

As her letters had indicated, Joe Davis refused to talk about his outlaw past and his long incarceration at Leavenworth, even in his old age. He was secretive and defensive to the end. Other people tried to interview Davis, but he refused to discuss his troubled past, and the family rarely mentioned his great "misfortune."

"I have spent fifty years trying to forget things that happened," Davis told Olivia E. Myers, who was researching an article she was writing on the Porum Range War in 1971 for *True West* magazine. "I was a kid, and I think I have paid my debt to society. I'd rather forget the whole thing."[19]

Over several days Betty Rushing patiently introduced me to elderly people who had known Joe Davis, including Virginia Vann Perry, who recalled meeting him when he first got out of prison in 1932. She said she once got up enough nerve to press Davis about how he had ended up in prison, but he abruptly cut her off, dismissing all the bank and train robberies as little more than "what kids did back then."[20] Perry was a remarkable individual who knew as much Cherokee history as any scholar. She proudly recalled how back in Georgia one of her ancestors, Joseph Vann, had been the wealthiest man in the Cherokee Nation, living in a magnificent red brick mansion, cultivating three hundred acres of fertile farmland, operating a mill, a ferry, and a tavern, and owning 110 slaves.[21] Perry led me into the genealogy room at the Muskogee Library and pulled a big map book of the Cherokee Nation off a shelf. She showed me all the land the Davis family had once owned in the southern part of Muskogee County. Vann and Davis were two of the biggest names on the Cherokee rolls, and the two families, along with the Starrs, had frequently intermarried, she proudly proclaimed.

### Green Country

Rushing took me to places of Joe Davis's youth and the towns where his bank robberies and courtroom dramas had captivated audiences and grabbed newspaper headlines across Oklahoma. We stopped at the senior center at Porum, a small community on the prairie thirty miles south of Muskogee that had been at the very epicenter of the brutal Porum Range War. For over a decade the area around Porum witnessed back-and-forth revenge killings, assassinations, and flagrant arson that law enforcement officials seemed unable or unwilling to control. During the early years of the Progressive Era, distrust and animosity plagued the southern part of Muskogee County, and the Davis and Hester factions of ranchers and farmers seemed determined to exterminate one another.[22]

At the senior center no one seemed to know anything about the Porum Range War. One older man did remember his uncle once telling him of a deadly gun battle on the edge of town. He described the story of how two outlaws, a cowboy named Davis and a gunman named Starr, had spurred their horses through town, arrogantly shouting and waving their pistols in the air. Some of the seniors seemed pained that Porum had ever been the scene of such violence, as if it cast a shadow of dishonor on their small community. Lincoln County, New Mexico, Tombstone, Arizona, and Dodge City, Kansas, could perhaps turn their gun-riddled past into profitable tourism dollars, but not Porum, Oklahoma.

Driving across the green-shrouded hills and through Porum Gap to the west, we paused again, this time at what little remained of the once bustling village of Texanna, not far from the shores of Lake Eufaula. This was near the place where Jack Davis owned his farm and ranch on the Canadian River, where his son Joe learned to read and write, began to rope and ride, came of age, and fell in love with Lula May Cobb. At a corner convenience store, a friendly young cashier wearing a sweatshirt directed us to an elderly woman living in a trailer home a few blocks away, saying that she knew as much local history as anyone. A short, gray-haired woman in her eighties or nineties appeared at the door and seemed excited to share her family history. She had lived in Texanna all her life and remembered hearing about the Davises. In fact, her father once told her "those damned Davises—they were all a bunch of outlaws."

Although the Davis Ranch was now under the waters of Lake Eufaula, I lingered in Texanna for a time to feel the weight of the history on the land and to try and grasp what life must have been like there a century ago. There is something almost magical about eastern Oklahoma and its heritage of the Five Civilized Tribes. Once we were back in the car on the road to Eufaula, before heading north to Checotah and Muskogee in the heat of the graying Oklahoma dusk, Rushing could only laugh, saying with a giggle that perhaps "those damned Davises" were a bunch of outlaws after all.

Joe Davis was part Cherokee, Rushing revealed. Like so many Oklahomans and her friend Virginia Vann Perry, she was proud of her Cherokee ancestry and the fact that she was on the tribal rolls. "You should go to Park Hill to enroll yourself," she told me excitedly. "All you have to do is prove your family was on the Dawes Rolls."

As it turned out, there was no Osage blood in my family after all. What little Native American blood there was turned out to be Cherokee.

In the years that followed, I made several history-seeking pilgrimages to Oklahoma's majestic green country in an attempt to better understand my grandfather and to walk the ground where he had robbed what seemed to be an improbable number of banks and trains. With her abundant energy, Betty Rushing had no idea she had opened more than one window into the fascinating life of her uncle, the outlaw Joe Lynch Davis, the grandfather I had never known.

### Cherokee Lineage

Over time, beyond the Dawes Rolls and all the other Cherokee records, a much clearer picture of Davis came to light from the prison and parole records at the National Archives in Washington, DC, as well as records at the branch archives at Fort Worth, Texas, Seattle, Washington, Laguna Niguel, California, and Kansas City, Missouri. Davis's banditry was chronicled in at least a hundred small-town Oklahoma newspapers, library holdings, court proceedings, transcripts, and various historical recollections and collections. It was evident that he was no ordinary outlaw. Davis had been at the very center of the bloody Porum Range

War, an excessively violent Oklahoma feud in which at least nineteen men were killed. That was almost as many as in New Mexico's Lincoln County War, the celebrated Johnson County War in Northern Wyoming, or the bloody Graham-Tewksbury genocide in Arizona's Pleasant Valley.

Robbing several trains and banks—and part of the time riding with the notorious Cherokee outlaw Henry Starr, who was the undisputed king of all the bank robbers—Davis left a wide-ranging trail that at first seemed easy to follow. In fact, Davis was one of only two outlaws to escape capture following the spectacular and widely publicized March 1915 robbery of two banks, at the same time on the same day, in Stroud, Oklahoma. As it turned out, Davis robbed more than just a bank in Stroud and the Golden State Limited in the arid and windswept desert of Arizona.[23] Davis held up at least five other trains, mostly in northeastern Oklahoma, and he used dynamite and nitroglycerine to blow up safes. He robbed more than fifteen small-town Oklahoma, Arkansas, and Kansas banks. It was also evident, as Ila Holley had speculated, that he was accused of far more robberies and crimes than he conceivably could have committed.

What was surprising was that Joe Davis came from one of the wealthiest and more influential families in eastern Oklahoma, a family who owned vast tracts of land and possessed considerable economic and political clout. Although there were many Cherokee, even those of mixed blood such as Joe Davis, who hated the railroads and the naked capitalism that gave rise to greed and inequality, Davis was certainly no "social bandit." What led him to a life of lawlessness as a teenager that eventually sent him at the age of twenty-two to Leavenworth to serve fourteen years? To unravel that mystery would take more than casual archival treks to northeastern Oklahoma; it would take two decades of serious historical sleuthing.

It was disconcerting to learn of my mother's painful and difficult childhood. She went through psychological hell in her youth. It was evident why she had carefully concealed any information about her murdered mother and her outlaw father. It seemed likely, as the shoebox letters seemed to indicate, that she never fully understood the degree of her father's troubled life. There was little doubt that witnessing her mother's physical abuse and death at the hands of her violent stepfather haunted her for years, despite the love she received from a compassionate grandmother.

From the beginning of my quest, it was obvious there were gaps in Davis's life that had to be filled in. Although I had completed biographies of several Civil War generals, a Mexican-Texan hero, and a Mexican revolutionary, I was well aware that writing biographies can be difficult. I was also fearful of being consumed by the story of Joe Davis. I was particularly worried about my kinship connection and losing any sense of direction and objectivity.

→ ←

In 1923, when Joe Davis was in his sixth year at Leavenworth, he applied for executive clemency. The Davis family was hoping that Theodore "Ted" Roosevelt Jr., son of the famous Rough Rider president who was assistant secretary of the navy at the time, could intervene with Attorney General Harry M. Daugherty. But Joe Davis was, the attorney general asserted in his terse denial, "equal of Jesse James in his palmist days."[24]

If "half of what has been told of him were true, he had no equal in Oklahoma as a cool, deliberate, and rather nervy bank and train robber," said Thomas A. Flynn of the young outlaw in 1917. Flynn was the US attorney who successfully prosecuted Davis in Arizona (and later corresponded with him at Leavenworth). A miscellaneous newspaper clipping in Davis's Leavenworth prison file seems to affirm such accusations. Davis was, the paper said, "one of the last of [the] really western men of the 'gun-man' variety."[25]

→ ←

A bulletin of the American Bankers' Association described Davis as "one of Oklahoma's most notorious characters." The name Joe Davis always appeared in the records of the association, the bulletin continued, in all the reports of crimes received from agents in Oklahoma. If the "ill deeds of Davis," especially those evil deeds he committed while riding with Henry Starr, "were written in book form they would fill a volume."[26] While the extent of his banditry easily eclipsed that of Belle Starr, the Dalton Gang, the Marlow Brothers, Cherokee Bill, even the James Younger Gang, and other more notorious outlaws, it was surprising there had been no meaningful scholarship undertaken on Davis. His life story certainly seemed worth telling. Without a doubt he was among the last of the Oklahoma outlaws. What follows is the violent and tragic story of Joe Lynch Davis, his many crimes, and the personal price he paid for such indiscretions, first at McNeil Island Penitentiary in Washington State, then during a fourteen-year incarceration at Leavenworth Federal Penitentiary.

# → 1 ←

# DEATH AT A GATE BY A CORNFIELD

I said "Cicero" and he turned to look at me. Then I said
you son of a bitch and I shot him two or three times.

— D. King quoting Mack Alford

**L**ike so many other Cherokee narratives, the history of the Davis family begins in the pine-covered hills and narrow green valleys of northern Georgia, long before most Native Americans ever learned of the Indian Territory or a place called Oklahoma.[1] Although their indigenous blood was thin, the history of the Davis family, in both Georgia and Indian Territory, was tied to that of the Cherokee Nation. At one time the Cherokee numbered as many as forty thousand, and they ranged over a vast area from the Appalachian Mountains in the east to the Mississippi River in the west, and from the Ohio River in the north to the Piedmont of present-day Georgia and Alabama. The English and American conquests of their lands devastated their society, and by the time of the terrible Trail of Tears in 1838, they numbered less than twenty thousand.[2]

Although the Davises were of mixed blood, they easily played themselves off as white and were able to avoid President Andrew Jackson's expulsion. While many of the Cherokee, including those who were forced into a new life west of the Mississippi, were also acculturated into white society and well educated, the Davises had the added advantage of being wealthy and influential.

Family legend holds that Joe Lynch Davis got his middle name from Jeter Lynch, a Cherokee of Gargantuan stature, the son of a Cherokee woman and a German peddler. As a Cherokee chief, Lynch gained a reputation for torturing and hanging lawless Carolina whites who drifted into the Cherokee lands in northeast Georgia. The "Chopped Oak" where Lynch hanged a number of his victims had gashes in the bark where warriors recorded the number of captured scalps with their hatchets.

The Cherokee roots of the Davis family were in Dahlonega in Lumpkin County, in the foothills of the Blue Ridge Mountains, where John M. Davis—Joe Davis's grandfather, the son of Daniel Davis and Rachel Sabre Martin—was born in the Cherokee Nation in 1813. John and his brother Martin later moved to Walker County, in the rugged mountains of northwestern Georgia, just south of Chattanooga, Tennessee.[3]

In northern Walker County, the famous Cherokee chief John Ross lived in a large log house that served as a post office, country store, and schoolhouse. Although only one-eighth Cherokee, like so many other members of the Five Civilized Tribes who became serial victims of America's bad faith, Ross went west on the Trail of Tears and served as principal chief of the tribe and their advocate for justice for over fifty years.[4]

### Escaping the Trail of Tears

Interestingly, John and Martin Davis were married to sisters, Julia Anne and Saphronia Tate. Saphronia was seventeen years younger than John when the couple wed in nearby Cherokee County during the war with Mexico in 1847.[5] A few years before the Civil War, John and Saphronia moved to the western part of Walker County, where they built a dog-trot log cabin and established a farm on the west bank of West Chickamauga Creek. In time, the surrounding farming community became known as Davis Crossroads.[6] Even in Georgia, the Davises always seemed to be moving west.

Nearby, Martin Davis also built a cabin and established a large working farm where twenty-one slaves toiled endlessly to produce as much as two hundred bushels of wheat, two thousand bushels of corn, and one hundred bushels of oats annually. The cash value of the farm in 1850 was five thousand dollars. Martin planted a peach orchard near his house, where he often relaxed and smoked his pipe. It was here among his fruit trees that he died in 1859, still clenching his pipe firmly between his teeth. As Julia and their six children stood by, he was buried on the spot where he died, which became the Davis Cemetery.

FIGURE 1. John Davis in his Civil War uniform. Ambrotype.
*Author's Collection.*

In the 1850 slave census for West Chickamauga, Walker County, John Davis is enumerated as owning ten slaves on a farm of some sixteen hundred acres.[7] Ten years later he and Saphronia are listed as having real estate of five thousand dollars and property, including nineteen slaves, worth nineteen thousand dollars, making him—along with his sister-in-law, Julia Davis, who lived nearby—one of the wealthiest farmers in the county.[8] John and Saphronia Davis raised ten children on the family farm. The eighth child, also named John (called Jack), was Joe Davis's father.[9]

As was the case for many southerners, the Civil War was catastrophic for the Davis family. Thousands of angry men in blue and gray swept over the Davis farms. During the summer of 1863, while John Davis was away at war with the Georgia Volunteers, Confederate cavalry frequently foraged on the property. By early September, rumors reached the farm that a large federal army was on the other side of the majestic Lookout Mountain at Chattanooga and was expected to cross at any time. With the area around Davis Crossroads and Chickamauga Creek abuzz with rumors and scouting forays, John Davis, who had been taken prisoner at Vicksburg but paroled and exchanged, rushed home to remove his slaves outside the reach of President Lincoln's Emancipation Proclamation. As John and his slaves fled to safer grounds, Saphronia and her sister-in-law, Julia, remained behind with some of the older servants.

On September 15, 1863, four days before the bloody Battle of Chickamauga, the Union forces of Major General William T. Sherman's Army of Tennessee began arriving at the Davis farm. Captain Jeremiah C. Donahower, a long-bearded twenty-seven-year-old commander of Company E of the Second Minnesota Volunteer Infantry, thought it less than manly that John Davis would be preoccupied with removing his slaves while having little concern for the "safety and welfare of his wife." Over the next few weeks, Captain Donahower came to admire Saphronia, "an intelligent and handsome woman" who was caring for "three very pretty and interesting children," as well as one "old Mamy, a negress about seventy years of age." When she responded to the captain's rap on her door, Saphronia was informed that the Federals would "occupy her front porch, and that no one would intrude, and that she was quite safe from harm . . . and when bed time came to fear no evil." Saphronia was, Donahower recorded, a "lady and a very frank one," but someone who lived in fear of the Federals and their "rumored cruel and horrible treatment of Southern women." Her greatest concern was not the liberation of the family slaves but that the Davis farm would be confiscated.

"Madam," Donahower assured her, "President Lincoln is a kind and tender hearted man" and "not the rude and boorish man your newspapers picture him, but a big brained and wise man, with a noble soul in his awkward body, and he will not take your land from you, but he will punish the South by subduing it . . . and your thirty-five or more slaves will soon be thanking God for Abraham Lincoln."[10]

After fierce fighting at Chattanooga and Chickamauga and the Confederate defeat on Lookout Mountain and Missionary Ridge in late November 1863, the vast armies in blue and gray moved toward Atlanta. When Atlanta fell to Major General Sherman in August 1864, the Deep South was opened to his indefatigable army in blue. Sherman's scorched-earth march through Georgia to Savannah and his equally devastating trample through the Carolinas did much to end the war.

For the last two years of the conflict Federals remained in the mountains around Davis Crossroads. Constantly foraging for food, they raided the family cellar, taking potatoes, hams, and canned jam. "We are getting along as well as we could under existing circumstances," Mary Davis, Julia's daughter, wrote in March 1864. "Have plenty of Yankees in this cove yet." The Federals "paid us a visit last week and took a few bushels of corn. . . . O, how I wanted to kill some of them," she continued.[11]

### Cherokee by Blood

John Davis, Joe's father, who had no middle name or initial, was born in Georgia at the end of the war on August 5, 1865, two months after General Robert E. Lee's capitulation at Appomattox Court House, Virginia, changed American history forever. The family called him Jack to distinguish him from his father. Like other Eastern Cherokee at the end of the war, the Davises found themselves thrust into an uncertain future. Some in the family looked west, but the Cherokee in Indian Territory had made the mistake of aligning themselves with the Confederacy. Like almost everywhere else in the beleaguered Confederacy, the years immediately after the war were characterized by "disease, death, and displacement."[12] John and Saphronia struggled to manage what was left of their farm. Emancipation meant the loss of most of his wealth, but in 1870 they still had real estate worth nine thousand dollars and personal property of thirty-five hundred dollars.[13]

The Eastern Band of Cherokee, numbering 2,335, was racially and culturally diverse. Yet tensions developed between those who were thoroughly acculturated, like the Davises, and whites who pretended to be Indian or attempted to gain Cherokee rights through intermarriage. Although petitioning for membership in the Eastern Band of Cherokee after the war, many of the Davises turned west and sought adoption into the Cherokee Nation in Indian Territory. With unwelcome intruders a constant problem, Cherokee in the west were leery of any unity with their Eastern brothers. Those hoping to settle in Indian Territory often claimed to be Cherokee citizens because their parents or grandparents had told them they were descended from the Cherokee. In fact many in the Cherokee government worried that large numbers of those in the East who sought membership in the tribe were not Indian at all, but white men "playing the Indian." A turning point came in 1888 when the Cherokee National Council declared that Cherokee citizenship required permanent residence within the Nation.[14]

As early as 1870 the Cherokee National Council agreed to a joint resolution declaring that all the Eastern Cherokee would be deemed citizens, providing they enroll with the Chief Justice of the Cherokee Supreme Court within two months of arriving in Indian Territory and produce satisfactory evidence of being Cherokee. The principal chief, Charles Thompson, declared that all Eastern Cherokee were welcome to "come home," but they must bind themselves to the sovereign land of the Cherokee Nation.[15] Three years later, John Davis left his wife and eight children and headed west to the Indian Territory, where he made application at Tahlequah for Cherokee citizenship. Witnesses testified that Davis was "Cherokee by blood by his mother." When John Davis returned to Georgia, he and his family were tallied on the rolls of the Eastern Cherokee at Cassandra in Walker County.[16] By 1868 the family was listed on the rolls of the Eastern Cherokee in Lumpkin, Georgia. By 1880, when Jack was fifteen and attending school, the family had moved to Cedar Grove in Walker County, Georgia.[17]

## Call of the West

Feeling the call of the West, realizing that their future was in Indian Territory and not in Georgia, and fearful they would not meet the criteria for obtaining lands, the Davises began migrating to the Cherokee Nation in the Indian Territory. One of the first to arrive was Jack's older brother, Cicero. After registering as Cherokee, he moved on to Colorado where he remained for eighteen months, seeking employment, before he returned to the Cherokee Nation.[18] Three other brothers—Samuel, Daniel, and Robert—went west and were able to obtain land. Both Samuel and Robert played a significant role in the history of eastern Oklahoma; Daniel disappears from the record.

As the Davises gradually arrived in Indian Territory, railroads were being built across the territory—especially the Missouri-Kansas-Texas Railroad (MKT), which was to play a large role in the young Joe Davis's outlaw years. These railroads were changing the lives of the Cherokees. The MKT (the "Katy") reached the northern boundary of Indian Territory in 1870 and received the first permit to build across the territory. Angling through Vinita and then Muskogee, the Katy was built through Checotah and across the Canadian River, just west of Texanna, before reaching McAlester and then progressing south past what is today Durant, across the Red River, and finally to Denison, Texas.[19] Despite the fact that the railroads brought an exciting new mode of transportation, many of the Cherokee resented the iron rails crossing their lands. It was yet another government intrusion into their lives that greatly accelerated the settlement of indigenous lands by thousands of unwelcome white settlers.

Although the white "intruders" were forced to pay a head tax for permission to live in the Cherokee Nation, they were viewed as aliens. In Cherokee matters they could not vote, hold office, serve on juries, or participate in tribal politics. Some of the newcomers, especially those who settled along the Canadian River in the southern part of Muskogee County, were fugitives from the law, and the Cherokee and Choctaw called them "Criminal Intruders." By 1900 thousands of whites occupied hundreds of small farms throughout Indian Territory in a land that was intended for Native Americans.

Jack Davis, Joe's father, rode west to the Indian Territory for the first time in 1881 and settled on the Canadian River near the small village of Texanna.[20] Here the old Texas Road—known as the Osage Trace in the early days—stretched north to St. Louis and south across the Red River into Texas. Originally an Indian highway, the trail carried trappers, traders, and settlers into Mexican Texas and, after 1836, more settlers into the newly established Republic of Texas.[21] Later referred to as the Shawnee Trail, the road next carried vast herds of Texas cattle north across Indian Territory to Kansas and Missouri.

### Younger's Bend

All along the Canadian River, especially at Younger's Bend east of the Jack Davis ranch, in the area around Briartown, five miles south of Porum, the countryside was rugged and broken with dense vegetation, trees, and caves. The densely wooded area became "a place for the rustler, the law defier, and the criminal"—a perfect haven for those fleeing the law.[22] The area's most famous resident was Belle Starr, born Myra Belle Shirley in Carthage, Missouri, in 1848. Starr had an illegitimate child with the outlaw Cole Younger before marrying Jim Reed, a horse thief. Upon Reed's death she moved to Younger's Bend and became involved in all kinds of illegal activities. It was here that she met and married a Cherokee outlaw, Sam Starr, and after his death in 1886 she wed Jim July, a Creek Indian. Her friends the notorious Jameses, Youngers, Reeds, and Daltons were frequent visitors to the area. On February 3, 1889, Starr was killed by an unidentified assailant on a remote road not far from her farm. In death she became larger than life—a legend, especially among the Davis family.

Following the genocide and their expulsion from Texas in 1839, a few Cherokee established a village around a large spring near what later became the village of Texanna.[23] A few years before Jack Davis arrived, the Cherokee had built a one-room log schoolhouse near the community. The logs were carefully hewn, and there was a rock fireplace at one end of the school. Cherokee children sat on split log benches with no backrests. Two miles southeast in the forest was an old Indian burial ground on a hill.[24] Nearby was a ferry on the Canadian River that was used by both immigrants and cattlemen. As late as 1900 Texanna had little more than one hundred citizens, most of them Cherokee. There were no African Americans in the community, and few in the general area. Tucked away in the forest in the extreme southwestern corner of the Cherokee Nation, the small community had a Baptist church and a Methodist church, a school, two physicians, a general store and cotton gin, two blacksmith shops, and a notary.[25]

One settler remembered Texanna as "a thriving little inland town . . . located on the Old Ft. Smith and Guthrie trail."[26]

Most of the farms in the area grew cotton, and by the turn of the century the cotton gin in Texanna was doing an annual business of a hundred thousand dollars. For fifty cents one could catch the daily stage that carried the mail to Checotah, twelve miles northwest in McIntosh County. Here family members frequently boarded the Katy Railroad for Muskogee.[27] Nine miles south of Checotah was Eufaula, the county seat of McIntosh County. Both communities would take center stage in the complicated life of Joe Lynch Davis.

### Jack Davis and Bessie Satterwhite

At nearby Webbers Falls on the Arkansas River, Jack Davis met and fell in love with Bessie Satterwhite. The two were married in a civil ceremony there on May 2, 1888.[28] After the death of her parents in Newberry, South Carolina, Bessie had gone west with relatives to Indian Territory. She was tough as nails, hardworking, nurturing, proud, and defensive of her family. She and Jack made the perfect couple. With the help of a midwife, five children were born to the couple at the ranch near Texanna. The oldest child, Sue Jane ("Susie" as she was known to the family), was born on April 6, 1889. Joe Lynch followed on January 6, 1891. A younger brother, Samuel Tate, came into the world on May 6, 1893, and Joe's favorite sister, Caroline ("Carrie"), was born on July 23, 1896. The last child, John Jr., was born on January 26, 1898, but he was seriously handicapped with cerebral palsy and was barely able to talk and walk. Jacy, as he was called, remained an invalid and could always be seen by his father's side.[29]

When he was twenty-seven Jack Davis received a letter at Texanna from Walker County, Georgia, saying that his father had died on February 3, 1892, at the age of seventy-nine. His mother, Jane Saphronia, lived for another twelve years. She frequently traveled west to visit her sons. When she died at the age of seventy-nine in May 1904, she was put to rest beside her husband in the family cemetery at Davis Crossroads in the mountains of northern Georgia.[30]

When the Davises first arrived in Indian Territory, much of the land was communally held and tribal members were allowed to occupy and use as much land as they could fence or cultivate. The Davises came to occupy vast grasslands and raised huge herds of cattle. The brothers—Cicero, Jack, Sam, and Robert—employed either whites or blacks as ranch hands or tenant farmers. At the same time the Davis brothers and other large ranchers, it was reported, were forced to "resort to greater extremities to protect themselves." In the process they employed

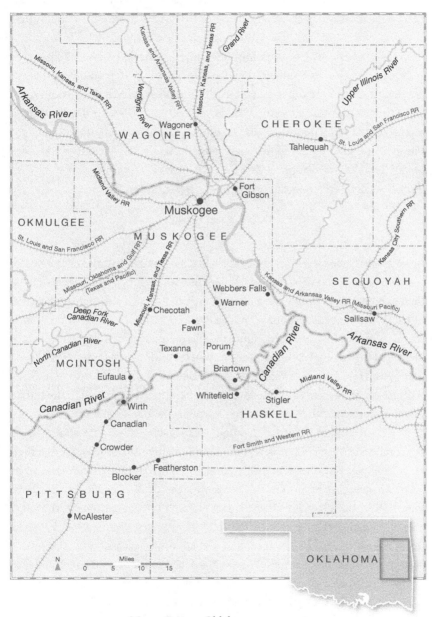

**MAP 1.** Eastern Oklahoma, 1900–1915
*Map by Carol Zuber-Mallison*

"a band of cut-throats willing at all times to do their bidding." Here, along the Canadian River, "was produced professional assassins who for a stipulated price guaranteed the death of an enemy." These organized bands would eventually turn on one another, and "this feud country grew to be a veritable hell."[31]

In 1894 the Dawes Commission to the Five Civilized Tribes established its headquarters north of Younger's Bend at Muskogee. Located on the crest of the prairie four miles from the Arkansas River, Muskogee was a thriving community at the time, with more than three thousand citizens, and within a few years it had the largest black population in Oklahoma.[32] The commission undertook the enormous task of helping to negotiate new treaties, enroll tribal members, and assign individual land allotments. Many Dawes applications were rejected when the petitioners were unable to prove they possessed Cherokee blood.

### Dawes Commission

On March 1, 1901, when Joe Davis was only nine years old, he rode north with his father to Muskogee where Jack appeared before the Dawes Commission to give oral testimony and enroll himself and his five children. When Jack first appeared in Muskogee, he correctly told the commissioners that he was one-eighth Cherokee. In 1910, when it became more advantageous to be Cherokee, he told the census enumerator that he was seven-eighths Cherokee and his children were fifteen-sixteenths Cherokee.[33] Although the family took pride at being mixed blood and were enumerated on the US and Cherokee census as such, their pride in being Native American seems to have developed more after they moved to the Indian Territory in the decades from 1870 to 1890 than when they were still in Georgia.

At the time of his Dawes application, Jack Davis was not sure of his age but thought he was thirty-six, having been born in either 1864 or 1865. He had lived in the Cherokee Nation since 1881, he testified.[34] He had no certificate of marriage, but he was sure that his union with Bessie was recorded in the clerk's office in the Canadian District. Jack provided the ages of the children and the years they were born, but he did not have proof of birth for the youngest child, Jack Jr. When he was asked why he was not on the 1889 Cherokee rolls, Jack explained that he was in school in Georgia at the time. He was listed, nevertheless, on the 1886 and 1894 Cherokee pay rolls and the tribe's census rolls of 1890 and 1896.[35] Like many others, Jack Davis's application was suspended, and he was placed on a "doubtful card" until he could produce evidence of his marriage and the birth of his youngest child. Jack would return to Muskogee on October 4, 1902, with the information, and a few months later, his application was formally approved. He and his children were officially enrolled as members of the Cherokee Nation and given tribal numbers. Joe Lynch Davis, ten years old at the time, was No. 506 (Cherokee by Blood).[36] Bessie Satterwhite appeared before the Dawes Commission that same year, on October 4, 1902, to give her sworn testimony and apply for citizenship by marriage. Bessie was thirty-four and had lived in the Cherokee Nation for fourteen years, and she and Jack had been together since they were married.[37]

Since the Supreme Court of the Cherokee Nation had admitted John Davis as a member in 1871 and the family appeared on the Cherokee census, the Dawes Commission declared the family "Cherokee by Blood." But Jack and his brothers remained uncertain as to how much the family were really Cherokee. Either they did not know the full extent of their Cherokee blood or they were prone to exaggerate. For example, Cicero Davis in 1900 asserted that he was fifteen-sixteenths Cherokee, while Sam Davis and Jack Davis reported they were seven-eighths Cherokee, yet Jack in 1901 told the Dawes Commission (correctly) that he was only one-eighth Cherokee. Another time, Cicero said the brothers were only one-sixteenth Cherokee.[38]

### Eastern Cherokee

On May 28, 1905, the US Court of Claims decided in favor of the Eastern Cherokee in a case entitled *Eastern Cherokee vs. United States*, and the following year Congress appropriated more than one million dollars for the claims. Guion Miller, a Maryland-born, forty-year-old lawyer and special agent of the Interior Department, began compiling a roll of all Eastern Cherokee who were alive in 1906 and who could prove they were legitimate descendants of the Eastern Cherokee. Jack Davis was one of 45,847 applicants representing over 90,000 claimants. In July 1909 Jack not only applied for himself and his four eligible children, including Joe Lynch who was sixteen at the time, but for all his aunts and uncle. He noted on the application that he had previously drawn Cherokee money at Webbers Falls and that all the children except John Jr. had drawn "Strip" money in May 1896.[39] Jack also pointed out that his grandfather Daniel Davis had his property, including a gold mine valued at $13,558, destroyed by the US Army in 1830. Daniel had lived in the Cherokee Nation for a time in 1835. Jack also noted on his application that his father had been on the Eastern Cherokee payroll in 1851.[40] Although thousands of applicants were rejected, on June 10, 1909, Jack Davis, and his four eligible children, along with 3,203 other Eastern Cherokee, were successfully enrolled.[41]

When it came time for the division of the land, Jack Davis and his children received a large tract of over 480 acres on the north bank of the Canadian River in the Canadian District. It was here that Davis lived for almost two decades, in the far southwestern corner of the Cherokee Nation. The land was across the river from the Choctaw Nation and just downriver from Standing Rock, where the Cherokee Nation faced Creek lands to the west. Each member of the family, excluding Bessie, received eighty acres. All of the land was adjacent, but for some unexplained reason, in addition to land on the river, Joe received forty acres located a mile to the northwest, near Texanna.[42] Other family members received lands where they had also established ranches. Samuel Davis and his Cherokee wife, Lucinda, received a plot of land one mile north of Porum as well as a tract of land on the Canadian River just east of Jack's ranch, while Cicero was given land four miles northwest of Porum. The youngest brother, Robert, also received a piece of land near Porum. At the time, the land was valued at anywhere from $2.00 to $6.50 per acre, and no Cherokee citizen was granted property worth more than $320.00. Consequently, some Cherokee received 160 acres while others received as little as 50 acres.[43]

Joe first learned to read and write at the family ranch from a tutor hired by his father. But as he grew older he rode horseback to the old Cherokee log schoolhouse at Texanna. Each year, according to the *Cherokee Advocate*, Joe was allotted seventy-five dollars for the cost of his schooling. When the census enumerator arrived at the Davis Ranch near Texanna, in Township 10 of the Cherokee Nation in the summer of 1900, Jack gave his occupation as "farmer." The census taker noted that the oldest children, Susie, Joe Lynch, and Sam Tate, were all "at school."[44]

## A Place Called Porum

More important for Joe Davis than any other community was that of Porum, eleven miles northeast of the family ranch, said to be named after John Porum Davis, a rancher, Civil War veteran, and Cherokee Nation council member from the Canadian District. In the early days a pass through the mountains west of the town provided easy access to Texanna. A town site was first platted in 1903 halfway between the Davis and Starr ranches in anticipation of the building of the Midland Valley Railroad, which arrived two years later, connecting Kansas City with Fort Smith, Arkansas.[45] Located on the prairie thirty-one miles south of Muskogee, Porum had a population of one thousand by 1910. At that time the town had a weekly newspaper (the *Porum Press*), Baptist and Methodist churches, two banks, telephone and telegraph service, two saloons, four lawyers, two physicians, blacksmith shops, barbershops, a hardware store, and a large commercial

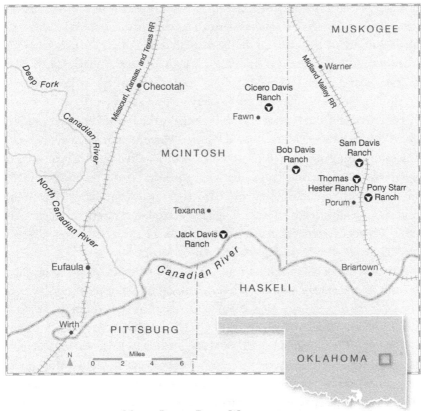

MAP 2. Porum Range War, 1905–1912
*Map by Carol Zuber-Mallison*

hotel. The community served as a trading point for the rich valleys of both the Arkansas and Canadian Rivers. The area was predominantly agricultural, with most farmers harvesting wheat, corn, or cotton. Ranching, primarily of beef cattle, also flourished. In time Porum was bragging that it was the "biggest little town in the West."[46]

It was on his father's ranch on the Canadian River that Joe Davis came of age, learned to break horses, brand, dehorn, castrate, and buy and sell cattle. It was a tough and demanding life and he loved it. By the time he was a teenager, he was already one of the best steer ropers in the region, competing at fairs and roping competition throughout eastern Oklahoma.

An old family photograph shows Davis as one of the older children in attendance at the Baptist Cherokee Mission in Tahlequah around 1905.[47] Four years later, a newspaper has Joe Davis attending Jones Academy near Hartshorne, a school for the Choctaw in southeastern Oklahoma, at the foot of the Ouachita Mountains, where he was a star on the baseball team.[48] A decade later he would tell prison officials and census enumerators, perhaps out of embarrassment, that he completed his high school education. This is far from certain, however, and his surviving correspondence seems to defy such an assertion.[49]

His prominent uncle Cicero Davis ran the large Circle-Bar Ranch, seven miles from Russell and seven miles south of Warner, where he branded as many as one thousand cattle every year. By 1900 Cicero had acquired hundreds of acres of good farm and ranch land, plus as many as 2,500 head of cattle, 23 horses, and 160 hogs. His ranching and banking interests were valued at one hundred thousand dollars (the equivalent to several million dollars today).[50] Cicero was referred to as the "Cherokee cowman," and he and his daughter Nannie were frequently seen striding the streets of Muskogee, Checotah, or Porum.[51]

Another one of Joe's uncles, Samuel Davis, the oldest of the Davis brothers and the most influential, owned the Half Circle Ranch four miles northwest of Porum at the foot of Black Haw Mountains. Sam Davis also branded as many as one thousand head of cattle annually.[52] He invested not only in ranching and farming near Porum but in banking and real estate as well. He was undoubtedly one of the wealthiest citizens in the area. He built a large white two-story house on the north side of Porum that was one of the nicest homes in the area. As early as 1894, the brothers were spotted on the streets of Muskogee with their mother and their sister Susanna, who were visiting from Georgia.[53]

Sam Davis was married to Lucinda Starr, who was nine years his senior and the daughter of Tom and Catherine Reese Starr.[54] Lucinda's brother Thomas Starr Jr. had a son, the gun-wielding Samuel Saguila "Pony" Starr, who in time became Joe Davis's steer-roping partner and closest friend. Pony was the oldest of ten children and nineteen years older than Joe. Over time no one was more closely allied to the Davises. In 1900 Pony Starr hired Eliza Catherine "Cassie" Horn to help him raise his younger brothers and sisters. Within a year the two were married, and the couple had two children of their own, Sophie and Nina Lois.[55]

## Open Range

When the Davis brothers first came to Indian Territory, the range was open. In the spring they sent their cowboys out to purchase cattle. Before the days of checkbooks, the cowboys stuffed several hundred dollars in their boots and strapped on a trusty .45 caliber Colt pistol. "This was a great cattle country in

FIGURE 2. Cicero Davis was known throughout eastern Oklahoma as the "Cherokee Cowman." He was murdered near the entrance to his ranch on September 11, 1906. A neighbor, Mack Alford, bragged of the murder and was brought to trial, twice, but was acquitted only to be assassinated himself ten months later. Cicero Davis is buried in Oak Cemetery in Fort Smith, Arkansas. *Author's Collection.*

those days," one cowboy remembered, "open range covered with blue stem prairie grass that grew as tall as a horse's back." There were no farms on the prairie, and barbed wire was an evil invention far in the future. All the cowboys participated in the fall roundup and were in the saddle for as long as three months. They rode for miles, usually south across the Canadian River as far as the Winding Stair Mountains, where they gathered thousands of head of cattle and swam the animals back across the river to the home range to be branded. Frequently, all the ranchers within miles would throw in together for the fall roundup.[56] During such roundups there were always plenty of beans, beef, and biscuits. The cowboys also feasted on deer, turkey, and even prairie chickens. It was during one of the roundups when Joe Davis and Pony Starr met and became close friends.

Problems developed when the ranchers began branding cattle that were not theirs. According to one report, the Davis brothers gained the "reputation for a quarter of a century of systematic cattle stealing, and the death of anyone who might be witnesses against them." Jack Davis, in particular, came to be known in law enforcement circles in Muskogee and McIntosh Counties as a "consistent violator of the laws" and a "terror to officers."[57]

For the Davises, the allotment of land meant an end to the open range. Although they were content to obtain titles to their land, they deeply resented the division of their big ranches, where they had freely grazed their cattle for decades. Many of the cowboys were now without jobs and some became outlaws. Some of the citizens in the southern part of Muskogee County were certain that the outlaws outnumbered the peace officers, and that it was only a matter of time before the desperadoes would overrun both the Indian and Oklahoma Territories. Bill Tilghman, a leading law enforcement officer at the time, was familiar with Jack Davis and his son Joe. It was in Indian Territory, Tilghman said, "that the bad men of the nation congregated." The outlaws were "reckless and desperate apostles of criminal liberty," he continued, "ready at all times to commit any crime on the calendar." Many were "horse thieves, cattle rustlers, and train robbers."[58]

### Lawlessness

Even before Joe Davis took up the outlaw trail, bank and train robberies were common in the Indian Territory. Bands of outlaws, usually well armed, easily overpowered train crews, dynamited bridges and train tracks, robbed express cars, and held up passengers, frequently making off with thousands of dollars. Bands of Cherokee and Creek lawmen often roamed over the land, looking for outlaws and horse thieves. These were not times for the timid. One of the more notorious outlaws in the Canadian District was Sam "The Verdigris Kid" McWilliams, who for a time was part of the Bill Cook Gang, mostly black men with Indian blood. McWilliams was ruthless and shot anyone who got in his way. The gang robbed stagecoaches, stores, banks, and railroads. They spread terror throughout eastern Oklahoma. In April 1895 the "Verdigris Kid" and members of the gang rode into Braggs, a small town nine miles south of Fort Gibson where they robbed a general store and shot up the town before a posse of marshals arrived and killed the nineteen-year-old McWilliams.[59]

A year earlier, after two members of the Bill Cook Gang had stolen a horse from Jack Davis (who at that time was a deputy marshal, on the right side of the law), Davis and two marshals tracked the outlaws to the home of a farmer named

John Bigsby. When the gang arrived at the Bigsby home, they concealed the stolen horse in the smokehouse and ordered Bigsby's wife to prepare something to eat. When the posse arrived a few minutes later, a gun battle ensued. Davis was shot in the shoulder and left for dead, but he was dragged into the Bigsby home and given a cup of coffee by the outlaws. When he refused the outlaws began cursing him and warned that if he did not drink the coffee they would kill him. He was still defiant, and one of the outlaws whipped out a pistol and blew a hole in Davis's right foot. In pain and bleeding badly, Davis drank the coffee. After the outlaws fled, Bigsby took Davis to a physician who dressed the wound, but it was months before he fully recovered. Several weeks after the incident, Davis was limping about in Texanna and was in good humor about the incident. The coffee "never tasted so good in all his life," Davis joked, especially when you have "a bullet lodged under your shoulder blade and a hole through your right foot."[60]

While riding through Younger's Bend in the summer of 1897, Jack Davis and a friend found the skeletons of three men. One skeleton had a bullet hole in the head, a second man had his skull crushed, while the remains of a third showed no signs of violence. That same year "Uncle Jack Davis," as he was known to many, noticed that someone had taken a large amount of wheat from his barn. Hurrying after the thieves, Davis caught them within hours and had them bound over to the grand jury.[61]

Two decades after Jack Davis established his ranch and farm on the Canadian River, the violence in the southern part of Muskogee County and nearby McIntosh County became so bad that he moved his family to Muskogee, where he bought a fashionable house on south Third Street, just south of the Midland Valley Railroad station. In Muskogee the family could enjoy a social life and escape the violence they had experienced on the Canadian River.

### Mack Alford Feud

Exactly who started stealing whose cattle first is uncertain. What is certain, however, is that by 1905 cattle rustling around Texanna, Eufaula, Checotah, and Porum had reached epidemic proportions. Law enforcement officials were either unwilling or unable to stop it; perhaps they were even complicit in the thievery. Here lay the origins of the bloody Porum Range War.

At the center of the early violence was a mixed-blood Cherokee named Mack Alford. Born in Alabama in 1870, Alford moved to Van Buren, Arkansas, with his father when he was only a child. At fifteen he came to the Indian Territory, where he married a Cherokee woman named Maggie and eventually settled in the timbered country four miles south of the Cicero Davis Ranch, in the hills northwest of Porum.[62] Illiterate and the father of seven children, Alford initially joined the Davises and worked to rid the country of the thieves and rustlers who were roaming the countryside stealing horses, cattle, mules, and anything else on four legs.

According to Alford, the Davises were frequently on the wrong side of the law, however. "I got to know so much about and seeing them with stolen property, they got afraid of me and wanted me out of the way," Alford confessed to a cell mate when he was jailed in Muskogee in 1906. Alford claimed that the Davises formed a gang that killed several people. If Alford is to be believed, in November 1884, Jack Davis received three hundred dollars from Sam Davis for killing a fifty-two-year-old man named James Simmons, simply because Simmons knew too much. Robert Davis allegedly told Alford that Jack Davis had lured Simmons out of his house to "have a friendly talk" but then "shot him in the back of the head." Cicero and Jack Davis were both indicted in the Western District of Arkansas, which included the Indian Territory at the time, for murdering Simmons, but they were never convicted.[63]

At about the same time, Alford claimed that Cicero Davis paid a man named John Seehorn to kill Charley Hufman, to whom Cicero owed seventeen thousand dollars. Shortly after Hufman's murder, Seehorn went to work for Jack Davis. A few months after that, he was found riddled with bullets and shotgun pellets. His body was taken to the Jack Davis ranch, cut open, filled with rocks, and tossed into the deepest part of the Canadian River.[64] Seehorn's property, including his saddle,

FIGURE 3. Porum around the time of the bloody range war. *Author's Collection.*

FIGURE 4. With money in ranching and banking, Sam Davis became the wealthiest of the Davis brothers. He was largely responsible for posting bail money in the frequent arrests of his brother Jack Davis and his nephew Joe Davis. Largely as a result of the Porum Range War in the southern part of Muskogee County, Davis sold his banking interests and his land and moved to Tahlequah, where he died on June 23, 1917, at age sixty-six. *Author's Collection.*

horse, and some money, was divided between members of the Davis Gang, which included Tuck Thornberry, Ben Graham, and Sam Shadrix. In some ways the Davis Gang was never really a gang, as the circle of associates constantly changed when new recruits joined and older hands fell afoul of the law or switched sides.

If Alford is to be believed, Jack and Cicero Davis also put out a contract on a man named Watt Ashley who was privy to too many of their crimes. Shadrix was hired by the Davises to kill Ashley. In turn he hired two men to do the dirty work, and they shot Ashley from ambush but only wounded him. Determined to kill Ashley, Shadrix went to Wagoner and bought a gallon of arsenic that he intended to pour into the well at the Ashley cabin. Alford claimed that he dissuaded Shadrix from such an evil act, arguing that Shadrix would kill the entire Ashley family, and if it became known who was behind the murders there would be a general lynching. Jack and Cicero Davis also put up $250 for anyone who would kill Harve Linsey, another Davis enemy. Not long thereafter, Linsey was shot by a man named Bill Hoover, and his body, like that of Hufman, was weighed down and dumped in the Canadian River. At this point in the bloodshed Alford became so fearful that he, too, would be killed that he fled to Mexico and hung out around the port of Tampico until it was safe to return. At the same time, Alford admitted, he himself was determined to kill Cicero and Jack Davis, as well as Tuck Thornberry and Ben Graham, before they killed him. Back in Oklahoma, Alford staked out the Jack Davis ranch and the Canadian bottomlands until he learned that Jack Davis was in Muskogee. He then decided to assassinate Cicero Davis, but Cicero, too, proved elusive.[65] By 1906 the hatred between Alford and the Davis brothers was well known throughout Muskogee County.

When the Graham brothers, Ben and Peter, broke with the Davis Gang, Alford formed a gang with the brothers and began rustling cows, some of them from Jack and Cicero Davis. His house in the brush northwest of Porum became a well-known hangout for rustlers and gunmen. Cicero Davis knew that Alford and his gang were stealing his cattle, and he put his cowboys on the alert, even having them ride the range at night. Cicero Davis also offered a reward for anyone caught stealing his cows and he advertised the fact in local newspapers.[66]

### Spivey Murder

In many ways the feuding that became the Porum Range War accelerated with the murder of George W. Spivey, an Alabama-born bachelor and farmer who rented property from Alford. Spivey lived in a crude log cabin in one of the more isolated spots in Muskogee County. It was widely rumored that he carried a large amount of cash in a money belt and that more money was hidden in his house. Alford confessed that he went with Bob Davis and the Davis Gang to Spivey's house shortly before midnight on December 31, 1903, to rob the old man, but a fight ensued and Spivey was killed. His body was saturated with coal oil and the house was burned to the ground. A neighbor by the name of Counts found the smoking embers of the house the next morning, along with Spivey's burned and blackened torso. Spivey had several bullet holes in his skull. Deputy US Marshal W. Frank Jones was sent from Muskogee to investigate the murder.[67]

Since eyewitnesses had seen Alford near the Spivey house the previous day, Marshal Jones immediately suspected him and staked out his house, hiding in the brush until the right moment to make an arrest. At about three in the afternoon, Jones spotted Alford going to his barn. With revolver drawn he met Alford as he exited the barn. Frightened, Alford dropped his gun, insisting that he was innocent of any murder. Jones yelled at Alford's wife to bring him his hat, and the two men rode to Checotah to catch the train to Muskogee where Alford was

**CICERO DAVIS' BRAND**

FAWN. I. T.

No cattle sold this side of the market. Range in the Cherokee and Choctaw nation Will pay a reward of $100 for the conviction of any one stealing my cattle.

FIGURE 5. Advertisement of Cicero Davis's brand, with reward for stolen cattle.

thrown in jail. During the entire trip Alford refused to talk, but Jones was sure that he knew who the other members of the gang were (including Ben Graham, Hack Thornberry, and Bob Davis), but he did not have enough evidence to arrest them. Not long thereafter Alford was indicted for the murder of Spivey at Eufaula.[68]

When Alford agreed to turn state's evidence and testify against the other members of the gang, Bob Davis, Thornberry, and Graham were arrested.[69] Alford admitted being party to Spivey's murder but claimed that he only held the horses while Davis, Graham, and Thornberry performed the deed.[70] "I heard a couple of shots and they all came running out and Bob Davis had the money, but he didn't divide it that night. It was three whole weeks before Bob got around to dividing it," Alford confessed. "There was only $1,500 or so . . . Bob claimed."[71] The murderers robbed and then shot Spivey several times in the head before pouring kerosene on his body and burning down his house around him, Alford claimed. One of the members of the gang, Sam Shadix, later testified that Alford pleaded with him to testify against Bob Davis, and that Alford was determined to "stick him" with the murder.[72]

Once Alford was acquitted of the murder in September 1906, the Davis family claimed that he was emboldened to steal even more cattle from Cicero Davis. The bitter feelings seemed to reach renewed heights when Alford applied for a bank loan in Warner and Cicero Davis used his influence to have the loan denied. Cicero warned anyone who would listen that the country was full of "desperate characters living in the vicinity who would not stop at doing anything." A few days later, Cicero Davis was riding with his wife in a wagon on a road near Warner when he ran into Alford, who was armed with a Winchester rifle. Alford leveled the gun at Davis's head, saying he was going to blow "his dirty brains" out, but Sidney Davis begged pitifully for her husband's life, and Alford failed to "carry out his evident intentions." Because of the increasing violence Cicero bought a magnificent, two-story home in Fort Smith, Arkansas, where his wife, Sidney, and their three daughters, Rachel, Nannie, and Christie, spent much of the year. The wealthy Davis also had plans to purchase another home at Fayetteville, where his teenage daughters could attend the university.[73]

## Death of Cicero Davis

On September 11, 1906, forty-seven-year-old Cicero Davis hitched up a double-team buggy and drove his family to Russell, where they boarded the morning train for Fort Smith. Leaving the team in a livery stable Davis decided to accompany his family as far as Stigler before returning on the evening train to Russell. Late in the afternoon, after saying goodbye to his wife and daughters, he retrieved his horses and buggy and set out for the seven-mile ride back to the ranch. On a dark and lonely stretch of road, near a cornfield at the entrance to his property less than a mile from where he lived, he stopped to open a wire gate. Three rifle shots suddenly rang out and the rotund Davis, struck in the chest, crumpled to the ground. Field hands working nearby heard the shots and the cries of a man in agony and rushed to the scene, only to find Davis dead in a pool of blood.[74]

Responding to "one of the most cold-blooded crimes perpetrated in Indian Territory," a heavily armed special posse headed by Deputy Marshal James Franklin "Bud" Ledbetter left Muskogee on the Midland Valley Railroad at ten o'clock that evening in pouring rain. Ledbetter was already a legend in the territory, having years earlier fought off the infamous Cook Gang when they tried to rob the Katy Flyer just north of Muskogee. He had also shot it out with the Al Jennings Gang and killed or captured the entire gang. Jack Davis had little doubt that Alford murdered his brother. He warned Ledbetter that if he did not arrest him, Davis would go to Alford's farm and "kill him before noon." It was still raining when the train carrying the posse pulled into Warner at midnight. Within minutes the men set out for the Davis ranch with a pack of bloodhounds, arriving at two in the morning.[75]

The bloodhounds were unable to pick up any scent in the rain. However, near the road behind a row of entangled shrubs, by the gate where Cicero Davis had fallen, the deputies found where the grass had been trampled down and trod upon. Someone had walked nervously back and forth on the grass and weeds, obviously waiting to ambush Davis. Perhaps more importantly and despite the rain, Ledbetter and his deputies were able to follow a set of well-defined footprints past Davis's cornfield, up the banks of a small creek, through Alford's cornfield and directly to his secluded farm. As the deputies surrounded the farm and crept closer, Alford was spotted calmly sitting on his porch, his rifle standing nearby against a wall. Realizing that the deputies had his house surrounded, Alford made no move to escape or resist. He was arrested along with two of his workers, Bud Roberts and D. King, who were digging a shaft near Alford's house looking for gold. The three men were placed in a buggy and taken to Checotah, where they were shackled in chains, put on the Katy night train to Muskogee, and thrown in the federal jail, charged with first-degree murder. As the prisoners and their guards approached the murder scene on the way to Checotah, one of the men turned to Alford and remarked, "Well, here is where that awful deed happened." Alford hung his head and fixed his eyes to the ground.[76]

At Fort Smith Sidney Davis was shocked with the chilling news of her husband's murder. A special train of the Midland Valley Railroad was chartered by the Davis family and sent to Fort Smith to pick up the grieving family. Sidney Davis and the children hurried west to Warner where Cicero's body had already been prepared for burial. She and her three grieving daughters, who were "terror stricken," then escorted the remains east. Davis was buried in the City Cemetery at Fort Smith.[77] His murder "created a sensation in Indian Territory at the time because of the dead man's prominence, wide acquaintance and high connections in the Territory and Arkansas," the *Checotah Times* reported. Disgusted with the bloodshed in Muskogee County, Sidney sold her husband's ranch and moved permanently to Fort Smith.[78] On September 26, 1906, the same day that the "Great Commoner" William Jennings Bryan arrived to the cheers of thousands in Muskogee, it was announced that Alford, despite his meager finances, had retained two of the more prominent and able criminal attorneys in Muskogee: W. M. Cravens, and Cravens's nephew, Samuel Morton Rutherford.[79]

## Alford on Trial

On October 5, all three men—Alford, King, and Roberts—were indicted for murder. The case was transferred to Eufaula on the grounds that it was nearer the scene of the murder, and the trial of the three men began on February 21, 1907, six months after Cicero's death. They were led into the small courtroom at McIntosh County Courthouse in chains. The clanking and rattling of the chains could be heard throughout the courtroom as Alford did his best to smile at the jury.[80]

Determined that Alford should hang, the Davises employed a special counsel to assist seventy-one-year-old US Attorney William Moore Mellette. To determine if Davis had been murdered with a shotgun, it was agreed in a preliminary hearing that his body would be exhumed from the City Cemetery in Fort Smith. The defense appointed Muskogee physician Dr. J. L. Blakemore to examine the body while the prosecution named E. L. Halsell, a well-known Muskogee County rancher and Davis relative, to assist Blakemore. On September 28, 1906, the body was exhumed and was found to be in an amazing state of preservation. Davis was full of shrapnel, not shotgun pellets, and it was concluded that he had been shot with a hollow-point bullet, just as Alford bragged. "That man Alford," Halsell said after examining the body, "was the worst sort of fiend." He had not only been "satisfied to kill Davis with an ordinary rifle ball but must use one which would blow his body to pieces." Moreover, Halsell complained, Davis had been shot in the back.[81]

The first witness for the prosecution was Cicero Davis's nephew C. S. Dunagan. Son of the oldest Davis sister, Georgia Ann Davis Dunagan, he was baling hay near the scene of the murder when he heard three shots in the direction of the main road. He rushed to the scene, where he found Davis lying dead in a pool of blood and an unspent 30-30 Winchester cartridge on the ground nearby. Dunagan sent a runner for assistance while he followed the tracks of the assailant for several hundred yards, in the direction of Alford's house. Sam Shadix testified that on the day of the murder he went to Alford's house at about ten in the morning, with the intention of borrowing a hay rake, and stayed for lunch. Shadix said that on several occasions Alford had threatened to kill Cicero Davis, and that he was bitter that Davis had prevented him from getting a bank loan in Warner.[82] Deputy Marshal Frank Jones told the jury that Alford once told him that Davis "needed killing." One of the members of the posse testified that Alford told a Cherokee boy that he was determined to kill Cicero Davis, as well as his brothers, and that he did not care what happened to him personally. "My old scalp isn't of much account anyway," he said.[83]

John Shadix also testified that Alford said he was not only going to kill Cicero Davis but Jack Davis as well. He said he would kill the Davis brothers before they killed him. Shadix had seen Jack Davis in Checotah and warned him that Alford was out to get him. Annie King, wife of D. King, was in the midst of testifying when the prosecution suddenly announced that the government was dropping the charges against her husband and Bud Roberts. The two men had agreed to turn state's evidence, and they were escorted out of the small courtroom and taken to an adjacent room. Annie King testified that she saw Alford, rifle in hand, leaving his house in the direction of Cicero Davis's place at about two o'clock in the afternoon on the day of the murder. He returned at about half past five, and King overheard Alford tell his wife not to get excited if a crowd of men came to the house to arrest him. Seventeen-year-old Clarence King, brother of D. King, backed up what his sister-in-law said. Hill Miller, Alford's brother-in-law, testified that he heard Alford make several threats, including the comment that he would "land Cicero Davis in hell." John Shadix's brother Sam claimed that Alford tried to get him to testify against Bob Davis, Tuck Thornberry, and Ben Graham, to "stick them" with the murder of Old Man Spivey. When Sam arrived at Alford's house, Alford told Shadix he was going to kill Davis, and that three days earlier he had hidden in the Davis orchard and shot at Cicero but missed. He went two days later in the afternoon to where he knew Davis would be returning home and would open the gate to his property, but Sidney Davis was with her husband at the time. At about five o'clock in the afternoon of the murder, Alford called John Shadix aside and said, "It's all off. I got him; I killed him." Alford confided to Shadix that he shot Davis three times, once with an expanded bullet that gave the indication that someone had used a shotgun.[84]

### No Damn Bloodhounds on Earth Can Track Me

Although Chester Pitts was convicted of larceny in Arkansas and had served jail time, he was allowed to testify for the prosecution. He quoted Alford as saying, "I am going to ditch that [Cicero Davis]. I've got Sam [Davis] right where I want him. When I get Cicero, I'll have things right where I want 'em. I've got just about enough of Cicero Davis knocking against me." Another local resident, Tom Conger, testified that Alford offered him two bits a head for all of Cicero Davis's cattle he could kill. D. King, who was living on Alford's place at the time of the murder, testified that he was sinking a shaft looking for gold and was blasting with dynamite and black powder. King recalled several instances of Alford threatening to kill Cicero. Alford admitted shooting at Cicero from the Davis's orchard only days before the murder, King said, but his aim was poor and he missed. On the day before the murder Alford had gone to the corner of a cornfield near the gate to Davis's property to kill Cicero, but Davis's wife and children were with him. Alford asked King to come to his house on Tuesday because he intended to kill Davis and needed an alibi. Moreover, King said, Alford had taken his rifle and left, headed northeast toward Davis's Circle-Bar Ranch, saying that he was going to kill Davis. "Mac, don't you know they'll track you with blood hounds?" King said. "No damn bloodhounds on earth can track me. I'll put rags and Cheyenne pepper on my feet," King remembered Alford saying.[85]

The prosecution introduced as evidence some coarse canvas, Cheyenne pepper scented rags that King said looked like those Alford had in his possession on the afternoon of the murder. When Alford came home at about five in the afternoon, he told King, "I got him this time. It's all off." The two men had walked together down to a small creek near the farm, and Alford related how he had used a special "explosive bullet" to kill Davis. Alford told King that he had lain in wait and when Cicero got out to open the gate by the big cornfield, he yelled out his name. Cicero looked around, saw Alford, threw up his hands and "hallowed," as Alford shouted out, "You dirty old————!"[86]

The defense worked hard to impeach King's testimony, forcing him to admit that his memory was bad. King, who had been a detective at one time in his life, seemed unable to explain why, if he knew Alford planned to kill Davis, he had not warned Cicero or done anything to prevent the murder. The defense claimed that King told his wife that Jack Davis had agreed to pay him a dollar for every day he spent in jail if he would "stick Mack Alford." One of the Davis Gang, Ben Graham, had shot at him, Alford told King, and he was sure it was at Cicero Davis's insistence.[87]

Much of the testimony led the *Checotah Times* to conclude that Alford was doomed. A "cruel chain has been drawn tighter and tighter around the man's soul." The testimony had stripped "bare the prisoner's heart, a heart not beautiful to gaze upon, foul in its moral decay." Alford appeared to be on the verge of a nervous breakdown. "In the upper outside pocket of his coat he carries a memorandum to which he frequently refers," but as he "lifts his hand to reach this paper his fingers visibly tremble and the sheet flutters in his hand. He bites his lips continually to hide their quiver," the *Checotah Times* went on to say. Courtroom spectators had no doubt that he was guilty and he would probably hang. Yet there was another side to Alford. "The gaze that he directs at every witness, seemingly frank and honest, almost boyish, may in itself, save his life, so strongly does it impress the jury," the *Checotah Times* continued.[88]

There was little doubt that the feud—which some saw as a fight between powerful, influential, and ruthless land barons and defenseless, poor, and impoverished farmers—had spilled over into the small courtroom and the prejudices of the jury. Many of the less fortunate sympathized with Alford and resented the Davises' arrogance and money . The feud was exemplified by two girls who sat next to one another on one of the crude courtroom benches at Eufaula. One was pretty, dressed in the latest fashion, her dress "smacked of style and smartness." She was the daughter of Cicero Davis. The second girl was dressed in "an old hat, her clothes were soiled and torn. Her face was darkly tanned. Tears welled in her big, brown, pathetic eyes." She was the daughter of Mack Alford.[89]

The defense introduced a long list of character witnesses, all of whom testified that Alford was a kind and gentle family man incapable of committing such a horrendous crime. After eleven hours of heated deliberations and closing arguments over what seemed to be overwhelming testimony that Alford was guilty of premeditated murder, on March 7, 1907, the jury reported they were helplessly deadlocked. The judge declared a mistrial. At the time, the jury stood seven for conviction and five for acquittal.[90]

After a change of venue, a second trial began in the US district court in Muskogee on May 1, 1907, with a new judge and the courtroom packed with family members and spectators. The contentiousness of the case had spread far and wide, and the first panel of potential jurors was exhausted, with only nine men seated. Witness for the prosecution Deputy Marshal Bud Ledbetter, despite objections from the defense, was sent into the Muskogee streets to find more jurors. Eventually five farmers, two salesmen, a real estate agent, a machinist, and three older retired men were seated. The trial was, the Muskogee press proclaimed, the "greatest murder trial of recent years in Indian Territory." The murder of Cicero Davis, the newspaper went on to say, was undoubtedly one of the worst in the history of the Indian Territory.

As they had done in Eufaula, the defense argued from the beginning of the trial that two men, one of whom had a shotgun, had committed the crime. Moreover, they worked hard again to impeach the testimony of D. King, the prosecution's lead witness. Alford was targeted, Rutherford and Cravens argued, by the Davises ever since he had turned state's evidence against Bob Davis in the Spivey murder case. Unlike the first trial, the prosecution led off with Sidney Davis, the murdered man's widow, who tearfully recalled her September 11, 1906, fateful journey to safe haven in Fort Smith, only to receive a telegram that her husband had been assassinated. The shirt of the murdered man was shown to the jury and the grieving widow sobbed uncontrollably as she recalled having washed the blood from the shirt and carefully sewn it back together after it was cut from the body of her dead husband. Sam Davis also identified his dead brother's shirt and answered questions relating to Cicero's fatal wounds.[91]

In the afternoon Bud Ledbetter, the legendary lawman, testified for two hours about how he had rushed to the scene of the murder, and under spirited cross examination, how he had followed the footprints in the rain from the murder scene to Alford's house where he arrested Alford, King, and Roberts. Ledbetter said he had carefully examined the gate and the post at the murder scene, and there was no evidence of any buckshot. He also recalled that when Alford was arrested, he had turned to his wife and children assembled on the porch of their cabin and said to them, "Remember we were here all day yesterday, remember that."[92]

### A Shot from the Orchard

On May 3, with hail and rain rattling the roof of the courthouse, D. King took the stand. Under a rigorous cross-examination, he seemed to stand up much better than he had in Eufaula. "I went up to Cicero's place today to kill him and took a shot at him from the orchard but didn't get him," King remembered Alford saying, "but I'm going after him again." On the day of the murder, Alford came home about 5:30 P.M. and told King, "I've got him this time. It's all off. I got him at the big gate by the corner of the cornfield. He came driving up and got out to open the gate. I said 'Cicero' and he turned to look at me. Then I said you son of a bitch and I shot him two or three times." The defense introduced several letters King had written Alford when they were incarcerated in Muskogee. Although he admitted the handwriting was similar to his, King asserted that the letters were forgeries.[93]

General Dunlap, a gunman and former deputy marshal in Crowder City, was a new witness for the prosecution. He had shared a cell with Alford at Muskogee, and he remembered the defendant saying he "killed the son of a bitch and I'm going to beat the case, too." In response, the defense alleged that Dunlap was a disgraced gunslinger and outlaw and the worst of criminals, and his testimony was little more than carefully crafted lies. Testifying for the defense, Jim Coggins, R. B. Lang, and Jim Morris all said that they had heard King brag that Jack Davis would pay him a dollar for every day he spent in jail if he would agree to testify against Alford. Davis had even agreed to give King five hundred dollars if Alford was convicted.[94]

One of the letters King had written while in jail seemed to confirm that Jack Davis had promised him five hundred dollars, and King warned that if Davis did not come through with the money he would defend Alford on the stand and tell the truth. Dave Coggins, a farmer who lived near Alford and admitted he was a friend of his, said that he had gone to see Alford on the day of the murder to lease some land. At about three in the afternoon, he met the defendant three-quarters of a mile from Alford's house in the opposite direction from where Davis was murdered, and the two men went into an orchard, ate some apples, and talked for over an hour before Alford headed south to check on some hogs he was raising.[95]

Susie Alford, the fourteen-year-old dark-haired daughter of the defendant, swore that she was eating watermelon with her father at the time of the murder. She also complained that Tom Conger, a witness for the prosecution, warned her that if she lied on the stand she would go to prison for perjury. Another daughter, thirteen-year-old Fannie Alford, told how she and her older sister, Susie, left the family farm on horseback to get some soda at a grocery store about a half-mile from their farm. They had returned and had gone into the cornfield to get some roasting ears, and it was there they met their father standing under a blackjack tree. He asked them to fetch a ripe watermelon. They sat in the shade of the tree from about four to five o'clock, leisurely consuming the watermelon, when they heard men's voices on the other side of the hill, about two hundred yards away.[96]

For many in the courtroom, the daughters seemed sincere. It appeared that the defense had firmly established a viable alibi in the minds of the jurors. The defense also put several witnesses on the stand to impeach the testimony of General Dunlap, whom the attorneys emphasized had been charged three years earlier in Muskogee with bootlegging. They all agreed that Dunlap was immoral, a criminal, and a chronic liar. One witness said that he was in a cell with Dunlap in Eufaula when the gunman confessed he thought the government was trying to smear Alford.[97]

Late on the afternoon of May 12, after almost two weeks of harrowing testimony, charges, countercharges, motions, counter-motions, the second Alford murder trail finally came to an end. The trial was "one of the longest and most sensational ever held in the Western District" of the Indian Territory, the Muskogee *New State Tribune* commented.[98] Some thought the final verdict would come down to whether the jury believed Alford's two daughters and if they were really eating watermelon with their father at the time of the murder. Asked what they would do if there was another hung jury, prosecuting attorneys vowed to retry the case.

Few had any doubts, especially the Muskogee, Checotah, and Eufaula reporters who covered the trial, that Alford was guilty. After days of suspense and long deliberations that lasted well into the night, the blurry-eyed and fatigued jury stumbled into the courtroom and delivered a verdict of "not guilty." A hush went through the handful of stunned spectators, but Alford "never moved or made any expression," the *New State Tribune* reported.[99] Despite a pile of contrary evidence, the jury believed the two young Alford daughters after all. Somehow, they were more credible than the long list of prosecution witnesses the Davises had helped the government amass. The Davises were bitterly disappointed. They had put a lot of effort and money into convicting Alford, and they had few doubts he killed

Cicero. Sidney Davis and the three daughters wept, and Jack Davis and other members of the extended family were furious. Quietly they vowed bloody revenge.

However, the acquittal did not lead to Alford's freedom nor to an end to his legal problems. Within hours of being pronounced innocent, he was arrested and charged with the murder of Old Man Spivey, who had been shot three years earlier. Once again, he was confined to the federal jail at Muskogee. In the second week of June 1907, out of desperation and thinking he would never get out of jail, Alford attempted to break out. He had been given liberty outside his cell, and with a knife, he tried to dig and cut his way through one of the walls. He succeeded in removing several bricks before being caught.[100]

Surprisingly, only weeks after his failed escape, on Saturday morning, June 29, 1907, when Alford's attorney submitted an application for release from prison, US Attorney William Mellette agreed to the motion of *nolle prosequi*, which amounted to a dismissal of charges by the prosecution. Looking pale and ill after ten months in jail, Alford stumbled into the sunlight and the bustling Muskogee streets a free man.[101] After studying the case carefully, federal prosecutors concluded that, since the government had used Alford as a witness in the Spivey murder case against Davis and Graham, it could not legally prosecute him for the murder.

### Bloody Vengeance

"What are your plans?" a newspaper reporter asked Alford. "I am going home," he said, smiling, "and when I get there I am going to farm and try to catch up again. I am going home on the Flyer and will eat dinner in Eufaula." Alford was timid and insecure and "extremely backward in talking," the newspaper went on to say. All his problems, Alford contended, grew out of an old feud that had "been in that section for a long time."[102]

From the time he returned to his farm, Alford must have known he was a marked man. With Cicero Davis's murder he had signed his own death warrant. Rumors around Porum were rampant that the Davises were out to get him. Alford concluded that the only way he could survive was by once again fleeing to Mexico. It was too late in the year for planting. His farm was in ruins. He was discouraged, penniless, and in constant fear of assassination.[103] The family began packing their belongings in two large farm wagons they intended to drive all the way to the Rio Grande.

On July 4, accompanied by two neighbors and his eleven-year-old son, Robert, Alford decided to make the six-mile trip to Porum in one of his farm wagons to help celebrate the holiday and buy some last-minute supplies, including a large quantity of steel cartridges. Meeting City Marshal A. M. Edwards on the main street in Porum, Alford said that all he wanted was for the Davises to leave him alone. They had spent a fortune prosecuting him and he was hoping to end the feud. Many in Porum had not seen Alford for almost a year because of his long imprisonment. They were fearful that with his presence, the violence would erupt again. Those individuals who had testified against him in court were particularly concerned.[104]

Late in the afternoon, as the sun set low over the hills west of Porum, Alford headed back to his farm, a Winchester across his knees. He had just reached a narrow lane in a heavily timbered area near a small creek, a mile from his farm and a half mile from where Cicero Davis was murdered ten months earlier, when three shots rang out in rapid succession. The first shot struck him square in the head, ripping into his brain, while the second and third bullets tore into his chest. Alford tumbled out of the wagon into the road a dead man.[105] The shots had come from a clump of bushes that skirted the road, yet no one saw the assassins, only hearing the sound of horses galloping off into the darkening distance. One of the men in the wagon, R. D. Lung, raced off to Checotah to inform Deputy Marshal W. Frank Jones of the murder. To delay the news of the murder, someone cut the telegraph wires about a mile north of Porum, near Sam Davis's mansion. Law enforcement officials who finally arrived on the scene claimed that the assassins were all well "known about Porum as wild and desperate characters."[106]

The day after the murder, Alford's forty-year-old wife, Maggie, and the family's four children arrived in Porum in tears, beseeching authorities to apprehend the murderers. Alford's brother also rode into Porum, complaining that armed men were riding around his brother's farm shooting at random and scaring off his tenants and hired help. Ironically, in Porum at the time, there was an "elaborate production" glorifying the life of the "most interesting character that American history had furnished"—Jesse James.[107]

In Muskogee, a special grand jury was impaneled that began investigating the Alford murder. On the streets it was rumored that indictments were only days away. The names of the murderers were certain to surprise everyone, it was said.[108] But the indictments never came and the murderers, if they were indeed known, were never arrested, although anyone with any knowledge of the Davis-Alford feud knew that Jack Davis and his brothers were certain to have had something to do with Alford's murder.

### Samuel Saguila "Pony" Starr

Within weeks the Alford murder case was pushed off the front page of Muskogee and area newspapers by the murder trial of Samuel Saguila "Pony" Starr. The thirty-five-year-old mixed-breed Porum rancher, farmer, and gunman was one of the gutsiest members of the Davis Gang. His grandfather the notorious Tom Starr was the individual who named the twisted timbers along the Canadian Younger's Bend after his friend Cole Younger. Starr grew up in Briartown and Younger's Bend, and he had rustled cattle with the Davises for almost a decade. For a few years he had also been a Muskogee County deputy sheriff. Starr ran a cattle ranch less than a mile northeast of Porum, and he operated a large farm three miles south of town where he grew some of the best corn, oats, alfalfa, and cotton in the territory.[109]

A loyal and well-to-do member of the Davis Gang, Starr was in constant trouble. At one time, five rustling cases were pending against him in Muskogee County alone. Found guilty in one of the cases, Starr was given a year in the state prison at McAlester, but he appealed the case to the Oklahoma Supreme Court. In October 1908, the appeal was rejected.[110]

Starr was charged with killing the twenty-five-year-old farm laborer Bob Covington in the woods near Porum on the morning of July 7, 1907, the day before Alford was assassinated. "Perched on Papa's Knee Tot Cheers Pony Starr on Trial for His Life," one Muskogee headline screamed, while noting "a large crowd of Indians are in attendance."[111] The "Tot" was Starr's five-year-old-daughter, Nina Lois.

Covington had been shot twice, once in the head and once in the neck. Starr was the only suspect because of the raging feud in and around Porum and a report that Covington and Starr were quarreling. Starr hired Samuel M. Rutherford, who had successfully defended Alford and who everyone agreed was the best criminal lawyer in Muskogee County. Rutherford had obtained several continuances in the case, arguing that he needed time to subpoena witnesses. When the case finally came up in the federal district court in Muskogee, several potential jurymen were excused, since they had already formed an opinion in the case or were opposed to the death penalty.[112] With a jury finally seated, the government brought forth at least thirty witnesses. Several said that they had seen Starr near the scene of the murder. Evidence also matched the tracks at the scene of the murder with Starr's horse. The prosecution produced a piece of thread recovered from a bush near the scene of the murder that was said to have come from one of Starr's saddle blankets. All the prosecution testimony was riveting but largely circumstantial. There were no eyewitnesses to the murder.

In Starr's defense Rutherford called forth a lengthy line of character witnesses, including the mayor of Porum and a deputy sheriff. All agreed that Starr was a moral, decent man who was not capable of committing such a horrendous murder. The prosecution countered that several of the witnesses for the defense had criminal records. As Joe Davis sat quietly in the gallery, other defense witnesses testified that, on the morning of July 3 at the time Starr was said to have committed the crime, Covington was observed illegally selling whiskey at a picnic near Porum. Others said they had seen Starr's horse on July 3 and the horse had not been shod, and so could not have made the tracks as alleged by the prosecution. Rutherford argued that Starr was the victim of a conspiracy, and that there were individuals, including relatives, who were out to get him and they would say anything to put him behind bars or see him hang.[113] The jury began deliberations late on the evening of November 6, 1908. Many in attendance who sat through all the sessions of the court had few doubts that Starr would be acquitted. The evidence was simply too contradictory and circumstantial. After the jury took time for dinner, they returned to the court to deliberate, and shortly before midnight pronounced Starr not guilty. The "verdict gives general satisfaction to the people of the community," the Muskogee press commented.[114]

### Thomas Luther Hester

After the Alford and Covington murders, the killings continued in the southern part of Muskogee County. Members of the Davis Gang frequently turned on one another. For example, in February 1909, Sam Shadix shot and killed Tuck Thornberry. At one time, both had been loyal members of the Davis Gang, and both had been implicated in the Spivey murder.[115]

As the feuding evolved into a larger conflict than anyone could have previously imagined, the opposition to the Davis brothers solidified and came to be led by Thomas Luther Hester, a merchant and rancher at Porum whom everyone out of respect referred to as "Judge." Like the Davises, Hester was born in Georgia. He gathered a large and loyal following in and around Porum, mostly small farmers, many of them members of the Anti–Horse Thief Association (AHTA). As early as 1906, the thirty-five-year-old Hester filed charges at Fort Smith against Sam Davis for cattle rustling.[116] In the years that followed, Hester filed case after case against the Davises, and they retaliated with filings of their own. With every new case, the violence and hatred seemed to intensify. Many around Porum, Texanna, and Briartown were forced into choosing sides. Either they were with the Davises or they backed Hester and the AHTA.

Hester branded his cattle TLH, while one of the brands the Davises used was the window sash. Hester claimed that the Davises consistently stole his cattle and simply used a running iron to connect the letters over his brand. The Davises, especially Jack and Joe, either increased the size of their own herds or shipped the animals off to markets in the north.[117]

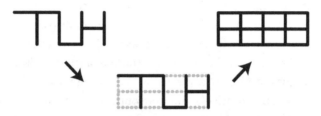

FIGURE 6. Illustration of Thomas Luther Hester's brand alteration.

All this violence, animosity, and mistrust led to a full-fledged and bloody range war. The Davises and their followers fought it out with Hester and the small farmers and ranchers of the AHTA. The conflict took place in courtrooms and with guns. It was the worst such conflict in Oklahoma history, and one of the worst in American history. The feuding spanned several years and led to one of the bloodiest gun battles ever seen in Oklahoma. Before the ferocity and viciousness had run its course, more than thirty men were dead, farms and ranches were in ruins, lives were ruined, and families in mourning. The anger and hatred resulting from the bloodshed would last for generations. The bloody Porum Range War also helped to usher in an era of banditry, a wild and tempestuous time, and Joe Lynch Davis was at its center stage. Those who lived through the tumultuous era would never forget.

## ✢ 2 ✦

# THE BLOODY PORUM RANGE WAR

We whipped the living hell out of them.

— Cassie Starr

As a young man coming of age on the family ranch on the Canadian River in the early years of the twentieth century, Joe Davis frequently made the twenty-minute horseback ride to the village of Texanna four miles northeast. It was here that he first came in contact with the Cobb family, poor Arkansas dirt farmers who were always looking for a better way of life. The Cobbs were struggling to operate J. W. Cobb and Company, a small store and hostelry on the main street in Texanna.[1] The head of the family, John William Cobb, had come from a well-to-do slaveholding family in McMinn County, Tennessee. His mother died when he was an infant and his father, Carter William Cobb, took the family to Texas after the Civil War. The Cobbs made their way by wagon across the Mississippi and Arkansas Rivers and southwest across the Red River to Fannin County in North Texas, not far from Bonham. The Lone Star State was as good a place as any to start over. In 1870 the family was enumerated on the Fannin County census with property of six hundred dollars, far less than the thirteen thousand dollars they had possessed, including several slaves, before the war back in Tennessee.[2] Struggling just to survive, the Cobbs eventually moved west to Cooke County, Texas.

FIGURE 7. Joe Davis shortly before the time of the Porum gun battle. At Pony Starr's ranch house on the outskirts of Porum, on May 29, 1911, Joe Davis's nineteenth birthday, the Porum Range War exploded into the worst violence in the history of Muskogee County. As Cassie Starr reloaded their Winchester rifles, Davis and Pony Starr fought off as many as thirty armed and angry men, most of them members of the Anti–Horse Thief Association. *Author's Collection.*

Following the death of his stepmother and with his father's third marriage, John William Cobb struck out on his own, traveling north and east across the Red River to Mulberry Township in the heart of the picturesque Ozark Mountains in one of the poorest sections of northwest Arkansas. It was here in February 1889 that Cobb met and married a young woman who was thirteen years his junior—the petite, bespectacled, God-fearing, iron-willed, and resolute Phenie Caroline Holmes.[3] On a small farm in the Ozarks, the Cobb family struggled to survive and raise six children—two boys and four girls. It was the oldest daughter, Lula May, born on March 13, 1893, who was to play a significant role in the life of Joe Davis.

In 1903 John William Cobb pulled up stakes in Arkansas and, with his family and all their possessions in a wagon, headed southwest to Texanna in Indian Territory where a seventh child, Johnny, was born in 1905. In Texanna John Cobb

FIGURE 8. The Cobb family, shown here around the turn of the century, came to Texanna in 1903 from Arkansas. In Texanna, John William Cobb operated J. W. Cobb and Company, a small store and hostelry on Main Street. Cobb became so popular in the community that he once ran for sheriff of McIntosh County. Standing (*left to right*) are Tom, Minnie, and Lula. Seated are John William with Ila and Phenie holding Myrtle. It was in Texanna that Lula and Joe Davis first met and fell in love. *Courtesy of Mary Jane Cobb Young.*

became popular enough to run for sheriff of McIntosh County. A township in the eastern part of the county was named for the family. For a time the oldest child, Thomas B., worked for Jack Davis on the Davis ranch, where he and Joe became good friends. Tom could ride and rope with the best of the Davis cowboys, and he worked his way up the ranching hierarchy to become foreman.

### Lula May Cobb

It was at the Cobb store in Texanna that eighteen-year-old Joe became infatuated with sixteen-year-old Lula May. Social life at the time consisted of dances, barbecues, camp meetings, church services, horse races, roping and riding contests, and simply visiting neighbors.[4] At first Phenie insisted that the teenagers do their courting at the family home, but such restrictions were quickly ignored by the couple. Between the two teenagers a relationship, perhaps sexual, developed that would change their lives forever.[5]

Even in her early teens Lula had a reputation for her strident independence, self-assurance, assertiveness, carefree disposition, and at times, audaciousness. Family members remembered her as being downright "wild." Joe Davis liked her spunk and feistiness. However, his father persistently disapproved of the relationship, certain that the Cobbs were little more than ignorant country people, socially and economically inferior to the Davises. The will of the heart prevailed, and Joe was smitten. There was little that Jack Davis or Phenie Cobb could do to separate the two. Three times they ran off to get married. Davis family legend holds that, when the two were courting, Joe bought Lula an expensive diamond engagement ring and that his sister Carrie was so jealous Joe bought her one, too.[6] Defense attorneys later claimed in federal court in Arizona that the two were married by a justice of the peace in the Creek Nation in 1913, but neither Joe nor Lula was ever able to produce a marriage license or any evidence they were legally married. When Joe entered the federal prison system, he continued to insist he was married.

Tom Cobb, the oldest son, was easily lured into the lawlessness around Texanna and Porum. Along with Pony Starr and Jack's younger brother Robert "Bob" Lee Davis, Tom and Joe rustled cattle from several small farmers in the area. By the winter of 1910–11, tensions in the southern part of Muskogee County reached fever pitch.

Exactly who stole whose cattle first is uncertain. What is certain is that, by 1910, many of the citizens in Muskogee and McIntosh Counties had come to see the violence as more than just cattle rustling. It had become a struggle between the small farmers who plowed the land for a living and the "Cattle Kings" who had

FIGURE 9. Lula Cobb and Joe Davis claimed they were married in the Choctaw Nation in 1913, but they were never able to produce a marriage certificate or any such evidence. Jack Davis never approved of Lula, once remarking that she was little more than a simple country girl. Following Joe's arrest in 1916, the father also objected to the Oklahoma press portraying her as a "Bandit Queen." Lula was murdered in Colorado Springs, Colorado, on May 27, 1923, while Joe was in Leavenworth. *Author's Collection.*

once grazed their large herds on the wide open range and who refused to adjust to the changing times. In eastern Oklahoma there were no bigger Cattle Kings than the Davis brothers.[7] When the Dawes Act divided the land shortly after the turn of the century and farmers and ranchers flooded into the area, the Davises continued to gather cattle from what they perceived as the open range, and the cattle were then shipped to slaughterhouses in the north. Many of the farmers began losing livestock, and the trouble began. What the Davis brothers saw as a way of life, the small farmers and law enforcement officials saw as rustling. Agitated farmers banded together in lodges of the Anti–Horse Thief Association (AHTA). Here they gained a measure of security and, in the process, become avowed enemies of the Davises.

### Fury of the Porum Range War

The Porum Range War that was already simmering and that boiled over after the murder of Cicero Davis in 1906 has traditionally been seen as a feud between the Davis brothers and the followers of Thomas Luther Hester. In reality it was much more than that. It was a struggle by the AHTA to bring some semblance of law and order to the southern part of Muskogee County and McIntosh County and to end the pervasive rustling.

In 1910–11 alone, the AHTA estimated that ten thousand dollars' worth of livestock was lost in Muskogee and adjoining counties. Resolutions condemning the Davises were sent to the Oklahoma attorney general and the court of criminal appeals in Oklahoma City. Despite numerous arrests Jack and Joe Davis were always able to hire the "ablest attorneys," the AHTA argued, and to buy witnesses who persistently lied under oath. The Davis brothers were little more than dangerous "walking arsenals" who were always free on bond. Many were convinced that the bloodshed around Porum would never end until the Davises were behind bars.[8]

At one time in 1911, the AHTA pointed out, there were five cases of cattle stealing pending against Joe Davis, three against his father, seven against his uncle Bob Davis, five against their close friend Pony Starr, and five cases against another member of their gang, Linton "Leonard" McCullough, that also included a perjury charge.[9] As many as twenty-five court cases involving the Davises were in various stages of litigation at one time. In their defense the Davis brothers argued that law enforcement officials were deliberately harassing the family by not charging them with one single charge of stealing cattle but, rather, by picking out a steer every day, filing multiple charges, and forcing them to post bond in each case.[10]

Jack and Joe Davis were fortunate to have one of the best attorneys in Oklahoma in their corner. There is little doubt that Samuel Morton Rutherford, one of the 169 lawyers in Muskogee in 1910, was the most respected and most successful criminal defense attorney not only in Muskogee County but perhaps in Oklahoma. For almost a decade the Davis family was dependent on his courtroom skills. From the time they watched him successfully defend Mack Alford and Pony Starr, they were certain he was the man to defend them. Rutherford had the capacity "for daring decisions and unflinching courage." An "outspoken individualist, a brilliant counsellor," he could keep a jury and courtroom spellbound for hours. Immaculate in his dress, slim as a rail, with a flaming red mustache, Rutherford possessed a courage and dignified assertiveness that was particularly attractive

FIGURE 10. One of the greatest criminal attorneys in Muskogee or eastern Oklahoma was Samuel Morton Rutherford who consistently defended Joe and Jack Davis. A graduate of Emory and Henry College in Virginia, Rutherford was the first US marshal for the Northern District of Indian Territory. As a leading Democrat, he was elected mayor of Muskogee in 1903. Men of Affairs and Representative Institutions of Oklahoma, 1916. *Courtesy of the Local History and Genealogy Department of the Muskogee Public Library.*

to juries. With the air of a southern gentleman about him, he would often enter a courtroom to wide applause, as if he were a movie star.[11]

Rutherford's grandfather had been superintendent of Indian affairs in the Trans-Mississippi and had established the first real settlement at the three forks near Fort Gibson in 1817. Born in Arkansas shortly before the Civil War, the attorney Samuel Morton Rutherford was educated at Emory and Henry College in Virginia and worked for several years in Fort Smith, Arkansas. Moving to Muskogee in 1895, he became the first US marshal for the Northern District of Indian Territory. Within six months of his appointment, he had sixty-five bandits behind bars at Fort Smith. Some of the most notorious outlaws in Indian Territory, such as Bill West, the Green Gang, the Crowel Gang, the Verdigris Kid's Gang, and the Buck Gang were jailed, and several outlaws were hanged. When the infamous Buck Gang terrorized Creek and Okmulgee Counties and were imprisoned in the federal jail at Muskogee in April 1895, a crowd gathered outside, intent on hanging the murderous outlaws. Waving a six-gun in each hand, Rutherford climbed a stockade wall and tried to calm the mob. When his eloquence failed, he waved the weapons in the air again and threatened to shoot the first man to defy him, telling the crowd that the prisoners would face justice at Fort Smith. The crowd dispersed, and the Buck Gang members were then tried and hanged.[12]

A few years later, when a black man was accused of killing a Muskogee policeman, a racist mob threatened to storm the jail and even brought an iron rail to batter down the jail doors. Rutherford climbed on a car, raised his arm in the air, and demanded silence. Instantly the crowd began melting away.[13] In 1903 he was easily elected mayor of Muskogee, and two years later he was selected as a delegate to the convention in Muskogee that drafted a constitution for the new state of Sequoyah. Rutherford was active in the Democratic Party and chairman of the Indian Territory delegation to the Democratic National Convention in St. Louis, Missouri, in 1904. Four years later he was a presidential elector for the new state of Oklahoma. In more than one case it was Rutherford's thoroughness and compelling courtroom oratory, especially his riveting closing arguments, that saved the Davises from long years in the state penitentiary. In cases of conviction Rutherford would use every legal recourse available, including endless motions and appeals. During the time he represented the Davises, their legal bill was certain to have exceeded a hundred thousand dollars (well over two and a half million in today's dollars).[14]

### Anti–Horse Thief Association

By January 1911 as many as three or four hundred men in the southern part of Muskogee County were carrying guns, many of them members of the AHTA. All anyone who wanted to carry a firearm had to do, especially if they were members of the Davis or Hester factions, was to get a constable to name them a deputy. Everyone seemed to be armed—not only farmers and ranchers but debt collectors, bank guards, businessmen, average citizens, even clergymen. One of the ways to stop the violence, Sheriff John L. Wisener and Muskogee County Attorney Wesley Ernest Disney concluded, was to disarm the deputy constables, and they issued orders accordingly. When three men refused to give up their guns, they were thrown in the county jail.[15]

In the southern part of Muskogee County and a large part of McIntosh County, the AHTA became the protecting guardians of small farmers. They banded together not only to protect their own lives and their possessions but to intervene in any matter they perceived as wrongdoing. Their vigilante justice frequently verged on lynch law and reflected the lack of an effective law enforcement system in the area. The problem in Muskogee County, the AHTA claimed, was that too many men, although found guilty, were allowed to be free while their cases were on appeal.[16]

In general a somewhat excitable group, the AHTA was first organized in Kansas and Missouri following the Civil War with the purpose of ousting horse thieves. Hundreds of lodges were established throughout the Midwest, as far west as New Mexico, Montana, Colorado, and Wyoming, and as far south as Texas.[17] By 1895 the AHTA was well organized in the Oklahoma and Indian Territories. Here the organization was composed of hardworking, determined, and hard-riding men, mostly farmers, whose objective was to bring the lawless to justice.

Members were required to be eighteen years of age or older and pay a fifty-cent initiation fee and annual dues of between three and five dollars. All members were required to vote on the admission of new members. Every voter cast either a white or a black ball; more than one black ball meant rejection. Members were expected to be ready to pursue suspected livestock thieves at a moment's notice.[18] The AHTA's emblem was a horseshoe standing for Humanity, Charity, and Justice. Their motto was to "protect the innocent and bring the guilty to justice."[19]

The *AHTA Weekly News* railed against lawbreaking, especially in Oklahoma, where crime left "a trail of ruined homes, wrecked lives, lost souls, and bleaching skeletons wherever it lays its bloody finger."[20] As far as the AHTA was concerned, the situation in Oklahoma was out of control. Jails were overflowing with criminals of all classes and had become the breeding ground for even more crime.

The AHTA reached its peak in 1912, with a national membership of over forty thousand. The organization was particularly strong in Oklahoma, where each chapter published a "Black List" with a large black cross on the cover and the names of "suspicious" characters. Black lists had the name, age, height, weight, complexion, eye and hair color, and residence of each suspect.

There were six lodges of the AHTA in the southern part of Muskogee County and in McIntosh County. Two of the most active were the Hickory Ridge Lodge, near the Cicero Davis Ranch six miles northwest of Porum, and the Twin Grove Lodge at Texanna.[21] In time Oklahoma had more AHTA members than even Kansas. In November 1911 at the annual meeting of the Indian Territory division more than five hundred AHTA members marched proudly down the main street in Tulsa, preceded by a marching band, AHTA officials in automobiles, the Tulsa fire department, and as many as two hundred men on horseback. With large cheering crowds lining the sidewalks, the procession ended at the Grand Opera House.[22]

Usually organized by school districts, all members of the AHTA were sworn to keep secret the signs and passwords of the organization and never to cheat, do wrong, or defraud a member of the order.[23] Much like the National Grange and the Farmers' Alliance, the AHTA was socially active at events such as their annual fish fry and picnic. Lodges had rabbit hunts where farmers armed with shotguns slaughtered thousands of rabbits. Those who shot the most cottontails were asked to serve dinner for those who shot the least. They also hunted livestock predators, especially wolves and coyotes. Most lodges had an end-of-year oyster supper where members joyfully sang the organization's anthem, "Home Sweet Home." In 1902 the AHTA began publishing the *Weekly News* out of St. Paul, Kansas. At the same time, the organization published a biweekly newspaper in Guthrie called the *Searchlight*.[24]

### Many a Poor Farmer

Some said that horse thievery was so common in the area around Porum and Briartown that simply tying a horse to a public hitching post was a risky enterprise. "Many a poor settler waked up in the morning to find that his team of horses or mules had been stolen during the night," one Oklahoman remembered. The AHTA proclaimed Oklahoma "one of the most violent states in the country [where] every week someone is shot with a revolver." The AHTA asked the legislature to pass a bill that would put revolvers "out of the reach of persons who shoot hastily and indiscriminately." Rewards of up to one hundred dollars were offered for the capture of any horse thief—and as much as five hundred dollars for the apprehension of anyone who murdered a member of the association. The homes of suspected horse or cattle thieves were constantly under surveillance. Members sometimes sat in the brush for days watching the homes of a suspected thief.[25] Sworn to "Protect the Innocent" and "Bring the Guilty to Justice," the AHTA seemed to have no boundaries. In reality it was an organized vigilante system that proved far more efficient than local law enforcement.

In early November 1910 Pony Starr, who was a deputy sheriff at the time, was arrested along with Bob Davis and charged with rustling cattle. Hearing they would be arrested, the two men hid out for several days in the heavy timber along the Canadian River near the Jack Davis Ranch and in the hills west of Porum. Oklahoma newspapers reported that the two "wealthy farmers" were accustomed to "going among various herds of cattle" where they "cut out the best steers and drove them away." They would then ship the animals to slaughterhouses in Kansas City.[26]

An accomplice in the rustling case, Clifford Sellers (who later turned state's witness), said that he was called to Starr's ranch near Porum, where he was warned not to testify, and that he and Dan Foster, another rustler implicated in the case, were told to leave the state. Davis and Starr told Sellers they were determined to beat the case and that "they never permitted any person to testify in court against them."[27] In a second meeting in Tahlequah, Davis and Starr gave Sellers and Foster one hundred dollars each and the two headed out for Montana.

Friction between the Davis Gang and Thomas Luther Hester and the AHTA was intensified by several events that took place around this time. A terrible fire swept across the business district of Porum on the night of February 6, 1911. The fire began on the second floor of a large two-story brick structure on Main Street and spread to several stores and offices, including those of an attorney, a dentist, and a physician, leaving only a heap of smoldering ruins.[28] The fact that the town mayor, J. M. Edwards, was found guilty of forgery in a Muskogee court two weeks later and sentenced to seven years in the state prison at McAlester did not help the relations between the factions either.[29]

Joe Davis later claimed that he first ran into trouble in Porum when he and Pony Starr were operating a still against the wishes of the local Ku Klux Klan. Although they were warned several times to stop making whiskey, they paid little heed to the KKK, several of whom were also AHTA members, and hostilities mounted thereafter. In the cattle-rustling case Davis and Starr, who were each under a four-thousand-dollar bond, retained the able services of Samuel Rutherford. As was the custom Sam Davis, the wealthiest of the Davis brothers, put up most of the bond money. Claiming that he had forty thousand dollars in livestock and twenty-five thousand dollars in real estate, Jack Davis also helped with the bond.[30]

### Rustling with Impunity

With Judge R. C. Allen presiding and pistol-carrying deputies stationed at every door of the Muskogee Courthouse searching anyone who entered, Starr went on trial first in November 1910. Davis went on trial before Judge R. P. DeGraffenreid three months later. Testimony against the two men was similar, but by the time Davis went before the court, the facts in the case had become clearer and the state had amassed more evidence. The prosecution alleged that, on the morning of June 14, 1910, E. V. Brashears, a farmer living near Briartown, noticed that two of his cows—a blue jersey branded "WW" and a black spotted cow branded "EV"—were missing. Further investigation revealed that Davis had shipped the cows from Checotah to a slaughterhouse in Kansas City on the Katy. Davis and Starr were accused of also rustling cattle from J. W. Jemison, another farmer living near Briartown. Jemison found the tracks of the two men he was sure had taken his cattle. One was riding a horse that was shod, while a second man was on a horse that was only partially shod. He followed the tracks west from Briartown over the hills into a canyon and then to Checotah, where he learned that Bob Davis had shipped the cattle to the slaughterhouse in Kansas City. An agent for the Katy testified that he shipped the cows for Davis, and a man in Kansas City told the jury that he received the Davis cattle, including cows branded "WW" and "EV." The hides of the two slaughtered animals were even displayed before the jury. Other prosecution witnesses swore that they saw Davis, along with Pony Starr and three other men, driving a herd of cattle a mile east of Checotah. Davis had told one cowman that he did not want to ship the cattle from Porum, since there was a warrant there for his arrest.[31]

In Starr's defense Rutherford called on several witnesses, including Clem Vann, who testified that Bob Davis had bought the cows from Dan Foster and Clifford Sellers, not knowing they were stolen. Foster and Sellers had driven a herd of seventeen or eighteen cattle to Bob Davis's ranch northeast of Texanna and were paid in greenbacks Davis retrieved from a woodpile. Linton McCullough took the stand to say that he, too, had assisted Starr and Davis in driving the cattle to Checotah. Moreover, he testified that he was present when Foster and Sellers sold the cattle to Davis. One witness quoted Sellers as saying, "I sold them cattle to Bob and got the money for them and I am going in and give up. I don't want anyone punished for what I done."[32]

Sellers testified that on June 14, 1910, he assisted Starr and Bob Davis in driving a herd of cattle from near Briartown to Checotah, where they were shipped to Kansas City. Sellers admitted that two of the animals in the herd belonged to a farmer near Briartown. Bob Davis went on the stand himself, asserting that he did not know the animals he purchased from Foster and Sellers were stolen. He had not paid any attention to the brands and paid $375 for the herd, money he acquired from selling hogs. Davis claimed that one of the prosecution witnesses, Peter Graham (who had turned state's witness), along with his brother Ben had become his sworn enemies and were "packing guns for me."[33]

In Starr's defense Rutherford reiterated that Starr had acquired the cattle in good faith, and it was not his fault the animals had been stolen. From the beginning there was little doubt in the minds of the jury, however, that Starr was guilty, and he was promptly convicted of grand larceny and sentenced to three years in the McAlester state penitentiary. As was his custom, Rutherford appealed the decision to the Oklahoma Court of Criminal Appeals. When Bob Davis went to trial in late February 1911, the courthouse in Muskogee was packed. The testimony against him was even stronger than it was against Starr. There was little Rutherford could do. Davis was found guilty and sentenced to two years at McAlester.[34] Rutherford asked Judge DeGraffenreid for a new trial, but the motion was denied. As with Starr, Rutherford promptly appealed the case. Early in 1912 the court of appeals ruled in favor of the prosecution, concluding that Davis knew the animals were stolen and there was more than enough evidence to convict him. There was little doubt, the court concluded, that he had received a fair trial.[35] Pony Starr's appeal was also rejected.

## Accomplice

Even before his case was received by the state appellate court in Oklahoma City, Bob Davis was arrested again for cattle rustling, this time from Porum and Warner, and for shipping stolen cattle to Kansas City. Joe Davis and Tom Cobb Jr., both nineteen at the time, were arrested as accomplices. Some of the cattle the three men rustled were from Robert Acker, a farmer living near Checotah, as well as two farmers who resided near Texanna. In Davis's trial at Muskogee, eighteen-year-old Lena Herron testified that on June 20, 1910, while she and her brother were picking wild blackberries near the family farm a short distance from Texanna, she saw three men driving a herd of twelve to fifteen cattle. One of the men sitting tall in the saddle was Joe Davis, who she remembered was riding a gray horse.[36] Her younger brother, twelve-year-old Chester, recognized one of the men as Tom Cobb. Twelve-year-old Fred Lewis, who lived nearby, said he was sure the men driving the herd were Joe Davis, Tom Cobb, and Bob Davis. Ben Maxwell and Pete Graham both testified that they saw the three men driving the cattle about a half hour before dusk not far from Warner. The Midland Valley Railroad agent at Warner went on the stand to confirm that Bob Davis shipped a carload of cows, steers, and yearling heifers with various brands to Kansas City. A deputy sheriff, Oscar Stegall, told the jury about seeing Bob Davis and Joe Davis at the shipping pens in Warner, preparing to send the cattle to Kansas City. In the herd there was a red cow and a calf, freshly branded "RA," that belonged to a man living near Texanna.[37]

On the stand Joe Davis admitted that he and Tom Cobb, along with his uncle, had driven cattle to Warner, but he insisted he had no idea the animals were stolen. On the stand Tom Cobb reinforced what his friend said. Bob Davis also admitted shipping cattle from Porum and Warner but argued that he had bought the livestock from Foster and Sellers. Again, a jury found Bob Davis guilty, and again Rutherford asked for a new trial. When the motion was denied, Rutherford again appealed the case to the Oklahoma Criminal Court of Appeals. In January 1913 the court agreed that Rutherford had filed "a most able and elaborate brief, [but the] supposed errors" in the case were trivial, mere irregularities that had no material influence on the case. The court went on to complain that Bob Davis was an "old and confirmed offender," a "persistent criminal," and that "the property rights of the people of Oklahoma should be protected against such characters." Moreover, hearing the case was a "waste of time." It did not matter that Foster and Sellers stole the cattle. There was no "material error in the record." The sentence was upheld.[38]

### Death of Deputy James Work

"Another chapter of the bloodstained history of the old Davis feud was written in the little town of Porum," the *McAlester News Capital* and the *Checotah Times* proclaimed in bold headlines on May 5, 1911. The day before at half past two in the afternoon a well-respected deputy sheriff, James Work, was shot and killed while trying to serve a warrant on Bob Davis.[39] Thirty-one years old, married, and the father of four children, Work was said to have been a good citizen, fearless, God-fearing, and a terror to bootleggers. He was also a loyal member of the AHTA. The Davises intensely disliked Work, as he blamed them for much of the violence around Porum. The trouble all started when County Attorney Wesley Ernest Disney heard rumors that bondsmen for Bob Davis were disposing of their property. He responded by asking Sheriff Weiner to issue new warrants that would require Davis to reappear in Muskogee and post a new bond. Work had arrested Bob Davis several times before for cattle rustling, once while Davis was on horseback at his ranch. Davis was compelled to get down from his horse and was not even given time to take the saddle and bridle off the animal before he was hustled off to Muskogee. Davis swore that Work would never arrest him again, that one day either Work or another officer "would overstep himself."[40]

On May 3, 1911, without incident, Work arrested Joe Davis for rustling and brought him to Muskogee on the Midland Valley Railroad, where he was booked into the county jail. That evening Work sat in the sheriff's office, laughing and joking with several deputies.

"Jim, why don't you carry a rifle?" one of the lawmen asked.

"They'll get you sure enough down there some time," Work admitted. "Oh, I'm not afraid of them," he went on to say. "One thing is sure though, if they ever get me, the boys down there will get them."

On several occasions Sheriff Wisener cautioned Work to be careful, that the Davises were armed and dangerous. "I'm awfully afraid that those desperadoes will get Jim," the sheriff admitted.[41]

On the morning of May 4, Work caught the Midland Valley Railroad to Porum. Gathering his horse at the livery stable, he rode to the farm of J. A. "Bud" Robertson and asked his friend to go with him to Bob Davis's Ranch, that he had three warrants for rustling that needed serving. Work was concerned he would be waylaid on the road, although he did not think Davis would resist once he arrived at the ranch house. Work had wanted to arrest Jim Eddy, another cattle thief, but Eddy was busy guarding Pony Starr, and Work was concerned there might be violence.

Work was armed with a lever action rifle and a six-gun, while Robertson carried only a small revolver. Nearing the Davis ranch, the two men dismounted and walked around a small hill and across Davis's hog pasture to the ranch. Reaching the edge of the timber, the two men sat down among the blackjack trees and waited for Davis to return home. Only minutes later Davis, accompanied by his twenty-two-year-old cousin Ammon Davis who lived in Whitefield, just across the Canadian River from Briartown and Linton McCullough came riding up to the Davis house. Work and Robertson calmly walked down the road toward Davis's house as Work yelled out for Bob to stop, that he had three warrants for his arrest. He pulled the warrants out of his pocket and waved them in the air. Davis turned and spurred his horse for the house.

Work yelled again for Davis to stop. "I've got a bench warrant for you," he shouted.

"They are going around the house," Robertson told Work.

"Let's head 'em off," Work replied.

When Ammon Davis first spotted Work, he stopped and threw up his hands. At the same time Bob Davis got off his horse, ran into the house, and grabbed a gun from under a bed.

Work turned to Robertson and remarked, "He's getting his gun."

At the same time, about one hundred yards from the house, Work brought his rifle down over his left hand. Still holding the warrants, Work shot twice at Ammon Davis. Fearing he was being shot at, Davis reined his horse for the back of the barn, where he began frantically tearing down a board fence in hopes of escaping.

"I believe I hit Bob," Robertson remembered Work saying, just as Davis opened fire from the porch before retreating to a window in the house and continuing to fire. As Robertson hid behind a rail fence, Work emptied his gun in a cloud of

FIGURE 11. Joe Davis's younger brother Samuel Tate shared the same name as his wealthy uncle. On the right is Joe's cousin Ammon who fled to Colorado with Bob Davis following the death of Deputy Jim Work. Ammon Davis died unexpectedly at Wagoner at the age of twenty-two during the Porum Riot trials on January 18, 1912, and was buried in the Davis Cemetery at Briartown. Never implicated in any of Joe Davis's many bank and train robberies, Sam Davis served honorably in World War I. He died at the age of eighty-one in March 1975 and was buried in the Davis plot in Rose Hill Cemetery in Ardmore. *Author's collection.*

smoke at the Davis house, where a pregnant May Davis hid in the back bedroom with her sons, four-year-old Kelley Roach and two-year-old Avo Earl. Work paused, turned around, and went to his knee to reload. Within seconds, a bullet ripped into his back.

He exclaimed, "I'm hit."

Although he insisted the wound was superficial, Work staggered backward as Robertson reached out to hold him. Although Work continued to insist that the wound was not serious, he fell over a rail fence and lay bleeding on the ground as Robertson rushed off in a panic to Porum for a physician.[42] When Robertson returned with a Porum doctor an hour later, Work was dead in a pool of blood. As it turned out, a bullet had pierced his heart.

After Work's wife, Eliza, arrived on the scene, her husband's body was wrapped in a sheet and placed in a wagon. With a small escort, the body was taken to Porum. The next day Work was buried in the local cemetery south of town. Every store and place of business in Porum was closed and some were draped in black crepe. A large part of the community attended the graveside services. "Threats of lynching were heard on every side," a Muskogee newspaper reported.[43]

Authorities were forced to admit that Bob Davis and his comrades "would never be taken alive."[44] Within hours of Work's death, posses were organized and lookouts were posted. Every road and trail in the area was guarded by armed and angry men. Three posses, mostly AHTA men in overalls, hurriedly gathered—one in Porum and two in Checotah. Several men rode to Bob Davis's ranch, but all May Davis would tell them was that her husband had left and she was sure he was safe. Acting almost as a public relations agent, Morton Rutherford told the press that the three wanted men were hiding in Younger's Bend, and that they would shoot it out and never give themselves up to any posse. Rutherford and Sam Davis both agreed that Bob Davis had been wounded, perhaps fatally.

"The woods to the east and south of Porum yesterday and last night swarmed with posses, heavily armed, ready and willing to bring back the riddled body of Bob Davis and his comrades," the *Muskogee Daily Phoenix* reported.[45]

Lusting for a lynching, the men were agitated by rumors that the Davis Gang was preparing to kill anyone who dared to testify against them in any of the pending cases.

### Porum Vigilantes

On the morning of May 9, 1911, five days after Work died, an AHTA posse found Robert Worthman, a stalwart member of the Davis Gang, hiding on the second floor of a vacant house not far from the Sam Davis residence just north of Porum. Worthman had in his possession seven feet of dynamite fuse, along with several rifles and hundreds of rounds of ammunition.

With a rope around his neck, Worthman was dragged through the streets of Porum for over two hours. He was told repeatedly that he would be lynched unless he confessed. At least half a dozen times, the mob halted and Worthman was forced to his knees to pray, being told that he had only minutes left to live. Worthman was finally taken to a large elm tree on the outskirts of town, and the rope around his neck was thrown over a limb.[46] As three men pulled on the rope, Worthman was certain he was about to be executed, and he broke down in tears, telling the posse that he was under orders to dynamite the homes of Thomas Luther Hester, J. A. Roberson, George Blackstone, and one of Joe Davis's cousins, Cicero Sumerlin ("Summie") Dunagan. All were leading AHTA members. In a strange twist of intrigue in the Porum Range War, Dunagan turned against his uncles and cousin.[47] At the very last moment, several deputies arrived and took possession of the terrified Worthman. With his hands manacled, he was rushed off on the Midland Valley Railroad to Muskogee, where he was confined in the county jail for his own safety.

The AHTA offered a five-hundred-dollar reward for Bob Davis's apprehension. At the same time, a large and incensed crowd gathered in Porum to hear the seventy-three-year-old North Carolina–born Reverend James Monroe McClure, one of the more influential members of the community, cry out "that the Davis gang was responsible for the many crimes committed in this country," as well as "many murders and untold number of thefts, killing witnesses and hiring men to perjure themselves."[48] In the Porum twilight, hundreds listened intently. "The Davises are a band of notorious cattle thieves, and I have at least five hundred good men at my back who are ready and willing to help drive that class of men out of the country," McClure went on to say.[49]

Most of the posses, including those organized by the AHTA, were on horse-back, but with the changing times, two groups of men roamed the countryside in automobiles. When several known friends of the Davises rode into Porum, it appeared for a while that they would be lynched by the mob. When Sheriff Wisener received news of Work's death in Muskogee, he telephoned all the towns in eastern Oklahoma to be on the lookout for the two Davises and McCullough. Passengers on the Midland Valley arriving and departing Porum were carefully searched by deputies at pistol point. Hearing a rumor that the three wanted men might be riding on top of one of the freight cars, all cars were carefully searched. Although forensic science was in its infancy, the sheriff was able to send the men's Bertillon anthropometric measurements, including their height, weight, ear and nose size and description, eye color, width of head, and length of arms and fingers, to county sheriffs and police chiefs throughout eastern Oklahoma and as far west as New Mexico Territory and Colorado. The men were certain to be wearing "high boots," the sheriff said, "slouch hats and clothing customarily worn by cattle men."[50] Bob Davis was forty at the time, five feet eleven inches in height, with brown hair and blue eyes, a light complexion, of medium build, and weighing 175 pounds. Ammon Davis and Linton McCullough greatly resembled one other, both being in their early twenties, six feet tall, weighing 170 pounds, of medium build, and light complexion.[51]

Some speculated that Bob Davis and his two companions were already on their way to Mexico, intending to ride horseback all the way to the Rio Grande. Others, including Rutherford, insisted that Davis was badly wounded and was hiding in the tangled bottomlands of Younger's Bend. There was even speculation that the three men had escaped across the Canadian River into Choctaw country and might be holed up in a cave in the mountains somewhere. One posse out of Eufaula, however, reported they were on a "hot trail."[52]

At nine o'clock on the evening after Work's death, five deputies looking for clues as to the men's whereabouts "raided" Jack Davis's home at 705 South Third Street in Muskogee. With all the telephone and telegraph lines cut and Porum in chaos and isolated from the outside world, Sheriff Wisener asked for a special train of the Midland Valley. With twenty-four heavily armed deputies in a caboose attached to the engine, the train sped across the prairie for Porum. Two hours later, a second train carrying another fifty Muskogee County deputies followed. Arriving in Porum, the deputies found a mob of several hundred heavily armed men carrying Winchesters, six-shooters, shotguns, and old Civil War weapons milling about the town. When the first train carrying the deputies pulled into the Porum station, men could be seen scurrying across the railroad tracks in the headlight of the train engine. "They crossed like a covey of quail," their "Winchesters gleaming under the glare of the electric headlights of the engine, each man carrying two weapons," one officer reported.[53] "Reign of Terror Exists at Porum" the *Muskogee Times-Democrat* proclaimed in a bold headline. Excitement in the community, it was said, was at a "fever pitch."[54] Several Davis partisans were holed up at the Sam Davis residence north of town, and an AHTA posse was threatening to attack the house. Reaching Porum, Sheriff Wisener surrounded the house with his deputies. Some thought the sheriff had arrived just in time to prevent a furious gun battle.

### Provoked and Mistreated

Always on the defensive Rutherford issued a statement giving the Davises' side of the controversy. Bob Davis had been repeatedly provoked and mistreated for years, he said. Hearing of the excitement at Porum, both Rutherford and Pony Starr had rushed south to negotiate the surrender of the two Davises and McCullough. No sooner had they stepped off the train than Starr began quietly visiting friends to inquire as to the whereabouts of the three men. When the

AHTA heard that Starr was in town, both he and Rutherford were forced to take refuge in Sam Davis's house.

With the understanding that he would not be turned over to the Porum mob, Linton McCullough came into Muskogee and surrendered to Sheriff Wisener and was taken to the county jail for his own safety. Bud Robertson was also taken to the county jail, but as a material witness in the case.

Some said the AHTA was bent on driving the Davises from the southern part of the county, and the Davises were equally determined to stand their ground. Porum had become a "seething hotbed of lawlessness." Tired of the depredations by the Davis Gang, the people were "maddened almost to a point of murderous frenzy," one newspaper reported. May Davis was forced to flee to Muskogee, as was Pony Starr's wife, Cassie.[55] After briefly appearing in Porum, Pony Starr and Rutherford also beat a hasty retreat to Muskogee. Sam Davis and his wife left town for Fort Smith, Arkansas.

As it turned out, after Work was shot, Bob Davis and his two accomplices had paused only briefly at the Davis farm. As Work lay dying, the older Davis grabbed some money and a gray suit of clothes that he rolled up and fastened on the back of his saddle. Davis said goodbye to his wife, then he, Ammon, and McCullough galloped off. Their escape was made possible by Kaiser Muskrat, a "notorious negro cattle and horse thief" who lived not far from the Davis ranch.[56] Muskrat was as tough and cunning as they came, having already been arrested several times and served five years in the state penitentiary. No one knew the back roads and trails of the post oak–blackjack country and tallgrass prairies of east-central Oklahoma as well as he did. On the night after Work was killed, the two Davises separated from McCullough, and Muskrat agreed to guide the two men north to safety.

"Well, they rode up and Bob Davis asked me if I could guide them over the hills," he later said. Having worked in the field all day, Muskrat was at first unable to find a horse but finally did so, and the three men rode off into the night. Muskrat later admitted he would "lay down and swear hell was an ice wagon or an ice house, if Bob Davis would come across with $500."[57]

Bob and Ammon somehow made their way to Claremore, thirty miles northeast of Tulsa, where a relative they would never identify joined them and took their horses back to Porum. In Claremore, in an attempt to disguise themselves, the two cowmen stripped off their "cowboy clothes" and donned a pair of "civilized shoes" and new suits. "We went around the posse and made it to Claremore. Here we bought those damned city clothes and civilized shoes. We changed into them as soon as we found a hiding place [and] were ready to board a train that was westbound. Those damned shoes pinched my feet and the city clothes were so tight I could hardly move," Ammon Davis later confessed. "I kept pinching at those tight shoes and I even pulled them off so my toes could rest. I'd rather have a hold of a longhorn steer than wear those things. The Indians never thought up worse torture than city clothes," he continued.[58]

At Claremore the two bought tickets to Kansas City, where they boarded the Atchison, Topeka, and Santa Fe (AT&SF) for Denver. Rattling west across the plains, they finally turned north at La Junta, Colorado and continued on to Pueblo, past Colorado Springs and a snowcapped Pikes Peak to Denver. The two had failed to purchase tickets in Kansas City and assumed they could acquire tickets on the train. When asked for their tickets, Bob Davis pulled out a big wad of bills and stripped off two ten-dollar bills. Told they would have to get off at the next station at Newton, Kansas, to purchase tickets, Davis began arguing so loudly that the conductor became suspicious he might be a bank robber. The conductor telegraphed ahead for a detective who boarded the train at Pueblo and immediately became suspicious, noticing that the two men were uncomfortable in the clothes they were wearing. As soon as the two men got off the train at Denver, they were arrested. While they were being held, express companies and banks throughout Colorado, Oklahoma, and the Southwest were contacted to determine if there had been a recent robbery or if anyone was missing a large sum of money. At the time Bob Davis had $1,997 in paper currency on the First National Bank of Muskogee.[59]

### To Muskogee in Irons

At police headquarters the two men were measured under the Bertillon system. After four days of relentless grueling, they finally broke down and admitted their real identities. Hearing of their arrest Sheriff Wisener dispatched Deputy Sheriff Joe Depew and Undersheriff W. I. Nicholson to Denver to escort them back to Muskogee. Waiving their rights to extradition and manacled together, the two Davises clanked their way onto the eastbound AT&SF. Once on the train, Bob asked Depew to remove the irons.

"All right but you know if you make a move to escape we'll get you so quick you won't know what's struck you," the deputy responded.

"We know," the older Davis laughed. "We'll be good."

Late on Sunday night, May 14, 1911, after transferring to the Katy, Bob and Ammon Davis stepped from the train at Muskogee only blocks from the Jack Davis residence on South Third Street. They were escorted under heavy guard to the county jail. A reporter on the scene reported that the two men were in the "best of spirits and in a much more cheerful frame of mind than the fagged and tired deputies who, for the past ten days have had but little sleep because of the hunt for the two men."[60] Ammon was released on bail. Bob Davis was denied bail and spent the next four and a half months in the Muskogee County jail.

The courts remained clogged with cases involving the Davises. Bob Davis had twice been acquitted on charges of rustling, and he had been convicted once. One case of larceny against Joe and Jack Davis was pending in Pittsburg County on a change of venue from McIntosh County. Rutherford had managed to get other cases against Joe and Bob Davis in Muskogee County dismissed. But there was more trouble on the horizon. On the day Bob Davis was finally granted bail, Jack Davis filed a suit against Blackstone and Company, a cattle company owned by Thomas Luther Hester and George Blackstone, to recover eighteen head of steers.[61]

In the meantime Joe Davis went on trial for cattle rustling in the district court in McAlester. There were 150 law enforcement officials on duty to keep the Davis and Hester factions apart. The threat of violence was so real that the district judge P. B. Cole issued orders for every man getting off the train to be searched and disarmed.[62] After several days of contested testimony from both sides, Joe Davis surprisingly was found not guilty. The Davises had won another round in their struggle with Thomas Hester and the AHTA.

In the midst of all their legal problems, Joe Davis had time to compete in the steer-roping contest at the Muskogee Fair, one of the great joys of his young life. Several thousand spectators jammed the stands each night. The fair also featured automobile and trotting horse races, "Montana Bessie" the bucking cow, fireworks, daily flights in Glenn Curtis's biplane, and a baby beauty contest. When rumors reached Porum that Pony Starr was a gatekeeper at the fair, the entire community threatened to boycott the fair.[63]

### Porum Range War Explodes

On Joe Davis's nineteenth birthday, Monday, May 29, 1911, the Porum Range War exploded into some of the worst violence yet. Joe Davis and Pony Starr were in the middle of it. It all started when Thomas Luther Hester claimed that Joe Davis stole some of his cattle and drove them across the Canadian River to Featherston, a small community on the Fort Smith and Western Railroad in eastern Pittsburg County, where Davis had purchased a small ranch. In turn, Joe and Jack Davis claimed that Hester was in possession of eleven head of their cattle. Joe rode to Hester's ranch, two and a half miles north of Porum, asking to inspect the cows, but Hester chased him off.[64] Joe Davis claimed he bought the cattle from an elderly

FIGURE 12. Pony Starr and Joe Davis pose on horseback at a steer roping contest
at the time of the Porum Range War. *Author's Collection.*

woman living west of Porum, and that the cattle were branded "P E" as well as
with the Davis's window sash on the left hip.[65] When Jack Davis had Rutherford
file a *writ of replevin* against Hester for the return of the cattle, a justice of the
peace in Muskogee sent Constable Orlando Dobson to Porum to serve the court
order and retrieve the cattle.[66]

Constable Dobson stayed overnight in Porum before going on to the Hester
ranch the next morning. Dobson and the local justice of the peace persuaded
Jesse E. Shumaker, a popular local butcher, and Charles McClure, a well-to-do
rancher and friend of the Davises, to accompany him to the Hester ranch. Early
on Monday morning the two men were deputized, and the three rode north out
of town. Joe Davis and Pony Starr met Dobson on the road, saying they wanted
to go along to identify the stock, but Dobson was afraid they might incite violence
and declined their offer.[67]

When Dobson first arrived in Porum, a rumor reached the local chapter of the
AHTA that the Davises were out to steal more livestock. Rumors swirled that Davis
and Starr were already at the stock pens north of Porum, preparing to ship a herd
of stolen stock. Many in the AHTA were determined to do everything possible to
stop the cattle rustling and wipe out the entire Davis Gang if necessary. Members

of the AHTA were particularly frustrated that, despite numerous arrests, law enforcement officials had failed to put Joe Davis and Pony Starr behind bars. Many small farmers and ranchers in the southern part of the county were convinced that the legal system was either broken or biased against them, and they were determined to take the law into their own hands.[68]

When Constable Dobson—along with Shumaker and McClure, both of whom were unarmed—first arrived at the Hester residence, they could see the disputed cattle in a corral behind the Hester house. Judge Hester was clearing oats from around several fruit trees. The three men hitched their horses to a wagon in front of the house and approached Hester, who came forward to greet them. When Dobson told Hester that they had come to serve a court order, the mood changed abruptly.[69]

"Go to hell" was Hester's terse response.

Dobson vividly recalled what happened next. "As I attempted to draw the envelope containing the warrants from an inside coat pocket, about thirty masked men rushed out toward us from both the house and the barn," he later told the *Muskogee Daily Phoenix.*

The men screamed, "Hands up," as they fired several warning shots into the air and the ground near the three men. Someone grabbed Dobson's gun, and the men were forced at gunpoint onto Hester's front porch. One man kept a pistol fully cocked against Dobson's chest. Five of the posse were left guarding the three men, while another thirty hurried off toward the railroad where their horses were tied and then galloped off at full speed in the direction of the Pony Starr ranch. Hester calmly told Dobson not to be afraid, that many in the posse had been mistreated and that they were only fighting for their rights.

"Dobson, we know you and [we] won't harm a hair on your head, but we've been imposed upon by the officers," one of the men on the porch said. "We are only fighting for our rights."[70]

The men said they were not "going to hurt Shumaker either, but will attend to that Son of a Bitch Charles McClure." Hester and his men were furious at McClure in particular for assisting the Davises in posting bonds and "swearing lies."[71]

### Yonder Comes Damn Old Wisener

Despite the guns pointed at him, Dobson tried to serve the warrants a second time.

"Let's see them," Hester angrily responded, while continuing to point a shotgun at the constable. Hester became particularly agitated after glancing over the papers.

"You take that paper and shove it up your [ass], there's no officer nor set of officers who can look at the brands on those cattle or take them away from here," he said. When the constable warned that Sheriff Wisener was certain to hear that he had been disarmed and threatened at gunpoint, and a "big load of officers" would appear soon, one of the AHTA men responded, "Damn Wisener, let them come; we expect them and are ready for them."

At that very moment, three men were spotted on horseback approaching from the direction of Porum. "Yonder comes damn old Wisener and two officers now," one man yelled, as Hester and his men took cover in the house and prepared for battle, only to learn that the three men approaching were friends from the AHTA.[72]

Early that morning as many as thirty-five angry men—most of them from the AHTA in Muskogee and McIntosh Counties, hearing of the *writ of replevin* that Dobson was intending to serve on Hester—had gathered at the Hester Ranch to resist the warrant and shoot down any member of the Davis Gang they encountered. The group from AHTA included the three Maxwell brothers, thirty-eight-year-old George Wesley, thirty-four-year-old Arthur Edward, both farmers and stock raisers who lived near Porum, and Jesse Gilbert (thirty-nine years old and a recent widower who had worked on the railroad for a time as a machinist and had recently moved to Porum with his three children from the Cobb Township). All were devoted members of the AHTA. The Maxwells claimed bitterly that they had lost a lot of stock to the Davises. They had sworn out complaints several times in the past, but nothing was done to retrieve their animals. Originally from Mississippi, the Maxwells had moved to Missouri and then to the Indian Territory. Within days after they filed charges against the Davises, they claimed, their barns went up in flames. They then filed arson charges against the Davises, who were arrested but then released—after which their homes went up in flames.[73]

### Angry Men in Mother Hubbard Dresses

To disguise themselves, the AHTA posse dressed in the strangest of attire. Several were in "Mother Hubbard" dresses complete with aprons; others had turned their coats inside out. A few wore black bandana masks and straw hats or sunbonnets. All were "armed to the teeth," carrying pistols and either shotguns or Winchester rifles across the pommels of their saddles. Many, like the Maxwell brothers, were determined to take Joe Davis and Pony Starr prisoner or, if they resisted, to kill them. Some of the men were from around Porum, but many had ridden over from McIntosh County.[74]

At the Starr residence, about two miles south of Hester's ranch, at about half past nine that Monday morning, Pony Starr and Joe Starr sat quietly on the front porch of the one-story house talking with Russell A. Bean, a thirty-eight-year-old full-blood Cherokee, and another associate named Jack Foreman. They were waiting to hear from Constable Dobson, hoping he had successfully delivered the court order to Judge Hester. Suddenly Pony Starr's wife, Cassie, looked up to see a large number of men on horseback approaching the house at a gallop.

She turned to Bean and Foreman and remarked, "What kind of men are those? They look like Negroes." Sensing trouble, Bean and Foreman ran out the front gate, swung onto their horses, and galloped off.[75]

"I saw the men coming up the road," Cassie Starr later said. "They were riding at a gallop. Joe and Pony . . . had expected trouble and they had their guns and plenty of ammunition ready for just such an occasion."

Davis remarked, "Come on Pony," as he jumped up and ran in the house and grabbed his Winchester.

"They are coming after me. I guess my time has come, but I will get some of them before they get me," Starr responded.[76]

Cassie Starr calmly walked to the front gate of the residence and confronted the masked men. When one of the leaders of the mob asked who was inside the house, Cassie replied, "No one except Joe Davis and Pony."

Tell the "sons-of-bitches to come out," the man shouted back.[77]

Cassie Starr vividly recalled what happened next: "When they got up to the house, I held up my hand and tried to stop them, but they would not listen and started shooting."[78]

Who fired the first shot in what proved to be one of the deadliest gun battles in Oklahoma history remains a mystery. Cassie Starr claimed that the posse first opened fire on Bean and Foreman as they fled the Starr residence. Members of the posse claimed under oath that when they approached the house Davis and Starr opened fire first from inside the residence.

"We did not want to fight," Pony would later tell friends. "When we saw the masked men coming towards the house our first impulse was to try to escape . . . but the mob opened fire and we saw there was no chance to get away at that time, so we stayed and fought. You can tell the world that I was scared."[79]

Another version of the story has Pony Starr calmly turning to Joe Davis and remarking, "Joe, what shall we do? Get on our horses and run?"

"No," Davis replied. "We will stand hitched and shoot it out with them."[80]

FIGURE 13. Joe Davis and Pony Starr at the time of the bloody Porum gun battle.
*Author's Collection.*

Joe Davis was wearing a blue shirt and khaki pants, a young woman remembered years later. "I saw him just as plain as everything. Joe ran to the back of the house and started shooting back [at those] men in those dresses! They were the Hesters; they called themselves the 'Citizen Group.'"[81]

### Death in the Morning

Both Davis and Starr were crack shots. From the southwest corner of the house, bracing his arm against the woodwork for accuracy, Davis opened deadly fire on the posse. He had a fine view of Hester's men, he would later say, and he picked them off one at a time. At the same time Pony Starr, scurrying back and forth from windows and doors, opened a killing fire from inside the house.

Starr would admit that he was so scared at the time he did not know where he was or what he was doing.[82] It was all gut reaction and self-preservation.

On horseback and out in the open, Hester's "Citizen Group" were at a distinct disadvantage. More than one man was shot from his horse. Several of the horses were struck, and they were seen to tumble and kick in death agony along the narrow lane that led from the house to the cattle pens on the Midland Valley Railroad. Davis and Starr had three lever-action Winchester rifles between them. "I ran to where the ammunition was kept and carried cartridges to the boys, and helped them load their guns as fast as they were empty," Cassie Starr remembered.[83]

With their untrained horses rearing and plunging, some of the vigilantes were bucked off, and they then became easy targets. Continuing to use his hand against the wall to help aim his rifle as he had learned to do through the years, Davis continued to pour lethal fire into the ranks of the posse. When he emptied the rifle or the barrel on his gun was overheated, he quickly grabbed a second rifle that Cassie Starr had reloaded. Years later Davis remembered how eighteen-year-old Clifford Hester, son of Judge Hester, tumbled to the earth when his horse was shot from under him. As young Hester rose to his feet in the tall grass, Davis sent a bullet ripping into his abdomen. For a moment Hester, who was wearing a red dress, regained his strength and rose again, only to be struck a second time in the stomach. The young man attempted to rise a third time but fell to the earth in a fatal twist.

George Maxwell was one of the first to die, tumbling from his horse, shot through the right eye. A large pool of coagulated blood marked the spot where he fell and stained the earth for weeks. His brother Arthur Maxwell was also shot off his horse. The third brother, Jesse Maxwell, a deputy sheriff in McIntosh County, took a bullet in the shoulder. Pete Graham, another active member of the AHTA and a farmer from near Texanna, was wounded in the right hip. The body of an unknown man dressed in a "weird outfit" was found on the morning after the gun battle under a bridge, a half mile north of the Starr Ranch.[84] Two other unnamed men killed in the fighting were said to have been carried off by their friends into the nearby woods. After the gun battle the body of a teenager named Jones who had formerly worked for Pony Starr was found in the wheat field near the Starr residence. He was carried to Porum in a wagon, as were all the other dead and wounded.[85]

Summie Dunagan, Joe Davis's cousin who had recently joined the Hester vigilantes and was wearing a red kimono, was shot in the hip. George Blackstone, one of Hester's partners, was wounded in the leg. At least fourteen men were injured in less than ten minutes. Riderless horses, some of them bleeding badly,

FIGURE 14. Sketch of Pony Starr's bullet-riddled ranch near Porum only days after the bloody gun battle. Muskogee Daily Phoenix, *May 30, 1911. Original sketch enhanced by Eddie Cantu.*

struggled through the Porum streets or out along country roads. Just north of the house, two dead horses lay in front of a big double gate that led to the Starr's barn.

The rapid rifle fire was easily heard in the streets of Porum, less than a mile from the Starr residence. Many of the citizens ran out of their homes and businesses and were able to see the fighting in the distance. A few of the overly zealous Hester partisans in the community grabbed their rifles and joined the fighting.

People who were waiting for the train at the Porum station on the outskirts of town, less than half a mile from the Starr home, could also hear and see the fighting. Some of the more daring climbed on top of boxcars near the depot for a better view. Three horses, each carrying two masked men, were spotted racing for the hills west of town. Clouds of smoke drifted over the Porum countryside while the northbound Midland Valley pulled into the station on its way to Muskogee from Fort Smith. Hearing and seeing the fighting, some of the travelers huddled in the cars, terror stricken, but others climbed to the top of the cars for a better view.[86]

During the heaviest of the fighting, several members of the posse were able to dismount and take a position lying down in the Starr wheat field, from where they opened a furious fusillade on the residence. Only once, however, did the vigilantes get close to Davis. This was when a board above where he was standing fell on his head and knocked him temporarily senseless.[87] The corner of the house from where his repeating rifle flashed causing so much death was riddled with bullets.

During the heaviest of the fighting, the Starrs' eight-year-old daughter, Nina Lois, came racing from a neighbor's house across the wheat field. She had been sent on an errand and now came fleeing back, crying and screaming that her mother was going to be killed.[88]

Caught in the open and realizing that Davis and Starr would never surrender, the posse finally rode away. As they disappeared Starr, slightly wounded in the finger, counted three cartridges in his Winchester. Davis said he was completely out of ammunition.[89] When the fighting finally ended, several Porum citizens hurried to the scene where they gathered the dead and wounded, placed them in wagons, and carried them back to Porum.

## Boys, You Have Got to Get Out

Low on ammunition and thinking the gun battle would never end, Davis and Starr at one time during the fighting concluded that they must somehow escape.

"Boys, you have got to get out," Cassie Starr told them, "for the ammunition is all out. I'll go and get the horses."

Referred to by the Muskogee press as a "comely looking little woman of the pretty Cherokee type," Cassie Starr, in a "rare display of cool nerve," calmly walked out the back door of the house and made her way some 150 yards to the barn.[90]

Seeing her emerge from the house, two men came charging out of the wheat field on horseback, one man firing his shotgun while the second man fired off four shots with a revolver. Two of the shots tore through Cassie's dress and apron.

"Don't let that damn woman get away," one of the men screamed.

Frustrated with his horse rearing and bucking plus his inability to shoot straight, the vigilante angrily threw his revolver at Starr. Cassie was able to grab the gun and fired the remaining shots at the man as he galloped off in great haste.

"I picked it up and fired two shots at him as he ran. I do not know whether I killed him or not, and did not wait to see," Cassie later told the Muskogee press.[91]

Reaching the barn Cassie was able to saddle one of the horses, but a second horse was loose in an adjacent pasture. She was forced to chase him around for several minutes before the animal was finally roped and saddled.

"It didn't take long to saddle them. I can throw a saddle over a horse as quickly as my husband can," she later bragged. "I led the horses up to the front door and the boys came out and rode away," she went on to say.[92] As they raced off, Davis and Starr claimed, they counted seven bodies lying in the lane near the house.

In ten minutes, at least two hundred shots were fired into the Starr home. Bullets tore through windows and doors, smashed furniture, and shattered a mirror on the wall into hundreds of little pieces. The screen door at the front of the house was pierced with thirty bullet holes, and the door and the door frame were in splinters. Bullets cut a broom handle in two, stripped the keys off an organ, cut the handle off a skillet, and ruined the family sewing machine. One bullet exploded an iron pot of turnip greens that was simmering on a woodstove in the kitchen and left the room full of steam. Shell casings covered the ground. Even the fence in front of the house was ripped apart.[93]

"This morning's battle was perhaps the fiercest ever recorded in the history of Oklahoma," several newspapers reported.[94]

### Fearful Flight

Brandishing their pistols and rifles in the air and spurring their horses, Davis and Starr galloped off toward Porum, where they raced down main street as frightened townsmen scurried for cover, although a few stood and stared in amazement. Just south of town the two gunmen ran into Dr. Charles Walter Vowell, who was returning to Porum after a visit to the Ross community. "Boys, what's all that shooting about?" Vowell asked.

"Doc, we have just rounded you up some business down there," Davis told the physician.

South of Briartown, Davis and Starr raced on for the safety of Younger's Bend, before the frightened outlaws turned west for the Davis Ranch. Late that evening, after helping to care for the wounded, Vowell turned to his son Carlile and remarked, "Now son, we have to live here and I want you to forget what you saw."[95]

Although someone cut the telephone and telegraph lines between Porum and Muskogee, news of the deadly gun battle reached Sheriff Wisener. A special train with twelve heavily armed deputies, along with two physicians, Claude Thompson and H. T. Tilley, plus a nurse, Margaret Welch, left Muskogee at half past one in the afternoon and hurried south, making the thirty-two-mile trip in less than an hour. Some feared that since the Davises had a large quantity of dynamite, they might blow up the train.[96] As soon as the Midland Valley pulled into Porum, the badly wounded were transferred to a baggage car. The train reversed course and sped back to Muskogee.

After the fighting, about fifteen of the Hester gunmen returned to Hester's ranch where Dobson, Shumaker, and McClure were still being held at gunpoint. Although seriously wounded, Jesse Maxwell pulled out his gun and was about to shoot McClure, shouting, "Charley McClure, you——, I'm going to blow your brains out!"

A second gunman grabbed Maxwell's gun to prevent him from killing McClure. Maxwell collapsed and was taken inside to a bed.[97] When the telephone in the house rang, Lillie Belle Hester rushed inside, coming back only to exclaim, "I thought they would have that old —— strung up before this."

A second telephone call informed her (falsely, as it turned out) that her son Clifford was not seriously wounded, as it had first been reported. Holding a pistol, Hester's sister spoke up. "We'll fix that old —— Charley McClure."

But one of the AHTA members grabbed the gun just as she cocked it. "Don't do it," he said, "we'll attend to him later."

Dobson asked one of the men who returned from the gun battle if Pony or Joe were hurt. "It's none of your damned business," the gunman replied.

Once again Hester began cursing the Davises and Sheriff Wisener, saying that he and the other ranchers and farmers were being imposed on and were only fighting for their rights. Hester ordered Dobson, Shumaker, and McClure out into the yard.

"Dobson, you and Jesse Shumaker can go," he said, but he refused to release McClure until he agreed not to "swear any more lies." McClure held up his right hand and gave his promise, only to be forced at gunpoint to repeat the oath a second time. The three men then mounted their horses and rode away.[98]

### Gunmen as Heroes

As Davis and Starr safely reached the Davis Ranch on the Canadian River, Cassie Starr was able to catch the Midland Valley to Muskogee, where the first thing she did was retain Morton Rutherford to defend her husband. The press flocked around her, asking for her version of the bloodshed at Porum. One newspaper account said it was obvious she had been weeping, yet another said she spoke "without a quaver in her voice."[99]

Five bullets had ripped through her dress and three more through her apron, but somehow she had survived without a scratch. The more the story was repeated across the state, the more exaggerated it became. Cassie Starr had now come to seize the pistol that was thrown at her in midair. Some newspapers wrote that she had even killed the man with his own weapon.[100] "She appears very well satisfied over the battle. It was a thrilling performance which could not but excite admiration," the *Muskogee Times-Democrat* remarked. Her quaintness extended to her language. "We whipped the living hell out of them," she said, according to the *McAlester News Capital*. She was not afraid to go back to Porum, she said: "I am perfectly able to care for myself. I am as good a shot as my husband," the

*Ada Evening News* reported. "Great Pluck Show" by "a slender Cherokee woman with eyes as black as midnight and of dauntless courage," the *Oklahoman* reported under glaring headlines of "Cherokee Woman Defeats Posse."[101]

In the eyes of the press, Cassie Starr had become a real heroine. At Fort Gibson, near Muskogee, and at other small towns and villages, Davis and Starr were also hailed as heroes. Many in the AHTA—including the president of the Oklahoma division, Campbell Russell—were fearful that the news of two men and a woman gallantly fighting off an attacking mob would sway public opinion in favor of the Davises. As far as Russell was concerned, the Davises were "one of the worst gang of thieves" in Oklahoma history.[102]

When the Midland Valley train reached Muskogee at five o'clock on the evening of the epic gun battle, the seriously wounded were placed in ambulances and taken to the general hospital. Shot twice through the abdomen, Clifford Hester never had a chance. Only hours after reaching Muskogee, he died before his family could reach his bedside. The doctors discovered that A. E. Maxwell had been shot through the bowels, and he underwent several operations. He lingered on unconscious while his wife and brother Ben stood by his side, but on Monday, June 3, he also died.[103] His brother Jesse, who was badly wounded in the shoulder, made a good recovery. A badly wounded cowboy named Jones died in Muskogee the day after the gun battle. As many as eight men died in the Porum gun battle. Although some in the Oklahoma press portrayed Joe Davis and Pony Starr as courageous heroes fighting off a berserk mob determined to kill them, many in Porum never forgave them.

### Hatred Knows No Bounds

When the gun battle erupted, commerce in Porum came to a halt while businesses closed their doors and citizens ran for cover. Afterward, small groups of grim and determined men, many of them heavily armed, stood on street corners listening to the latest rumors and discussing what had happened on the outskirts of their small town. "The usually peaceful and law-abiding citizens of the little village had been wrought up to a high pitch by the killing and the battle which had taken place right on the edge of town," reported the *Tulsa Daily World*. Many in Porum were greatly agitated by "what they consider are the wrongs they have suffered from the Davis crowd and further trouble is anticipated," reported the *Eufaula Indian Journal*. Soon the small groups became a mob, and the talk of vengeance became louder. Anyone associated with the Davises was warned to leave town. Moreover, they said that if Charlie McClure returned to town, they would kill him on sight.[104]

The morning after the gun battle, an angry throng led by Reverend J. M. McClure and including several survivors of the fighting marched to the home of Sam Davis, just north of Porum, where they seized an old man named Steve Little who had worked for Davis as a cook and hired hand for several years.[105] Several masked men placed a rope around his neck, threatening to hang him, and stood with drawn revolvers as Little was forced to go inside the Davis mansion and bring out all the guns. Little was dragged back to Porum, where the mob took him to an old blacksmith shop, tied his hands to a rafter, and stripped off his shirt. Six of the masked men flogged him unmercifully with a heavy leather strap until his body was bloody and black and blue. The hatred in the Porum Range War seemed to know no bounds. Almost unconscious, Little was dragged to the train station and placed on a southbound Midland Valley. He was told that if he ever returned to Porum he would be killed. Little got off at the first stop and found a northbound train. The conductor was kind enough to hide him in the toilet of the chair car and lock the door until the train passed through Porum. Arriving in Muskogee, Little managed to make his way to the home of Jack Davis, who took him to the family physician. Little was said to have been "an inoffensive old man about 50 years old."[106]

In Porum the angry mob also seized Bob Worthman, who had almost been lynched following the death of James Work, and again he was threatened with hanging. The mob also threatened to hang Buck Davis, whom they found hiding in a small two-story house with several rifles and ammunition. Fearing for his life, Davis confessed that Jack Davis had paid his way from Tahlequah, and that Pony Starr had given him guns and ammunition and instructed him to stay in Porum until Starr contacted him. Reverend McClure quoted Joe Davis as saying that "Porum would be blown to hell in three days."[107]

In Muskogee Jack Davis sought out Rutherford, who contacted the Muskogee County district attorney. An agreement was worked out that, if Joe Davis and Pony Starr surrendered, they would be assured safe conduct to Muskogee and released on bond, providing they agree to remain in the city to await their larceny trials. It was also agreed that Jack Davis would accompany Deputies Sam Tusk and Joe Depew to Eufaula where they would join deputies from McIntosh County and ride to the Davis Ranch to meet Joe Davis and Pony Starr. Tusk was a Muskogee policeman and cowboy who had ridden the range with Davis and Starr, and they trusted him. As a Muskogee County deputy sheriff, Depew had been in charge of bringing Bob and Ammon Davis back from Denver, and the Davises appreciated their fair treatment.[108]

After a rendezvous on the Canadian River, the party rode back to Eufaula, where Joe and Jack Davis, Starr, Depew, and Tusk caught the noon train for Muskogee. As the Katy pulled into the station at Checotah, Thomas Hester and Ben Graham were standing on the platform. Hester had just finished burying his son Clifford, and he was in a fighting mood. Although in the rear of the crowd, Hester spotted Pony Starr on the train. He instinctively whipped out his pistol and attempted to shoot Starr through the train window. Friends of Starr who were near Hester caught his arm and prevented yet another killing.[109] Another version of the story has Lula Davis, "Joe Davis's sweetheart," meeting him at Checotah, and as Davis leaned out the window of the train to kiss her, a man on the station platform drew a revolver intending to kill Davis before someone standing nearby caught his arm.[110]

A large crowd was at the station when the Katy pulled into Muskogee at twenty minutes to two in the afternoon of May 31. When Starr stepped off the train, his wife rushed forward and threw her arms around her husband, embracing him, kissing him, and clinging to his arm all the way to the sheriff's office. Pony had time to grab his young daughter Nina, lift her into the air, and kiss and hug her.[111] Friends were already waiting at the sheriff's office to make bond. After Rutherford and the district attorney met, it was announced that no warrant would be issued because the actions of the two men at Porum had been in self-defense.

### Special Grand Jury

Judge R. C. Allen agreed to convene a special grand jury to investigate the violence at Porum. As news of the Porum gun battle spread across the nation, many citizens in Muskogee County and elsewhere in eastern Oklahoma were embarrassed by how exaggerated the story had become, and that the press was referring to Porum as "Wildman's Town" or "Widowmaker Town."[112]

Many in both Muskogee and McIntosh Counties, including the Davises and the Hesters, waited anxiously for what was certain to be a series of indictments. After two weeks of testimony, thirty-four indictments were issued. Eventually there would be more than fifty, almost all of them for rioting. Twenty-two citizens of Porum were indicted for inciting and participating in the attack on Joe Davis and Pony Starr. The six masked men who brutally beat Steve Little were identified and indicted. Judge Hester was charged with "directing, advertising, and selecting persons to participate in the riot at Porum," as well as resisting an officer.[113]

When the Midland Valley carrying one of Sheriff Weisner's deputies arrived in Porum to serve the warrants, all those indicted, including Judge Hester and

Reverend McClure, were waiting on the platform to be served. Fifty other men from Porum, mostly businessmen and members of the AHTA, rushed to Muskogee to post the fifteen-hundred-dollar bond for each man. Even members of the AHTA from McIntosh and adjacent counties showed up to help with the bonds. When those indicted and their bondsmen crowded into the district clerk's office, it took more than ten hours to process the paperwork.[114] The grand jury also recommended that Sheriff Wisener permanently station six deputies in Porum to help keep the peace.

The lodges of the AHTA in the southern part of the county agreed to forego their annual celebratory picnic to concentrate on the Porum troubles. To assist Jesse Maxwell, who was under arrest and facing mounting legal bills, the AHTA members at Texanna all agreed to donate one dollar or a day's labor. Several teams and plows went to work, and in one day Maxwell's eleven-acre cotton field was plowed.[115] The four lodges in Muskogee County also agreed to levy a fee of two dollars and fifty cents on every member for the purpose of creating a fund of at least one thousand dollars or more to be used to help secure a murder indictment against Joe Davis and Pony Starr as a result of the Porum gun battle.[116]

At the same time the AHTA held a special meeting in Porum to deny any responsibility for the "vigilante attack on Pony Starr and Joe Davis." Although his son had been killed in the gun battle and more than thirty members of the AHTA had gathered at his ranch on the morning of the attack, Thomas Luther Hester denied knowing any of the members of the mob. The AHTA was for law and order, and they commended the calling of a special grand jury. In a series of resolutions, the association condemned the repeated release of men on bond who they claimed were thieves and murderers. In particular, they objected that the "Davis gang was being allowed to run loose," although they had "committed crimes and four murders."[117]

Rumors reached Muskogee that an armed and angry horde of as many as five hundred citizens—many of them members of the AHTA, including several who had survived the assault on the Starr ranch—were gathering on the streets of Porum. They were threatening not only to banish from town anyone associated with the Davises but also to march on Muskogee and kill all the Davises and their friends. When one Davis partisan who ran a hotel in Porum was accused of making remarks that were thought to favor the Davises, he found a note on his front door giving him twenty-four hours to get out of town. Ten minutes later the man was on the northbound train. Others friendly to the Davises, such as Charlie McClure and Charles Horn—fearing they would be beaten as Steve Little had been, or even hanged—were afraid even to board the train. They escaped by horseback in the night to Webbers Falls before going on to Muskogee.[118]

Phelix Latta, a Cherokee farmer and proprietor of the Peay Hotel in Porum, typified public opinion in Porum. Latta told one Oklahoma small town newspaper that the "Davis boys and Starr are thieving citizens and deserve the worst that could be given them." They were all "pretty smart Cherokees and wealthy, but . . . cattle thieves of the boldest type." On the other hand, the Davises had been persecuted consistently, Jack Davis told the Muskogee press, "continuously arrested and taken from their work while their fields went neglected and their cattle were left to graze the best they might."[119]

With a Porum mob threatening to march on Muskogee and hang Bob Davis and shoot Joe Davis and Pony Starr, the Davises, along with Pony and Cassie Starr, their daughter, Nina, and seven "Indian cowboys," took refuge in the Davis home on South Third Street. The house was an "armed camp," the Muskogee press reported, with the "men sleeping on their rifles." Among those who were armed and ready for battle were Cassie Starr and Bessie Davis. To avert any violence at least fifty deputies guarded the county jail where Bob Davis was still being held, as well as the Davis home.[120]

# ARSON, MURDER, AND MAYHEM

There are nine of us widows around Porum
and I don't know how many orphans.

— Daisy Maxwell

**A** week after the epic Porum gun battle, the courthouse in Muskogee was crowded with "jurors, witnesses, and curious people" as Bob Davis went on trial yet again for rustling cattle.[1] Many of the potential jurors admitted having formed an opinion in the case from reading the Muskogee newspapers, so it was difficult to seat a jury. When a jury was finally selected, Dan Foster led off for the prosecution, testifying that he and Cliff Sellers had helped Davis and Starr drive seventeen head of cattle from Younger's Bend to the shipping pens at Checotah, after which he received one hundred dollars from the Davises to leave the country. On cross-examination Rutherford forced Foster to admit that he had served four terms in the state penitentiary. Rutherford also got several prosecution witnesses to admit that they had contributed as much as fifty dollars to a fund to help put Bob Davis behind bars. Sensing he had the upper hand and the burden of proof was on the prosecution, Rutherford rested the defense case without calling a single witness.

Although he was ill at the time, Rutherford still possessed the fire that made him one of the best criminal defense attorneys in the state. In his closing argument to a packed audience, he screamed out that no responsible man would believe Foster or Sellers, both of whom were "confessed criminals."

"Would you," he asked the jury, "trust these men in a business way, would you be willing to loan them money? God forbid that the time will ever come when twelve jurors will be weak enough in wit and character as to be swayed by the same spirit which moves a mob." Men would never "ride to liberty over the ruins of the lives of Bob Davis and Pony Starr, and not only their lives but their wives and families."

In his closing remarks for the state, W. G. Robertson called Davis a "criminal beyond question." Robertson tried to dismiss the criminal records of Foster and Sellers by telling the jury that it was impossible to "convict a cattle thief with a Sunday school teacher."

After two days of testimony, it took the jury less than thirty minutes to acquit Bob Davis. But the very next day, Davis was put on trial in another instance of cattle rustling. Rutherford again rested the case for the defense without calling a single juror. This time Davis was acquitted in twenty minutes.[2]

A day later Pony Starr went on trial. Again, it was hard to seat a jury, and after the venire was exhausted, the sheriff was forced to go into the streets to find potential jurors. Claiming that they had found several new witnesses, the state charged Starr with taking two head of cattle from the same herd that Davis had been acquitted of rustling animals from.[3] Once again, Foster related how he had helped in the theft of the cattle and that he had been given money to keep quiet. Foster quoted Pony Starr as saying that "no witness had ever lived to testify against the Davis boys."[4] Sellers told the jury of his role in the theft and said that the Davises had warned him not to testify. Pony's first cousin, twenty-three-year-old Mollie Sellers, who was married to John R. Sellers, even testified for the prosecution. This time Rutherford put Starr on the stand in his own defense. Starr admitted that he had driven the cattle to the stock pens in Checotah, but he argued that he had purchased the cattle from Foster and Sellers. He also denied having threatened the two men. On June 10, 1911, the courtroom was filled to capacity as Nina Starr sat on Pony Starr's lap and Cassie Starr sat near her husband while Rutherford, arguing well into the afternoon, put forth his usual conspiracy theory that much of the evidence by Foster and Sellers was manufactured. When Rutherford tried to introduce evidence of the deadly Porum gun battle, the judge quickly sent the jury from the courtroom and admonished him. Closing for the state W. G. Robertson spoke for three hours, pleading with the jury to rely on the testimony of good and honest farmers and not "jail birds."[5]

### Guilty as Charged

On Monday morning, June 12, 1911, the jury found Pony Starr guilty. For once Rutherford had lost his magic. Starr did not flinch when the sealed verdict was read, although he did manage a faint smile at some friends. Starr was given one year in the state penitentiary. As was his custom, Rutherford asked for a new trial. When the motion was denied, he gave notice of appeal. "You can tell the world," he promised the Muskogee press, "that Pony Starr will never spend one day in the penitentiary."[6]

On the day after Starr was convicted, Bob Davis and Starr were arraigned in yet another case of rustling. Rutherford argued that the men were being placed under double jeopardy, and that they could not be tried for the same crime twice.[7] But the indictment was for the theft of a different herd of cattle near Texanna. In a minor victory, Rutherford was able to get a change of venue to Eufaula, where he hoped to find a more sympathetic jury. However, in Eufaula, Starr was found guilty again, and this time he was sentenced to six years in prison. Rutherford promptly appealed, alleging improper conduct on the part of the jury.[8]

While Starr was out on bond, he and Joe Davis were among the star attractions at the popular four-day roping and riding contests at Athletic Park in Muskogee. "Pony was one of the ropers but if his work was any criterion, he did not steal any cattle at all because it took Pony about six minutes to fail to rope his steer. He never did succeed in throwing it and finally had to give it up," the local press quipped. With a large crowd in attendance, the Stetson-crowned Joe Davis, although he did not get the award money, was "well up in the front."[9] It was said to have been one of the most successful roping contests ever held in the Southwest, and the star performer at the fair was world champion Henry Clay McGonigle, who was pitted against the Oklahoma champion and favorite son, "Blue" Gentry. By agreement, McGonigle was to rope and tie eleven steers in less time than Gentry could rope and tie ten. McGonigle won with a time of seven minutes and twenty-three seconds. Joe Davis admired McGonigle, who was thought to be the greatest steer roper of his time. He was also a celebrated personality who could throw a thousand-pound steer to the ground with one hand. Having stolen horses in Texas, where he also robbed a bank in Seminole, and rode off into a dust storm with eight thousand dollars, McGonigle lived on the edge of the law. He and Joe Davis would meet in Arizona five years later under very different circumstances. In 1902 McGonigle had accompanied Will Rodgers to Uruguay for the First International Rodeo, but two decades later he was convicted of killing two cattle inspectors at Seminole and was given a fifty-one-year prison term.[10]

Joe Davis did not take the convictions of Pony Starr lightly. Members of the Davis Gang were always acquitted; that was simply the way it was and he assumed that was the way it always would be. Rutherford always prevailed. Disappointed and casting aside numerous threats to his life, Joe Davis rode south from Muskogee—much against the wishes of his family—to check on the family property on the Canadian River before going on to Featherston to check on his own property.[11]

In June 1911, not long after the Starr rustling cases were concluded, Joe Davis and a cowboy named Buck Bertholf went on trial for stealing three colts from Joe's cousin Summie Dunagan. Rutherford was again in action, and after two days of grueling and "hard fought" testimony, it took the jury less than twenty minutes to acquit both men.[12]

The violence at Porum did not end with the deadly gun battle on May 29, 1911. Two days after Pony Starr was convicted of rustling, two gunmen yelling "Uncle Mac!" appeared at Reverend McClure's home late one night. When told by his wife that he was not present, they mounted their horses and rode away, but not before firing several shots into McClure's house. Three nights later, Bud Robertson, the state's key witness in the Jim Work murder case, was sitting on the front porch of a hotel in Porum when gunmen fired fifty shots in rapid succession at the hotel in an attempt to assassinate him. "Out of the night came the flash of a rifle," Robertson said as he fled inside. Jack Davis had no doubt that either McClure and Robertson were lying or the incidents were staged in an attempt to "create public sentiment in their favor."[13]

Several Davis partisans in Porum received letters warning them to leave town or suffer the consequences. John Robertson, who owned property in Porum and a farm adjacent to Sam Davis, received a half-literate letter: "We learn that you have been blowing your head . . . and cussin the AHTA . . . we will attend to your needs at once for we mean business and we will asur[e] you this is no child play for we believe you need attending to."[14] The letter was signed "Commity." Robertson was determined to stay and fight, so he offered a fifty-dollar reward for the identification of the man who wrote the letter. Fearing he was certain to be killed if he returned to Porum, Sam Davis sent a man named Bill Arnold to look after his farm. However, only days after arriving in Porum, Arnold received a note telling him to leave Porum or he would be killed. Arnold and his wife were working in the yard at the Davis property only days later when they were shot at. The couple fled to Muskogee the next morning, swearing they would never return to Porum.[15] Anti-Davis partisans posted men at the mansion, fearing that if the house was burned they would be blamed. Two friends of Pony Starr, Jesse Reynolds and John Miller, were threatened and chased out of the community by Dan Foster. A one-armed Cherokee named Bert Reynolds, who was thought to be a friend of the Davises, was also forced to flee.[16] Davis adversaries, brothers Bill and John "Toll" Redden, were warned to leave town within three days, otherwise they would be "sent to hell." When they refused, two men on horseback fired several shots into Toll Redden's house late one evening.[17]

### Muskogee Courtroom Drama

Bob Davis's trial for killing Jim Work began in Muskogee on September 16, 1911. The trial would prove to be one of the longest and most grueling in Muskogee history. The prosecution, led by County Attorney W. E. Disney, had lined up sixty witnesses. The able Morton Rutherford, as expected, was retained by the Davises. Emotions were running high, and Judge R. P. DeGraffenreid stationed deputies at every entrance and ordered everyone entering the court to be searched. Bob Davis's wife, May, and other wives of the Davises were there in fine attire, as were Pony Starr and his wife, Cassie. Jim Work's widow, Eliza, described as a "little red-haired woman dressed in black satin," was also present, along with relatives of the dead man. Bob Davis sat in a chair beside Rutherford, with "his pretty blue-eyed" two-year-old son Avo seated on his lap.[18]

The courtroom was packed with curious spectators, along with relatives and friends of the defendants and the victim. It took two days to seat a jury. Since it was impossible to find jurymen from the southern part of the county who were not biased, all the jury came from Muskogee or Fort Gibson. The case got off to a rocky start when Rutherford was successful in getting an entire panel of potential jurors disqualified because their names were improperly drawn. Deputies were sent into the streets of Muskogee to find a new venire. Rutherford was also able to get Sheriff Wisener disqualified in the selection of the jury and a prominent real estate agent appointed in his place. When a jury was finally seated, Judge DeGraffenreid ordered the twelve men sequestered and admonished them not to read any newspapers or discuss the case with anyone.

In the days before the trial opened several barns went up in flames near Porum and Warner. Steve McDaniels, a prominent farmer who lived a mile east of Warner and who served as jury commissioner and had helped draw the first panel of jurors, saw his barn, including four hundred tons of hay, burned to the ground. John A.

Martin, a constable and president of the local lodge of the AHTA who lived six miles northwest of Porum, had his barn destroyed. It was the third time Martin had lost his barn to arson. Oscar Stegall, a deputy sheriff at Warner who had previously testified against Bob Davis, said that there was also an attempt to burn his home.[19] At midnight a few days later, the cry of "fire" could be heard in the streets of Porum. Citizens watched as the residence of a man named Craft and the livery stable of Charles J. McClure went up in flames. The Crafts' six children were almost consumed in the flames. Although some of the arson was blamed on the followers of Luther Hester, everyone agreed that most of the fires were the work of the Davis Gang.[20]

In early December 1911 a large barn owned by J. M. McLemore four miles south of Warner was destroyed by fire. McLemore placed his losses, including several horses and mules, at over three thousand dollars. Bloodhounds were rushed to the scene from the Southwest Detective Agency in Muskogee, but the dogs were unable to pick up a scent. There was a "feeling of unrest and alarm among the farmers of that section regardless of the friendships," the *Muskogee Times-Democrat* reported.[21] Many of the citizens in the rich farming and grazing country south of Muskogee prayed that the newly elected governor, Lee Cruce, would declare martial law.

In his opening remarks at the Work murder trial, Rutherford sought to introduce evidence of the violence at Porum and the bitterness that existed in the southern part of the county, in particular the brutal whipping of Steve Little. There was little doubt, Rutherford said, that numerous individuals in Porum were scheming to send Bob Davis to the gallows. When Disney rose to object several times Rutherford shouted, "Sit down," clenching his fist in anger and glaring at the prosecuting attorney. Disney responded that he had no intention of sitting down. "Both of you men sit down," Judge DeGraffenreid bellowed as he ordered the jury from the room until some measure of civility could be restored.[22]

## Always Enthralling Rutherford

Rutherford argued that Bob Davis had returned fire in self-defense, and that Davis did not even know it was Work who was shooting at him. For some time he had feared for his life and thought a mob was coming for him. Davis believed that, if he surrendered, he was certain to be hanged. Rutherford also argued, as he frequently did in defense of the Davises, that Bob Davis was the victim of a conspiracy that existed in the southern part of the county.

In a typical prosecution strategy Disney opened the case for the state by calling Jim Work's grieving widow, Eliza, to the stand. There was not a whisper in the courtroom as she recalled seeing her husband's body being hauled off from the Davis farm in a wagon. As the widow sat in the stand dressed all in black, Disney unwrapped from a dirty newspaper Work's bloodied shirt and vest that he had been wearing on the day of his death. When the vest was lifted before her eyes, the widow broke down in sobs and could only nod in answer to a series of questions, brushing away tears with a cotton handkerchief. The next prosecution witness, J. A. "Bud" Robertson, not only recalled the death of his friend but claimed he had recently been shot at while sitting on the front porch of his house. Rutherford grilled Robertson in cross-examination for over two hours, arguing that Robertson was little more than a drunkard and that even once while intoxicated had shot into his own house. Robertson admitted that he had been drinking at the time but said he was shooting at a cat. Rutherford also got Robertson to admit that he had spent time in the Muskogee County jail. Robertson retorted that it was not because of a crime but because he was afraid the Davises would kill him and sought protection. Several witnesses for the prosecution said they overheard Bob Davis threatening to kill Work.

Sheriff John L. Wisener was the first witness for the defense. Rutherford, with his usual bombastic fireworks, peppered the sheriff with questions. On the stand in his own defense, Bob Davis said he was fearful that a mob would attack his house and hang him. He had not seen the face of the man who fired at him from the woods, only a cloud of smoke. He admitted firing three shots but said that he had no idea he was shooting at Deputy Work.[23]

### Never Set Foot in Porum Again

While the trial continued, Joe Davis and Pony Starr received a number of threatening letters signed simply "Black Hand." The two were warned to leave the country "before it is too late." "You leave, you damn Pony Starr, damn you, don't you ever set foot in Porum again. If you do you are a dead man. This is the last time we aim to warn you," one letter read.[24]

Rutherford put one witness on the stand who testified that he had ridden on the train from Muskogee to Porum with Work, and the deputy told him he was determined to arrest Pony Starr and Bob Davis and if they resisted he would kill them. Chester Pitts of Porum said that, during the recent campaign for sheriff, he and Bob Davis had gone behind a store in Porum for a drink of whiskey. Work later approached Pitts and demanded to know if they had been talking about him. "He said that if Bob was talking about him he aimed to kill him," Pitts said.[25]

Rutherford worked hard to impeach the testimony of Bud Robertson, and to show that Work was bitter against the Davises. R. B. Ramsey, a former sheriff, said that Work was always inquiring if there were warrants he could serve on the Davises. One witness said that on the morning of the shooting he had asked to borrow Work's rifle but was told, "No, I am going to get me a man with that."[26]

In the midst of the trial, W. E. Disney agreed to drop the charges against Ammon Davis and Robert Worthman. Rutherford then proceeded to call Bob and Ammon Davis to the stand.[27] Bob Davis said that Ammon arrived on the day of the shooting and told him there were rumors in Porum that a group of men were out to "get him." The two Davises and Robert Worthman were in the barn saddling their horses to round up some cattle at the time Work arrived at the ranch. Bob Davis said that he had just walked past the corner of his house when someone shot at him. He reiterated that he had no idea the man shooting at him was Jim Work.

In the scorching Muskogee summer the trial had to be moved to the superior court, where the temperature was less severe. A few days later proceedings came to a screeching halt when a large number of the jury came down with food poisoning. Everyone blamed it on tainted food from a thirty-five-cent meal (the price limit set by county commissioners) they had consumed at a local restaurant. When the trial resumed a day later, only five jurors were in the box; the remainder were scattered about the courtroom lying on cots.[28] The courtroom had become little more than a hospital ward, complete with a trained nurse in a gray-blue uniform and a white apron who hurried from patient to patient. Wild rumors were rampant in Muskogee that the jury had been poisoned, perhaps by the Davises. Two of the bailiffs were also incapacitated with food poisoning, and Judge DeGraffenreid had the nurse take the oath as bailiff. It was thought to be the first time in Oklahoma history that a woman served in such a capacity.[29]

The next day, in the midst of the testimony of Robert Worthman, who admitted that he had served time in McAlester, two jurors were so ill that they almost collapsed in court. After several minutes of deliberation Judge DeGraffenreid agreed to call for a physician. Eight members of the jury were now on cots, violently ill, vomiting, and complaining of intense abdominal pain. Several jurors remained on cots in the courtroom over the weekend. By Monday two jurymen were still confined to their beds, while the others looked "pale and haggard," and the judge threatened a mistrial. Amidst all the suffering and drama, two of Bob Davis's children joyously played with a rubber ball in the back of the courtroom.[30]

May Davis, described as "a frail little woman with very dark hair streaked with gray and pansy blue eyes," testified while holding her two-month-old daughter, Lorene. She heard shots, she said, and saw her husband run into the house, grab his rifle, and fire one shot at a man from the porch of their house. Terrified, May, who was pregnant at the time, grabbed her two children and ran to the back of the house for safety.[31]

### Go Back Home Bob . . . to That Little Wife of Yours

His red mustache ablaze, Rutherford was brilliant in his final argument, according to the local press. He even suggested that Work could have been accidentally shot in the back by Robertson. "I know with great confidence in my heart," he told the jury, "as to what your verdict will be . . . I know that you will say to him, 'Go home Bob, go back to that little home which you defended, back to that little wife of yours who waits for your return, back to that little boy, aye to that little babe snuggled in your wife's arms, go back to her Bob, take that little wife in your arms and receive the kisses she is waiting to bestow on you. Go back to that little home which you so bravely defended against lawlessness and riot and live in happiness and peace." As the trial came to an end, Bob Davis seemed to be the "most unconcerned man in the courtroom," gazing "listlessly at the jury," while his brother Sam sat by his side, nodded his head up and down, confirming Rutherford's every assertion.[32]

After two weeks of intense testimony and grueling arguments—with two jurymen still on cots—the case finally ground to an end and went to the jury on October 3. Many thought that Judge DeGraffenreid's jury instructions favored Davis: if Davis knew that Work was a lawman, they should find him guilty; if he did not know the man shooting at him was a lawman, he had the right to defend himself. As the judge read the instructions, Bob Davis, the Muskogee press reported, sat with his "pretty blue-eyed son upon his knee." His "faithful wife sat near in a big picture hat. In her arms was a dark haired baby of a few months."[33]

In Muskogee, it was feared there would be trouble should Davis be acquitted. Numerous deputy sheriffs lined the courtroom and crowded the halls. In Porum, citizens anxiously awaited the latest news from Muskogee. It had been one of the "most bitterly fought cases in the annals of the local courts," the *Daily Phoenix* reported. It was also "one of the longest drawn out . . . and more dramatic than in any case ever tried in the state courts in Muskogee."[34]

Late in the evening on Tuesday, October 3, a little over five months after Jim Work was killed, it took the jury less than thirty minutes to acquit Bob Davis.

The vote on the first ballot was 12–0. Although Sam Davis commenced weeping, Bob Davis sat unemotional. As the clerk announced the verdict, his "face was cold and absolutely expressionless," the *Indian Journal* said. "His lips did not twitch nor did his eyes drop."[35] Davis was "as calm as he was during the long days spent in the court room and no one could have told that he had been under one of the greatest strains a man can ever be called upon to bear," the *Daily Phoenix* reported.[36] Rutherford nodded at Bob Davis as if to say, "I told you so."[37] Within minutes Davis was strutting down the streets of Muskogee with brothers Jack and Sam by his side like a conquering hero.

Only hours later Bob Davis was arrested and escorted back to the Muskogee jail by seven deputies. It seemed as if the Davises' legal problems would never end. Although he had twice been acquitted of larceny, a sentence of seven years for cattle rustling still hung over his head in McIntosh County. The next day, Jack and Sam Davis posted a twenty-five-hundred-dollar bond, and Bob Davis again walked the streets of Muskogee. Under advice from Rutherford, Davis had little to say except that he was "glad to be out and breathe the cool air."[38] He would not say what his plans were, but almost everyone agreed that he could never return to Porum.

### Tainted Legacy

With Ciccro Davis dead, Sam Davis tired of the endless court drama, Bob Davis caught up in innumerable court proceedings, and Jack Davis living in Muskogee, nineteen-year-old Joe Davis began to emerge as the heir apparent of the family's badly tattered and tarnished legacy.[39] Joe seemed to have the daring and reliability of his father and uncles. Many in the family thought he would go far. But Joe seemed to have inherited from his father and uncles an arrogant sense of entitlement, the belief that power and money were everything, and that outlawry was sometimes necessary. Regardless of what crime was committed, somehow jury members and witnesses could always be bought and bribed, and with Rutherford's help he would always be acquitted.

Following Bob Davis's acquittal, the AHTA continued to press for justice. The situation in Porum became so tense that violence was expected at any moment. Since the "Battle of Porum" in May, both the Davis and Hester factions were on edge. Both were heavily armed, "in battle array and ready to fight to the death," it was reported.[40]

When someone wrote the *AHTA Weekly News* inquiring what had become of the Davis Gang, one Texanna farmer responded sarcastically that it was hard to tell, "for some of them are like birds, here and there. There are two or three of them at Muskogee boarding at the Muskogee County boarding house."[41]

In early August 1911 articles splashed across the front page of Oklahoma newspapers announcing that Joe Davis and Pony Starr had given up on Porum and were headed west for a new life in sunny Arizona Territory. The two said that they had purchased a ranch seventy miles west of Phoenix where they would engage in the cattle business, "beginning life over again and striving to forget the past while they hew a future for themselves out of the desert sands." In the vastness of the American West they hoped to find "new pastures" where they would raise "fat beef cattle[,] . . . lead a more tranquil and peaceful life," and in some ways "retrieve their shattered fortunes."[42] They would only return to Oklahoma when necessary for pending cattle rustling court cases against them.

Sick of the bloodshed and violence and fearful of being assassinated, the two said they were determined to leave Oklahoma for good. With the news that the two gunmen were leaving Oklahoma, "a sigh of relief" went up from the southern part of Muskogee County and the bordering portions of McIntosh and Haskell Counties, for the "presence of Davis and Starr there meant a constant menace of bloodshed," the *Ada Evening News* reported.[43]

### Arizona Gentlemen

Davis and Starr arrived back in Muskogee the third week of August, saying they were making plans to stock their Arizona ranch with "high grade cattle." They said that the ranch was purchased at fifteen dollars an acre and consisted of about two thousand acres of semi-desert land. The ranch had several ponds, one near the crater of an extinct volcano that was fed by a live spring and was full of fish. Deer and wild turkey were abundant, and they had killed a fine buck and a half dozen turkey. Once their Oklahoma cases were concluded, they would return to Arizona to lead lives of "country gentlemen."[44] Speculation that Davis and Starr were intent on moving to Arizona proved to be little more than boisterous rhetoric with little substance, however.

Fearful of returning to Porum, Starr eventually got a job selling clothes in Muskogee. "Doin' nothin' got next to my nerves, and I just had to do something," he told a local reporter. "Of course I may not be as handy at this as I was with a rope and—some other things," he continued, a twinkle in his eyes, "but I hope to get used to it after a while." Starr admitted that his life would not be worth "one chance in a thousand" should he go back to Porum.[45]

No sooner was Joe Davis back in Oklahoma when the Porum Range War claimed yet another victim. Charles J. McClure, a close friend of Jack Davis who always sided with the Davises, had received a letter warning him to leave Porum. McClure was one of the key witnesses in cattle stealing cases against Joe Davis and Pony Starr that were scheduled for the fall term of the district court in Muskogee, as well as in the case against the thirty men who were charged with rioting following the Porum gun battle. Cherokee, forty-eight years old, and married with five children, McClure was said to have been a "quiet, unassuming sort of a fellow" and a "staunch friend of the Davis boys." In late August 1911 he was riding through a strip of woods near Porum when an assassin fired at him but missed. Another time at a farm three miles south of town, while sitting on his horse, three shots were fired at him but he again escaped.[46] Threatened by people in the neighborhood, McClure was convinced at last that he had to leave Porum, so he began preparations to depart.

### Face Down in the Road

At 6:40 P.M. on Saturday, August 26, 1911, McClure had been to the home of Sam Davis just north of town and was returning to his home east of Porum. As he was passing by the three-story community school on the northwest side of town, two masked assassins, later identified as Toll Reddin and Ben Call, opened fire from a window on the northwest corner of the second floor of the school. McClure had come to a fork in the road about 150 feet east of the school when four bullets ripped into his back and through his lungs in what the *Porum Journal* called a "cold, premeditated murder."[47] McClure tumbled dead from his horse and landed face down in the roadway, his rifle beneath him. John Moore, one of the first men on the scene, rushed to town for aid, but there was little anyone could do. The two men, one wearing a red mask and the other a black mask, fled from the building, their coats turned inside out, racing north and separating in a field.

Seven-year-old Carlile Vowell later recalled seeing the bullets ripping through McClure's body and hitting the ground in front of him, kicking up dust. Years later he recalled how he stumbled into the two murderers as they ran from the schoolhouse. "They didn't say anything to me. They came out of the school and down the path, one kept bearing out to the left and he was getting way out there when the other called out and said, 'You SOB you're going [to] stay with me.' I was too young or thoughtless to be scared. I just kept running . . . and when I got to Mr. McClure . . . he was laying on his stomach his head on one side, and I'm sure he was dead."[48]

The footprints of the murderers were found on top of the desks they had piled in the schoolhouse so they could shoot out a window, along with tobacco spittle, indicating that they had been waiting for their victim for some time. In Muskogee Joe Davis and his father rushed to the office of the district attorney, certain that members of the mob had killed McClure, demanding the murderers be apprehended.[49] Furious that a close friend had been murdered, Jack Davis offered a reward of one thousand dollars for the arrest and conviction of the men who killed McClure. "Disarm every citizen in Porum and then keep them, forever, from carrying weapons and perhaps the trouble at Porum may be stopped," Jack Davis theorized. Porum was a "feud town where they have killings for meals of the day and hold-ups for late dinners," it was said.[50]

Deputies Joe Depew and Henry Robbins rushed to Porum but were unable to find any trace of the murderers. The masked men were reported to have gone into a house not far from town, but the owner denied seeing anyone. In fact, the deputies were unable to find a single witness to the murder or anyone who was willing to talk. Young Carlile Vowell would not admit that he saw the criminals until years later. Sheriff Wisener and County Attorney Disney were sure the murderers were not from Muskogee County but were members of the AHTA, probably from McIntosh County, who were on their way to a county meeting at Hickory Ridge, about six miles northwest of Porum. A detective working on the case somehow concluded the two murderers were hitmen from Dequeen, Arkansas.[51] Several individuals were arrested and brought back to Muskogee for interrogation, but little was learned and they were released. Over a hundred angry mourners, including Joe and Jack Davis, helped to bury McClure in the small cemetery at Briartown.

Four months later a Muskogee grand jury indicted John "Toll" Reddin and Dan Foster for the murder of McClure. Webb Easton, Charles Terrell, and Toll Reddin's brother Will were all indicted as accomplices for providing the assassins with weapons, helping them change clothes, and assisting them to escape. Deputies came by automobile from Muskogee and swooped down on Charles Terrell while he was working at a Porum livery stable. Terrell, it was said, had driven a buggy that dumped Dan Foster and Toll Reddin off at the schoolhouse the evening McClure was murdered. Toll Reddin had enlisted in the army under an assumed name but was returned to Muskogee from California. Both men hated the Davises. By this time many of the participants in the twisted drama of the vicious Porum feud had begun to turn on one another. Call was convicted of murdering Foster, fearing that he was about to reveal the details of the murder. Three years later, in October 1914, all the charges against Toll Reddin were dropped.[52]

At about the same time McClure was murdered the body of another Porum feudist, a young farmer named Baker, was found buried in a shallow grave in the woods near the village. It was later learned that Baker had fallen out with another feudist, and he had been killed at night, his body taken to the woods and buried. A Muskogee grand jury worked hard to discover who had murdered the young farmer, but they were unsuccessful.[53]

## Spectacle at Eufaula

Less than a week after McClure was murdered, yet another Pony Starr rustling case took center stage at Eufaula. Starr was charged with stealing fifty-one head of cattle from Jim Simpson and Jim Crabtree near Eufaula. Many in Eufaula feared that their town was being sucked into the Porum Range War. Near the confluence of the Canadian and the North Canadian Rivers, Eufaula had once been in a bloody conflict with Checotah over the location of the county seat for McIntosh County, and everyone in the community yearned for peace.

Hundreds of Davis and anti-Davis followers gathered in the small town for the Starr trial. Seventy-five Davis and Starr supporters were quartered at the two-story Tulley Hotel, while the followers of "Old Man Hester" and the AHTA were housed at the three-story, red-brick Foley Hotel, both on Main Street. Both sides came heavily armed. There was little doubt the small town was teetering on the edge of a volcano, ready to explode at any moment. While their Winchesters were kept concealed in their hotel rooms, most of the factions could be seen carrying six-shooters as they strutted about town and dined in Eufaula's restaurants. The "click of a gun would have brought the whole arsenal flashing into action at an instant's notice," the *McAlester News Capital* reported.[54] No one was more concerned than Judge Preslie B. Cole, who ordered Sheriff J. W. McCune to disarm everybody in town. The court order was thought to be one of the most sweeping in Oklahoma history. "A sigh of relief went up not only from the citizens of Eufaula, but from the factionists themselves, as they all realized that a single false move by some hot-head would precipitate a bloody fight that would cost many lives," the *Muskogee Times-Democrat* reported.[55] In all, more than thirty weapons were confiscated from the two hotels. The next morning everyone entering the small McIntosh Courthouse was searched, and several individuals were arrested for carrying weapons.

As expected, Morton Rutherford represented Starr, while a seasoned W. G. Robertson prosecuted for the state. The witnesses were the same as in previous trials and the arguments by the attorneys were similar. At first the jury reported that they were unable to reach a decision, but Judge Cole asked them to continue deliberations. Hopes in the Davis camp rose that the jury would be unable to reach a verdict, but early on the afternoon of Saturday, September 9, the jury returned with a verdict of guilty. When the jury was unable to agree on the punishment, Judge Cole sentenced Starr to six years in the state penitentiary.[56] Rutherford gave notice of appeal and within hours Starr, with the help of the Davises, posted an eight-thousand-dollar bond and hurried back to Muskogee, where he and Joe Davis were scheduled to rope twenty steers the next day at Athletic Park.

Back in Eufaula the following Monday, the cases of Joe and Jack, his father, were scheduled before Judge Cole. Joe was charged with stealing the same cattle near Warner that Bob Davis had been convicted of rustling. Jack was charged with stealing cattle from Thomas Luther Hester the previous spring. With the opposing factions again poised for legal combat, Rutherford asked for a change of venue to Pittsburg County. Most citizens of McIntosh County had formed an opinion in the case and were prejudiced against the Davises, he argued. Rutherford and Robinson "scrapped" all day over the motion before Judge Cole agreed to a special term of the court to begin at McAlester on October 16.

It was feared there would be violence on the northbound Katy that evening. Hester and his followers were content to crowd into the "smoker" at the front of the train while the Davis faction rode in the "chair" car toward the rear of the train. Even when the two groups got off the train in Muskogee, it was feared there would be trouble, but at least a dozen deputies were there to keep the groups apart.[57] Despite threats to his life, Sam Davis returned to Porum to take care of some business. Jack, also hearing of threats against his life, hired two officers to escort him to Muskogee in an automobile.[58]

### Shot in the Back

On Tuesday, September 19, 1911, the Porum Range War claimed another victim. In 1910 twenty-year-old Thomas Cobb—oldest son of John William Cobb and Phenie Caroline Holmes, and the older brother of Lula, Joe Davis's lover—had moved with his family from Texanna to the more prosperous Checotah, where the family had opened a pharmacy.[59] Besides being an excellent cowhand, Tom was perhaps best known in the county for his prowess at winning spelling contests. On the evening of September 19, 1911, Cobb stood in line to buy a ticket to see the Yankee Robinson Circus. Fayette Ludovic Robinson had started the circus in Minnesota in 1875, and it was one of the greatest shows in the country. Half circus and half variety show, the spectacle had arrived in Checotah from Broken Bow and was headed to Atoka before going on to Hugo and then into Arkansas.[60] "The Oldest Show Traveling" featured three rings and two elevated stages and "Consul II, the Man Monkey," along with "Tom-Tom," who was said to be the largest elephant on earth. There were five other elephants: Dutch, Queen, Many, Little Tom, and Bolivar. Complete with lions and tigers, the circus had paraded down the main street in Checotah to the cheers of hundreds. Ticket sales were brisk.

Cobb left the show early and was walking home alone. He had just crossed the Katy tracks, not far from the big show tent, when someone shot him in the back in what the press labeled a "mysterious affair."[61] Although there was a large crowd nearby, no one witnessed the shooting or came forth to identify the shooter. In the dark Cobb had not seen the man who shot him, but he was certain it was because of his association with the Davises. The bullet entered his groin and came out just above his thigh bone. Although Tom was seriously wounded, he managed to hobble home alone. A doctor was called, but there was little that could be done other than cleaning and bandaging the wound. For weeks Cobb suffered in great pain and at times he grew weak. For days on end, he seemed near death.[62]

Tom's father, John William Cobb, died of typhoid fever at the age of fifty-three on May 27, 1916, at Coalton, a small coal town near Henryetta. He was buried in an unmarked grave in West Lawn Cemetery in Henryetta. Four months after his father's death it was widely reported that Tom, who had recovered from his Checotah wound, was also dead. But a week later, the newspapers apologized and said that Tom was not dead after all, but alive and well and "enjoying good health." In December 1915, however, five years after being shot in Checotah and seven months after his father's death, there was no mistaking that the twenty-five-year-old Tom was dead at Coalton, leaving a wife and a young child. He was buried by his father's side in Henryetta. Family tradition holds that he never completely recovered from his gunshot wound and that it hastened his death.[63]

### Just Typical Cowmen

In early October 1911, the legal sparring between Jack and Joe Davis and Luther Hester continued when Jack Davis filed suit—again—against the cattle company of Thomas Luther Hester and George Blackstone. Reviving the previous case in the Muskogee district court, Davis was hoping to recover eighteen head of three-year-old steers branded with the Davis window sash.[64]

On Sunday, October 15, the Davis family, along with dozens of defense witnesses, caught the Katy to McAlester for Joe's trial for cattle rustling, which was scheduled to begin the next day. Rutherford would be able to get the case against Jack

Davis dismissed, but many feared that Joe would be convicted. Besides prosecution witnesses, many in the Hester faction, including a host of Porum citizens, were determined to get a conviction and send Joe to the state penitentiary. All the Davises—including Sam, Bob, and of course, Jack, as well as Pony Starr—were present. As many as 150 law enforcement officials were on high alert, either guarding the courthouse, patrolling the streets, or as one newspaper put it, to "keep the factions from killing one another."[65]

As had been the case in Eufaula, Judge Cole ordered every man getting off the Katy to give up his weapons, and anyone entering the Pittsburg County Courthouse to be searched. Several Winchesters were seized from the Davis followers. "Feelings between the two sides was high," the *Checotah Times* reported. "There is much bad blood between them and a clash is expected every time any of the two clans get together," the *Eufaula Republican* said. Another newspaper classified many of those arriving in McAlester as "bad men."[66] Sheriff Dave Tatum and the McAlester police chief feared that violence could erupt at any moment.

When the southbound Katy train failed to arrive on the morning of the trial, Judge Cole agreed to put the case off until the afternoon. Although he was unable to introduce evidence relating to the Porum violence and the mob attack on the Starr ranch, Rutherford was again at his best. On the evening of the second day, the case went to the jury. They quickly returned a verdict of not guilty. In the Davis camp there were cheers and great relief. As the court adjourned, Joe Davis rushed forward to thank the jury personally, jubilantly shaking the hands of those who had testified on his behalf, and even Judge Cole.[67] Rutherford told the press that McAlester was the first place the Davis family had been fairly treated by the court and the press. "They are all typical cowmen," the *McAlester Capital* reported, and their appearance and deportment gave no evidence of them being "anything but successful men in their business."[68] Quite joyously, the Davises boarded the night train for Muskogee in triumph, although Joe got off at Eufaula to catch the train to his ranch at Featherston. But the legal bills continued to mount, and the strain of the family's finances increased accordingly.

### Davis vs. Hester

Less than two weeks after Joe Davis was acquitted in McAlester, the "famous Hester cattle case" in which Jack Davis was hoping to recover the eighteen head of cattle came to trial in the superior court in Muskogee. Heightening the tensions between the two feuding factions was a fire that swept through Porum on the morning of November 11. It consumed several buildings, including the popular

Commercial Hotel. The fire was thought to have started in a pool hall and was not arson, as was feared. The Davis building that Sam Davis had helped finance survived, although the heat was so intense that glass windows in the building were shattered. With no public waterworks and no fire department, there was little that citizens could do but watch helplessly.[69]

Again, the two sides squared off. No fewer than forty witnesses were prepared to testify. Although feelings among the "Porumites" ran high, it was reported that, for one of the first times observed in these cases, "members of both factions mingled freely with each other, joking, and talking over 'crops.'"[70] As expected, Rutherford was there to represent Jack Davis, while the veteran barrister and former judge W. G. Robertson represented Hester.

Under orders of the superior court, the disputed herd had been driven to Muskogee so the jury could see the animals and examine their brands. Hester testified that on eleven previous occasions witnesses had sworn under oath that the cattle were his. Rutherford pointed out the Davis brand of the window sash on the cattle. Linton McCullough, who had once ridden with the Davis Gang, testified that the Davises had stolen several cattle that were part of Hester's herd. His God-fearing mother had reformed him after he served a term in the county jail, McCullough said, and she told him that he was to always tell the truth or he was certain to go to hell.

For two days Rutherford and Robertson battled back and forth over the marks, brands, and color of the cattle. Forty witnesses from Porum swore there was no doubt that Hester was the rightful owner of the herd. An equal number of witnesses testified that Jack Davis owned the cattle. In the end the jury was deadlocked and the case was dismissed.[71]

### Reticent Young Man

Even more excitement and continued agitation came with the opening of the trials of those involved in the attack on the Starr ranch. With both sides convinced it would be impossible to find an impartial jury in Muskogee, it was agreed to change the venue to Wagoner. Eighteen miles north of Muskogee, Wagoner was a farming and railroad town with twenty trains a day passing through the community, and cotton crops as far as the eye could see. Compared to Porum, Wagoner was quiet and peaceful, and many of the citizens resented the problems from Muskogee County spilling over into their community. Although many in Wagoner gathered to hear nationally known socialist leader Clyde J. Wright speak at the county courthouse, the biggest shows in town were the trials of the Porum mob.

"All the Davis boys are here" and "half of the town of Porum," it was reported. With Judge R. C. Allen presiding, the trial opened on the afternoon of January 15, 1912. It was strange to see Jack and Sam Davis sitting at the bar with the prosecuting attorneys for a change. Five men—Ben Graham, Charles Brooks, Barney Call, Pete Graham, and Lon Baker—had been singled out for prosecution, with Pete Graham to be tried first. While wearing a "Mother Hubbard" dress and a mask, Graham had been seriously wounded in the gun battle and was carried to Muskogee where he eventually recovered.[72]

Joe Davis, "a reticent young man" who "told the story" of the epic gun battle for the first time in public, was the first witness for the prosecution. Joe calmly related how Cassie Starr had confronted the posse at the front gate of the Starr residence, how the mob had opened fire, and how he and Pony Starr had fought it out with the attackers. They were left no alternative but to stand and fight, he said, and they had done so until their ammunition ran out. They then fled on horseback after Cassie Starr saddled their horses. On the stand Pony Starr repeated much of what Davis said. He had fought from inside the house while Davis was at the corner of the house. Starr related how he and Joe had surrendered and returned to Muskogee. Jesse Shumaker testified that he had gone with Dobson to deliver the replevin papers to Hester and to examine the brands on the disputed cattle and they were confronted by a mob of thirty-five to forty armed and masked men wearing Mother Hubbard dresses. Lucy Starr, Pony's sister, related how she had seen the mob of men riding from Hester's farm to her brother's home. She recognized one of the men as Ben Graham. In the "notorious battle of Porum" W. A. Battles, a Porum schoolteacher, described the scene after the fighting and how he had cared for the wounded and helped carry off the dead. One man who was shot from his horse and lost his mask, Battles said, was either Pete or Ben Graham. Over two long days, the prosecution questioned ten witnesses.[73]

### Bad Blood Enhanced

The defense argued that Pete Graham, J. G. Maxwell, and Cliff Hester were not with the masked mob but three hundred yards in front, and that they were passing Starr's house when they were fired upon. In all, the defense put forth twenty-five witnesses. "Every inch is being hotly contested," the local newspaper reported. Every defense witness claimed that Davis and Starr had opened fire first. In the end members of the prosecution thought they had built a strong case, but the jury had no problem acquitting Graham.[74]

Even before the Graham verdict was announced the next case proceeded, with Barney Call on trial. Joe Davis and Pony Starr again told their version of the gun battle, but from the beginning it was evident that the state had less of a case against Call than they had against Graham. The defense argued that Call was in Porum at the time the gun battle started but had ridden to the scene of the fighting and was administering aid to several of the wounded when he was fired on from the Starr residence. In fact, he was trying to help the mortally wounded Clifford Hester when a bullet ripped off his hat. While Call's hat was introduced as evidence, it was said that he recalled the gun battle with a "spirit of bravado."[75] When Call was acquitted, few in the courtroom, including the prosecution, were surprised. All the cases had done so far was to demonstrate the degree of "bad blood among the two factions in Muskogee County." The trials had done little more, the local press concluded, than prove that Joe Davis and Pony Starr, "two extensive cattle dealers near Porum had treated the small farmers very badly, driving off parts of their little herds, changing the brands on them and making life so miserable that they felt compelled to organize with the results that several lives were lost."[76] Within days, the prosecution had dropped the remaining thirty-three cases on the grounds of insufficient evidence. That evening, the Midland Valley south to Porum was full of great cheer. The "riot cases" had been little more than a "waste of taxpayer's time and money," the *Porum Journal* concluded.[77]

For the Davises there was greater tragedy that happened at Wagoner. Twenty-two-year-old Ammon Davis—who lived in Whitefield, just across the Canadian River from Briartown—had been called to Wagoner to testify. He collapsed while calmly walking down a Wagoner street and was diagnosed with pneumonia. Although he was given the best medical care that Davis money could procure, he died. Ammon was said to be a "fine looking young man," and a loyal member of the clan, who was "very popular with his relatives and their friends." Unlike his uncle Bob, he managed to escape prosecution in the Jim Work killing.[78] Because Ammon was unmarried, with his parents dead and no brothers or sisters, Bob and Jack Davis were forced to make the funeral arrangements. Ammon was laid to rest beside his father in the Davis Cemetery near Briartown.[79]

In the southern part of Muskogee County, only weeks after the Wagoner cases were concluded, the Porum Range War continued its violent course. In late March 1912 someone poured coal oil over the northwest corner of the home of Charley Brooks, six miles outside Porum, and set his house on fire. Brooks was one of the more prominent members of the AHTA and had been indicted in the "riot case."

The roof of his house was collapsing when the family was aroused and escaped. Brooks's twelve-year-old son, however, was seriously burned over much of his body and died within hours. In all the arson incidents during the range war, this was the first death, which only served to heighten the anger toward the Davises. At the same time the John T. Whisenhunt place between Texanna and Porum went up in flames.[80]

### Daring the Fate that Befell Him

Late on April 9, 1912, Jack Davis was riding alone on his way to his ranch on the Canadian River. On several occasions he had been warned that to return to his ranch meant certain death. "Defying the enemies that lurked about him," he was determined to return, nevertheless. Jack Davis was a stubborn and proud man. Two shots echoed in the quiet afternoon and Davis fell off his horse in the roadway. One of the shots tore through his arm while a second gashed through his side. Although badly bloodied, Davis managed to stagger to the ranch house where there was a telephone, and a physician was hurriedly summoned from Texanna. When the news reached 705 South Third Street in Muskogee, there was great fear that Davis might die.[81] Joe, Bessie, and several family members hurried south by train and then buggy. The next day Jack was bundled up and placed in a light wagon and taken to Eufaula, where he was put on the northbound Katy. At home in Muskogee under the diligent care of Dr. Claude Thompson, he slowly recovered. He had "dared the fate that befell him," it was said, and he had survived.[82]

Jack Davis said at the time that he was not sure who was trying to kill him, and he was not certain where the shots came from. McIntosh County deputies from Eufaula rushed to the scene but could find no clues. Everyone in Texanna was tight-lipped. "The specter of the bloody feud of Porum belched forth its fiery breath again," the Muskogee press reported.[83] A week after his near assassination Davis was seen walking the streets of Muskogee again although he carried his right arm in a sling.

Six days after Jack Davis was shot, a few minutes before noon on Monday, April 15, 1912 (the same day the *Titanic* struck an iceberg in the North Atlantic), Davis left the family home on South Third Street to walk to the office of Dr. Thompson, a few blocks away on the second floor of the English Building on Broadway, near the corner of Main Street. His heavily bandaged arm hanging limp by his side, Jack was scheduled to have his wound examined and re-bandaged. Constantly fearing assassination, he carried a lever-action Winchester rifle under his good arm. When Dr. Thompson asked why he was carrying the gun, Davis responded tersely, "Those fellows who shot me are in town today, and I am afraid they are going to kill me." While looking out a window overlooking Broadway, Davis suddenly exclaimed, "Yonder comes the men who shot me."[84] Grabbing his rifle, he raced down the stairwell.

Twenty-one-year-old Linton McCullough, who lived near Webbers Falls, had been with Bob and Ammon Davis when Jim Work was killed, but he had turned state's evidence and testified against Bob Davis in one of the cattle rustling cases. Jesse Maxwell had been a McIntosh County deputy and a constable in Texanna and a thorn in the side of the Davises for years. McCullough and Maxwell had caught the Midland Valley morning train to testify in a whiskey-smuggling case in Muskogee. The two men disembarked at about nine, made several calls, played a few games of pool, and ate lunch at the American Café on North Second Street. Walking south down the street from the restaurant, they spotted Jack Davis in front of the American National Bank, rifle in hand.

"If it comes to a fight, Davis will have us bested a thousand ways with that Winchester," Maxwell remembered remarking. Hastily retracing their steps, the two men, both armed with Colt .45 revolvers, made their way along Court Street before crossing a viaduct to the Forrest Hardware Company, where McCullough purchased a saddle, before crossing the Katy tracks to Broadway. It was then that Davis spotted them. "We were just walking along when the shooting started," McCullough testified.[85]

"We were walking along the street not expecting anything. I saw Jack Davis standing in the stairway with the rifle in his hand. I was just a little way behind Maxwell and he turned slightly to say something to me which caused me to look up and that is when I saw Davis. His gun barrel was not more than four feet from me, or at least that is the way it looked to me."[86]

### Praying for the Soul of Jack Davis

Everyone agreed that Maxwell and McCullough were walking west on Broadway and had just passed the stairway near the impressive "Welcome to Muskogee" electric arch. They were only a few feet away when Davis opened fire. Sheltered by the walls of the stairway and holding his rifle in his left hand, as if it was a pistol, Davis sent one bullet ripping into Jesse Maxwell's spine. As Maxwell turned to run, Davis put a second bullet through his right arm that tore through his chest before cutting into his left arm. Maxwell managed to stagger into the Muskogee Drug Store before he collapsed in a bloody heap. Carried to the Baptist Hospital, he remained conscious and was able to dictate a deathbed statement to County Attorney W. E. Disney. As his wife, Daisy, and his brother Ben rushed to his bedside from Porum, Maxwell slowly drifted into unconsciousness and died at half past twelve on Tuesday morning.[87] Before he died, Maxwell was said to have prayed for the soul of Jack Davis.

Two of his brothers, George Wesley and Arthur Edward, had died in the Porum violence, and now Jesse was dead, too. Friends and relatives came to Muskogee to take his body back to Texanna for burial. Besides his mourning family, forty armed and angry men stood by as his casket was lowered into the soft Oklahoma earth.

As McCullough turned to run, his hands in the air, Davis fired a third steel bullet that ripped into his back, passing from side to side through his body. Wounded, McCullough managed to make his way west along Broadway before turning north toward the corner of the First National Bank. He was carried to Dr. Thompson's office on Broadway and then to the McAllister Sanitarium. Hundreds of people were on Broadway at the time of the shooting, and many thought it a miracle that others were not killed or wounded.[88] Both McCullough and Maxwell were carrying revolvers, but they did not have time to use them.

After the shooting Jack Davis walked calmly up the stairs to the law offices of J. A. Dial, W. C. Jackson, and Perry Miller, where he called his brother Sam on the telephone to say that he had just shot two men. Jack always consulted with his older brother in times of trouble.[89]

W. P. Miller, who was mayor of Muskogee at the time, was only yards away from the shooting and was in Davis's line of fire. Fearful that he would be shot by accident, he ran into the drugstore on Broadway before following Davis up the stairs with a city policeman on his heels. Seeing the mayor Davis handed him his rifle, saying, "I'll surrender to you."

With several deputies now on the scene, Davis was hurried through alleys and a side street to the county jail. Davis protested in vain, declaring that he had the right to walk down any street in the city. Interviewed that evening by the Muskogee press, Davis said that he could have killed McCullough, but he did not have the heart to kill a man with his hands in the air.

Morton Rutherford was in St. Louis at the time of the shooting, but a Davis telegram sent him on his way back to Muskogee. Interestingly enough, about fifteen minutes before the shooting, a mysterious telephone call was received at the sheriff's office.

"If you don't want to see trouble, you had better keep Maxwell and McCullough on that side of the track."

When asked who was calling the person replied, "None of your damned business."[90]

As Daisy Maxwell took her husband's body back to Texanna for burial, rumors spread throughout Muskogee that a mob would be arriving from Porum to lynch Jack Davis. Sheriff Wisener posted guards around the Davis house on South Third Street and put additional deputies on duty at the jail.

### Davis Ranch in Flames

Fewer than fifteen minutes after news of the shooting reached Porum, angry men were on the streets, milling around and talking of retribution. That night the Jack Davis ranch house burned to the ground. At first the elderly ranch foreman John Pearce tried to fight the fire, but he was burned badly, and there was little he could do but watch the flames light up the night sky.[91] Officers in Muskogee and Eufaula intimated that the Davis ranch might have been intentionally set on fire by the Davises to create sympathy for Jack Davis and to turn public sentiment in their favor. The Davises thought such assertions were sheer nonsense.

That same night in Porum, Ben McCall, a member of the anti-Davis faction, watched as his two-story hotel on the north side of town was devoured by flames. A drizzling rain hindered the fire, so much of the furniture and household belongings were saved. The next night someone set fire to Sally Starr's residence, an old landmark three miles east of Porum. Bloodhounds were brought quickly from Muskogee on the Midland Valley, but they were only able to trail the arsonist to where he had mounted his horse.[92] By May 1912 at least a dozen homes in the Porum area had gone up in flames.

The day after Davis killed Maxwell and wounded McCullough, he was arraigned before Justice Mel Bailey and charged with murder. With Rutherford still on his way from St. Louis, Davis was represented by W. C. Jackson and J. A. Dial.[93] The prominent defense attorney DeRoose Bailey was also hired. Sheriff Wisener and Joe Depew (now chief of police) issued orders prohibiting anyone from carrying weapons on the streets of Muskogee. The next morning the first two Winchesters to be confiscated were those of Joe Davis and Bob Worthman.

Two days after the Muskogee shooting, a wild rumor made its rounds in the city that both Joe Davis and Worthman had been killed in a pitched battle with anti-Davis forces near Texanna. "The first I heard of anybody getting killed," Joe said, "was when a man asked me as I came up the street if we had had a fight down at the place. He said he heard I had been killed. That was the first I heard of it."[94]

As Rutherford protested vociferously, Judge DeGraffenreid denied Jack Davis bail. For days Rutherford continued to plea for bail, threatening to take the matter to the Oklahoma Supreme Court, but DeGraffenreid was uncompromising. Several of Davis's friends told Rutherford they were fearful that, if Davis was released, it would only be a matter of time before he would be killed.[95]

The only time Jack Davis became agitated while in the Muskogee County jail was when his son Joe came to say he intended to return to Texanna and "bring out" the horses and cattle. "I am the only man who can do it," young Davis insisted. "To ask one of our friends to go is asking them to take too many chances. These things I am going to do, have to be done and I am the only one who can go to do them. I may not come back, but if I do, I will return with some information which will be of use in your trial and I will bring out the cattle." Jack pleaded with Joe not to take any chances, saying that there were numerous individuals around Texanna and Porum who had sworn to take his life in a second. With Bob Worthman by his side, Joe went south by rail and then on horseback, arriving in Texanna only hours before Jesse Maxwell was buried. Within days he was successful in driving most of the Davis stock north to Muskogee, without incident.

Pony Starr, said to be a "man of means and a man of action" and "one of the bravest men in the Porum feud," also gathered his stock and drove them from Porum south to the booming railroad town of Hugo, where he leased a ranch east of town. Starr had been hoping to relocate his stock ever since he and Joe Davis purchased the ranch in Arizona. "He has taken up his home in a land far from the trouble, determined to be at peace with his fellows," the Hugo newspaper reported.[96]

### Most Important Murder Case in Eastern Oklahoma

Once prosecuting attorneys announced they would seek the death penalty, the murder case against Jack Davis quickly became, according to the *Muskogee Times-Democrat*, "the most important murder case ever set for trial in eastern Oklahoma."[97] Playing every legal card available, Rutherford asked Judge R. C. Allen to recuse himself, saying that the judge was prejudiced against the Davises and asking that the case be transferred to the superior court of Judge Farrar L. McCain. Rutherford also asked for an indefinite continuance, saying that it was impossible for him to go to Porum to secure witnesses or even send friends there to do so. Judge Allen denied all of his requests and put the Davis murder trial at the top of his docket.[98] A major obstacle arose when the prosecution was unable to find an important witness, Dr. Claude Thompson. Chief prosecutor W. E. Disney was quoted as saying that Thompson had overheard Davis say, "I am going to kill those fellows," shortly before he shot Maxwell and McCullough. Weeks went by and Thompson could not be found. He was reported to be in Cherokee County, but deputies could not locate him there. A week later, Thompson was scheduled to

FIGURE 15. Newspaper sketch of Jack Davis as he sat in a Muskogee courtroom. On trial for his life, Davis has his arm in a sling, having surviving an assassination attempt only weeks earlier. Muskogee Daily Phoenix, *May 10, 1912. Original sketch enhanced by Eddie Cantu.*

appear at a meeting of the state medical association in Shawnee. When deputies rushed there to subpoena him Thompson failed to show.[99] Judge Allen insisted that the case must proceed without Thompson.

By early May Thompson was located, and Judge Allen set the trial for May 9, with 150 potential jurymen being called. Against fears that someone would try to assassinate him, Davis was driven to and from the county jail in a "closed carriage" escorted by a dozen deputies. Everyone entering the courthouse was searched for weapons by a slew of deputies. Other deputies in civilian clothes mingled among the crowd. With the court packed to capacity, juror after juror was disqualified. Some objected to capital punishment; others admitted to being prejudiced or having already formed an opinion based on the extensive press coverage.

Jack Davis sat beside Rutherford, his arm in a sling, paying "great attention" to the proceedings. Joe Davis, Sam Davis, Bob Davis, Pony Starr, and more than a dozen members of the Davis family crowded the front seats. At considerable expense, the Davises had retained Jackson and Dial to assist

Rutherford.[100] After two days of wrangling, twelve men were finally seated on the jury.

In their attempt to hang Davis, W. G. Robertson argued in opening remarks that when Davis heard that Maxwell and McCullough were in Muskogee he had hurried to his home, secured his rifle, and gone to the business district, where he laid in wait, then killing Maxwell in cold blood and wounding McCullough. There was little doubt, the state argued, that the murder was premeditated and with malice.[101]

Opening for the defense, Rutherford tried unsuccessfully to introduce events of the range war, plus Joe Davis and Pony Starr's gallant defense against the Porum mob. He was able to introduce evidence describing how Jack Davis had escaped assassination near his ranch in early April. Jack had told Dr. Thompson he was certain the men who tried to kill him were Maxwell and McCullough, and Rutherford was working to secure their indictment, he told the jury. Jack had few doubts that Maxwell and McCullough had come to Muskogee to kill him or his son. He had gone downstairs from Dr. Thompson's office to defend "his boy." He was "afraid they were about to meet Joe and take his life."[102] When Davis finally encountered the two men, they made a move for their guns, Rutherford argued, and so he had shot them in self-defense. The jury was also taken to the scene of the shooting on Broadway. Rutherford was successful in forcing the prosecution into devoting much of its energy into proving it was not Maxwell and McCullough who had ambushed Davis near Texanna. One witness swore that Maxwell was in Porum during the entire day when Jack Davis was shot.[103]

## The Blood-Stained Vest

As was the custom in murder cases at the time, the bloody clothes worn by the deceased were introduced into evidence. In the brilliantly lit courtroom, the blood stains on Maxwell's vest were clearly visible to the spectators. The prosecution and defense argued as to whether the deadly bullets had entered Maxwell's body from the front or the back.[104] To add to the drama Daisy Maxwell, dressed all in black, sat with two other Porum Range War widows as a dozen or more fatherless children played nearby. Lillie Belle Hester, having lost her young son Cliff in the violence, sat nearby. Many in the courtroom lusted for revenge against the Davises. Robertson frequently referred to the women in black, saying that the Porum carnage had robbed them of their life and left them destitute.[105]

Linton McCullough was the lead witness for the prosecution. He recalled the reasons that he came to Muskogee on April 15. He described how Davis killed

Maxwell and how he had been wounded. On cross-examination, he admitted that he was carrying a gun because he was afraid of the Davises. The second witness, Dr. Thompson, was of little help to the prosecution. Thompson recalled Davis saying "the fellows who had shot him were in town and that he was afraid they were going to kill him." Thompson testified that Davis was looking out the window when he turned away suddenly, grabbed his rifle, and hurried downstairs. Edward L. Halsell testified that he had seen Davis in Thompson's office on the morning of the shooting and heard Davis complain that the two men who had shot him near his ranch were in town and he was waiting for his son, adding that he was determined to "have it out with Maxwell and the others." Davis said that if he was going to die, he wanted to face his killers and "not have it out in the brush."[106]

Dr. J. O. Callahan testified that he was called to the Muskogee Drug Store where he found Jesse Maxwell "pulseless and dying." He had remained with Maxwell as he was taken to the Baptist Hospital where he expired later that night from internal hemorrhaging. H. H. Brown, the county jailer, said that when Davis was first brought to jail, he remarked, "Doc, a fellow don't know what he will do until he gets up against it."[107]

For the defense George M. Wilkins, a stockbroker, recalled how he was on Broadway when he saw Maxwell and McCullough both move toward Davis with their hands on their hips. Wilkins also said that at least two men had overheard Maxwell and McCullough plotting to kill Davis and his son. Wilkins was directly across the street from where the shooting occurred, and he saw the entire affair. He was leaning on the big electric "Welcome to Muskogee" sign when Maxwell and McCullough made a motion as if to draw their pistols. McCullough then ran past him saying, "I am hurt! Help me!" On cross-examination, Wilkins admitted that he had served a term in the state penitentiary.[108] Other witnesses said that Maxwell and McCullough were both attempting to draw their guns when they were shot. Martin G. Miller, the mayor's brother, said that the two men were moving toward Davis when they were shot and that Maxwell, the smaller of the two, was reaching for his gun. Another witness, a former police detective, described seeing the two men on the morning of the shooting and related that they were passing a bottle between them. He had heard McCullough say that "if he had shot at Davis instead of his horse the other day he would not be here at this time." Maxwell had responded, "Well that don't make any difference, we will get him today."

Pat Griffin, a city employee, said he was walking east on Broadway on the day of the shooting when Maxwell and McCullough stopped him, and Maxwell asked, "You live here don't you?"

When Griffin responded that he did, Maxwell asked him if he knew where Jack Davis "hung out." When Griffin said that he had seen Davis several times in the English Block, the two men walked away and he heard Maxwell remark, "That is the —— we are looking for."

Bill Carr said that he was in Eufaula after Davis was shot near his ranch, and he heard Maxwell say, "We will get Jack Davis yet."

### I Had My Gun in My Hands So I Got Them

Rutherford called Joe Davis to the stand, but the state vigorously challenged much of his well-rehearsed testimony. There was little he could say to defend his father. He had not been with Jack when his father was shot near Texanna, nor was he with him at the time of the Muskogee shooting. Next came the defendant himself. Jack Davis recalled how he was ambushed and wounded while on horseback near his ranch. Contradicting what he had said at the time, he testified that he was sure the men who tried to kill him were Maxwell and McCullough. Davis refused to name a third man he suspected of also being involved in the assassination attempt, but under grilling by the prosecution he said that the third man was Dan Foster. He recalled that a friend, John Campbell, had told him on the morning of the shooting that Maxwell and McCullough were intending to kill him and that he had better "look out."

It was by pure coincidence that he happened to look out the window of Thompson's office and see Maxwell and McCullough on the street, he testified. When asked why he grabbed his gun and ran down the stairs to confront the two men, Davis replied that he did not know if his son "Joe was armed," and he was "afraid they would kill him." He claimed that he had shot Maxwell and McCullough in self-defense.

"They both stopped and both made a motion toward their hips for their guns," Davis insisted. "I had my gun in my hands so I got them."[109]

Reporters covering the trial thought the "most dramatic and thrilling incident of the trial" was when Rutherford reenacted the shooting of Maxwell and McCullough as Davis recalled it. "Davis spoke in a quick manner . . . in explaining the way he used the gun . . . his eyes flashed fire and his face took on a stern almost sinister expression," the *Times-Democrat* reported. He had stopped shooting when McCullough put up his hands.

"When a man has his hands up that is my time to quit firing," Davis told the jury. Davis's "conduct on the stand showed that he is a man of nerve and quick decision," the newspaper went on to say.[110] A rigorous cross-examination failed to break his story.

"To Hang or Go Scot Free" was the headline in the *Muskogee Times-Democrat* on the evening the Davis murder case went to the jury.[111] Some thought the closing argument by DeRoose Bailey in Davis's defense was the best they had ever heard in a courtroom.[112] Many thought Judge Allen, in his directions to the jury, gave the defense an advantage. If the jury believed that Davis had been advised there were threats to his life, the judge said, then he was justified in defending himself.

After the case went to the jury, there were numerous wagers on the streets of Muskogee, as if citizens were gambling on a horse race or betting on the stock market. Odds were for a conviction. The Davis family members were nervous, fearing a possible death sentence. Most conventional wisdom was that Davis was guilty and would be convicted. At three o'clock on the afternoon of the second day of deliberation, the jury returned to the courtroom and asked to see Maxwell's bloody vest once again. Each juror carefully examined the blood-stained garment, passing it from hand to hand, carefully examining the holes the bullets had torn in the cloth as Davis watched intently. Rutherford had argued that the first bullet struck Maxwell in the front part of the shoulder, while the prosecution insisted that he was shot in the back.[113] With only the lawyers, defendant, and Judge Allen present, they also asked that Davis's testimony, along with that of Mayor Miller and several others, be read to them.

From the beginning of deliberations the jury was hopelessly deadlocked. Had Davis killed Maxwell out of revenge, or was it in self-defense? On the first ballot the vote was eight to four for conviction. After twenty-four hours, the jury stood seven to five for a guilty verdict. Late on the third night, with little progress being made, Judge Allen declared a mistrial. Although Rutherford professed disappointment that Davis was not declared innocent, the Davises were greatly relieved. The defense attorneys and the Davis family had feared the worst. Within hours Davis was out of the county jail on fifteen-thousand-dollar bail and was spotted casually walking the streets of Muskogee as if on a Sunday stroll.[114]

The county attorney announced that a second trial would begin on June 5, 1912, and that Thomas H. Owen, a prominent local attorney, had been added to the prosecution team. With one criminal case after another, Muskogee County was running short on funds, so several prominent citizens of Porum agreed to pay for Owen's services.[115]

To add to the anxiety of the Davis family, only days after the Muskogee mistrial, news came from the Oklahoma Criminal Court of Appeals that Bob Davis's conviction for rustling had been upheld and he would have to serve two years in the state penitentiary.[116] At the same time, news arrived that a cousin of the Davis brothers, Jeff Davis, said to be found in possession of his neighbors' cattle, had been shot and killed at Collinsville in Rogers County.[117]

As the Davises waited for Jack's second trial to commence, Pony Starr was almost assassinated in Durant. By coincidence, Starr was at the home of a friend when he ran into William Work, brother of the deceased Jim Work.

"Hello Pony," Work said as he grabbed a pistol and shot Starr in the leg. "I shot Pony Starr because I thought he was after me. If I had it to do over again, I certainly would not do it differently," Work proclaimed. "My only regret is that the shot was not a better one, for I believe Starr and his gang are after me."

Work had sold his farm in McIntosh County on the advice of friends who warned him the Davises would kill him on sight. He moved to Bryan County. A year later, in 1913, Work was found guilty of assault to murder and was given six months in the state prison.[118] After the shooting, the "much-shot-at Starr" returned to Hugo, where he was seen hobbling about the streets on crutches.[119]

### A Second Murder Trial

When the second Davis murder trial finally opened in early June, Rutherford succeeded in getting Judge Allen replaced by Judge R. P. DeGraffenried. Rutherford also tried, unsuccessfully, to disqualify Sheriff Wisener, who he alleged had allowed Dan Foster, an open enemy of the Davises and four-time convict, to serve subpoenas on members of the Davis family.[120] Rutherford did get an entire venire of 150 men quashed before a jury was finally seated. The trial began on June 6, 1912. With his arm in a sling Jack Davis sat patiently by Rutherford's side. Pony Starr was seen hobbling in and out of the courtroom on crutches. The day before the trial began Daisy Maxwell, the dead man's widow, gave birth to a son at the Rockefeller Hotel across the street from the courthouse. Born in the mountains in Arkansas, Daisy had said she was hoping to return to Porum with her children and live in peace. "There has been so much death and sorrow," the *Daily Phoenix* reported her saying, as her blue-eyed, seven-year-old son, Guy, stood by her side.[121] The day before, her son had come into the hotel room where the family was staying, "shaking his chubby fist" in his younger brother's face and saying, "You just wait; we'll get Jack Davis yet."

"No son, you must not talk like that," his mother cautioned.

When the son asked to go down the street and play with other boys, the mother responded, "No darling, I can't afford to lose you too."

Daisy Maxwell claimed that the Davises put a fifteen-hundred-dollar bounty on her husband, and that some men had thrown rocks at their house, hoping her husband would come to a door or a window so they could shoot him. "There are nine of us widows around Porum," she said, "and I don't know how many orphans." The three Maxwell widows alone had fourteen children who were left without a father. "I will make a living some way," she continued, "I don't know just how, but I will."[122]

In his opening remarks Rutherford was at last able to sneak in information about the range war, much to the objection of the prosecution. The testimony by the different witnesses was much the same as in the first trial. Dr. J. O. Callahan testified that the bullet that killed Maxwell had entered the back of his body, but Rutherford got the doctor to admit that the deadly soft-nosed bullet that Davis fired would make a small hole on entry and would tear a bigger hole in passing out of the flesh—the hole in the front of Maxwell's vest was much smaller than the hole in the back. In cross-examination, McCullough admitted that he bought a revolver in Muskogee "for the Davises."[123] With the courtroom packed to capacity, the *Daily Phoenix* reported, "the trial shows every evidence of being a hard-fought one."[124]

### In the Early Morning Heat

One difference in the second trial was that Judge DeGraffenreid gave the jury the option of finding Davis guilty of manslaughter, which would carry a sentence of from four to twenty years. They could also acquit Davis or find him guilty of first degree murder, with either death or life in prison as the sentence. Again, the jury asked that much of the trial transcript be read back to them, especially Jack Davis's testimony. The betting on the streets of Muskogee this time was that the jury would either return a verdict of manslaughter or be unable to render a verdict, as in the first trial. In the early morning Oklahoma heat on Saturday, June 15, 1912, after forty hours of deliberation, the jury announced that they had a verdict. Everyone rushed to the courthouse. Jack and Joe Davis met Rutherford on the steps as tensions reached epic proportions. The commotion was so great that the judge threatened to have anyone arrested who did not remain quiet. The verdict was a surprise to almost everyone who had sat through the trial. In a glaring headline the five-cent *Times-Democrat* said simply, "Jack Davis Not Guilty."[125] On the first ballot in the jury room, the vote had been ten to two for acquittal.

An eleventh juror was won over on Friday afternoon. On Saturday morning a final juror, a farmer from Haskell, went over to the majority.[126]

When the verdict was announced, a breathless silence fell over the court as Jack Davis broke into a big smile and rose to grasp Rutherford's hand. Much like a conquering hero in ancient Rome, Davis strode forward to shake the hands of the jury and thank them personally for his acquittal. Rutherford said that he and the Davises always "put up a wonderful fight."[127] The *Porum Press* said Rutherford was the "greatest defender of criminals, murderers and outlaws" that had ever been seen in Oklahoma. The newspaper ripped into Rutherford for saying that the people in Muskogee were far more civilized than those living in Porum.[128]

Rushing out of the courthouse, Joe Davis hurried to the nearest telephone to call his mother and other family members with the good news. Bessie, always the loyal wife and mother, never had any doubt that her husband was innocent. Jack and Joe Davis, along with Pony Starr and a small crowd, followed Rutherford to his office, where Davis spoke briefly to the press. "I shot Maxwell in self-defense and honestly believe that he was about to kill me. . . . I am not an outlaw as some would picture me and all I have ever asked for was to be left alone." Jack said that he was trying to sell his farm near Texanna and wanted "nothing more to do with the people in the southeastern part of the county." From the beginning, Rutherford told the press, he was convinced he "was defending an innocent man."[129]

Daisy Maxwell "wept bitterly" upon receiving the news in her hotel room. She had never wanted revenge, she said, but she had no doubt that her husband "was shot in cold blood and without warning and I believe the man who took his life should be punished."[130] A lengthy editorial in the *Times-Democrat* asked the citizens of Muskogee County to accept the verdict and remain calm. Many in the city were concerned, nevertheless, that it was possible for a man to "shoot down his enemies on the public streets without fear of conviction."[131]

Muskogee's two largest newspapers, the *Daily Phoenix* and the *Times-Democrat*, both editorialized in hope of somehow stopping the violence that had for the first time spilled over into the streets of the city. "The Davises and anti-Davises . . . should avoid the other. There has been sufficient trouble and blood shed on each side. There can be no good reason for a continuation of hostilities. Let both sides obey the law and let their carnage of blood shed cease," the *Times-Democrat* wrote.[132]

A little over three weeks after Jack Davis was acquitted, the Porum Range War claimed yet another victim. Tom Smith, a farmer who had been a witness for the defense in the Muskogee murder trial, was shot and killed near Porum.[133] It seemed as if the vehement passions around Porum would never subside.

### Death in a Thunderstorm

During the Porum Range War the unflappable and consistently conniving Dan Foster, said to have been a "notorious character," seemed always somehow to be involved. At one time the fearless, Hoosier-born Foster, who talked little, had been an ally of the Davises. However, over several years he had become a bitter enemy. Although Foster was a constable at Porum, Jack Davis was convinced that he was one of the men who tried to kill him at his ranch in early April. Foster had also been an important witness for the prosecution in several of the Davis-Starr cattle rustling cases, and it was widely rumored in Porum that the Davises had put a price on his head.[134] Many on both sides of the feud did not trust Foster and saw him as a double-crosser.

On July 25, 1912, he was riding with Bill Reddin, one of the men accused of murdering Charles McClure a year earlier, when the two men were ambushed and shot at by Barney Call.[135] "We were riding toward Porum," Reddin said, "when two shots were fired at us in quick succession." Foster's and Reddin's horses reared and jumped about, but the two men were able to turn in their saddles and get off several shots at Call, who they said wore a tall white hat. Although they fired several times at Call, he escaped into the underbrush.[136] Foster took the train to Muskogee to complain to the county attorney, but all Disney would do was suggest he "better leave the country or he would get shot."[137]

Two weeks later, on the afternoon of August 8, 1912, two and a half miles south of Porum on the road to Briartown, Dan Foster was shot and killed during a violent thunderstorm. Jack Davis assured the press that the homicide could not be traced to the Davises, though he expressed no regret that Foster was dead. In fact Foster "ought to have been killed ten years ago," he continued. Although he had served four terms in the state penitentiary, Foster worked for several years as a constable in Porum and at one time was married to a Starr. He had been visiting a friend south of town and was encouraged to wait out the storm, but he decided to ride back to Porum. Late in the afternoon, he was riding alone, his head partly concealed in his coat to avoid the sheets of rain pouring down, when there was a flash from near the roadway, a deafening crack of thunder, and then a second flash. Foster was seen by an observer to totter in the saddle and fall to the ground. Only minutes after his riderless horse galloped through the rainstorm into Porum, there was news that an unknown man was lying in the roadway south of town.

A sewing machine salesman returning to Porum in his carriage found the body in the roadway. At first it was thought that Foster had been struck by lightning, but an inquest the next day in Porum determined that a soft-nosed bullet, probably fired from a Winchester, had gone through his right arm and into his shoulder, shattering a rib, and passed clear through his heart, finally lodging in the skin on his left side. Death was instantaneous. Deputies found where an assassin had laid in ambush in a field of oats for several hours near the roadway. Footprints were traced through the underbrush and the mud to where a horse had been tied to a tree about seventy-five yards from the scene of the murder.[138] Foster was the fifteenth man to die in the bloody range war.

Foster's body was taken to the Jesse Maxwell house where Foster had been a boarder. He was buried the next day in the cemetery south of town. Many in Porum had hoped that the violence would end with the death of Maxwell in Muskogee, but Foster's murder quashed any hopes of peace and quiet.

### Ninety-Nine Years in State Prison

Everyone in Porum was sure that it was Barney Call who murdered Foster, despite the fact he was a "clean-shaven young man."[139] When deputies arrived from Muskogee on the day after the murder, they found a pool of blood in the roadway and the assassin's hiding place in the oat field, along with two spent 30-30 Winchester cartridges. Call had left his home in Porum a short time before the shooting and was seen returning on horseback a few minutes after the fatal shots were fired. Call's horse was tracked by the deputies from his barn to the scene of the killing and back again. The horse tracks were those of a horse shod only on two feet, and Call's horse had two shoes only. From the murder scene the trail led down a small creek, through a cornfield, across the Midland Valley Railroad tracks, and directly to Call's barn. In several places fences had been cut, and a pair of wire-cutters was found in Call's saddle bags. Moreover, when the deputies arrived, Call's saddle in his barn was still wet.

With a mountain of evidence and numerous witnesses, prosecutors were able to convict Barney Call of first-degree murder. He was given ninety-nine years in the state penitentiary. In the Muskogee courtroom, his nineteen-year-old girlfriend, Isabelle Higgins, sat by in tears.[140] After all the deaths in the southern part of the county, Call was the first man to be convicted.

In December 1912 county attorney Disney hauled Call and his girlfriend before a grand jury to obtain their knowledge of the range war and the killings around Porum. Higgins knew little and Call, already under a life sentence, would only testify if given immunity from additional charges. News that his father, Ben Call, was indicted as an accomplice in the murder of Charlie McClure did not help his mental state. Within days Call suffered a mental breakdown.[141] A month later, while still at the Muskogee County jail, Call came down with spinal meningitis and became delirious. With the fear that he would infect other inmates, the jail was quarantined and the inmates transferred to the city jail. Call was spirited away to a small old house on the north slope of Standpipe Hill where, the local press reported, "the chill blasts from the north whistle through the gaping weather boards and warped windows and doors." In this house Call fought a losing battle with death. His family came north from Porum and were shocked at his emaciated condition. He slipped in and out of consciousness and died with his girlfriend by his side.[142] Although indirectly, the Porum Range War had claimed another victim.

County Attorney Disney was able to convene a second grand jury a few days before Christmas. Disney was determined to bring to trial those responsible for the mayhem and suffering and to end the fighting. Caught in the fiery politics of the era, the grand jury also agreed to look into the conduct of Sheriff W. R. Robinson, as well as the collusion between county and city officers in the gambling and bootlegging that flourished in Muskogee. But the Porum Range War retained center stage, and dozens and dozens of witnesses were subpoenaed. A chief witness was James Robbins, a city detective who had worked as deputy sheriff for several years and who spent weeks investigating the Porum troubles. "One by one the blood stained pages were turned before them," the *Daily Phoenix* reported with respect to the grand jury, "sometimes slowly, at times with [so] much rapidity that it left them aghast."[143]

A number of the wives of the Porum feudists were subpoenaed. Several of the women refused to answer any questions and were promptly jailed. Bud Robinson and a farmer named Houston Curry also refused to answer any questions. They, too, were sent to jail. Witnesses were called and recalled. So intense was the grilling that some left the jury room in tears. Several witnesses were indicted for perjury, and they too were jailed. The sister of Barney Call and Sarah McClure, Charlie McClure's wife, did agree to testify. Even working on Christmas Day, the grand jury was determined to get to the bottom of the range war. Four men were indicted for killing McClure, but the jury could never learn who killed the young farmer named Baker, whose body was found in the woods near Porum.[144]

Two days after Christmas a new grand jury convened and began investigating how the previous grand jury had collected evidence. More Porum residents who refused to talk were thrown in jail. New evidence was uncovered, and the new sheriff—James Franklin "Bud" Ledbetter, a local hero with a reputation for righteousness and justice—appeared to bring a new degree of honesty and fairness to the county.[145] Although the Muskogee County grand juries did bring some of those responsible for the Porum mayhem and violence to justice, they never really got to the bottom of the Porum Range War—and they never touched the Davises.

### A New and Unsettled Country

Fearing that he would never be able to return safely to the family ranch near Standing Rock, Jack Davis put the family's 520 acres up for sale. There were at least two offers of fifteen thousand dollars for the property, but the offers were declined. Finally, in August 1912, Davis found a buyer in Muskogee and sold the ranch for eighteen thousand dollars. Shortly thereafter he also sold the family home in Muskogee.[146] "With his fortune almost gone and a price upon his head, Jack Davis, leader of the Davis faction of the feudists will move to Ardmore," the *Daily Phoenix* reported. Davis had "escaped death many times" and had been "shot at from ambush." Davis's right "arm now hangs almost useless from a bullet wound," the newspaper went on to say.[147]

But Jack Davis's family did not move to Ardmore as speculated. Instead, Davis announced he had found a place near Monument, New Mexico, southwest of Hobbs, "in the wilds of Eddy County and more than 50 miles from a railroad." Here he could at last find peace. The "passing of Jack Davis means that Muskogee County is soon to lose the last member of the family by that name—a family which has attained more notoriety than any other one family in Oklahoma," the *Times-Democrat* reported.[148]

After twenty years of fighting with rustlers, homesteaders, and lawmen, as well as being a sign of the "onward march of civilization," Jack Davis decided to give up his struggle in Muskogee and McIntosh Counties in a "desire to secure peace [and] migrate to a new and unsettled country." The conviction of Pony Starr and his brother Bob along with the deaths of his archenemies Jesse Maxwell and Dan Foster combined with his growing unpopularity and infamy in Porum and Muskogee played heavily on Jack Davis and his decision to "quit the game." Jack visited Bob in prison in McAlester, and it was hoped his brother would join him in New Mexico as soon as he was released. Some speculated that Sam would also move to New Mexico. Fearing for his life Samuel Tate Davis sold his two-story mansion, his farm, and all his property in Porum and moved to Tahlequah.[149]

In October 1914 Bob Davis, who was serving a five-year term for rustling, and Pony Starr, who was serving a second sentence of six years for the same crime, were among the forty-four criminals paroled by Acting Governor J. J. McAlester. Governor Lee Cruce, who was out of the state at the time, protested that Governor

McAlester's actions were unconstitutional, since McAlester had not gone through the state prison board, nor had the secretary of state affixed the Oklahoma seal to the documents.[150] The Davis family helped circulate a petition asking that Bob Davis be granted a pardon also, but the AHTA raised a counterpetition opposing any such pardon, arguing that Davis was dangerous.

Only weeks later, Jack Davis told the newspapers that he was not moving to New Mexico after all. Pony Starr had persuaded him to buy a ranch located thirty miles northeast of Hugo in the heart of the Choctaw Nation, on Glover River, ten miles from Noah and Ider and fifteen miles from Little Creek. The new ranch was in the pine-shrouded Kiamichi Mountains in the wild western part of McCurtain County.[151] Here Davis built a large fortress-like ranch house on a rise in a little prairie, five miles from the nearest habitation. The walls of the house were cut full of loopholes so guns could be fired.[152]

Davis had decided to stay in Oklahoma after all. "He hopes to live there in peace and will start anew," the *Hugo Husonian* reported.[153] At the same time, Davis bought a large home on the southeast corner of Third Street and Main in Hugo and began moving his family from Muskogee. Jack Davis is a "picturesque character in Oklahoma and one of the heavy financial men of the east side," the Hugo newspaper reported. With his vanity sometimes getting the better of him, Davis told the newspaper that his sons were all "college men."[154]

By August 1912 Jack and Joe Davis had also begun moving the family's large herd of over five hundred cattle from the Canadian River to the new ranch. Although most of the cattle were driven overland, some of them were shipped from Eufaula. Joe and hired hands Buck Burtholf, Bob Worthman, and an unnamed black man as a cook went first to Muskogee to retrieve several saddle horses. Including ponies from the ranch on the Canadian River, they drove a large herd of over fifty horses and mules across country on a weeklong drive to the McCurtain County ranch.[155]

Only days later, with his vanity again run amok, Jack Davis announced in a telephone interview with the *Daily Phoenix* that he was forming a motion picture company to produce a "picture show" of the epic Porum Range War, complete "with its tragedies, with its heartaches and sorrows, and with its loves and hates." No professional actors would be needed. The central figures, including himself and his son, would simply play themselves. With passion and ferocity, they would all "live over the scenes that have burned into the souls of the Porum feudist." Moreover, Jack was contemplating entering the motion picture business as a professional actor. He had not decided where he would film the scenes, but he said he would form his own company and take his own pictures with his "bunch" as the main actors. "Love amidst the hatred of the feud will be depicted," Davis went on to say, complete with "the haunts and fears that drive a man who commits a crime to live in constant dread that his crime will find him out." The movie, Davis said, "will be a sort of psychological study of the feudist mind." Although he professed to do so, it was hard for Jack Davis to let go of the past. At times it seemed almost to haunt him. Whether he was actually contemplating such a "picture show" or was simply playing games with the Oklahoma press remains a mystery.[156]

## The Wilds of McCurtain County

The *Daily Phoenix* pondered, partly in jest, if Davis would be depicting the earliest years of the violence. According to the confessions of Mack Alford, whole families were wiped out when their wells were poisoned. Men were butchered and thrown in the Canadian River while the "murderers drew lots for their valuables." There had been "midnight rides when victims, drugged, were dropped off in a river" and were said to have drowned. This is all according to Alford.[157]

The *Porum Journal* poked fun at the *Daily Phoenix* and the newspaper's "scoop" in interviewing Davis about his proposed movie and acting career. "Scoop" and Davis have "prolific imaginations," the newspaper quipped. "Me and Pony is going to act before the camery and put on a picher show of the Porum feud," the *Journal* mocked Davis as saying. "Me and Pony can go over the whole thing in real life. Then we will put on the show in Muskogee and use bean sacks to hold the coin."[158]

Always anxious to talk to the press, Davis told the *Times-Democrat* that he was perfectly happy living in Hugo and at his new ranch. "I am living in peace and prosperity," he said. "I have fine neighbors, my family is in good health and we are living happily." Davis looked "prosperous and contented," the newspaper concluded.[159]

Even before Jack Davis moved away from the Porum bloodshed to the wilds of McCurtain County, a new chapter was unfolding in the life of his son Joe Lynch Davis. What lay ahead would perhaps eclipse the drama of the Porum Range War. In the end it would lead Joe Lynch Davis straight to the federal penitentiary at Leavenworth, Kansas.

# → 4 ←

# "ALIBI JOE" IN THE
# LAND OF THE SIX-SHOOTER

Oh, we tried to live right after we left Porum,
but they wouldn't let us alone.

— Bessie Davis

In the early morning darkness of October 28, 1912—only hours before the Great Commoner William Jennings Bryan passionately and extemporaneously enthralled thousands of rural Oklahomans at Eufaula—the Katy Limited No. 9 rambled south from Checotah on its run from St. Louis, Missouri, to Galveston, Texas, on the Gulf of Mexico. Fifteen minutes behind schedule, near the small station of Wirth, on a clear moonlit night at precisely 2:35 A.M., just as the train eased into the Canadian River Valley, Ed Thomas, the engineer, looked out to see a bright reflection in the sky. Closer examination revealed a railroad bridge was on fire. The brakes on the Katy Limited screamed into the cold Oklahoma night as more than one hundred sleeping passengers were jolted awake in the Pullman cars.[1]

Once the train screeched to a halt, the Katy crew, including the conductor, John N. Dolan, and a fireman, William Kelm, rushed forward with buckets of water to extinguish the fire. "We can put this fire out—it's just started," Kelm shouted to Dolan. Suddenly three baby-faced masked men, little more than mere boys, appeared out of the darkness from the west and poked Winchester rifles in the ribs of the trainmen.[2]

"No, I'm sorry you can't put it out," a short, heavyset outlaw calmly said. "Stick up your mitts and keep quiet. We don't want to have to kill you. We don't intend to rob anyone who has to work for a living." More excitedly, a taller bandit shouted out: "To hell with the bridge, up with your hands." A third outlaw jokingly told the crew they "had other work for them."[3]

Badly in need of money for their mounting and insurmountable legal fees, especially after Jack Davis's high profile Muskogee murder trial, Jack and Joe Davis had decided to rob the Katy Limited. "The Davis boys have spent a fortune on lawyers," one Oklahoma newspaper observed in September 1912.[4] Both father and son had inherited the Cherokee hatred for the railroads, and they carefully selected a spot just north of where the Katy crossed the Canadian River, a few miles south of Eufaula.

By late October 1912 Jack and Joe Davis had put together a reliable gang of veteran outlaws. Robert Worthman was still working for the Davises at the time and they trusted him. He had ridden with Joe Davis for several years and the two had rustled cattle together. Twice he was convicted of larceny and he had served two terms in the state penitentiary.[5] For a while William "Buck" Bertholf had been the foreman on the Davis Ranch on the Canadian River. He had also rustled cattle with Joe Davis and he, too, had spent time in the state penitentiary. For several years Jack Davis paid Bertholf two dollars for every "stray" he could find and drive to the Davis Ranch, "the old bottom place, the old ranch place," as Bertholf remembered.[6] A leading Muskogee entrepreneur described Bertholf as "a low down thief and drunkard."[7] Another member of the gang, Tom "Montana Slim" Spencer, was a notorious criminal who had worked for the Davises for several years and had been in a number of scrapes. He had the reputation for being one of the best "yeggmen," or safecrackers, in the West.[8]

The day prior to the robbery of the Katy, Spencer rode into Eufaula and purchased twenty-four sticks of dynamite, all he could find in the town, saying he was digging a well.[9] At the same time, Buck Bertholf took three horses to a blacksmith in Blocker, a small town on the Fort Smith and Western Railroad in Pittsburgh County, fifteen miles northeast of McAlester, asking for light shoes, saying there was some "hard riding for them that evening."[10] About a week before the robbery Bertholf approached Roy Van Brunt—a farmer, convicted criminal, and whiskey peddler who ran a gambling house in Eufaula and someone the Davises knew was good at using dynamite—saying that "Uncle Jack" wanted to see him in Muskogee. When Jack Davis and Van Brunt met a few days later, Davis asked Van Brunt if he was making any money. "Roy, we can make a good piece of money. We are going to hold up this Katy Limited train and get some moncy out of it," Davis said.[11]

Van Brunt said he was good with explosives, but he did not think dynamite would blow one of the safes on the train. Moreover, if they did rob the Katy, they were likely to be "picked up" and "get it bad."[12]

"You know the boys are all right," Davis responded. "Well you keep this under your hat. We will get into this and get a piece of money," Davis continued.[13] The day before the robbery, even, Bertholf went to Eufaula to persuade Van Brunt to join in on the heist but Van Brunt remained reluctant.

On the early morning of October 4, 1912, four masked men held up the northbound Kansas Southern and Rock Island Railroad on the Tarby Prairie, three and a half miles north of Poteau, only a few miles from the Arkansas border. They blew open the safe in the express car, ransacked the mail, and escaped into the woods with several thousand dollars.[14] The men were never caught. G. E. Lewis, US postal inspector at Muskogee who was in charge of investigating train robberies in eastern Oklahoma, had little doubt that Joe Davis and his gang of outlaws were responsible.[15] There is no historical evidence to substantiate Lewis's claim, however.

### Robbing the Katy Limited

Jack Davis was clearly the mastermind of the small gang of outlaws that robbed the Katy Limited. He and Joe had carefully studied the Katy timetable and decided on the place for the theft. Although Joe was assuming a larger role in family affairs, Jack was still the kingpin. Spencer would blow the safe in the Katy baggage car while Joe and Worthman guarded the train crew. Bertholf would hold the horses in a small grove of trees near the railroad.

Realizing there was a robbery in progress, one Katy employee rushed through the passenger section of the train warning the passengers to hide their valuables. A black porter on the Katy named A. J. Henderson was forced to uncouple the passenger section of two chair cars and four Pullmans from the rest on the train. Fearing he would be scalded, Henderson had a difficult time disconnecting the steam hose. Every time he hesitated Worthman punched him with the butt of a Winchester and yelled at him to hurry up. Once Worthman threatened to shoot Henderson, saying he had always wanted to "kill a negro."[16] Allowed to go to the opposite side of the train where he could more ably disconnect the hoses, Henderson was warned that if he tried to run, he would be shot. After several minutes the hoses were finally uncoupled.

One outlaw—a tall slender young man wearing cowboy boots, a large Stetson hat, a light coat with a white mask over his face, and wielding a pistol—forced the locomotive fireman, thirty-year-old William Kelm, into the cab of the engine and ordered him to pull the train forward until he was told to stop. When Kelm protested that the burning bridge would not support the weight of the engine, the bandit screamed out, "Damn the bridge. Go ahead till I tell you to stop."[17]

Kelm asked the outlaw how far down the track he was to take the train. "Anywhere this side of the big bridge," a reference to the lengthy bridge over the Canadian River, the cowboy responded. At first Kelm was unable to move the locomotive, realizing the brakes were locked and there were pins that had to be pulled. In the delay, the outlaw grew impatient and angry, and Kelm was afraid the young cowboy would shoot him. The cab was well lit, Kelm remembered, and he got a good look at the man. The cowboy cursed him and talked a "good deal." In court at Eufaula and Muskogee Kelm would identify the outlaw as twenty-three-year-old Joe Lynch Davis.[18]

Steaming across the burning bridge, Kelm brought the train to a halt a half mile down the track, just short of the Canadian River. Worthman and Spencer ordered the train men out of the train and they were lined up along the locomotive tender with their hands in the air.

"Let your hands down, boys, that is kind of tiresome," Joe Davis told the trainmen. A few minutes later, he told them to, "Sit down on the ground there . . . it would take a while to do this little job."[19]

Dolan, a twenty-nine-year veteran fireman who was said to be one of the "scrappiest trainmen on the Katy road," lost his nerve completely during the robbery. Dolan said he had been taking some medicine and asked if he could relieve himself. Sure, one of the outlaws said, but there was no need to go off into the darkness since there were no women present. Dolan hurried to behind a mound of cinders near the tracks, squatted, and left a pile a "greyhound couldn't run and jump."[20]

Dolan later began a conversation with Davis: "You've got that old pocket book of mine and there is nothing in it but a few cards and stuff of no interest to anybody but me."

Davis responded that he had no intention of taking anything "except from those who can stand to lose it."

"Cap, we don't want any of your money," Davis continued.

"Thank you, you are a gentleman," Dolan responded.[21]

## Stick 'Em Up!

Hearing several loud voices the express manager, Sidney Wolf, opened the door of the express car and was immediately covered by one of the outlaws. "Stick 'em up!" a bandit yelled. "Don't act a fool. We don't want to hurt you." As Wolf jumped down from the train, Spencer leaped into the express car and began working on the safe. Several minutes later Spencer, with a red bandana over his face and wearing a black cap and a dirty green vest, jumped down, and there was a small explosion. Finally, on the fourth time, Spencer put in a double charge and blasted the express car into splinters. The safe slammed against a wall of the express car and the door to the safe was jammed. Spencer hurried to the locomotive where he retrieved a coal pick and a shaker bar and was able to jar the door loose. Within seconds, Spencer jumped down holding two large sacks of money and yelled out, "Let's go."[22] The safe also contained several boxes of jewelry but Davis decided they were not worth carrying. A combination car consisting of the mail and a "Jim Crow" car were not entered. Several African Americans in the segregated car who were much closer to the explosions during the robbery spent the time praying.

Fireman Kelm was slow in cutting off the headlight to the locomotive as he was ordered to do and one of the bandits, while passing in front of the locomotive, fired three shots with a revolver into the headlight. With almost seven thousand dollars, the men raced off into the darkness where Bertholf waited anxiously with the horses. The men rode east at a gallop before heading southeast across the Canadian River. In all the robbery had taken fifty-five minutes. "It was a skillful piece of work on the part of the bandits, carefully planned and executed without a hitch," the *Eufaula Republican* reported. The robbery was "one of the most daring and spectacular hold-ups committed in Oklahoma in recent years," the *Eufaula Indian Journal* proclaimed.[23] Most Oklahoma newspapers agreed, as did law enforcement officials throughout Oklahoma.

As soon as the outlaws disappeared into the darkness, Engineer Thomas jumped into the locomotive and sped south to Crowder where the news of the robbery was flashed by telegraph along the entire line of the Katy. The story was quickly picked up by newspapers across Oklahoma and adjacent states.

Realizing there was a robbery underway, a brakeman on the train named Sandy Frame tumbled out of the train and ran four miles into Eufaula, reaching the town in "nothing flat," according to his version of the sprint.[24] Frame arrived in Eufaula at about the same time Thomas reached Crowder. At daylight a switch engine was dispatched that pulled the passenger section of the train into Eufaula. No sooner had the train rattled into the depot than a large number of excited passengers disembarked with pieces of the demolished express car as souvenirs. Postcard dealers in the town were soon out of cards.[25] In less than twenty-four hours, a work crew had repaired the burned trestle and Katy trains were once again carrying mail south to the sea.

Three-time presidential candidate William Jennings Bryan, who was nearing the end of an exhausting twenty-two-state, seven-week barn-storming campaign on behalf of presidential candidate Woodrow Wilson, spoke to a crowd of thousands in Eufaula on the afternoon of the robbery. The theft was appalling, the Great Commoner shouted out, but it was "infinitesimal as compared with the theft of the Americans by the trusts." The "difference between the train robbers and the little coterie of men who systematically rob the government by means of special tariff favors gained through enormous campaign contributions is that the latter are befriended by men who have been elected president of the United States."[26] There was little doubt, the *Eufaula Indian Journal* announced, that Bryan was the "greatest orator that ever stepped upon a platform."[27]

### Lawmen in Abundance

A Eufaula posse led by Undersheriff Walter Grayson and Deputy W. J. Irwin were the first to reach the scene of the robbery. The footprints of the outlaws in the soft sand led to where four horses had been tied. Asked how he knew there were four horses, Irwin explained to the press how he had carefully examined the urine and dung.[28] Sheriff J. W. McCune was in the north end of the county at the time of the robbery but hurried south early on Tuesday morning. With a posse of men in automobiles, Sheriff Dave J. Tatum of Pittsburg County raced to the scene. A special train carrying Muskogee County sheriff W. R. Robinson, Katy special agent Crockett Lee, and his associate, Grayson, along with several deputies and two bloodhounds from the Burns Detective Agency, left Muskogee at 5:25 A.M. and arrived at the scene an hour later at daylight.[29]

The bloodhounds quickly picked up the scent of the outlaws and followed it into the woods east of Wirth where the horses were tied and then down a road toward the river before losing the scent. A brown money wrapper was found, and the deputies spotted where telephone wires had been cut. In the wilderness and rugged country south of the Canadian River, Sheriff Tatum and his posse were forced to abandon their automobiles. The lawmen continued on foot into the wilderness along a narrow winding trail over rocky hills and through dense thickets. Sheriff Tatum sent word that the trail was "growing more and more difficult." Many law enforcement officials were sure the outlaws were headed for the rugged Kiamachi Mountains, and every town in the region was telephoned to be on the lookout. In the meantime the Katy Railroad offered a five-hundred-dollar reward for the apprehension of the outlaws, American Express put up another five hundred dollars, and the US postal authorities added one thousand dollars.[30]

On October 31, 1912, only two days after the robbery, citizens in Muskogee woke up to a headline in the *Times-Democrat*—"Joe Davis Arrested."[31] By interviewing farmers who said they had seen the bandits, Sheriff Tatum concluded the outlaws were making their way toward Blocker, not far from Joe Davis's ranch at Featherston. Law enforcement officials suspected all along that the Davises were behind the holdup, and when Joe and Buck Bertholf rode into Blocker, they were intercepted by Sheriff Tatum, Crockett Lee, and several deputies. They were immediately hustled off to the federal jail in McAlester and charged with obstructing the US mail. Davis was allowed to call his father in Muskogee, and Jack rushed off to McAlester to post bond, but not before putting in a call to Rutherford. In McAlester, Jack Davis had no problem posting a two-thousand-dollar bond for the two men. Learning that an arrest warrant had been issued for Bob Worthman, Jack Davis helped him make his bond as well.[32]

Rutherford not only was the defense attorney for the Davises, he continued to act as their public relations agent. "I will bet there is absolutely nothing in the case," Rutherford told the *Times-Democrat*. "While Joe may have had the nerve, he did not have the brains or ingenuity to plan such a robbery . . . as for breaking into a safe, he could not effect an entrance if he had the combination and the keys," Rutherford continued.[33] Instead of arresting Tom Spencer, however, law enforcement officials mistakenly took into custody a close Davis associate from the Porum Range War, John McClure, who had nothing to do with the Katy robbery.

Rutherford's partner J. A. Dial, who would be helping to defend the Davis Gang, criticized law enforcement officials, saying the only reason Davis, Worthman, Bertholf, and McClure had been arrested was that they "corresponded in a general way to the descriptions given by some of the trainmen." The robbers wore cowboy boots, the Katy men all agreed, but naturally Davis and the others wore boots because they did so "all the time around the ranch," Dial pointed out.[34]

### Suitcase Full of Money

At a preliminary hearing in McAlester only days after the arrests, prosecutors could only come up with some questionable circumstantial evidence. Several employees of the Katy, including Dolan, Kelm, and Henderson, were unable to identify either Davis, Bertholf, or Worthman. "I will tell you they look like the people but I can't say they are," Dolan told Lee, the Katy agent. Although the suspects were asked to walk around, sit down, stand up, and then walk around again, there were no positive identifications. There was more confusion when Henderson identified McClure, a small, heavyset individual, as the outlaw who blew up the safe, although all the other trainmen agreed the individual was of slim build and close to six feet tall.[35] Lee, the Katy special agent who was positive the Davis Gang was responsible for the robbery, was furious.

Joe Davis and Bertholf had none of the robbery money on them at the time of their arrest. Moreover, Davis said he had plenty of witnesses to prove that he had been in and around Featherston and Blocker for almost a month, gathering cattle. The night the Katy was robbed he was at a farmhouse more than twenty miles from the scene of the crime, he said, and the next day he had ridden into McAlester. Everyone knew McIntosh County officials had it in for him, he said.[36]

On November 8, 1912, the day Woodrow Wilson was elected president, Rutherford was in federal court in McAlester asking for a hearing before the US commissioner. At another hearing a month later, prosecutors admitted they had few clues and little evidence, and they agreed to drop all the charges. Headlines across eastern Oklahoma were similar: "Joe Davis and His Friends Were Not Katy Bandits."[37]

The stolen money was divided by the outlaws and carefully hidden. Joe Davis and Spencer each got twelve hundred dollars. Worthman, who Spencer later referred to as a "god-damn son of a bitch," made off with three thousand, while Bertholf was given six hundred for holding the horses. The mastermind, Jack Davis, received twelve hundred dollars. Six hundred dollars were set aside to buy witnesses, if necessary.[38]

Another acquittal only added to the confidence of Joe and Jack Davis. Somehow, they always seemed to get away. Such confidence led to a degree of carelessness that would inevitably land them in legal jeopardy. One of their biggest problems was that the stolen money was all in one- and two-dollar bills. What eventually led to the Davises' undoing proved to be a fifty-one-year-old former employee of theirs named Jim M. Blevins. Referred to as a "queer whip-shrewd old Tennessean," Blevins was working on the Davis ranch in McCurtain County in early November when Joe Davis, Worthman, and Spencer arrived, only weeks after the Katy robbery.[39] Blevins listened in silence as Spencer bragged of the robbery and how, after four explosions, he had successfully blown the safe and the outlaws had made off with almost seven thousand dollars.

## A Hole at the Base of a Tree Stump

From the McCurtain County ranch, Jack Davis had sent Spencer to Muskogee, where the Davises were still living at the time, and Spencer returned in a buggy with a suitcase full of money.[40] Spencer had even shown Blevins his share of the loot.

"How does that look to you, old man?" Spencer said.[41]

Spencer had buried some of his share in a baking powder can in a hole at the base of a tree stump in the backyard and the rest in a coffee can in the barn. At the time, Blevins was helping to repair the ranch house, and Jack Davis gave him a pile of one-dollar bills to buy lumber in Hugo. Fearful that he knew too much and that he would be murdered, Blevins slipped away one day and made his way to Eufaula where he told Sheriff J. W. McCune "many a dark tale and swore they were the gospel truth."[42]

Sheriff McCune summoned Lee, who was convinced all along the Davis Gang was responsible for the Katy robbery. To keep Blevins safe and undercover, he was given a job by the Katy as a freight handler at Parsons, while Lee threw all his efforts into an extensive investigation. Slowly but surely, he was able to build a case against the Davises and their small gang. In more than one interview, Lee convinced several of the Katy trainmen that the men they had failed to identify in McAlester were indeed the robbers.

The flood of one- and two-dollar bills that suddenly appeared in McCurtain County and at Hugo in Choctaw County also focused attention on the Davises. Joe Davis and Tom Spencer were said to have used the small denominations "so frequently and injudiciously . . . that suspicions of officers fell on them."[43] Jack Davis bought two hundred bushels of corn from a farmer paying mostly in one- and two-dollar bills. Jim Blevins and Tom Spencer purchased lumber in Hugo and Idabel, also with small bills. Joe and Jack Davis did business with a general store in Hugo, always paying for goods with one- and two-dollar bills.[44] Joe Davis had even acquired several head of cattle and had paid for the animals with small bills.

By March 1913 Agent Lee was convinced he had enough evidence to convict Joe Davis and the Davis Gang on state charges. Two Pittsburg County deputies, Chaney Haynes and Lee Pollock, quietly arrested Buck Bertholf at Blocker and he was thrown in jail in Eufaula. Bob Worthman was arrested at Tahlequah by a deputy from McIntosh County, and he too was taken to Eufaula. A friend of the Davises, Thomas Meek, was arrested at a ranch in the northern part of Pittsburg County but was released. John McClure was arrested again, but Lee finally concluded he had not been involved.

Fearful that Joe and Jack Davis and their gang might either put up a fight or flee a large contingency of law enforcement officials gathered quietly at Hugo. The party included Sheriff J. W. McCune of McIntosh County, Sheriff Dave Tatum of Pittsburg County, Sheriff R. W. Cornell of Choctaw County, Sheriff Dan Holman of McCurtain County—along with Crockett Lee and Charles Anderson, special agents for the Katy, and at least two deputy sheriffs. The party left Hugo with a wagonload of supplies, including a complete camping outfit and a number of extra saddle horses.[45] The route took them over mountains and through some of the roughest country in the state. After several days' ride they were able to swoop down on the Davis Ranch near Corrine and capture Tom Spencer and his brother Walter, who were at the dinner table eating a cold dinner at the time. Joe Davis was said to be in Arkansas buying cattle and was not at the ranch. The officers found a large supply of salted pork at the ranch and they built a big fire in a stove and "cooked themselves a meal." Tom Spencer later said he never "saw men eat so much grub." The ranch house was an arsenal full of Winchesters, six-shooters, shotguns, and "every kind of firearm imaginable" along with enough ammunition, it was said, to "kill all the people in McAlester."[46]

At the time of his arrest Tom Spencer had a pistol in his pocket and another in his belt. A Winchester lay across the table. Walter Spencer had forty-five dollars in his pocket, mostly in one-dollar bills. Under heavy guard, the two men were taken back to Hugo and then to jail in Eufaula. Hoping to find the buried loot Blevins had described, the officers dug all around and under the ranch house as well as the barn. They were able to find a hole near the root of a stump, just as Blevins said, but the hole was empty.[47]

After several days Lee and Anderson traced Joe Davis to Hope, Arkansas, where he was arrested without a fight. Davis had just shipped two carloads of cattle and was preparing to ship a third.[48] Heavily guarded, he was taken on the train to the county jail in Eufaula where he was greeted by the other members of the gang. As was his custom, Jack Davis rushed to Eufaula to post bail. As expected, Rutherford was also there.

At a preliminary hearing in Eufaula on April 1, 1913, before McIntosh County judge Benjamin David Gross, the prosecuting attorney John W. Robertson (who was more than familiar with the Davis Gang) put forth a convincing and compelling case. Before a packed courtroom, Jim M. Blevins—who Jack Davis claimed was an idiot and a drunkard—proved to be a prosecution star. At first the defendants laughed at Blevins as he spoke in a deep, uneducated southern drawl that was difficult to understand, much as they had made fun of him on the ranch. "They laughed and chuckled till they grew red in the face," one newspaper said.[49] But then, with great theater and suspense and as the courtroom grew silent, Blevins told a "long story so simple it was intensely dramatic." Rutherford tried, but he seemed unable to shake Blevins who, he argued, was a "trained" witness carefully coached by Lee. Blevins responded with shrewd, sharp answers. "I ran away from the Davis Ranch because I got to knowing too much," he said. "Talking Tom Spencer [told] me many secrets and I'd heard after a man got to knowing too much on the Davis outfit the gang put him out of the way."[50] The eyes of the outlaws "narrowed and Worthman's face grew red," reported the *Husonian*.[51]

For eight hours Judge Gross listened to thirteen prosecution witnesses, including several Katy trainmen. Kelm, the fireman, who had been forced to drive the locomotive across the burning trestle, now identified Joe Davis as the man who made him do it. Wolf, the express manager, pointed out Spencer as the robber who handled the explosives and blew the safe. Lee took the stand and related how he had trailed the outlaws for two miles and found where four horses had been hitched less than eighty yards from the site of the robbery. Lee told how he had helped to arrest "Talking Tom" and Walter Spencer on the Davis Ranch. Lee also produced the one- and two-dollar bills he had confiscated from Walter Spencer. The Katy agent related how he and Anderson had gone to Arkansas and arrested Joe Davis. Despite Rutherford's gallant efforts at countering the testimony, at the end of the day Judge Gross agreed to hold the gang over for trial. Bond was set at four thousand dollars each for Joe Davis, Worthman, and Spencer and at twenty-five hundred dollars for Bertholf.

## On Trial Again

In hopes of being granted a change of venue as he had done before, Rutherford produced 89 affidavits from men who agreed the Davis Gang could not get a fair trial in Eufaula. When the state produced 189 similar affidavits, many from prominent individuals, arguing otherwise, Judge Gross denied the motion, and a trial date was set for September 29, 1913.[52] Rutherford was successful, however, in obtaining a delay and in getting Sheriff McCune disqualified from selecting the jury venire. "I do not object to being disqualified in this case for I have taken an active part in collecting the evidence which will lead to a conviction," the sheriff responded unapologetically. "This case is attracting considerable attention and promises to be a lively battle," the local press proclaimed.[53]

With Judge Preslie B. Cole presiding, the trial began a week behind schedule on the morning of October 6, 1913. As many as one hundred witnesses were scheduled to testify. Much to his disgust Joe Davis was missing the steer roping contest at the state fair in Muskogee. Judge Gross ordered everyone entering the small McIntosh County courtroom to be thoroughly searched and disarmed. As members of the Davis family and friends filed into the courthouse, deputies with Winchester rifles and Colt revolvers stood motionless at the entrance. Rutherford was able to get sixty of the one hundred venire rejected before a jury could be seated. All twelve men were farmers. Before a crowded courtroom Sidney Wolf, the Katy express manager, was the first witness for the prosecution. He identified Tom Spencer as the man who had ordered him at gunpoint out of the baggage car. Under heavy guard for fear of his being assassinated, Blevins was again the star witness for the prosecution. Once again he related how Joe Davis and Tom Spencer had boasted of the robbery. He left the Davis Ranch in McCurtain County, he said, wanting to do the right thing as "the bunch were murderers, robbers, and cattle thieves."[54]

A new witness, damaging for the defense, proved to be Roy Van Brunt, who had recently been paroled from the state penitentiary. Van Brunt related how Jack Davis had tried to recruit him to aid in robbing the Katy and that Bertholf had come to his home in Eufaula the night before the holdup, hoping to persuade him to blow the safe on the Katy. Van Brunt admitted he had seriously considered the offer but in the end was afraid he would get caught. In all, the state called forty-one witnesses.

Jack Davis took the stand to brand Van Brunt a liar and a convict, saying he was bitter toward the Davises because he had once refused to go Van Brunt's bond. Bertholf also denied ever having contacted Van Brunt. All the defendants denied any involvement in the robbery and all offered verifiable alibis. Tom Spencer admitted he had been using a false name for several years and that his real name was Fred Spess, yet he seemed unable to explain how his brother's name was Walter Spencer. Originally from Missouri, the Spesses were poor Pawnee County dirt farmers, several of whom had gone bad. Their father, L. E. Spess, was widowed at an early age, and the family never seemed able to get on the right side of the law.[55] Both Tom Spencer and Bertholf admitted they had served time in the state penitentiary. Several of the defense witnesses seemed to contradict one another, the *Eufaula Democrat* observed.[56] No sooner had the defense rested than one potenial juror, Andy Kerkeundahl of Wilburton, was arrested on a charge of perjury for saying he had never been convicted of a crime, and evidence was produced to the contrary.[57] A few days later, another potential juror, John Lane, was arrested for perjury and placed under a one-thousand-dollar bond. During his questioning as a possible juror, Lane told the court he did not live within four miles of where the robbery had taken place, but as it turned out, he lived two miles away.[58] It was obvious the prosecution was attempting to send a message to any potential jurors—especially anyone willing to perjure themselves, no matter how trivial their mistruths might be.

### Undoubtedly Guilty

The trial was said to be one of the hardest fought ever seen in McIntosh County. There was little doubt on the streets of Eufaula that the Davis Gang were guilty and that the jury would convict them. After seven days and thirteen hours of deliberations, late at night on October 15, 1913, the jury returned to the courtroom and without hesitation pronounced the Davis Gang innocent. "The not guilty verdict of the jury caught most citizens by surprise, especially those who had set through the trial," one of the state's leading newspapers reported. The verdict hit the public like a "bolt of lightning from the clouds and speculation has been running riot since."[59] How could all the officers, detectives, and witnesses for the prosecution have been wrong or have lied? There was only one possible answer. The Davises had bought enough witnesses to sow enough doubt in the minds of enough jurors—most of them individuals scrabbling for a living who identified with anyone who they perceived to be striking at a system that had dealt them a bad hand in life.

Joe and Jack Davis were once again vindicated, and their glee seemed to know no bounds. One more time they had beaten the system. But just as Joe Davis and Bob Worthman walked out of the McIntosh County Courthouse, they were arrested on warrants out of Osage County and whisked off by Undersheriff Wiley G. Haines to Pawhuska where they were arraigned and charged with horse stealing.[60] Davis, Bertholf, and Worthman "have to do more compulsory traveling than any other young men in Oklahoma," the *Muskogee Times-Democrat* announced.[61]

### Broad-Brimmed Stetson

On the night of September 4, 1913, a southbound Katy passenger train had been stopped three miles south of the village of Hominy in the southern part of Osage County by a fire burning on the tracks. The cross ties had been torn up for yards beyond the fire and the ties piled on the track and set on fire. Katy trainmen expected bandits to appear out of the darkness at any moment, but no one appeared. The next morning two horses were found tethered in a small thicket, not far from the fire. Nearby sat two bottles of nitroglycerin. It was obvious a robbery had been in the offing, but for some reason the outlaws were scared off. As it turned out the horses had been stolen from Charles Whitehorn, an Osage farmer living near Hominy.[62] A large white broad-brimmed cowboy hat—identical to the kind Joe Davis was known to wear, bearing the stamp of the Model clothing store in McAlester—had been left on one of the saddle horns. On the night of the robbery two men had mounted the baggage car on the front end. The train crew had suspected them and stopped the train to put them off, but the two men had fled into the night.

Getting off the train in Pawhuska, Davis and Worthman were met by Harve M. Freas, Osage County's three-hundred-pound frontier sheriff who was said to be a "terror to evil doers."[63] At the beautiful new courthouse on the hill overlooking the oil boomtown and county seat, bail was set at five hundred and with Rutherford's assistant Jack Harley representing the men, they were soon on their way home.

Following the not guilty verdict in Eufaula, Crockett Lee began working on the Hominy case full time. The Stetson hat was easily traced to the Model clothing store in McAlester where a clerk told Lee he sold it to Joe Davis.[64] There was little doubt in Lee's mind that the same gang who pulled off the train robbery near Wirth was the same troupe of outlaws who planned the Hominy holdup and he was able to expand the charges to train robbery. He had no doubt the Davises were intent to rob another train to secure funds to pay their legal expenses. As far as Lee was concerned, the Davises were in a downward spiral that knew no end.

At a hearing in Pawhuska the second week of November 1913, Joe Davis walked into the courtroom wearing a broad-brimmed Stetson hat purchased from the clothing store in McAlester that was identical to the hat being produced by the state as Exhibit A. With no other evidence, however, the two men walked free, as Lee sat stunned and motionless but determined more than ever to convict Joe Davis and his father.[65] Headlines in eastern Oklahoma were similar to those in the *Hugo Husonian*: "Joe Davis Given Complete Freedom."[66] Walking out of the courtroom at Pawhuska, Davis told the *Times-Democrat* that his days in Oklahoma were over. "We have been persecuted and hunted in Oklahoma and I am through," he proclaimed. Within weeks he was leaving for Montana to "begin life anew."[67] Many in Porum and Texanna cheered the news. But, just as Jack Davis had once announced he was taking his family to the wilds of New Mexico, Joe Davis in this case was more talk than action.

## Robbing Banks

Exactly when—in late 1913 or early 1914—Joe Davis began robbing banks in Oklahoma remains uncertain. There is little doubt, however, that in 1914–15, Joe Davis, Worthman, Bertholf, and Tom Spencer were responsible for a rash of bank robberies that swept across the Sooner State. Yet Joe Davis in particular was accused of far more bank robberies than he conceivably could have committed. When exactly he joined the notorious Henry Starr, the Cherokee Bad Boy as he came to be known, is also somewhat of a mystery.

On the morning of January 12, 1914, the First National Bank at Terlton was robbed and a deputy sheriff was killed in a running gun battle. The Terlton robbery was followed by bank robberies at Vera, Garber, and Pittsburg. Many in the Oklahoma legislature and citizens throughout the infant state had by now had enough. "If the state of Oklahoma is ever going to get away from the reputation of being a wild western state, uncivilized and inhabited by criminals, it is time something definite and effective is done to put a stop to these kinds of depredations," the *Oklahoma Leader* editorialized. According to the newspaper, one of the biggest problems in Oklahoma was that "people in general encourage the bank robbers by placing them on a pedestal." The "rising generation of bandits should be made to realize . . . that the day of the gunman has passed," the newspaper continued.[68]

Many blamed the lawlessness on Al Jennings, a former train robber and outlaw, who was now running for governor. Jennings's book *Beating Back* was said to have inspired more than one outlaw.[69] In a riotous tour of eastern Oklahoma, the popular Jennings spoke to overflowing crowds. People by the hundreds rode in farm wagons, came on horseback, walked for hours, and stood in line just to shake his hand. On February 18, 1914, Jennings spoke to a large crowd from a platform in front of the Severs Hotel in Muskogee.[70]

There appears little doubt that it was indeed the Davis Gang who robbed the Bank of Millerton on May 21, 1914, and made off with several thousand dollars. Millerton was a small town on the St. Louis and San Francisco (Frisco) Railroad less than thirteen miles west of Idabel, the county seat of McCurtain County. One of the masked outlaws kept the bank employees covered while the second bandit scooped up the cash. The bank employees were marched outside with their hands in the air, then the outlaws jumped on their horses and galloped off in the direction of the Kiamichi Mountains. The McCurtain County sheriff, who was in his office at Idabel at the time, immediately organized a posse and took up the trail of the outlaws. The posse caught up with them on Little River, eight miles from Millerton, where a running gun battle ensued. While fleeing, the robbers lost a bag of money amounting to fifteen hundred dollars. Some speculated the bag was dropped intentionally along the riverbank so as to slow the pursuit.[71]

Through the mountains the chase went on into the night. Several in the posse got so close to the outlaws they claimed they recognized Spencer and Worthman.

As a consequence Sheriff Robert W. Cornell at Hugo in Choctaw County was wired to arrest Joe and Jack Davis. Sheriff Cornell arrested not only Jack but also his friend Thomas Sawyer, a cattle seller who just happened to be in Hugo trying to sell Jack Davis some cattle. Both men were able to prove they were nowhere near Millerton at the time of the robbery. "This is one time I ask for speedy justice," Jack Davis said. He was in Hugo having a plow fixed and had been invited to dinner. "Our innocence is easy to prove," he continued. Joe Davis heard of the arrest warrants when he was at Corrine, and he hurried west to Hugo to give himself up, arriving three hours later. At the same time Jack Davis left a telephone message in Corrine for Worthman saying he was being charged with the robbery and he, too, should come to Hugo to post bond. Worthman called Sheriff Cornell that evening to verify if there was an arrest warrant and when he was assured there was, he promised to be in Hugo "as fast as a horse can carry me."[72] Jack Davis had no idea as to the whereabouts of Spencer, since he was no longer employed on the ranch.

Late in the afternoon of September 8, 1914, two men leisurely walked into the Keystone State Bank at Keystone, a small community twelve miles west of Tulsa at the confluence of the Cimarron and Arkansas Rivers, and made off with twenty-seven hundred dollars. A junction on the Katy, Keystone was a rough settlement catering to cowboys, bootleggers, Creek Indians, oilfield roughnecks, and railroad workers. The bandits forced one of the bank cashiers to carry a bag of money containing several hundred dollars in coins to the banks of the Cimarron River where the robbers were joined by a colleague who was holding their horses, and the three men rode rapidly away. A posse of Keystone citizens followed the outlaws into the rough country six miles southeast of town but lost the trail in the darkness and difficult terrain and returned to town.[73] Although there was never any proof, some lawmen were sure that Joe Davis was one of the robbers.

Joe Davis and Henry Starr were also accused of robbing the bank in Cove, Arkansas, in the rugged Ouachita Mountains in the western part of Polk County, not far from the Oklahoma border, and making off with fifteen hundred dollars.[74] Again there was little evidence tying the two to the crime, and Arkansas authorities made no effort to extradite them.

### Baxter Springs, Kansas

There is little doubt, however, that six days after the Keystone robbery, on the afternoon of September 22, 1914, Joe Davis was involved in the raid on the First National Bank at Baxter Springs, Kansas. The robbery was said to have been "one of the most sensational in the history of the Southwest" and was "pulled off without a hitch."[75] At 2:30 P.M. two masked outlaws hitched their horses a block or more from the bank and calmly strode into the bank. One of the outlaws—said to be tall, less than thirty years of age, and armed with a Winchester shotgun and a pistol (probably Davis)—entered the bank as a third outlaw who had ridden up stood in front of the building to keep everyone away.

Baxter Springs was one of the wildest cow towns in the West dating back to before the Civil War. William Clarke Quantrill's guerillas and the federals had fought here during the Civil War. After the war cattle drovers found the community a welcome break after months on the dusty trail. Numerous saloons and palaces of diversion provided all the amenities a poor cowboy would want.[76]

Davis placed a gun at the back of the assistant cashier and said, "Get busy, damn you!" Two customers in the bank at the time, a hardware merchant and a farmer, were told to put their hands up. A second robber held out a grain sack as Davis ordered the cashier to dump in all the cash, even the money from an open vault. The customers and the cashier were locked in the vault as the robbers calmly walked away with $8,534. Meeting a young woman on the street, the bandits tipped their hats in a courteous fashion, stepped aside, and proceeded on their way. The bank bookkeeper returned to the bank a few minutes later to find it deserted. While pondering the situation, he heard a faint murmur from the vault and someone cried out, "Let us out."[77] As soon as the alarm was sounded parties from the town began following the robbers, but they had long since disappeared.

The three outlaws raced east across Spring River before turning south into the timber and hills and into the night. The posse later found where the robbers had divided the money. One of the grain sacks lay on the ground and several money wrappers were scattered about. In Oklahoma, near the Missouri line, the outlaws continued south, cutting fences in at least a dozen places. They were last seen riding hard late at night near Peoria, fifteen miles southeast of Baxter Springs in Ottawa County, before disappearing in the heavy timber again.[78]

Two weeks later, at half past two on the afternoon of September 30, 1914, three masked men hitched their horses a block or so away and entered the Central State Bank in the oilfield town of Kiefer, south of Sapulpa in Creek County. "Throw up your hands," one of the robbers shouted as the cashier, assistant cashier, and three customers were herded into the vault and warned that if they came out, they would be shot.[79] After rifling the safe, the counter, and the money drawer of fifty-two hundred dollars, the outlaws locked the cashiers and customers inside the vault and rode off at top speed, "yelling and shooting." Only yards away, a picture show depicting the outlaw days of the Wild West was in progress. Several automobiles full of armed citizens pursued the bandits northwest out of town toward Sapulpa, but the outlaws fled into the Red Fork Hills south of Tulsa and the trail was lost. At one point, the outlaws were said to be surrounded, but somehow they got away. Although Joe Davis was the only outlaw positively identified, it is likely the other two men were Henry Starr and Tom Spencer.[80]

Bank heists in northeastern Oklahoma in the outlaw summer of 1914 were similar. Three men, with similar descriptions, rode boldly into town and hitched their horses near the bank. One of the men held the horses or stood outside, while the other two robbed the bank. In each case they safely escaped.

### Murder of Fred Spess

Two weeks after the Kiefer theft, on October 9, 1914, some teenagers were out hunting along a road near Beaver Creek a mile south of Blocker when they found the body of a man lying in some underbrush, partly covered with leaves. He had a bullet hole in his head and more than two hundred dollars in a coat pocket. It appeared as if a large package had been ripped out of the inner lining of his coat. The body was carried into Blocker and identified as that of Fred Spess, alias Tom Spencer, a prominent member of the Davis Gang. Law enforcement officials immediately speculated that Spencer was the third outlaw in the robbery of the Kiefer bank. It was widely rumored in outlaw circles that Spencer got away with more than his fair share of the loot and that Joe Davis followed and killed him.[81]

Suspecting the dead man might be Tom Spencer, officials contacted Walter and Gus Spess who came to Blocker and identified the body as that of their brother. Moreover, they admitted their brother had been a member of the Davis Gang—and that he had been with Joe Davis robbing the bank at Cove, Arkansas, as well as the Keystone State Bank, the Keifer Central Bank, and the bank at Baxter Springs, Kansas. The Oklahoma press reported that a woman running a boardinghouse in Tulsa overheard a conversation between two men, likely Starr and Davis, discussing how Spencer got away with most of the money after the Kiefer robbery.[82]

On Friday night, November 13, 1914, Davis rode into McAlester and was at a café when Sheriff Dave Tatum and a deputy, Otto H. Reed, pulled up in an automobile and motioned for him to come outside. At the time Davis was arrested for murder he was armed and had fifty dollars rolled up in one of his socks. He was taken to the county jail, and a preliminary hearing was scheduled for the following week. "I don't know a damned thing about it," Davis told the press. "A man seems to have been killed up here somewhere and they are charging me with it. No, I don't know where Tom Spencer is and I don't give a damn. I'm not his keeper."[83]

With Rutherford by Davis's side, the preliminary hearing in the justice of the peace court was held, a week later, as scheduled, in McAlester. Judge Brooks Fort was fearful the Spess brothers would show up and a gun battle would erupt that "might rival the famous Porum feud." As was now the custom in eastern Oklahoma, Fort issued an order to disarm anyone entering the court. In the hearing the judge found there was insufficient evidence to hold Davis and he went free. Once again he grabbed the headlines. "Joe Davis Freed of Murder Charge" was typical.[84]

"The Spess boys," Jack Davis told the press, were "trying to saddle the blame onto Joe in order to relieve themselves." Tom Spencer was not dead. The brothers were playing for time so Tom could get "farther away from the pursuit." If Tom Spencer was really dead, why didn't Walt and Gus come to McAlester to testify? "They are afraid to show up," Jack Davis proclaimed.[85]

"Talk about crimes, this arrest of Joe was one of the blackest I ever saw," the father went on to say.[86]

In reality the law enforcement officials had all agreed not to pursue the murder charge, all of them agreeing that there was little evidence to tie Davis to the murder of Spess. They were far more likely to convict him of bank robbery. As Joe Davis triumphantly walked out of the Pittsburg County Courthouse, Sheriff Henry C. King of Creek County served him with an arrest warrant, for robbing the Capital State Bank of Keifer. In handcuffs and under a heavy guard, Joe was taken to Sapulpa for arraignment the following morning. Undersheriff L. D. Kern of Pawnee was also in McAlester with an arrest warrant for the robbery of the First State Bank of Keystone. Sheriff R. E. Martin of Cherokee County, Kansas, also came south to McAlester, hoping to extradite Davis to Kansas where witnesses waited to identify him in the Baxter Springs robbery.[87]

### Extradition

Authorities in Cherokee County, Kansas, were determined to extradite Davis. County Attorney F. W. Boss had been at the Pawnee hearing, along with Rutherford, and both went to Oklahoma City for a meeting with Governor Lee Cruce. Boss carried papers from the governor of Kansas, George H. Hodges, requesting Davis's extradition. Pointing in particular to the Spess confession, Boss told the governor there was little doubt that Davis helped to rob the bank and there was even less doubt Boss could obtain a conviction. Walter Spess had been brought to Baxter Springs where he identified several items left by the outlaws near the river bridge outside the town where the outlaws had camped the night before the robbery. Moreover, both the Pinkerton and Burns detective agencies were working on the case and were continuing to develop credible evidence against Davis. Redmond S. Cole, the county attorney in Pawnee County, Kansas, told Governor Cruce he had examined the Baxter Springs evidence and thought it more likely that Davis could be convicted in Kansas. Cruce promised to do everything possible to cooperate with the Kansas authorities, but he wanted Davis tried in Pawnee County first. The governor also complained that no one from Baxter Springs was present in Oklahoma City to identify Davis, although Cole assured him the cashier at the Baxter Springs bank could identify Davis.[88]

At a hearing in the stately Creek County Courthouse in Sapulpa in late November, employees of the Keifer Central Bank failed to identify Davis, and he walked free yet again. But this time officials from Pawnee County waited with a warrant charging him with robbing the Keystone bank, and they spirited him away to Pawnee on the St. Louis and San Francisco Railroad. With his father and Rutherford by his side, Davis arrived in Pawnee a week before Christmas 1914 to answer charges for the Keystone robbery.[89] At the preliminary hearing the "Hugo youth furnished the authorities evidence that he had not been near any of the points where the crimes were committed." Davis once again walked free. "Joe Davis Free of All Charges," the *Hugo Husonian* proclaimed.[90]

Seasoned lawman Bill Tilghman claimed that anytime Joe Davis was arrested he always had a ready alibi. Joe would bribe a hotel clerk to leave a line blank among the many names on the register, Tilghman claimed, and he would fill in his name later. Livery stable keepers would do the same. So common was the tactic that law enforcement officials began calling Davis "Alibi Joe."[91] Producing several witnesses who would testify the defendant was elsewhere at the time of the robbery was a common defense tactic in Oklahoma and elsewhere—it was not unique to Joe Davis.

### No Social Bandit

Only twenty-four years of age, Davis had established a record unsurpassed perhaps in the criminal annals of Oklahoma or any other state. Within three months he had been arrested four times on four different felony charges, on warrants out of four different jurisdictions, and each time he was released. "Officers scratch their heads and look wise and say that Davis is undoubtedly the man they want but they seem unable to get the evidence," the *Pawnee Courier-Dispatch* reported.

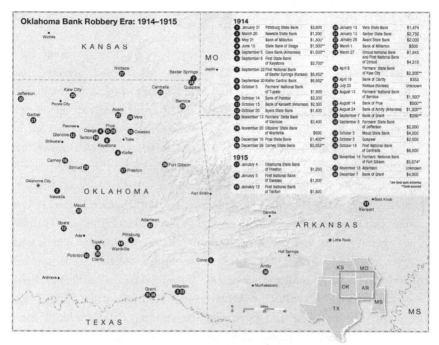

MAP 3. Oklahoma bank robbery era, 1914–1915
*Map by Carol Zuber-Mallison*

The only time he had ever been convicted was in Eufaula for carrying a gun illegally. Of Georgia Cherokee extraction, he was beginning to take on the aura of the social bandit. He was, the paper said, "a fine specimen of young manhood" and "one of the best cowmen in the Southwest," a "dead shot," and someone who had obtained quite a reputation "in handling the rope." He was "reputed to have killed a number of men," the newspaper went on to say.[92]

Joe Davis was certainly no social bandit, however. In the socioeconomic and political order of eastern Oklahoma during the Progressive Era, his banditry was not so much an example of lower-class social resistance but more about protecting wealth and power. He did not live on the edge of society, and he certainly did not identify with the lower class. His uncles were wealthy ranchers. Sam Davis owned businesses and was the largest shareholder in one of the Porum banks. Joe was certainly honored to be part Cherokee, and he took great pride in striking against the railroads and the banks, but he did so as much for the thrill as for the money. Although some in Oklahoma marveled at his bravery in the Porum gun battle, most viewed him as just another outlaw who was feared more than admired. The AHTA hated him.[93]

Law enforcement officials were always leery of Joe and Jack Davis and their political influence in eastern Oklahoma. For years, they claimed, Jack Davis had made himself a terror to officers. While living a comfortable lifestyle, he had "bluffed the officers in eastern Oklahoma . . . until they were really afraid to arrest him or concern themselves where they knew he was interested." The fact that he had been a "consistent violator of the laws for many years" was well known.[94]

Between the Keystone theft on September 8, 1914, and the robbery of the First National Bank at Terlton on January 12, 1915, and the robberies of the Vera State Bank and the Garber State Bank the next two days, bank robberies of epic proportions had become a way of life in small-town eastern Oklahoma. Outlaws now began using nitroglycerin. In the Garber bank, besides making off with seventy-five hundred dollars the robbers blew up part of the building. Bank robberies were also becoming more violent. When Pawnee County deputy sheriff Robert Moore gave chase after the Terlton robbery, the outlaws shot him through the heart.[95] Moore left behind a grieving wife and four children. In all, there were fifteen different bank robberies, the vast majority attributed to Joe Davis and Henry Starr. All were daylight robberies, carried off quickly and efficiently at two-week intervals.[96] It was the worst streak of bank robberies in Oklahoma history. Insurance companies threatened to refuse insurance to banks in eastern Oklahoma. As a consequence, some of the larger banks began employing armed guards who stood outside with shotguns.

Despite opposition from five socialists in the state house of representatives, the Oklahoma legislature, at the urging of the railroads and the bank industry, persuaded the new governor, Robert Lee Williams, to sign the "Bank Robber Bill," which appropriated fifteen thousand dollars for the capture of bank robbers. A one-thousand-dollar bounty was put on Starr's head. The reward was payable "Dead or Alive."[97] With Davis frequently by his side, Starr had become the undisputed king of the Oklahoma bank robberies. During his thirty-two years in crime, he robbed more banks than the James Younger Gang and the Doolin Dalton Gang put together. In twenty-one bank robberies, Starr would net over sixty thousand dollars.

Crockett Lee, the indefatigable Katy agent, remained convinced that federal authorities could charge and convict the Davis Gang with obstructing the mails in the Katy robbery at Wirth. He worked on the case for months and was not giving up. Finally, in early January 1915, Joe and Jack Davis, along with Bob Worthman and Buck Bertholf, were indicted by a federal grand jury in Muskogee for conspiring to "obstruct and retard the passage of the train of the Missouri, Kansas and Texas Railroad Company known as the Katy Limited," for burning a bridge on the Katy, and for assaulting with "guns, pistols, revolvers and so forth . . . J. H. Dolan, conductor of the train."[98]

With the US attorney for the Eastern District of Oklahoma, Daniel Haden Linebaugh, in the lead, the government threw four seasoned attorneys at the Davises. For one of the very first times in recent memory Rutherford would meet his match. Linebaugh was a popular Muskogee Democrat who had recently been named US attorney by President Wilson. He had been a former traveling salesman who was said to be of "high intellectual and professional attainment." Linebaugh was also a prominent Methodist and a Grand Chancellor of the Oklahoma Grand Lodge of the Knights of Pithias. During the trial, he was ably assisted by W. P. McGinnis and advised by George Miller Jr., US attorney and the former McIntosh County attorney.[99]

### Charged in Federal Court

Joe and Jack were arrested at the family home in Hugo, but Worthman could not be found. Otto H. Reed was deputized as a federal marshal for the explicit purpose of arresting him, and Walter Spess was employed at three dollars a day to guide Reed to the Davis Ranch in the mountains near Idabel where it was thought he was hiding. Spess rode into the ranch first and waited for Worthman, who showed up two days later. He was tricked into going to a nearby ranch where Reed was waiting to arrest him.[100]

While visiting in Ardmore, Jack Davis stopped at the office of the *Daily Ardmoreite* and presented the Davis mantra that "prosecuting attorneys were out to get him and Joe." In little more than a month, he pointed out, his son had been arrested and accused of three bank robberies and one train robbery and acquitted in all the cases. In one instance when Joe was said to have robbed a bank, "the young man was waiting on his mother in a serious sick spell and two physicians were with her at the time the boy was at home." Jack Davis was, the newspaper reported, "a young looking man weighing 245 pounds . . . congenial and pleasant and does not have the appearance of a man who is leading the wrong kind of life."[101]

As was the custom, the Davises were doing everything to woo public opinion. Bob Davis wrote a letter to the *Tulsa Daily World* saying that bank robbers Jim and Walter Spess, along with Bill Inhofe, were all "snitches . . . traitors and double-crossers . . . traitorous and unloyal . . . thieves and outlaws."[102] The Spess brothers were now blaming Henry Starr for the murder of their brother and they were out to kill him and obtain the reward. They knew Starr's hiding places in the Osage Hills and in the Creek country.

The Osage Hills, a vast stretch of heavily timbered and rocky canyons, mostly in Osage County, were about as safe an outlaw haven as there existed in the state. The Spess brothers had even gone to where Starr was thought to be hiding in a barn as law enforcement officials waited in the brush nearby but the elusive outlaw was not there. Bob Davis went on to say, "If the officers want Starr, why don't they go out and get him and kill him and not hire a bunch of outlaws and murderers like Walter and Jim Spess and Bill Inhofe to do the dirty work?" Joe's uncle, who had moved his family to Tahlequah for safety, was hoping his letter was a clear warning to Henry Starr to be on the lookout for the Spess brothers and Inhofe. What perhaps angered the Davises the most was that Walter Spess had agreed to turn state's evidence and would be testifying in the forthcoming trial.

### US vs. Joe Davis, et al.

The Katy trial was set for the last week of January 1915 but had to be delayed until early February after a smallpox epidemic swept into Muskogee. Before a packed courtroom in the grand Federal Courthouse on February 16, 1915, Judge Ralph E. Campbell called the case of the US vs. Joe Davis, et al. into session. The courtroom was so crowded with spectators and family members standing along the walls and in the aisles that Judge Campbell ordered the marshals to bar the doors. After numerous disqualifications, a jury, primarily of Muskogee businessmen, was finally seated.

W. J. Irwin, McIntosh County deputy sheriff, was the first prosecution witness. Irwin related how he had gone to the scene of the robbery on the morning of the day that William Jennings Bryan spoke in Eufaula and how he had followed the tracks of the outlaws across the Canadian River. W. R. Robinson, sheriff of Muskogee County at the time of the robbery, said that Crockett Lee was on the scene when he and two of his deputies arrived, and he, too, had seen where the horses were hitched and helped track the outlaws to where the trail ran out south of the Canadian River. William B. Webb, chief clerk on the Katy, testified that the Katy Limited No. 9 was a regular mail train that carried mail on the day of the robbery.[103]

Described as a "witty Irishman with a fine sense of humor, [who] fairly sparkled with mirth," John M. Dolan was back to testify for the third time.[104] Now, however, unlike his testimony at the preliminary hearing in McAlester in 1912, with plenty of coaxing from Crockett Lee, he distinctly remembered that Joe Davis was the outlaw with the large white Stetson hat and a white kerchief around his face who forced him at gunpoint to take the locomotive across the burning bridge. He remembered Joe Davis, he said, "by his movements, by the way he walked, and by his voice."[105] Davis had cursed him, and every time Dolan heard his voice the more he became convinced Davis was the man. Dolan also identified Spencer as the outlaw with the black cap and visor who blew the safe, as well as Worthman who wore a red kerchief. In cross-examination, Rutherford was able to get Dolan to admit that he had met with Crockett Lee several times and that Lee had continuously urged that Davis, Bertholf, Worthman, and Spencer were the outlaws who robbed the Katy. Dolan also admitted that, at the preliminary hearing in McAlester three days after the robbery, he had been unable to identify any of the bandits. Rutherford also engaged Dolan in a lengthy discussion of where the moon was on the night of the robbery and if it was a full moon, a half moon, or a quarter moon. Rutherford introduced evidence of how, in the lineup at McAlester, A. J. Henderson, the black porter, had identified John McClure, a small, heavyset man, as the individual who blew the safe although Spencer, who was close to six feet in height, was now said to be that individual.[106]

On the third day of the trial, with spectators continuing to crowd the courtroom as if it were a circus, thirty-three-year-old William Kelm, the locomotive fireman, related his story of trying to put out the fire when someone poked a Wincheser into his ribs. Like Dolan, he now had no problem identifying the outlaws. Joe Davis, the man with the big white hat, seemed to be in charge, giving directions and threatening the trainmen. When the money was taken from the baggage car, Davis—who Kelm was afraid would kill him—told him to turn out the light on the engine and when he did not do so fast enough, one of the outlaws fired several shots into the headlight. On cross-examination, Rutherford was able to get Kelm to admit that at the McAlester preliminary hearing he had been unable to identify any of robbers, but he could somehow now identify Davis by the "way he walks and talks . . . his eyes, nose and everything."[107]

Charles C. Cissna, a railway postal clerk, testified there was a mail car on the train, and although the mail had not been disturbed it was certainly delayed. At the time of the robbery, Cissna heard someone on the outside of the train shout, "Put up your hands. Stick them up." Seconds later someone fired through the car window. He later found a spent bullet on the inside of the mail car and the slug was introduced as evidence.[108]

A teller at the Southwest National Bank of Commerce in Kansas City, Missouri, James M. Green said he had shipped two packets of money in one- and two-dollar bills on the Katy to the Greenville National Bank in Greenville, Texas. One packet contained thirty-five hundred dollars and the second had four thousand. The money was tied with string and wrapped in wrapping paper, retied, and sealed with tape.[109]

### If I Was There I Guess I Was

Jack Lane, a farmer who lived near Crowder, said about sunup on the day after the robbery, he was fishing on Gaines Creek, about two miles east of Crowder, when he saw a man come down to the creek and take off his big white hat and dip it into the water. Asked to look around the courtroom and identify the man, to the prosecution's surprise Lane did look around and then responded, "I don't believe I see him." Lane did testify, however, that Jack Davis had approached him on a Muskogee street the night before the trial.

"I hear you are going to swear to a lot of junk against me," Lane remembered Davis saying.

"Just you keep still," Lane replied, "I won't swear much against you."[110]

As had been the case in the Eufaula trial, Roy Van Brunt proved one of the more effective witnesses for the government. Van Brunt told how "Uncle Jack" had sent Buck Bertholf to Eufaula to try to recruit him to help rob the Katy and blow the safe, and Van Brunt had even gone to Muskogee and met Davis in person. He thought the endeavor was too risky and the robbers were likely to be caught. Realizing the outcome of the case was likely to fall on his ability to impeach Van Brunt's testimony, Rutherford ripped into him unmercifully. Van Brunt admitted to having served in the state penitentiary on a five-year sentence for attempted murder and to being a "gambler, a whiskey peddler and a pretty tough character." He admitted to having sold whiskey in the Choctaw Nation, where Van Brunt said he was born. Rutherford tried to get him to admit he had been in an all-day poker game in Eufaula the day he claimed he met with Jack Davis in Muskogee. To the prosecution's shock, Van Brunt shot back, "If I was there I guess I was."[111] Rutherford went on to assert that Van Brunt had been promised a parole for his testimony. Moreover, he personally had it in for Jack Davis, who had once bought whiskey from him but who had refused to post his bail in Eufaula. Van Brunt was now going to "put the screws" to Davis.

"Have you ever heard of Joe Davis or Jack Davis peddling whiskey," Rutherford shouted out.

"No," Van Brunt responded, "but I have heard of them stealing."[112]

More damaging to the defense was the testimony of twenty-six-year-old Walter Spess, the brother of the dead Fred Spess, alias Tom Spencer, who said he was a farmer in Pawnee County. He had worked on the Davis Ranch in McCurtain County for twenty-five dollars a month where his brother was the foreman and he was there after the robbery and heard his brother and Joe Davis brag about the heist. But it was only after meeting with Crockett Lee several times that he was able to give the jury specifics as to the course and conduct of the robbery, Rutherford argued. Jack Davis had sent Spess's brother Tom to Muskogee and he had come back along with Blevins in a buggy with a suitcase full of money, Walter Spess went on to say. Most of the money was buried at the ranch, but some of it was used to buy lumber, corn for the horses, and ranch supplies.[113]

Under cross-examination, Rutherford got Spess to admit he hated Joe Davis and had turned him in for the Kiefer and Keystone bank robberies. He also told authorities in Baxter Springs, Kansas, that Davis was involved in that robbery, too. He was sure Davis had killed his brother although Rutherford questioned whether the dead man found near Featherston was really Tom Spencer. Rutherford questioned why neither Gus Spess, who lived at nearby Eufaula, nor Walter had ever tried to reclaim the body, although two hundred dollars was found in the dead man's pocket. It was far from certain, Rutherford asserted, if Fred Spess (Tom Spencer) was even dead. Spess said the sheriff of Pawnee County warned him that Joe Davis was out to kill him, but Rutherford countered that it was Spess who was out to kill Davis.[114]

### I Thought They Ought to Be Stuck

Another chief witness for the prosecution was fifty-two-year-old Jim Blevins who lived a few miles from Texanna and who worked as a foreman on the Davis Ranch on the Canadian River. When Jack Davis moved his ranching operations to McCurtain County, Blevins worked there for three months and helped renovate the house on the property. It was while he was at the ranch that he heard about the robbery of the Katy. Several times Joe Davis and Tom Spencer discussed details of the robbery and how the money was divided, including the six hundred dollars that were held out to buy witnesses. Blevins said that twelve hundred dollars were buried in a baking powder can in the yard in a hole at the foot of an old stump and in a lard bucket in the barn. Rutherford had great fun in asking Blevins how someone could conceivably get twelve hundred dollars in one- and two-dollar bills in such containers. Blevins also admitted that while he was visiting a friend in Hugo named Bill Ogden, he discussed how there was "a big reward offered for the fellows that robbed that Katy train and I think it would be a good scheme for a man to work at it and get it." When Rutherford asserted that Blevins expected to get five hundred dollars in reward money Blevins shot back, "I thought they ought to be stuck." When asked why he had gone to Parsons, Blevins responded, "They taken me up there to keep them from killing me."[115]

M. F. Cosby, a blacksmith from Blocker, told the jury how Buck Bertholf brought two or three horses to his shop on the Monday preceding the robbery and asked him to shoe the horses. Bertholf later returned and asked that the light shoes be replaced with heavy shoes. W. F. Logan, a farmer living near Featherston who was on a fishing trip at the time of the robbery, said he saw Joe Davis southwest of the small village on the afternoon before the robbery. Davis was traveling north leading a blaze-faced sorrel horse. J. C. Hubert, who lived near Featherston, said that after the robbery he saw a blaze-faced sorrel horse belonging to Joe Davis in a pasture three hundred yards south of the Fort Smith and Western Railroad depot looking like it had been ridden hard. Hubert readily admitted the horse could have been used to round up cattle, and Rutherford pointed out that the Davises had shipped two carloads of cattle from the Featherston stockyards two weeks after the robbery.[116]

Tom McGuire, who lived on a farm twelve miles northeast of McAlester, said he saw Joe Davis and Buck Bertholf heading east along the road passing Bob Sawyer's house.[117] Y. R. "Gus" Davenport, who lived near Blocker, told the jury he saw Worthman riding on horseback carrying either a Winchester or a shotgun about a mile from Blocker on the afternoon of the robbery.[118]

A farmer in McCurtain County named Blakenship told the court he sold two hundred bushels of corn to Jack Davis during the winter of 1912–13 and that Davis paid for the corn with a twenty-dollar bill, a check, and lots of one- and two-dollar bills. R. Y. Snow, who ran a sawmill near Idabel, said he sold Blevins twelve dollars' worth of lumber for the Davis Ranch that was paid for in small bills. Walter Spencer later bought more lumber and paid for it with a ten-dollar and five-dollar gold pieces and lots of one-dollar bills, Snow said. Welch Evans, a bookkeeper at the M. L. Wood's mercantile store in Hugo who said he knew Jack Davis personally, testified that Davis frequently bought groceries at the store and paid for them with small bills.[119]

W. C. Grayson, the undersheriff of McIntosh County, told the jury how he had gone to the site of the robbery near Wirth with Crockett Lee and Dennis Price and how they followed the tracks of four horses east and then across the Canadian River until the tracks were lost on the dry hard earth on the north-south wagon road. They found a couple of one-dollar bills along the track and a money wrapper. Dan Holman (sheriff of McCurtain County) remembered how he and the sheriff of Choctaw County, R. W. Cornell (a deputy for Holman at the time), along with Crockett Lee, Charlie Anderson, and two other deputies went to the Davis Ranch "in pretty wild country" where they arrested Tom and Walter Spencer. They found forty-five dollars on Walter and four dollars on Tom, mostly one- and two-dollar bills. They found three Winchesters in the house and took revolvers from both men. They also found a hole near the stump, just as Blevins said they would, and they dug up a large part of the front yard, under the house, and in and around the barn but failed to find any of the loot.[120]

### Alibis and More Alibis

Beginning on the morning of February 18, 1915 (the day Frank James died peacefully at the age of seventy-two in Kearney, Missouri), Rutherford began presenting a long line of defense witnesses, twenty in all, including the defendants themselves. Most were either friends of the Davises or convicted criminals who provided alibis. It is very likely that some of their testimony had been concocted and rehearsed and was paid for by Jack Davis.

Bessie Boatright, a twenty-seven-year-old farmer's wife who lived near Blocker, said she knew Davis, Bertholf, and Worthman, and all three men were at her place the day before the train was robbed. The men said they were going to brand cattle, she said.[121]

"Wasn't Bob there under cover?" Linebaugh asked in cross-examination in reference to Worthman. "If he was there he slept under cover," Boatright responded.[122]

A man named Neal, who lived five miles northwest of Canadian and who knew Bertholf and Worthman, said they stayed at a nearby ranch on the Saturday before the robbery. Howard Ross, a Jack Davis sharecropper who lived eight miles east of Eufaula near Texanna, said Worthman was at his farm the night before the robbery and was there the next morning when Ross left to hear Bryan speak in Eufaula. Emma Ogden—who with her husband, William Ogden, ran a small farm a mile from the Davis Ranch on the Canadian River—said Worthman was at their farm on the day of the robbery. She remembered the date because it was the same day Bryan spoke in Eufaula. William Ogden testified that he arrived in Eufaula with a wagonload of cotton at about nine or ten in the morning. After the robbery Jim Blevins was staying at his house picking cotton, and he remembered Blevins sitting in front of the fireplace and remarking that there was a big reward for the Katy robbers.[123]

William Hall, a livestock buyer and professional roper who knew Joe Davis well and who had just returned from the Calgary Stampede in Alberta, Canada, was camped with Davis and Bertholf on the night of the robbery. The two had left the next morning saying they were going to McAlester. Davis was riding a bay horse and Bertholf a brown pony. A cowman from the Clayton Valley in the wilds of Pushmataha County named T. "Black Bill" Matlock—who once ran the movie theater in Okmulgee and in Lehigh, and who had recently moved to New Mexico—testified that he was camped about three miles from Featherston on the night of the robbery and the day before he saw Davis and a "big fellow" riding together.[124]

Simeon W. Lewis, a black Choctaw freedman characterized by the Muskogee press as a "shiny-faced negro with a white cowboy hat and a pair of high cowboy boots" who lived three miles south of Blocker, said he saw Davis and Bertholf on the morning of the robbery east of his farm riding toward McAlester. Davis was on a bay horse and Bertholf was riding a brown horse.[125] A. C. Dusenbury, a resident of McAlester said on the morning of the robbery, about eight or nine o'clock, he saw Davis and Bertholf on horseback about three or four miles north of McAlester. Both men wore white hats and he had stopped to talk with them in the middle of the road. Dusenbury said he told the two young cowboys that the Katy had been robbed.[126]

E. S. Norton, a rancher from Broken Bow in McCurtain County, said he was in a wagon looking for a mule that had been stolen from him and he was camped on the Canadian River at the time of the robbery. In the early morning he heard shooting nearby and later heard the train headed south. Norton arose and began building a fire. Within minutes three men on horseback rode by his camp and told him the train had been robbed and there was certain to be a "whole gang of marshals there soon." Two of the individuals were mere boys, small in stature, while a third was tall. Norton said he knew Davis, Bertholf, and Worthman, and the men who came to his camp were not them. On cross-examination Norton admitted that Jack Davis had paid his way to Muskogee.[127]

Bob Baldwin, a cowman from McCurtain County who ran five or six hundred head of cattle, testified that Tom Spencer helped drive some steers from the Davis Ranch on October 28, the day before the robbery, and stayed overnight at Baldwin's ranch the following night. Pat Robinson, a shoemaker from McAlester who had served a three-year term for robbery, quoted Van Brunt, who was in prison at the same time, as saying he was "swearing crooked" to get out of prison. Crockett Lee had promised him parole if he would testify against the Davises. Van Brunt also tried to recruit an inmate named John Culver to testify against Jack Davis. "I don't know anything about it and I won't do it," Robinson remembered Culver saying. Culver took the stand to say that, while he was in the McAlester prison, Van Brunt said he received a letter from Eufaula, asking him to testify against the Davises. Van Brunt wanted Culver to swear he had witnessed Van Brunt talking to Jack Davis in Muskogee.[128]

### The Truth or Not

A lawyer from McAlester, T. D. Taylor, told the jury how Van Brunt had come into the office of James Jackson McAlester—founder of the city and the man who developed the coal industry in eastern Oklahoma, the lieutenant governor at the time and running for reelection. Van Brunt wanted to know whether if he testified against the Davises he would have to go back to prison. "I am going to stick to it, enough to get out; it don't make any difference if it is the truth or not," Van Brunt was heard to say. Van Brunt said he would do anything, even "swearing to a lie," to avoid having to go back to prison.[129]

In some of the more dramatic testimony, Sig T. Wilkerson, a former evangelist and cattleman who lived near Blocker, said he was part of the coroner's jury that examined the body of the man found shot in the head a mile south of Blocker in November 1914. The body had started to decompose and the stench was unbearable, but Wilkerson had cut the shoes and part of the clothing off the man. He had taken a stick and opened the man's mouth and examined the wound behind the right ear that had killed him. Wilkerson said the body was definitely not that of Tom Spencer.[130]

Bob Worthman was the first of the outlaws to take the stand. He said he had worked for Jack Davis since 1912 and was working for Davis at the time of the robbery. He had stayed at Bessie Boatright's farm on Sunday night, had left there on Monday at about eight o'clock and had gone to another ranch where he ate dinner before going on to the Davis Ranch on the Canadian River. There he had helped gather cattle that were to be shipped from Blocker to the new ranch in McCurtain County. The first he heard of the robbery was when Joe Davis told him that he and Bertholf had been arrested and that lawmen were looking for him. He immediately went into Muskogee to see Jack Davis. The next day he and Jack Davis went to McAlester on the train and Davis helped him make bond. Under cross-examination, Linebaugh got Worthman to admit he had served two terms in the state penitentiary, both times for larceny.[131]

On the stand Bertholf related how he had spent the last six months working on a cattle ranch near Benson, Arizona, and he knew nothing about the robbery until he was arrested. The only time he had ever been to Van Brunt's house in

Eufaula was to buy whiskey and beer. On the Monday before the robbery, he had been with Joe Davis branding cattle for a man named Boles. Moreover, he had never taken any horses to M. F. Cosby in Blocker to be shod.[132]

Before a packed courtroom, twenty-three-year-old Joe Davis told the court he was a citizen of the Cherokee Nation. Stock raising and farming was his life. He was raised on his father's ranch on the Canadian River and it was there he had been arrested. In the days before the robbery he was helping his father establish a new ranch in McCurtain County. A few days before the Katy was robbed he left Muskogee, where his father and mother were still living at the time, and he rode horseback all the way to Checotah, on to Texanna, and finally to Eufaula. There he had caught the night train to Crowder where Claude Sawyer came up from McAlester and the two had "called on some young ladies." They stayed in the Missouri Hotel, and Davis caught the train to Featherston and then to Blocker, where he branded some livestock for Boles. On the night of the robbery he and a man named Bill Hale were in camp.[133]

In response to the testimony of the Davises' using one- and two-dollar bills to pay their ranching expenses, Rutherford had Joe Davis identify checks on the Hugo National Bank and the Oklahoma State Bank at Hugo that were made payable to Walter Spencer and to Jim Blevins. He denied telling Blevins anything about any robbery, and he was sure Bertholf did not have any horses shod in Blocker. He and his father were not trying to keep Worthman and Bertholf from being arrested, and he did not have anything to do with Bertholf going to Arizona, though he wired him a ticket to return to Oklahoma. Joe had tried to find out where Tom Spencer was but could not find him. He had no knowledge of Spencer and he certainly didn't murder him.[134]

### They Diten Got Buck

At every opportunity Rutherford tried to sneak into the minds of the jurors the idea that the men had previously been acquitted of robbing the Katy, although Judge Campbell consistently ruled such testimony out of order. A dramatic moment in the trial came when Linbaugh handed Joe Davis a letter and asked him to read it. The letter was from Davis to Mrs. Fred Spess and was scribbled on stationary from the Brothers of the Sacred Heart at St. Josephs College in Muskogee, although the letter was actually written from Hugo.

July 27, 1914

I write you [a] few lines in regards to Fred. They arrested Bob and myself and want Fred on the MKT charge. The US taken it up on the mail mat[t]ers.

So tell Him to keep out of the way until he hears from me again. I was brought back from New Mexico, but don't think it will amount to much. They diten [sic] got Buck. He go away. Give this to Fred, or let him know about [it] as soon as possible.

Your Friend

Joe Davis

Hugo, Okla.[135]

Jack Davis was the last witness for the defense. Davis said he had lived in Muskogee for thirty years and had moved to Hugo two years ago after he sold his ranch in Muskogee County. Rutherford made several attempts to introduce evidence of how and why Davis had been forced to leave Muskogee County or, as the trial transcript put it, the "troubles that have befallen this defendant," but Judge Campbell ruled such testimony irrelevant. Davis denied contacting Van Brunt. Moreover, he was sick in bed in Muskogee on the Monday of the robbery and the first he learned of the Katy being held up was when the ice man told him about it and he read the news in the newspaper a few minutes later.[136]

Linebaugh called four men as rebuttal witnesses. Surprisingly, H. B. Garrison, who lived at Quinton in Pittsburg County, admitted that Simeon Lewis, witness for the defense, had a good reputation in the community for truth and veracity. Lewis owned his own property and was considered "well-to-do for a Negro." Garrison said that in Pittsburg County blacks and whites sometimes went to the same country dances where there was crap shooting and whiskey peddlers were in abundance. On the other hand, George McKee, who ran a livery stable in Quinton, thirteen miles northeast of Blocker, said Lewis had a "bad reputation." R. W. Cornell, the sheriff of Choctaw County, took the stand again to say that Bob Baldwin, the McCurtain County cowman who had testified for the Davises, "had a bad reputation." Rutherford hounded the sheriff into admitting that he was determined to arrest the Davises and that Jack Davis had bitterly opposed him in the last election. Cornell admitted that he had taken an active part in "running down every clue" he could find against the "boys."[137]

## Bad Blood Up

The night before the conclusion of the trial, a fracas erupted at the Paris Café on North Third Street in Muskogee. While Van Brunt, Walter Spess, and Blevins along with several government witnesses were eating dinner, Joe Davis and several of his friends walked in. Words were exchanged. Claude Sawyer slapped Van Brunt across the face with a newspaper.

"Get your guns," someone shouted.

"Yes, get your guns," Joe Davis declared, "and take the consequences." Sawyer, who was dating Joe's younger sister Carrie at the time, claimed that Van Brunt reached for a gun in his back pocket.

"Come on with it, you louse," Sawyer cried out.

Tensions eased when US deputy marshal Tom Hosmer, who was in charge of the federal witnesses, led them all out of the restaurant. When everyone arrived at the court for a night session they found the doors guarded.

"There's bad blood up. We can't let anyone in," a deputy remarked.[138]

At the conclusion of the testimony, Rutherford rose to ask that the charges against the defendants be dismissed, that the facts in the indictment did not constitute a crime. Judge Campbell promptly overruled the motion.[139]

At the beginning of the government's closing argument, Linebaugh apologized to the jury for being ill and fatigued, and he spoke for only forty-five minutes. He praised the detective work of Crockett Lee and reviewed the testimony of several witnesses, especially Blevins, who had been the foreman at the Davis Ranch in McCurtain County for three months following the robbery. Linebaugh also took time to reread the incriminating letter Joe Davis had written to Mrs. Fred Spess.

### Rutherford at His Best

In his closing arguments Rutherford spoke for well over three hours, bitterly attacking several of the prosecution witnesses. How was it that Dolan and Kelm had been unable to identify Joe Davis, Bertholf, and Worthman until they met several times with Crockett Lee? He opened with a tirade against Lee, a "little two-by-four with a big six-shooter trying to earn perhaps $100 a month and [who] in his zeal hounded and sacrificed the defendants as the martyrs of old." Lee was only hoping to advance his career, Rutherford argued. "Oh, how would Crockett Lee like to have the scalps of these boys dangling from his belt with his six-shooter which weighs him down from one end to the other of the Katy railroad," Rutherford shouted out in hissing tones. Van Brunt was a "jail bird and a low dirty hound." Blevins was like "a dog" that bites "the hand of the man who fed him," someone who "swore falsely for a money reward." Walter Spess was a crook who was trying to get in the good graces of the government.[140]

At one point Rutherford put on a big white cowboy hat, tied a white kerchief about his face, and paraded before the jury box, showing how it would have been impossible for Dolan, Kelm, or any members of the train crew to identify him. "If my head were cut off at the top of this handkerchief and paraded down the street on the end of a pole, would you recognize it?" Rutherford asked. Reviewing the whereabouts of Bertholf, Worthman, and Joe Davis in the days prior to the robbery, Rutherford was sure it would have been impossible for them to have taken part in the robbery. He also presented his usual theory that the Davises were victims of a conspiracy that had existed in Muskogee County for over a decade.[141]

With fifteen pages of instructions from Judge Campbell, the case of the *US vs. Joe Davis, et al.* went to the jury at nine o'clock on a Friday morning, February 19, 1915, the day the bloody Battle of Gallipoli opened in distant Turkey. By evening the jury had not reached a verdict, and they retired to the Torson Hotel in bustling downtown Muskogee at Sixth Street and Boston, where they had been sequestered for the duration of the trial. Rumors leaked out of the courthouse that the jury stood nine to three for acquittal. That evening the bailiff, J. S. O'Brien, led the jurors to the Broadway Theatre on West Broadway to see a "picture show." There, on the big screen, was a holdup that was in many ways similar to the robbery of the Katy Limited. Masked bandits held up a frontier stagecoach carrying the US mails, stole the money from the express box, and escaped on horseback.[142] O'Brien claimed he had no idea as to the nature of the show when he bought the tickets.

### The Dance Isn't Over 'Till the Fiddler Stops His Tune

On Saturday morning at 9:45 there was a tapping on the door of the jury room and the bailiff was told that—after twenty-four hours of deliberations, a day and a night after they were given the case—the jury at last had a verdict. Joe and Jack Davis, Bertholf, Worthman, Rutherford, Linebaugh, and the other attorneys, all rushed to the courtroom. Everyone expected there would be acquittals, especially of Jack Davis. Ten minutes later the verdict was announced; all the defendants were declared guilty. Jack Davis "shrank back in his chair, seemingly unable to believe what he heard." The other three defendants took the results as if the entire case had been little more than a lengthy charade. Joe Davis and Buck Bertholf looked at each other for a moment "then threw back their heads and laughed." Worthman's "lip curled into a sneer."[143] Rutherford immediately asked for a new trial, and when this was denied he told Judge Campbell he would appeal.[144] The only family member in the court at the time was Bob Davis, recently released from the state penitentiary.

### Two Years in Leavenworth

Jack Davis was found guilty on a single charge of conspiracy to obstruct the mail, but Joe Davis, Bertholf, and Worthman were guilty of conspiracy as well as actually robbing the train. "For the first time in the many years that they have run the gauntlet of the laws, Jack Davis, long reputed to be the leader of the gang of Oklahoma outlaws, Joe Davis, his son, and Buck Bertholf and Bob Worthman, alleged members of the gang, sat in a court room here yesterday and heard a jury pronounce them guilty of a crime," the *Muskogee Daily Phoenix* told its readers.[145] Worthman would later say that it was Blevins and Van Brunt who "swore away his liberty."

The four men spoke scarcely a word as they were taken to the federal jail. At the jail they were searched and relieved of all their valuables. Joe Davis emptied his pockets and shoved the contents across the counter to the jailer, saying he had $150. The jailer carefully counted a roll of bills and determined he had $200. Jack Davis had only a pocketknife and some small change. Worthman had several letters and a memorandum book. Jack Davis and Worthman were placed in one cell and Joe Davis and Bertholf in another. The four had been in their cells for only a few minutes when Bessie and Carrie rushed into the jail.

They were still crying an hour later when a newspaper reporter caught up with them:

"It's not true," Bessie said, speaking "slowly and with great effort."

"It can't be," she said. "They don't make men go to prison for what they didn't do, and my boy didn't do this." Brushing away an occasional tear, "Jack doesn't know about it," she continued. "He would have told me if he had. Oh, we tried to live right after we left Porum, but they wouldn't let us alone."

Unable to control her emotions or conceal her tears, Carrie Davis "seemed strangely out of place among the men whom her father is accused of leading into lawless deeds," the newspaper reported. Dressed fashionably in a purple suit with a black velvet hat, the "tall athletic blonde, every feature finely marked, refined and intelligent," seemed unable to control her emotions.

"Mother, mother, dad's in jail—they say he was guilty," she sobbed. Nothing seemed to comfort her.

"Did he do it?—please, oh, please tell me," she implored. Then her faith in her father and brother seemed to reassert itself, and she proclaimed there was little doubt they were innocent. "He didn't," she spoke of her father. "He couldn't, for he loves me too much and he knows I wouldn't like it."[146]

In fact, the criminal activities of Jack and Joe Davis played heavily on the family and left deep psychological scars. From the time she was a young woman, Carrie slept with a loaded .45 caliber revolver under her pillow.[147]

At the jail Jack Davis spoke with his usual braggadocio self, perhaps with a bit more humility. "There's an old saying," Davis told the Muskogee press, "that the dance isn't over 'till the fiddler stops his tune."[148]

"The case isn't over; we'll show 'em a trick or two now. I'm not guilty and that statement goes as long as I live. I felt they'd get me from the minute I walked into the court room. It just sort o' seemed like the atmosphere was against me."

But, Davis claimed, "We've just begun to fight."

Joe Davis, Bertholf, and Worthman stood quietly as Jack Davis spoke. "My boys were all acquitted of this robbery when they were tried at Eufaula. That shows we were being hounded . . . we were half convicted as soon as we were charged." Both Jack Davis and Rutherford blamed the conviction on Van Brunt, Blevins, and "that picture show Friday night."

"They took that jury into the show and let the men see a stage coach robbery where the robbers got away with an express package. Tell me the officers didn't know what the picture was going to be. . . . Of course it had an influence on them. Of course it did." As for Blevins, he "was talking for the money, reward, that's all."

A reporter jokingly asked the forty-nine-year-old Davis when Van Brunt's murder was scheduled. In an instant Davis's entire demeanor changed and his voice was pitched lower. He seemed in earnest as he spoke.

"Listen," he said, "I know the kind of name I have. But I want to tell you that the people who accuse me without knowing the facts do me an injustice. I've lived my life among people who are rough and who want to fight at the drop of a hat. I've been successful in my business and I've made enemies."[149]

"I know I've killed men, but I never shot at anybody unless I thought that I was about to be shot myself. The men I have killed died because they were trying to kill a man who was just a little bit quicker—that is all there is to it."[150]

Davis continued, "If my life would have been spent among [a] different kind of people I would have been a different kind of man . . . I'm not a lawbreaker . . . I'm not a robber."[151]

"We will give them another round," Davis asserted. "Of course we will appeal."[152] Rutherford immediately went to work compiling a mountain of affidavits. His office "was filled all day yesterday with a constant stream of people," the *Daily Phoenix* reported in late February 1915.[153] One of those who worked hard in accumulating affidavits for the appeal was Joe's uncle Bob Davis. "I do not fear the results of my efforts to secure a new trial," Rutherford said, "waving his hand at the pile of law books which he had upon his desk." These "defendants have been hounded by the sleuths of the government and by the secret agents of the Katy railroad," he went on to say, "until this conviction was secured."[154]

On February 28, 1915, the outlaws stood before Judge Campbell for sentencing. Jack Davis, "once reported to be among the wealthiest cattlemen of the Indian Territory," when asked if he had anything to say before sentence was pronounced, could only mutter "Nothing, only that I am an innocent man."[155] The Jack Davis "who stood before the bar of the federal court yesterday to be sentenced was an old man" the *Daily Phoenix* told its readers. "Although he held his head erect, his demeanor told of his forty-nine years and his voice carried a tone of regret."[156] Jack Davis was a beaten man. He was sentenced to two years at Leavenworth and fined $5,000.

For Joe Davis, Bertholf, and Worthman, the snickering was over. Joe Davis and Worthman were given two years in Leavenworth and assessed fines of $4,000 each, while Bertholf received two years and was fined $2,500. Bond was fixed at $15,000 for Joe Davis, Bertholf, and Worthman, while Jack Davis's bond was placed at $12,500.[157] Rutherford strenuously objected to the amount of the bonds, saying they were prohibitively large, but Judge Campbell paid him little heed. "Jack Davis at one time had been comparatively wealthy," Rutherford was forced to admit, "but now he is virtually a pauper."[158]

The case for a new trial began on the afternoon of February 28, 1915, with Rutherford presenting a pile of affidavits. He vehemently argued that the guilty verdict was not only contrary to law but in conflict with the evidence, which was insufficient. Judge Campbell had made mistakes, but more importantly, the jury had not been fair or impartial.[159]

According to one sworn statement, R. E. Lee, who had served as the jury foreman, was overheard saying that "the Davis gang, if they had their just deserts, would be hung, as well as a good many others."[160] On another occasion, two men heard Lee utter another prejudicial statement: "There is a lot of old timers here attending court and I see Crockett Lee here who is interested in a case and I hope Crockett will win, as he is a good man."[161] While referring to Joe and Jack Davis, another juror, F. C. Ferre, was heard to remark that "the country would be better off without such a gang of thieves and outlaws." John R. Harris and Caleb Starr had stopped at Ferre's bakery in Grove, Oklahoma, to buy some bread, and Starr had a newspaper with an account of attempts by the authorities in Kansas to extradite Joe Davis for the Baxter Springs bank robbery and heard Ferre make the remark.[162]

One affidavit was signed by Morton Rutherford himself alleging considerable mismanagement and misconduct of the jury during the trial. He had stepped into the lobby of the Torson Hotel to buy a cigar one evening and was shocked by what he witnessed. The hotel was one of the best in the city, and the jury frequently gathered here in the mornings and evenings. "Promiscuously scattered around and through" the lobby, Rutherford asserted, were newspapers of all descriptions in which the trial was frequently in the headlines. The newspapers consistently referred to the defendants as the "Davis Gang." The newspapers also contained, in "minute detail," accounts of other crimes the defendants had allegedly committed.[163] Moreover, the jurors were allowed to mingle freely and talk with other guests at the hotel, some of whom were known to be prejudiced and unfriendly toward the defendants. In addition, jurors were allowed to walk the crowded streets of Muskogee where they were exposed to adverse comments.[164]

### Damn Davis Boys Should Be Lynched

Perhaps more significantly, on the night before the jury began deliberations, they had attended the Broadway Theatre, which was filled to capacity. There on the movie screen were two young men dressed in cowboy attire with white broad-brimmed hats and high boots and wearing kerchiefs over their faces. The blowing of a safe and the taking of two bags of money were graphically depicted. No one could deny that the entire movie eerily resembled the robbery of the Katy Limited. The actors not only were dressed like Joe Davis, Bertholf, and Worthman but actually looked like them. Joe's eighteen-year-old sister, Carrie, was one of those present at the Broadway Theatre that evening and saw the jury there and heard the prejudicial comments by the audience.[165] Remarks, often derogatory, by the audience during the movie were constant and audible throughout the theatre.[166] One moviegoer was heard to utter that "such pictures should not be allowed, for they contribute to the lawlessness and the making of outlaws like the Davises." One moviegoer loudly declared that the "damn Davis boys" should be lynched. A woman had also gone to the New Yale Theatre where a similar film was being shown and someone commented that the lead actor looked exactly like Joe Davis.[167]

Finally, Rutherford argued, the defendants were denied a public trial as guaranteed by the Constitution when, on the final day of the trial, Judge Campbell cleared the courtroom of over 150 spectators and denied the public admittance.[168]

Struggling to make bond, even after it was reduced to ten thousand dollars, Joe and Jack Davis were finally released on March 4, 1915, thanks to Sam Davis and friends of the Davises such as Rains Matlock of Pushmataha County and Frank Vore of Muskogee. As Jack left the jail at half past three in the afternoon, a chorus of prisoners sang out, "Good-Bye, Uncle Jack—come again." With a broad smile,

"Uncle Jack" retorted that he did not plan to be back. Pausing on the steps of the jail, as if he had never been to Muskogee before, he remarked, "I hardly know which way to go."[169] No relatives were there to greet him. A few hours later when he returned to the jail, Joe was released and the father and son walked silently to their hotel. They were out of money and growing desperate. The convictions at Muskogee proved a turning of the tide in the lives of Joe and Jack Davis and led to yet another desperate violent chapter in the life of the son.

## → 5 ←

# FEARLESS TO A RECKLESS DEGREE

Stand aside and let me get that bastard up there!

— Henry Starr

Henry Starr once told a reporter how he and Joe Davis had played together when they were children. Since there was a twenty-year age difference between the two, this story, like many of Starr's other stories, was either greatly exaggerated or downright untrue. There is little doubt that Starr was one of Davis's role models and was someone Joe emulated—a bandit who robbed banks and got away with it. The two did have a lot in common. They were both mixed-blood Cherokee; they both were adventuresome, daring, and compulsive train and bank robbers. The two men were close but Starr admitted they were "strangely different" in many ways. Henry drank and chased women; Davis never "swore, drank, chewed tobacco, smoked, or followed after women."[1] If trial transcripts accurately reflect the historical record and prosecution witnesses are truthful, Starr was exaggerating again. The two outlaws shared one trait that was undeniable: they were addicted to robbing banks. The more banks they robbed, the more they wanted to rob, and at times they seemed unable to resist doing so.

There is little doubt both men were involved in several bank robberies that swept across eastern Oklahoma in the late fall and early winter of 1915–16. They were certainly responsible for the robbery of the Central State Bank at Kiefer on

September 30, 1914, after which Tom Spencer was allegedly killed by Davis when he made off with more than his share of the $5,682 loot.[2]

## Bad Boy of the Cherokee

In the early 1890s, although he was only a teenager at the time, Henry Starr formed a notorious gang that terrorized and robbed stores, banks, and train stations throughout northwestern Arkansas. When a US marshal tried to arrest him in 1892, Starr killed him. Starr was eventually arrested, and he was twice sentenced to be hanged by Judge Isaac Charles Parker, the famous "Hanging Judge" of Fort Smith fame. Parker called Starr a "marvel of wickedness," someone who was "full of hatred and vengeance."[3] After a series of appeals, Starr managed to beat the hangman and wound up with a sentence of fifteen years on a manslaughter charge. While imprisoned at Fort Smith in 1903, a disreputable outlaw named Cherokee Bill attempted to break out of the jail using a gun smuggled to him by a trustee. In a vicious firefight one of the guards was killed. Starr managed to intervene, and he persuaded Cherokee Bill to give himself up, with the understanding that the guards would not kill him.

Starr's actions gained him the attention of President Theodore Roosevelt, and a short time later a telegram arrived from the White House: "Will you be good if I set you free?" Starr wired back, "Yes," and Roosevelt commuted his sentence. Released from prison, Henry married a second time and had a son whom he named Theodore "Ted" Roosevelt Starr. When Arkansas pressed for his extradition for the robbery of the Bentonville bank he had robbed in 1893, Henry fled his home in Tulsa and went to the Osage Hills. "I preferred a quiet and unostentatious internment in a respectable cemetery rather than a life on the Arkansas convict farm," he said.[4]

By 1908, however, the "Bad Boy of the Cherokee" was back to his old tricks, this time involving a bank in Tyro, Kansas. Although he was pursued by a posse of twenty men, he managed to escape. Eventually he fled to Colorado, where he fell in with another notorious Oklahoma outlaw, Kid Wilson. Together, they robbed the bank at Amity, a small farming community in the southeastern part of the state only a few miles from the Kansas border. Starr spent the summer and fall hiding out in the wilds of New Mexico and Arizona, but eventually he returned to Oklahoma only to be betrayed and arrested. He was extradited to Colorado, where he pleaded guilty to the Amity robbery and was given seven years in the Canon City prison. Here he had the opportunity to study law and wrote his autobiography, *Thrilling Events: Life of Henry Starr.*[5] After promising Governor

Elias M. Ammons he would not leave the state, he was paroled in 1913. Within days Starr was back in Tulsa.

## Last of His Type

From September 1914 to March 1915, eighteen banks were robbed in northeastern Oklahoma, many of them by Starr and Joe Davis. Starr would often brag that he robbed more banks than the James Younger and Doolin Dalton Gangs combined. "Henry Starr is about the last of his type of wild west outlaws . . . that made pale that of the Dalton for outlawry," one Oklahoma newspaper agreed.[6] He was the kind of outlaw that "even the officers who trailed him would enjoy sitting down to a meal with him or ride trail with him." Although he broke the law, he never killed a man in a robbery nor harmed a woman or child, and he held "certain ideals that men admire." Or so it was said. This helped to make Starr, one Oklahoma scholar concluded, "one of the most dangerous criminals this or any other country produced."[7]

Convinced that Starr was hiding in the Osage Hills, the brushy Bigheart Mountains, or perhaps in the tangled forests of the Verdigris and Big Caney Valleys, the law relentlessly searched in all of Starr's old hideouts. They were certain he was in Oklahoma, but they could not find him. While hundreds of law enforcement officers were tramping through the wilds of Oklahoma in their search, Henry was in reality living comfortably in Tulsa in a five-room bungalow, complete with electric lights, a telephone, and hot and cold running water. The house was two blocks from the home of the Tulsa County sheriff and four blocks from the residence of the mayor. Henry enjoyed nightly joy rides in a new five-passenger Ford and frequently spent a quiet evening at the cinema. Life in general was good. He even took on an assumed name—R. L. Williams, which was the name of the governor of Oklahoma.[8]

Davis and Starr first conceived the idea of robbing two banks at the same time while meeting at the Tulsa fairgrounds on the north side of the city, a mile from where Starr was living.[9] The banks they decided to hit were the First National Bank and the Stroud National Bank, which were only a block apart in Stroud, a small cow town in Lincoln County with a population of thirteen hundred, on the Frisco Railroad some fifty-eight miles northeast of Oklahoma City and fifty miles southwest of Tulsa. After the Stroud heists, they thought they would pull off two other robberies at the same time in Sapulpa, thirty-eight miles northeast of Stroud.[10] Davis enlisted a friend, Claude J. Sawyer, son of a well-to-do McAlester cowman, who was described as six foot two inches, clean-cut, and a "slim, fine looking young man."[11] The two had roped steers and robbed more than one bank together. Starr recruited Bud Maxfield, an oilfield worker who lived in the small community of Turley, eight miles north of Tulsa. In turn Maxfield enrolled Lewis Estes, a restless young man who had come to Oklahoma from Coburn, Missouri, looking for work and who had been with Starr since his return from Colorado. At the time Estes was working for Maxfield in the Bird Creek Oil Field as a teamster. Charles Johnson, who owned a small ranch near Bartlesville, also joined the gang, as did another criminal from a family of outlaws, Liege "Bull" Higgins.[12]

### Two Banks on the Same Day at the Same Time

The outlaws gathered at Maxfield's home, a mile east of Turley, where they stored camping equipment in one of Maxfield's large covered oilfield wagons. Some of the outlaws would ride in the wagon while their horses were tied behind. A couple were on horseback. At least two outlaws who drove the wagon planned to use the horses pulling the wagon as saddle horses in their flight from Stroud after the heist. After leaving Tulsa, the party turned east near Owasso and then south, stopping along the Frisco Railroad before fording the Arkansas River at Bisbee, where they camped for the night and bought more horses. Passing through Mounds, they turned west to Millay and then headed straight for Stroud.[13]

The gang quietly camped at George Rodgers's farm two miles east of Stroud. Over the next two days, they rode into town several times to scout out the place and to buy provisions, along with three cotton-flour sacks from a bakery. Starr had wanted to rob the banks on Friday, but two of the gang were superstitious, so the men agreed on Saturday, March 27, 1915.[14] George Rodgers grew suspicious of the men, and on Friday night he telephoned Andrew W. Lycan, the town marshal. Lycan theorized that the men were probably hunters, and Rodgers was told not to worry.[15] It was decided that Davis, Sawyer, and Estes would rob the First National Bank at the southwest corner of Main and Fourth Avenue, while Starr, Higgins, and Johnson would raid the Stroud National Bank, one block away on the northwest corner of Main and Third Avenue. Starr was always the showman—on the day before the robbery, he mailed postcards to both banks saying he intended to rob the banks and use the money to "feed the poor people."[16]

The William J. Burns Detective Agency out of Tulsa and hundreds of peace officers throughout the Sooner State had been searching for Starr for months. More successfully, the Burns Agency had been watching Davis, Sawyer, and one or two others in the gang, whom they referred to as the "Long Riders." For weeks the agency had sent out warnings to banks in different towns in eastern Oklahoma to be on the lookout for the outlaws, but for some reason the two banks in Stroud were never contacted, or so they said.[17]

## Stroud

On Saturday morning the outlaws broke camp and drove their covered wagon to the stockyards two blocks south of Main Street. The two horses pulling the wagon were unhitched, saddled, and tied to the stockyard fence, as were five other horses that had been either ridden or tied to the wagon. A string of boxcars hid them from sight of anyone on the streets in the town.

The two groups of three men each calmly walked toward the two banks, only blocks from the stockyards. Davis, Sawyer, and Estes proceeded up Fourth Avenue while Starr, Higgins, and Johnson went east to Third Avenue, where they turned north. They crossed Main Street to the Stroud National Bank. Bud Maxfield was left with the horses. At first everything went like clockwork. No one seemed suspicious. They were careful to keep their weapons concealed, and most citizens of Stroud thought they were just another group of cowboys who had come to town to enjoy the bars, brothels, or restaurants.

Signaling to the other group, they simultaneously entered the two banks, guns drawn, with masks over their faces. It was 9:30 A.M., just as they had planned. In the Stroud National Bank at the time was the bank's vice president Lee Patrick, a bookkeeper, J. E. Charles Jr., and J. M. Reed, a customer. One of the outlaws stood guard outside the bank on the stone steps. On the front door of the bank, only steps away, was a large printed placard with Governor Williams's name at the bottom that offered a one-thousand-dollar reward for Henry Starr, "dead or alive," and one thousand dollars for any man captured or killed during a bank robbery.[18]

Pointing a pistol Starr ordered Charles, the bookkeeper, to gather up what amounted to $186 in silver on one of the counters and place it in one of the flour sacks. Starr threw a second sack at Charles and ordered him to open the large vault behind the counter. Charles said that the vault had a time lock.

"You open the safe or I will kill you," Starr shouted out.

"I can't open that, it's time locked," Patrick, the vice president, pleaded. "Don't you know what a time lock is?"

"You open it or I'll blow your head off," Starr cried out.

"You will have to kill me then," Patrick courageously replied. "I cannot open the safe because I do not know the combination."

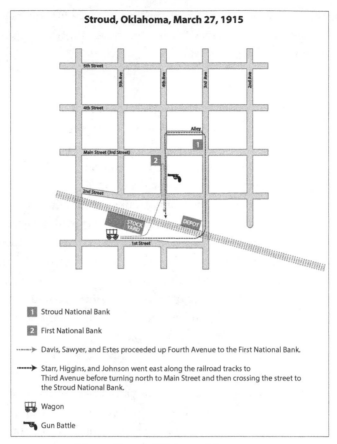

MAP 4. Stroud, Oklahoma, May 27, 1915
*Map by Ana Clamont*

"It's 9:30 now and you ought to have it open; you better open it damned quick or I'll kill you," Starr said as he waved a big automatic revolver in the air.[19]

### Stick around for the Big Show

In the midst of all the drama, seemingly unaware of what was happening, Lorena Hughes, the six-year-old daughter of a local merchant, George Hughes, who lived next door, walked into the bank. Somewhat agitated, Starr stepped over to the counter and handed her some pennies.

"Here kiddie, take these and go and buy some ice cream," Starr said. The young girl took the coins, but instead of leaving the bank she climbed on a chair and sat there.

"Oh hell!" Starr exclaimed. "She's balling up the game. All right kiddie, stick [around] for the big show." The child played undisturbed as the robbery continued.[20]

Finally convinced that the big vault could not be opened, Starr turned to a smaller safe and ordered Patrick to open it.[21]

"What else is there?" Starr demanded. As Patrick got down on his knees, Starr again handed him the flour sack. Patrick pulled out shelf after shelf to show Starr they were all empty, but there was a pile of silver dollars on a corner shelf that Patrick began putting in the sack.

"Hurry up there, you're too damned slow, and don't rattle that coin too loud, you're making too much noise," Starr commanded.

"You hold the sack and I can do it faster," Patrick responded.

"All right," Starr said.

Patrick asked if Starr wanted a pile of eighty dollars in quarters on a shelf in the safe.

"No!" Starr responded.

"Do you want this pile of dimes?" Patrick asked.

"No!" Starr said, somewhat agitated.

"Then you've got it all," Patrick said. "You've cleaned us out."

"You can put your hands down now," Starr said, and "make sure to do just what I tell you to do or I'll kill you, by God!"

Starr spotted a diamond stud in Patrick's tie and snatched it.

"Pardon me," Patrick pleaded, "my mother gave me that diamond just before she died. I'd like to keep it."

"Yes, I've heard that mother story before, but it don't do with me," Starr retorted, as he placed the diamond in the inside pocket of his overcoat.

"All right, let's go," Starr said as he turned to the other outlaw. Stuffing one sack with $1,000 in currency into his overcoat pocked, he handed another sack of $663 to Charles and ordered him to carry it. A stack of $160 in silver sat on the counter unnoticed.

Taking Patrick, Charles, and Reed as hostages and leaving Lorena Hughes to play with her pennies, the bandits exited by a side door with their hostages. They went north up Third Avenue before turning west down an alley to Fourth Avenue and back to Main Street in sight of the First National Bank, where they hoped to join Davis, Sawyer, and Liege. As they passed through the alley, Patrick continued to beg for his diamond.

"I'd like mighty well to get that diamond back," he pleaded.

"I want it myself. Got a girl I want to give it to," Starr responded.

"I'll trade you my gold watch for it," Patrick continued.

"Don't want your watch," Starr replied.[22]

The scene at the First National Bank was similar to what was happening at the Stroud National. Everything was carefully planned. In the bank at the time was the bank's president, O. E. Grecian, a director called R. J. Miller, the cashier H. E. Breeding, the bookkeeper W. A. Chastain, a clerk called Claude Hood, customers Joseph Evans, H. M. Fendle, Charles L. Woods, Julian Gallaway, and Russell Stephens, a county schoolteacher who was in the bank to cash a check.

Lewis Estes entered the front of the bank, while Davis and Sawyer slipped in a back door. Sawyer and Estes wore masks while Davis, who carried a Winchester rifle and a pistol, wore a black hat, a yellow-looking raincoat, and a pair of goggles.[23] Everything seemed routine in the bank until one of the outlaws shouted, "Hands up!"

Witnesses later agreed that Davis was the "yellow faced fellow" who slipped the Winchester rifle from under his coat and went to the rear of the bank, while Estes closed the front door and stood there. Well-dressed and wearing the amber goggles, Davis walked behind the cage and thumped his rifle against the floor.

"Where is the cash?" he shouted out. "We want the money—get the gold," he demanded, leaning his rifle against the counter and pulling out a revolver.[24]

"Who [is] the cashier?" Davis asked.

"I am," Breeding hesitantly replied.

"Get the money out of the safe at once and give it to me," Davis responded.

Sawyer walked up and down outside the cage, drawing his revolver across the iron bars of the cage "as a boy would draw a stick over a picket fence." Inside the vault, Breeding dumped $4,315 in gold and silver coins into a flour sack Davis handed him. In his nervousness Breeding dropped a cigar box of silver dollars and the coins rolled around on the floor.

"Make yourself useful, pick 'em up," Davis demanded, as he pointed his revolver at President Grecian, who quickly went on his knees to gather the coins. When Davis turned away, Breeding pitched a big bundle of currency into a box near the safe.

"Here's a box of pennies," Breeding said.

"Don't want them," Davis responded.

"Then you've got it all and you might as well go," the cashier said courageously.

"No, we'll be ready in a minute, we're going to wait for the other boys up the street," Davis said. "We are taking both banks today."

Pausing, Davis turned to Breeding and asked, "How much is in that sack?"

"About $4,000," the cashier responded.

"Hell—is that all? If I'd known that, we shouldn't have come to town."[25]

## A Town Aroused

As Davis, Estes, and Sawyer paused at the First National Bank waiting for Starr and the other outlaws, the town was already aroused. Men were scurrying about, either seeking shelter or looking for weapons. The employees at the First National sensed that there was likely to be a confrontation, perhaps a violent one, and they became uneasy and fidgeted.

"Here, you fellows don't move!" Davis shouted out, "How would some of you fellows like to smell this?" pointing his revolver in the air.

With one of the bank customers carrying the heavy sack of money for them, the outlaws stepped onto Main Street. Davis shouted, "All right!" to Starr, Higgins, and Johnson as they emerged with their hostages from the Stroud National Bank down Main Street. "You fellows march right along," Davis called out to the hostages as the two groups converged.[26]

As word of a bank robbery spread throughout the downtown area, several townsmen began arming themselves and gathering in small groups. As the outlaws and their hostages headed for the far side of the stockyards, a general alarm had already been sounded.

"There never was a wild west show or a moving picture so exciting as today's events at Stroud," an eyewitness—a traveling salesman for the Armour Packing Company, J. M. Parks—told a newspaper reporter.[27] Parks was on his way to buy groceries when he heard someone shout that the First National Bank was being robbed. The salesman was able to gain a vantage point where he could see the interior of the bank. He watched as two outlaws went behind the bank counter and raked up the money that was stacked in piles.

As the bandits started down Fourth Avenue, they were careful to keep the hostages between themselves and the townsmen. Starr brought up the rear using Vice President Lee Patrick as a shield. The robbers had made it about one block when the shooting started. "The shooting was lively from then on, the bandits returning the fire with a vengeance and although they walked rapidly toward their horses, they never ran," an eyewitness reported.[28] Charles Guild, a horse buyer who was in Stroud on that memorable Saturday, appeared at one of the street corners with a double-barreled shotgun. Seeing Guild, Starr turned to Patrick. "Stand aside and let me get that bastard up there." Starr fired one shot that ripped through the front of Guild's coat and across his vest, after which he sent two more shots in Guild's direction. Guild scurried for cover.

On the opposite corner of the street, Deputy Sheriff Isaac Dodrill stood half concealed behind the corner of a stone building with his Colt revolver. The deputy fired three or four times at Starr, each bullet going high, through the windows on the First National Bank. In the meantime, local barber Harry W. Fender was grabbed by one of the outlaws at the entrance to his shop and forced to carry one of the money sacks. Fender, who was carrying the money bag from the First National, fell to the street during all the excitement. He was poked in the ribs with a rifle by one of the outlaws and ordered to his feet. The town marshal, Andrew W. Lycan, ran out of a drugstore with a revolver in his hand. Starr, who was walking backward at the rear of the procession, spied him and pointed his pistol at the marshal. Lycan dodged back into the store.

As the outlaws were attempting to escape, Walter Martin, a Lincoln County farmer, appeared suddenly from across the street. Starr shouted at him, "Get back!" but Martin seemed dumbfounded and stood still. "Get back, you!" Starr screamed again. Martin froze in place, and Starr fired at him. The dust flew from his coat as the bullet tore into Martin's shoulder and he fell back into a doorway.

"You got that man," Patrick said, standing next to Starr.

"Yes, and I'll get the other one back there," Starr replied, as he aimed his pistol at Deputy Dodrill, who was down the street.

## A Bullet in the Hip with a Hog-Killing Rifle

As the sound of gunfire echoed up and down the streets of Stroud, men began rushing about, armed with shotguns, rifles, revolvers, and anything else they could get their hands on. Paul Holiday Curry, brown-eyed, brown-haired, the twenty-year-old son of a local grocer who was said to be a crack shot, raced up and down Main Street looking for a gun. He finally found one, a "murderous looking short barrel rifle that carried a big snub-nosed lead bullet" that was used by a Stroud butcher to kill hogs. Curry ran into his father's grocery store and out the back door, where he took a position behind a rain barrel just as Starr came down the street guarding the rear of the procession. Starr saw Curry in plenty of time but said he "didn't think the blamed kid" would shoot. Curry did shoot, and a bullet sped into Starr's hip, just above the left leg. Starr stumbled to the ground against a wire fence and lay there, motionless, not saying a word.

"Lay your gun down or I will kill you," Curry shouted. As the Cherokee outlaw flung his pistol aside, Curry rushed over to him.

One of "your men is shot," R. J. Miller, the bank director, told Lewis Estes. "Keep your mouth shut and move on," Estes replied.[29]

Several witnesses said that the outlaws never looked back as Starr lay wounded. Estes took up the rear guard. Only seconds later someone, perhaps Curry, shot Estes in the neck. Blood spurted out and down his side, then over the big revolver he wore.

"Here," Estes told Miller, the bank director, "I'm hit, help me. Take my arm!" Estes also ordered Grecian, the bank president, to take his other arm as they broke into a hurried hobble down the street. "The first man that starts to duck, I'll kill him!" one of the bandits shouted.[30] At the stockyards, the robbers grabbed the money bags from their hostages, unhitched their horses, and galloped off. By an almost super human effort Estes, too, managed to reach the stockyards. He was able to mount his horse and raced off, still bleeding badly.

Half the male population of Stroud, some on horseback and others on foot, pursued the outlaws, shooting at them as they disappeared over a hill southeast of town. Only minutes after the outlaws rode off, several automobiles filled with angry and heavily armed citizens were already in pursuit. Speeding down the dirt road that led south out of town, one car veered off the road and into a tree stump. Several of the men were injured and had to be carried back to town.

As the outlaws fled Liege Higgins accidently dropped one of the money bags. He dismounted to recover the money, only to have his spooked horse race off without him. Carrying the money, he hastily mounted behind the badly bleeding Lewis Estes, and they galloped down the road that led out of town. After two miles Estes became so weak from blood loss that he was fearful he would fall off the horse, and he dismounted as Higgins continued on horseback into the timber.[31] Two men in a Ford touring car who were chasing after the outlaws found Estes leaning against a tree, bleeding profusely, holding one arm in the air in an attempt to surrender. Seventy-five dollars in silver coins were found scattered over the ground. He was carried back to Stroud and taken to Dr. James J. Evans's office over the bank, where Starr lay on a cot.[32]

Posses were organized not only at Stroud but also at Chandler, the county seat of Lincoln County, fourteen miles down the Frisco Railroad toward Oklahoma City. Only twenty-three minutes after Captain H. B. Gilstrap picked up the telephone in Chandler, a special train of the Frisco with eleven state militia members on board left for Stroud. Arriving in Stroud, they were put into automobiles and rushed into the hills to join the pursuit.[33] Eventually abandoning the cars and led by men on horseback, the militiamen were several miles south of Stroud when they discovered they had forgotten to bring ammunition for their rifles, so they were forced to return to town. In Oklahoma City, when Governor Robert L. Williams learned of the Stroud robberies, the governor immediately offered an additional two-hundred-dollar reward for the capture of any of the robbers.[34] Although Starr and Estes lay wounded, the bank heists in Stroud were said to have been "the boldest ever executed in Oklahoma."[35]

## Pursuit

Telephone calls brought armed farmers to Stroud on horseback and on foot. Many were anxious to join in the pursuit. Much of the day following the twin heists was spent in confusion and disorganization as they attempted to pick up the trail of the outlaws in the rough blackjack timber country south and east of Stroud, where several farmers said they had seen the outlaws. The robbers did not follow any roads but took to the backcountry, cutting their way through fences.

At first it was thought that the outlaws, who were said to have field glasses and wire cutters, had fled to the Osage Hills. Thinking they were headed in that direction Creek County sheriff Lew Wilder wasted little time in organizing a posse in Drumright, twenty-two miles north of Stroud, and another posse at Oilton on the Cimarron River, eight miles farther north. At one point it was reported that Wilder had the bandits surrounded in the Osage Hills and that their surrender was imminent.

When reports reached the Oklahoma press that the outlaws had escaped, Wilder was furious, saying it was impossible. "They are trying to make a fall guy out of me," he angrily proclaimed. "We had posses out from Sapulpa, Kellyville and Bristow, and no set of men could have gotten away with it."[36] If the outlaws did escape, they had to be somewhere in the Osage Hills, Wilder insisted. Other senior law enforcement officials were sure that the outlaws were headed to the Kiamichi Mountains in the southeastern part of the state where game abounded, caves were numerous, and crude huts could serve as hideouts. The area was an unexplored wilderness, an outlaw's haven, where only by accident could the outlaws be found.[37] Joe Davis was said to have found safety here more than once, and it was here that he and his gang were thought to have "planned" several of their robberies. Nearby, in the towering timbers of Choctaw country, was Robbers Cave, where Pony Starr once carved his initials.[38]

Most reports had the outlaws surrounded in the woods a few miles south of town. Newspapers went wild. "Bandits Surrounded," one newspaper cried out in bold headlines. Another newspaper reported that after a furious gun battle, the outlaws had all been killed. When someone told Starr that his gang was surrounded in a blackjack thicket not far from town, the Cherokee outlaw could only laugh.[39]

"Hell's bells," he responded, "them boys don't stop in no thickets."[40] Starr knew they were heavily armed and would never allow themselves to be surrounded.

Every road leading out of Stroud was guarded day and night and Lincoln County sheriff George Edward Arnold insisted it was impossible for the outlaws to have got away. But within a few days, Arnold withdrew the posses, believing that the robbers were already in the Ozarks, probably headed for Joplin, Missouri. "There is scarcely a chance they are in Oklahoma," Arnold said. "They have been riding hard now since Saturday morning and men in their business don't lose any time if they can help it."[41]

### Escape

It was finally determined that the outlaws had passed through the rough timbered country south of Bristow, seventeen miles east of Stroud, where they cut their way through several farmers' fences. Near midnight on Saturday they sliced through a fence at the Jess Allen Ranch, and a few minutes later cut the fence on the A. C. Smith farm seven miles east of Bristow. It was evident that the outlaws had changed their course from south to southeast. When it was first learned they were near Bristow, a posse of nine men in two automobiles went out to search for them. Several farmers east of Bristow said they had seen the outlaws only minutes before the lawmen arrived, making their way through several fences. The outlaws left behind a well-defined trail of gaps in wire fences.

At one farm five miles southeast of Bristow, the outlaws asked a farmer for directions on how to get to Kellyville. Continuing on, the posse found where the bandits had paused for a meal at a farm two miles southeast of the crossroads of Mills Chapel.[42] At one point the posse abandoned their automobiles and began pursuit on foot, claiming they got within forty yards of the outlaws before the bandits sensed they were being followed and changed direction. Several times, in fact, the bandits were forced to double back. The posse also found where the five outlaws had separated, two bandits going in one direction and three in another. Several times the Chandler men said they passed farmhouses where the bandits had been seen only minutes before. The Bristow posse finally lost the trail and gave up the pursuit in the vastness of the hills and ravines east of Bristow. They returned Monday morning, worn out, covered with dust and mud, blaming local farmers for refusing to give them horses to further pursue the bandits.[43] Fourteen men in three automobiles with sharpshooters from the state militia arrived on the scene, but there was little they could do at this point.

New reports had one group of the outlaws passing near Kellyville before daylight on Sunday morning, heading in the direction of Sapulpa. On Monday a farmer's son found three jaded horses, all showing signs of having been ridden hard, tied to a clump of trees near Kellyville.[44] In the end there were no new reports, however. It was evident that the Stroud bank robbers had gotten away.

In Stroud only minutes after the robberies and the subsequent gun battle, several citizens carried the wounded Henry Starr into Dr. James J. Evans's office over the Stroud National Bank. "Yes, I'm Starr. The jig's up now," Starr said, after several people recognized him.[45] One of the first men to arrive at Evans's office was Lee Patrick, vice president of the Stroud National Bank. "You can have that diamond your mother gave you," Starr told Patrick, apologetically. Patrick took the diamond out of Starr's pocket as well as a sack of money from one of the outlaw's inner pockets. An hour later, the badly wounded Estes was brought into the same office. Estes was in much worse condition than Starr, and for several hours it was thought he would not survive.

"Doctor," Starr told Evans, "you take my horse and saddle for this work you're doing on my leg. . . . You take it and try and save the kid there. I paid $600 for that horse." Dr. Evans told Starr he thought it was strange that his gang would desert him.

"That's all right," Starr responded. "We agreed before we started in that it would be every man for himself."

At Dr. Evans's office, Starr and Estes lay on cots. When Estes was first brought into the office, Starr told him, "Estes, I'd rather have been killed myself than had them catch you."

As his leg was being dressed, Starr never flinched. He told Dr. Evans, "That Estes kid is sure some fine kid." But when Estes began to talk about the robbery, adding that he had a wife and two brothers back in Missouri, Starr told him, "Clamp down on that conversation, kid. Don't talk at all."

With his leg bone shattered near the hip, Starr was seriously wounded. However, his life was never in danger, although for a time it was thought the leg would have to be amputated. Starr asked what Curry had shot him with and when he was told it was a "hog-killing rifle," he replied, "A hog gun and a kid too! I wouldn't have minded it so much if a man had shot me."[46]

At first Starr and Estes refused to reveal the names of their accomplices. "There are no suckers in the bunch," Starr said, "They are all good ones."[47]

### Starr and Estes

There was talk in the streets of Stroud of lynching the robbers, and the two wounded outlaws heard the gossip. "Doc, have you got any poison?" Starr asked Evans, putting on a show of bravado in front of a reporter for the *Stroud Messenger.* "I don't give a damn about dying but I don't want to be strung up."[48]

The day after the robbery, Starr and Estes were carried on their cots in wagons to an express car of the Frisco Railroad and taken to Chandler. At the Chandler depot, three hundred curious onlookers waited patiently to catch a glimpse of the outlaws. Starr and Estes, still on their cots, were placed in a hay wagon and taken to the Lincoln County jail in the basement of the courthouse.[49] The entire crowd followed. William "Bill" Tilghman and his Eagle Film Company were there to film the arrival of the outlaws. Ironically, at the time, Tilghman was preparing to film another reel of his successful "Passing of the Oklahoma Outlaws" at his ranch near Chandler. In the days that followed, curious onlookers, some on horseback, some in wagons or automobiles, and some on foot, all came to Chandler from far and wide to catch a glimpse of Starr or Estes.

George Hollis, owner of a hotel in Kiefer who was on his way to Oklahoma City on business, stopped in Chandler to see Starr. Hollis had been in the Central State Bank in Kiefer at the time of the robbery seven months earlier.

He took one look at Starr and said, "That's the man!" Approaching the outlaw on his cot, Hollis continued, "Don't you know me?"

Starr replied that he had never seen Hollis before in his life.

"You are the man who robbed the Kiefer bank when I was in there last summer."

"You are mistaken," Starr replied. "I have been out of the state for eight years and I returned only a few days before I was shot at Stroud."[50]

There were rumors in Chandler that Sheriff Arnold had received a letter saying that a gang of outlaws was coming to liberate Starr. Everyone remained on edge. Deputies were sent to carefully watch the main roads leading into town.[51] Three men—Walter Spess, Steve Russell, and Puss Irwin, all known outlaws—drove into town in an automobile and were arrested by several deputies. The sheriff was sure they had come to rescue Starr. Days earlier, a farmer in the northern part of the county had noticed the three men camped in a tent on the edge of the woods. Two of the men would retire when anyone approached. The third man would walk forward to converse, but he always carried a Winchester rifle in the crook of his arm.

The towns of Stroud and Chandler became a circus after the robberies. Detectives from the Burns Detective Agency in Tulsa arrived in Chandler to identify all the "Long Riders" and to provide mug shots.[52] Lying on the cot in the jail, Starr agreed to have his photograph taken. A local photographer quickly advertised a postcard of the wounded outlaw as well as images of the two banks that had been robbed: "Price ten cents each or three for 25 cents." Starr was allowed to telegraph his wife, with whom he had returned to Oklahoma from Colorado, as well as his mother in Tulsa, asking them to come to his aid. "I am bad hurt," he wired.[53]

### Paul Curry as Hero

Paul Curry, the young man who shot Starr, received almost as much attention in the press as did Starr. No sooner had the gun smoke in Stroud settled than Curry wired Governor Williams, hoping to claim the reward: "Both the bank of Stroud and the First National Bank were robbed by Henry Starr and bunch," Curry told the governor. "I shot Starr through the leg and captured him. I also shot one other robber and he was captured. Will hold for your disposal and claim reward."[54]

Curry was deluged with letters from admirers praising his bravery. There were even offers for Curry to perform on the stage. "The boy is only a country youth with little education but he is bearing the praise and notoriety that have come to him very modestly," the *Oklahoma Leader* reported. Curry wanted to go to Oklahoma A&M College in Stillwater, where thousands of "foreigners, freaks and just ordinary Oklahoma boys" had received an education through the years, but never a "boy bandit catcher."[55] Using his reward money to pay his tuition, Curry hoped for a career as a mechanical engineer. Besides being a crack shot, he was an excellent athlete. He held several local records in the pole vault and in the sprints, and he was sure he would do well in Stillwater.

A musical touring group from Tulsa stopped in Chandler to play the outlaws a lively tune or two. In Tulsa, sixty-five miles to the northeast, a "For Sale" sign hung in front of Starr's home at 1534 East Second Street. "I don't want a lot of detectives, policemen and curiosity seekers ransacking my home," Starr pleaded. Reporters invaded the home nevertheless, and one pressman spotted a record on Starr's graphophone: "Where the River Shannon Flows."[56]

By late May 1915, Starr was able to hobble around on crutches, although he complained that his wounded leg was three-fourths of an inch shorter than his good leg. "I am getting along all right, but it takes a little time to get over a smash like I got," he was heard to say.[57] In July his son, "Little Roosevelt" Starr, arrived to visit his father.

A report that Starr would plead guilty and throw himself on the mercy of the court was little more than a tactic by the prosecution, Starr told the *Tulsa Daily World*. "Going to have fried chicken for dinner," he told the newspaper. Starr had lost thirty pounds while in jail, and he was hoping to gain some of the weight back. "I am also strong for the roasting ears. I like the big field corn," he went on to say.[58]

Sheriff Arnold placed a dictaphone over Este's and Starr's cells in the basement, but a "dope fiend" in an adjacent cell saw the law enforcement officials installing the device and warned Starr.[59] There were only scattered pieces of conversation on the machine: "We must prove an alibi. You can't tell what they have on us and we must be able to prove where we were at the time of the robbery," Starr was heard to say.[60]

Both men appeared in court in Chandler without counsel. Their bail was fixed at fifteen thousand dollars, but neither man could post that amount. Despite cautions from Starr to remain quiet, after a week or so Estes agreed to turn state's evidence. In return he was promised immunity from prosecution for the robbery of the banks at Carney and Keystone and leniency for the Stroud robberies.[61] Although law enforcement officials had a good idea all along of who the other Stroud robbers were, they now knew the names of all the outlaws.[62]

### Convictions and Acquittals

Sheriff James Woolley of Tulsa County began working on the Stroud case immediately after the robberies, and he was able to gather reliable information on the outlaws.[63] In early April, less than two weeks after the Stroud bank heists, despite heavy winds and a pounding rainstorm, Sheriff Woolley and several of his deputies seized Bud Maxfield at his home northeast of Tulsa. Also caught in the dragnet was Sam Estes, who had been to Stroud to visit his wounded brother in jail. Sam Estes was on his way back to Muskogee and had stopped at Maxfield's house. The oil field wagon the outlaws had abandoned at the stockyards in Stroud was easily traced back to Tulsa and to Maxfield. Sheriff Woolley promised to apprehend other members of the gang within twenty-four hours.[64]

Sure enough, a few days later Bill Tilghman of Eagle Film Company and law enforcement fame, now a special agent assigned to the case, along with Sheriff Arnold of Lincoln County and one of his deputies, Frank Miles, arrested Claude J. Sawyer at a livery stable in McAlester. The six-foot-two-inch Sawyer was wearing a thirty-five-dollar hat at the time; he asked only that he be able to call his father, who was at the family ranch ten miles south of the city. Tilghman and Arnold were fearful that Sawyer would summon companions to his rescue. Within minutes of the phone call, they rushed the young outlaw off to Tulsa and then to Chandler on the Frisco Railroad.[65]

Forty-year-old Charles Johnson was the next to be arrested. Hi Frisbie, a deputy in Osage County who was hoping for a five-hundred-dollar reward, picked up Johnson's trail with the help of an Indian tracker. They followed the trail through a heavy rain and windstorm into the rough country east of Pawhuska, said to be the hiding place of many an outlaw. When Johnson appeared, Frisbie flipped a six-shooter on him with the command "Stick 'em up!"[66] Johnson was taken back to Pawkuska and then to Chandler by train.

Twenty-one-year-old Sawyer, described as a "clean cut and good looking" young man dressed in a "natty blue sere suite, white shirt and collar and carrying one of his expensive sombreros," was the first to go on trial in Chandler.[67] When several defense witnesses arrived in town, the prosecuting attorneys, including Lincoln County attorney Streeter Speakman and an assistant from the attorney general's office in Oklahoma City, warned that they would convict the first witness who perjured himself. With his usual vigor, Samuel Morton Rutherford arrived in Chandler to defend Sawyer. As expected, Estes, who seemed nervous and unable to maintain eye contact with Sawyer, was the key witness for the state. On the stand Estes recalled having come to Oklahoma from Missouri, as well as details of the robberies, including how the gang had met at Maxfield's house near Tulsa and their ride to Stroud. He described how he and Starr had been shot and captured.[68]

Bank officials from the First National Bank took the stand to identify Sawyer as one of the men who robbed their bank. Mrs. Edward Burgess, who lived five miles north of Henryetta at the village of Schulter, identified Sawyer as one of the two men who came to her home on the morning after the robbery to ask for food, saying they knew her brother-in-law. The men's horses were jaded and the men were fatigued, she went on to say. They slept there during the day and left that evening, leaving her a ten-dollar gold piece.[69]

On the stand, Sheriff Arnold related how he and Tilghman captured Sawyer at McAlester. Sawyer had $310 in his possession at the time, most of the money being bank notes from the First National Bank in Stroud. Several witnesses swore that they saw the robbers enter Stroud, but no one could positively identify Sawyer.

No sooner had Rutherford begun his defense than the proceedings were halted to await a physician's report on fifty-nine-year-old Robert Sawyer, Claude's father and a key defense witness. He was confined to his bed at a local hotel as the result of a nervous breakdown. When the trial reconvened, Rutherford presented witness after witness who testified that Sawyer was not in Stroud at the time of the robberies.

An old cowboy who worked on the Sawyer ranch testified that, on the day of the robberies, he was branding cattle with Joe Davis and Claude Sawyer. An "old driller" testified that he remembered Sawyer's stepmother reading an account of the robberies in the newspaper and remarking to Davis, "This is one affair they cannot charge you with."[70]

### Twenty-Five Years in McAlester Prison

Days later Henry Starr, still on crutches, was hauled into court, where he pleaded guilty and was sentenced to twenty-five years. "I am a bank robber and have been caught, that's all there is to it," he was heard to say. "I couldn't beat back like Al Jennings."[71]

Bud Graham, a liveryman from McAlester, testified that Sawyer had stabled his horse at his place the day before the robbery. He produced a ledger to prove it. In his own defense Sawyer swore that he was branding cattle at the family ranch on the day of the robbery. The dollars he had at the time of his arrest were the proceeds from a horse he sold, Sawyer said. Many of those in attendance thought the young cowboy made a favorable impression on the jury, but it did not take them long to find him guilty. He was sentenced to five years at McAlester state penitentiary.[72]

Charlie Johnson was the next to go on trial. As was the case with Sawyer, Estes was the prosecution's main witness. Employees of the Stroud National Bank lined up to identify Johnson as one of the men who robbed their bank. But Henry Wells testified that on the morning of the robbery he saw Johnson in the vicinity of Bartlesville, one hundred miles north of Stroud. No sooner had Wells stepped down from the stand than he was arrested for the robbery of the Kaw City Bank.[73] Mr. and Mrs. Frank Wells, who lived ten miles south of Bartlesville, both testified that they, too, had seen Johnson on the day of the robbery. A farmer named Frank Simmons said he had seen Johnson at the Johnson family farm on the day of the Stroud robberies. Johnson also testified in his own defense, insisting that he was at the Johnson farm and was nowhere near Stroud. Witnesses probably mistook him for Liege Higgins, he thought. Surprisingly, Johnson was pronounced not guilty.[74] But he was no sooner out of the courthouse than he was arrested for having received money stolen from the First National Bank.

Bud Maxfield was the fourth of the robbers to go on trial in Chandler. His covered wagon was even placed into evidence. Maxfield argued that he had sold the wagon to Henry Starr a week before the robbery. His defense was similar to that of Sawyer and Johnson—that on the day of the robbery he was nowhere near Stroud. In fact, his story was that on the day the banks were robbed, he had gone into Tulsa, where he became drunk. But O. E. Grecian, forty-two-year-old president of the First National Bank, who had been held hostage and taken at gunpoint to the Stroud cattle pens, positively identified Maxfield as the unmasked man holding the horses. The bookkeeper at the Stroud National Bank, J. E. Charles, said there was no doubt that Maxfield was the man at the stockyards. It did not help the defense that Maxfield admitted to serving eight years in the Arkansas state penitentiary.[75] The jury retired at seven in the evening of August 12 and returned near midnight with a guilty verdict, and Maxfield was off to seven years in McAlester prison.

Joe Davis and Liege Higgins could still not be found. Bill Tilghman and others in law enforcement were convinced that Davis had fled into the Arkansas Ozarks, though most lawmen admitted his whereabouts were "unknown."[76] It is more likely that when the outlaws split up near Bristow, some turning east and others riding south, Davis headed into the timbered country along the Canadian River that he was familiar with, probably in company with Sawyer. He may have somehow made his way into the more secluded area of McCurtain County, where he found safe haven at or near the Davis Ranch.

Some thought Davis was one of the men involved in the robbery of the Farmers National Bank at Kaw City, a small farming community in an oxbow bend of the Arkansas River, ninety-four miles north of Stroud, on the afternoon of April 6, 1915. Three masked men, one of them tall (possibly Davis), and two others both short and heavyset, locked the cashier and his assistant in the vault. They made off with $2,025 before racing across the river into Osage County toward the Osage Hills and then turning east toward Pawhuska. At first, they rode along the public roads, waving their firearms in the air and forcing drivers off the road.[77] Three horses thought to have been ridden by the outlaws were later found in Osage County. A spokesman for the Oklahoma Bankers Association, W. B. Harrison, had no doubt that the men who robbed the bank in Kaw City were the same men who were at Stroud. They were last seen near Dewey, twelve miles northeast of Bartlesville, he said. A posse was hastily organized at Dewey, but they could find no trace of the outlaws.[78]

Always prepared to defend the Davises, Rutherford in May told the press that Davis had never left McCurtain County, and that he was "down in the Choctaw country near the Jack Davis Ranch" all along, herding cattle at the time of the Stroud robberies.[79] Lawmen, nevertheless, were certain that Joe Davis was involved in a spate of bank robberies in the days following the Stroud fiasco. On the afternoon of August 13, 1915, three outlaws rode into Bernice, a small town in Delaware County, in the extreme northeastern part of the state. They forced the cashier and bookkeeper to open the safe and made off with fifteen hundred dollars.[80] It was rumored that the outlaws had scouted both Bartlesville and Tahlequah in the week preceding the Bernice theft, but those banks were too heavily guarded.

### Bank Robberies without End

Almost two weeks after the Bernice heist, two unmasked men, said to be "cowboys from Oklahoma," held up the Bank of Amity, Arkansas. Amity was a small village near Hot Springs. They locked the cashier in the vault, but the cashier was able to set off an alarm, and townsmen rushed into the street to exchange gunfire with the bandits as they fled toward the Oklahoma border with twelve hundred dollars.[81] A day later, the Bank of Prue in Prue, Oklahoma, twenty-seven miles west of Tulsa on the Arkansas River, was robbed by two masked men of five hundred dollars. One of the outlaws was described as about twenty-eight years old, clean shaven, with light hair and a "large felt hat of light color."[82]

Some blamed Davis for the robbery of the Farmers' State Bank at Jefferson, forty-four miles west of Ponca City, on September 8, 1915, but this seems unlikely. After the "yeggmen" blew the safe open with nitroglycerin, the front wall of the bank collapsed. The outlaws fled across the state line through Kay County into Kansas in an automobile.[83] The robbery of the Bank of Grant in the small town of Grant, six miles south of Hugo, not far from the Red River and the Texas border, by two unmasked men on the afternoon of September 7, 1915, may well have been Davis's doing, however. After forcing the cashier into the vault, the robbers made off with $250. The cashier was able to get out of the safe and chase after the outlaws on foot, firing at them with a shotgun. Although Sheriff W. H. Loftin of Cherokee County formed a posse and pursued the bandits, the heavy timber and cane breaks along the Red River made it difficult to track them down. All that was found was a coat discarded by one of them that had been purchased in Hugo. Citizens in the small town remembered the outlaws as having lounged around town before the robbery, visiting almost every store, consuming sodas, and leisurely enjoying lunch.[84]

On October 5, 1915, in Maud, in Pottawatomie County, fifty-eight miles southeast of Oklahoma City the Maud State Bank was robbed of four thousand dollars, and a bank at Quapaw in Ottawa County in the extreme northeastern part of the state, just across the Kansas border from Baxter Springs, was robbed of two thousand dollars. It was evident that more than one band of outlaws was operating in the state. Neither bore the imprint of Joe Davis. At Maud the bank vault was blown four times before it was finally opened, and the outlaws raced out of town. A posse found the tracks of four horses leading eastward past Bowlegs toward Weworka, the county seat of Seminole County. In the Quapaw robbery, the masked bandits thanked the cashier courteously, as Davis was known to do, before they cranked up a large Chalmers automobile and "whirled up the street" to the southwest, in the direction of the Osage Hills.[85] Davis, however, was never known to flee a bank robbery in an automobile. The First National Bank of Centralia, forty miles southwest of Quapaw in Craig County, was hit two weeks later. Three bandits forced four bank officials and two customers to lie on the floor of the bank as they rifled the vault of six thousand dollars. They sped off in an automobile.[86]

There is little doubt that Davis led the robbery of the southbound Katy Limited No. 9 at Onapa, eight miles south of Checotah, not long after midnight on October 27, 1915. In fact, the holdup came close to being the third anniversary of the robbery of the same Katy Limited at Wirth back on October 26, 1912. Some thought that the Onapa robbery was intended by Joe and Jack Davis to send a message to Crockett Lee and Katy officials that, despite having been convicted in the Muskogee federal court, they could still strike at the Katy with impunity. The manner in which the holdup was conducted, the place selected for the heist (twelve miles north of the Wirth holdup), and the descriptions of the men who called themselves the "Black Sox," all left no doubt it was the work of Joe Davis and his gang. In many ways, the robbery seemed to be more for revenge than for money. The night before the holdup, the police department in Muskogee received a mysterious phone call from a man refusing to identify himself but asking if the police had received a report that Joe Davis had been killed in Dallas, Texas. Joe Davis or a member of his gang, the police speculated, was "merely beginning his jollity before he left for the scene of the holdup."[87]

## Robbery of the Katy Limited at Onapa

Two of the Davis Gang boarded the Katy Limited at Muskogee and hid on top of a boxcar.[88] When the train reached Sandy Crossing near Onapa, a few miles south of Checotah at a quarter after one in the morning, the two men, wearing white bandanas, climbed over the tinder into the locomotive. They forced the engineer and fireman at gunpoint to stop the train. The engineer was ordered to run the engine and express cars down the track to where five other gunmen with black stockings over their heads appeared out of the darkness carrying Winchesters and revolvers. Four of the outlaws forced E. M. Sears to open the express cars and then carry the nitroglycerin, while three others stood guard over the train crew. During the holdup, one of the brakemen ran off into the woods. He was shot at, and his small finger nipped.

To keep passengers from leaving the passenger cars, one of the bandits randomly fired a pistol into the air. The crew were forced to hold their hands above their heads, but after several minutes, one of the outlaws remarked, "you look tired," and ordered the men to sit on the ground.

Over the next hour, the outlaws laughed and joked. While the nitroglycerine was being prepared, one bandit leaned against a telegraph pole and entertained his fellow outlaws and trainmen with funny stories and popular songs, inviting everyone to join in on the chorus.[89] The frivolity of it all seemed vintage Joe Davis.

The engineer on the Katy, Ed Thomas, told the press that he was going to quit running the train on the route on October 27 or 28. "I always get into trouble on those dates," he said. "You know it was three years ago, lacking one day, that the gang held me up at the Canadian River, not far from where they got me this time, and they turned the trick about the same time."[90]

The robbers tried to blow three safes with the "soup," an adulterated mixture of dynamite and nitroglycerin. They finally succeeded in opening one safe, that of the American Express Company. They were unable to blow a second safe in a second car and two other safes in a third car. After five blasts scattered glass from the windows of the express cars for yards along the right-of-way, the outlaws ran off into the woods with nine thousand dollars in two sacks. Just before they disappeared into the darkness, they thanked the train crew and wished them a hearty "good night."[91] What happened at Onapa on October 27, 1915, was said to be the "boldest train robbery of recent years," a "well-rehearsed drama," and the most "desperate and best plan ever attempted." It was pulled off with the "smoothness of a motion picture plot," announced the *Muskogee Times-Democrat.*[92]

During the robbery, a freight train came roaring down the track through the night from the north. It would have collided with the Katy Limited had not two of the outlaws successfully flagged the train to a stop. One of the trainmen on the freight train jumped down and came forward to ascertain what the trouble was, only to be captured by the outlaws. Suspecting there was trouble, the engineer backed the freight train into Onapa, where news of the robbery was sent by telephone and telegraph to every constable, town marshal, and deputy sheriff within a one-hundred-mile radius.[93]

Sheriff John S. Barger, in a special train with a posse from Muskogee, arrived on the scene in the half light of dawn. A second posse, led by McIntosh County sheriff John W. McCune, boarded the northbound Katy at Eufaula. Hours later, a second train arrived from McAlester with yet another posse, along with bloodhounds and horses from the state penitentiary. Deputy Sheriff Jim Brown brought a posse north from Pittsburg County on a freight train that stopped at the Canadian River, where the lawmen headed east into heavily forested river bottomlands. A posse was also organized at Stigler in Haskell County. General manager of the American Express Company at Kansas City, H. H. Meek, later arrived on the scene, as did Crockett Lee and other Katy railroad detectives. The Katy and the American Express Company immediately announced they would pay a reward of three hundred dollars for every bandit captured and convicted.[94]

### Bloodhounds and Black Stockings

At the scene of the robbery two black stockings were found by Sheriff Barger and his men. The bloodhounds from McAlester sniffed these and a glove left by one of the outlaws and quickly picked up a trail that led off into the woods north of the tracks. The hounds followed the scent through the woods for half a mile then came to a barking halt where the outlaws had mounted their horses. The posse continued east to where a set of buggy tracks was found. Here it was obvious the gang had gone in different directions.

One of the outlaw trails led across the Canadian River into the vastness of the Cheney Mountains, a group of thickly wooded hills extending to the south. The outlaws in the buggy, probably carrying the bulkier portion of the loot, drove north to the first section line and then turned east. They headed into the mountains several miles east of where the men on horseback had ridden.[95] Sheriff McCune took his posse directly east from Onapa and posted men at every crossing and ferry on the Canadian River. With the remainder of his men he beat the bushes along the river, telling the press that it was impossible for the gang to cross the river without being detected, especially the men in the hack. For hours the posses scoured the winding trails and rough country east and southeast of Onapa, often not knowing which direction to turn. One posse returned with five partially empty whiskey bottles that the trainmen said the outlaws had rifled from an express car. Although most of the posses gave up within twenty-four hours, Sheriff McCune's posse continued on. After a couple of days, however, he also gave up. McCune was forced to admit that the gang had reached the vastness of the Winding Stair Mountains, where the "old Davis gang of outlaws which terrorized eastern Oklahoma several years ago" were known to hang out.[96]

Sheriff Dave Tatum of Pittsburg County was continuing to search the countryside for any evidence relating to the Onapa robbery. An arrest warrant was issued for Bob Worthman, but the veteran outlaw could not be found. Officials said there was little doubt the "Davis Boys" were responsible for the Katy robbery, but they could not be found, and there was no evidence to arrest them. Under the headline "Bandits of Kiamichis Are Bad Ones," the *Oklahoma Leader* related how the Davis Gang could be anywhere from "the densely wooded bottom around Warner and Porum to the wild Kiamichi Mountains in southeastern Oklahoma." The Davises were "kinfolks to half the people who live in these hills." To some in the press, it was evident that the new version of the Davis Gang would "surpass the deeds of which the others are remembered."[97] On November 5, the local press reported that Joe Davis and Buck Bertholf had quietly returned to the Davis Ranch near Featherston, where they were gathering cattle for shipment.[98]

### Fort Gibson

On November 14, 1915, four men rode into Fort Gibson and at twenty past two in the afternoon robbed the Farmers' National Bank of $5,574. One man guarded the entrance to the bank and the horses. The other three—two white and one black, wearing heavy black mufflers on the lower part of their faces—went inside and leveled their weapons at bank officials. A merchant, a farmer, and a railroad man were caught inside the bank at the time. They were forced at gunpoint to line up. When told that the vault was on a time lock and could not be opened, the leader of the gang shouted out, "I don't give a damn about the time lock; open that vault." After one of the bandits put the muzzle of his rifle against the temple of one of the cashiers, the vault was opened. The assistant cashier was forced to scoop the money into a sack. One of the sacks that was thrown out of the vault was said to be gold coins worth two thousand dollars. "Put that damn stuff back, I ain't got time to fool with silver," the robber commanded.[99]

While the robbery was in progress, a young clerk from a nearby drugstore approached the bank and was shocked to learn that a robbery was in progress. He attempted to run away but was grabbed by the collar by the outlaw at the entrance to the bank, and a pistol was thrust in his face. He was forced inside. Along with the cashiers and customers, the clerk was shoved into the walk-in vault before the outlaws galloped out of town. Riding hard in a southeasterly direction toward the Cookson Hills, the outlaws encountered a black man driving a wagon. They yelled at him to get out of the way or they would kill him. One of the bandits was seen to be carrying a heavy sack. Only minutes later, a customer came into the bank and heard pounding on the vault door, and the prisoners were liberated. The news was telephoned to Muskogee. Sheriff John Barger, with two deputies, hurried the eight miles to Fort Gibson in an automobile.[100]

In another automobile, Deputy Sheriff Henry Reese was thought to be only fifteen minutes behind the bandits, but the driver, Deputy R. M. Mountcastel, took a wrong fork in the road and the lawmen were soon lost. Sheriff Barger in a second automobile, with heavily armed posses on horseback, headed into the Greenleaf and Sugar Mountains, trying to pick up the outlaws' trail. The men riding in the automobile were forced to abandon the vehicles but were able to borrow horses from local farmers. They continued into the night into the Sugar Mountains.[101] By the morning of the second day, it was evident the outlaws had escaped.

The robbery was the largest and boldest that ever occurred in Fort Gibson. In the days that followed, it was determined that at least four of the men had been seen in Fort Gibson the week preceding the robbery, undoubtedly scouting. It was thought that the "negro" was probably a Cherokee with a walnut-stained face. Others thought he was really a white man who had stained his face black. One of the men suspected of being in the gang was Napoleon P. Vann, a handsome young Cherokee who was wanted for the murder of a marshal in Caney, Kansas, two years earlier.

Two weeks after the Fort Gibson holdup, a black man named Sam Hendricks walked into a bank in Claremore in Roger County and asked to deposit $202 in silver he had in a flour sack. In an era of rampant racism, a black man with a large amount of cash caused officials to immediately think that Hendricks was one of the robbers. Arrested and grilled for hours, Hendricks refused to talk, and he was finally released.[102]

Ever since the robbery of the Katy at Wirth three years earlier, Crockett Lee and post office inspectors out of Kansas City, fearing other such robberies, tried in vain to keep a watch on Joe Davis. Ever since the Porum gun battle Davis had been involved in crime after crime, they insisted. They were sure that he was involved in the Stroud robberies and several of the following bank heists as well as the more recent Onapa holdup. But there was little evidence, and they seemed unable to find and arrest Davis, although he was frequently "at his father's home in Hugo."[103] Several of the inspectors were forced to conclude that many of the local law enforcement officials were simply afraid of the vengeance of the Davis family.

Post office inspectors were also sure that Joe Davis had led the gang that robbed the bank at Fort Gibson. Henry Starr's mother, who lived near Fort Gibson, told the inspectors she had seen the robbers come into town, and that Joe Davis was riding one of her son's horses. Other evidence compiled by the inspectors left little doubt that Davis was the gang leader. He was a "terror to the eastern part of Oklahoma since he has grown to manhood," the inspectors concluded, and "it does not appear that a man could be a worse criminal." Davis was the "acknowledged leader of a band of bandits" who, for years, had given "the officers of Oklahoma in and around Muskogee much trouble." At the same time, the inspectors were forced to admit that Davis was "accused of many crimes that he did not commit . . . but on the other hand there is every reason to believe that he committed many, many crimes for which he was not accused."[104]

With a price on his head and ever more railroad detectives, postal inspectors, and county sheriffs on his trail, Joe Davis decided once again to leave Oklahoma. Sometime in March 1916, with several thousand dollars in a large duffle bag, he headed west to Arizona by rail, into the heart of the desert Southwest, the land of endless sunshine, where he became Joe L. Mayes, an Oklahoma cowboy looking for work. He would ask Lula Cobb to join him and he would make a new life for himself—or at least wait until his notoriety in Oklahoma began to ebb.

## → 6 ←

# BOY BANDIT IN THE
# LAND OF ENDLESS SUNSHINE

I am a poor hobo, if you kill me, you are killing a good man.

—Ray "Steamboat" Preston

Family legend has it that Jack Davis sent his son Joe to Arizona to "keep him out of trouble." In reality, his twenty-four-year-old son knew full well that railroad agents, federal law enforcement officials, and Oklahoma lawmen were closing in on him. In March 1916, using the alias Joe L. Mayes, Joe Davis boarded a westbound train. Davis got off the train at Benson, Arizona, where he found work two miles south of the small community of Fairbank on the Little Boquillas Ranch, in western Cochise County on the San Pedro River, nine miles west of Tombstone. Here he joined his childhood friend and fellow outlaw, William Triplet "Buck" Bertholf, and John Carroll, an Oklahoma cowboy whom Davis affectionately called "Little Britches" because of his diminutive stature. Joe deposited four thousand dollars in the Bank of Benson and later transferred the money to the Bank of Arizona in Prescott.

After four months at the Little Boquillas Ranch, the trio drifted over to Seligman, a dusty out-of-the-way railroad and cow town seventy-six miles west of Flagstaff. Here Bertholf got a job working at a restaurant, while Davis and Carroll signed on as cowboys at a nearby ranch. Life was peaceful as the three Oklahomans made their way to Prescott for the annual Frontier Days celebration in early July.

Hundreds of cowboys arrived from all over the country for the steer roping and bareback bronc riding contests. Thirty-four cowboys participated in the steer roping contest, with a first prize of four hundred dollars, but neither the name Joe Davis nor Joe Mayes was among those listed in the local newspaper.[1] Davis was tempted to participate but feared exposing himself to such publicity was risking arrest.

Eventually, the three young cowboys wandered back to Benson and then on to Clay McGonigle's ranch in the treeless, windswept eastern foothills of the Peloncillo Mountains, five miles north of Pratt, New Mexico, northeast of the small desert community of Rodeo, just a stone's throw from the Arizona border. Davis greatly admired McGonigle, whom he first saw at a rodeo in Muskogee. He closely identified with the world champion rodeo performer who was "one hell of a cowboy." Thomas Jefferson "Jeff" Spurlock, another Oklahoma cowboy and member of the Davis Gang, joined the group and they moved on to John Henderson's ranch a half mile south of the McGonigles' spread in New Mexico's Bootheel, in one of the more remote areas of the state.[2]

### Joe L. Mayes

Davis and his pals spent considerable time in the border town of Douglas, where Spurlock worked for a time at a bootleg whiskey operation. Unlike Spurlock, Davis seemed to have plenty of money from his Oklahoma bank and train heists, and he frequently stayed at the fashionable Gadsden Hotel. Douglas was a boomtown at the time, with two large Phelps Dodge copper smelters and railroads that stretched west across the desert to Bisbee and the Pacific, south into the interior of Mexico, and east along the border to El Paso and beyond. With the turquoise-colored ore spurring the economy, gambling of all sorts was prevalent, as was business in a large red-light district where saloons abounded. By 1916, as in almost all border communities, there was a large military presence because of the simmering revolution in Mexico, which frequently spilled over the border into the United States.[3] In Douglas, Davis purchased a new Willys Overland Model 83 touring car from the D. B. Hutchins dealership. He paid for the fashionable automobile with a $725 check drawn on the Bank of Arizona in Prescott. The Hutchins dealership even provided driving lessons.[4]

While they hunkered down in southwestern New Mexico during the summer of 1916, Davis began discussing with Carroll, Bertholf, and Spurlock the possibility of holding up the Golden State Limited, a crack unit of the Chicago, Rock Island, and Pacific Railroad that made a regular run on the nearby El Paso &

Southwestern Railroad. It was almost as if robbing trains was in Davis's blood. It was always dangerous, and he seemed to enjoy such adventures. Davis speculated that the train would be carrying thousands of dollars in payroll funds for either the American troops patrolling the Arizona–Sonora border (especially the garrison at Camp Harry J. Jones just east of Douglas), the smelter workers at Douglas, or the copper miners at Bisbee.

## Apache Station

While motoring from Douglas to Pratt in Davis's touring car, the gang selected a likely ambush site where the railroad crossed a small arroyo and passed near a low and barren volcanic hill about five miles southwest of Apache Station, on the southeastern rim of the vast, arid San Simon Valley. A few days later, Davis sent John Carroll to Oklahoma with instructions to acquire enough nitroglycerine ("soup," as they called it) to blow the safe in the baggage car of the Golden State Limited. Meanwhile, Buck Bertholf, using the alias Bill Smith, bought ten feet of fuse and eight dynamite caps at a hardware store in Douglas. While he was in the border town Bertholf also purchased hats, caps, overalls, handkerchiefs, and automobile goggles for use in the robbery. The stage was set when Carroll returned from Oklahoma with a suitcase containing the nitroglycerine wrapped in sheepskin. Davis poured half "the soup" into a pint bottle and buried the remainder near a large volcanic rock on the Henderson Ranch.[5]

During his sojourn in the far Southwest, Davis's twenty-three-year-old lover, Lula Cobb, frequently came west to be with him. Lula was living with relatives on a cattle ranch near Claude, a small railroad town in the Texas Panhandle. Joe always sent her money, and she was always anxious to come west. Joe Davis and Lula Cobb had been romantically involved for years. They had allegedly married in the Creek Nation in 1913, although no marriage certificate was ever produced or has ever been found. Sometime in late June or early July 1916 Lula become pregnant with twins, probably while she was in Arizona.[6] Her pregnancy did not appear to tame her wild and adventuresome spirit, which had always attracted Davis. On July 23, 1916, from the Gadsden Hotel in Douglas Joe wrote to Lula, who was back in Texas at the time, hinting at his plans in the Arizona desert. The letter is one of few that survive in his handwriting.

> My Dear One: . . . Britches [Carroll] just got back this morning. Was gone three weeks instead of eight days. I have bought a car and will leave for you about the 3rd of September so be ready to go when I come. I will be there if

I am alive and I feel good and sure that I get by with the deal, if not, I will be found there and I write a letter to you and leave it where I start from and if I am killed it will be mailed to you and tell you where all my stuff is. If I make it the letter won't be mailed. I guess you are having a good time. Put a letter in the post office at Claude and say where you are so I don't have to be inquiring about where you are and I come right straight and get you; don't let anyone know when I am coming. . . . Just came over in Old Mexico yesterday, things is pretty rough over there. Buck is backing up on everything and had to get another man, he don't know where you are. If he comes and you see him tell him you don't know where I am at. So be a good girl and we [will] be together soon and stay that way. You don't know how bad I want to see you, more so than ever. I got a nice car for us to ride in. It [is] an Overland, so be good and have a good time for us both.[7]

Davis took time in late August to drive with Jeff Spurlock across the desert to Deming, New Mexico, where the two took rooms at the Commercial Hotel, and Joe tried to call Lula on the telephone. A bad connection made it impossible to carry on a meaningful conversation, and the next day, August 30, 1916, Joe sent Lula a registered letter. "Could not hear you over the phone," he explained, "roads bad, cannot drive car in mud. Will start about 7th of September and write tomorrow and send money. Stay there until you hear from me again. Little pants forged a check on me for 700 and left."[8]

### Things May Be Pretty Hot

The following day Joe wrote a longer letter, asking Lula to join him in Arizona:

The rains is so bad and much mud almost impossible to get any further. So I am going back this morning and you come to Douglas . . . and stop at the Gadsden Hotel and stay there until I come or send for you. Come by the 9th of September. Come by way of El Paso and write me a letter and put in separate envelope and address to John Henderson, Animas, New Mexico and tell me when you are starting. . . . Go by the name of Mayes at Douglas. It may be the 10th or 11th before I get to see you as things may be pretty hot about the 6th or 7th. I come or send a letter and you can come by the one I send the letter by. It will be an old man about fifty and getting gray, he come in a car for you if I don't. I won't be far from there and we make a trip through the country in the car. Another boy and myself stayed four hours yesterday in one mud hole. We thought we could make the trip there and be back by the 6th but couldn't on account of roads so bad so we came back this morning. Will send you some money as women needs money sometimes. I could hear money over the phone but did not know that it was so I send some in case of accident, so be sure and come and write when you start. Leave there about Tuesday and you will get to Douglas Wednesday night. I come or send for you ten or eleven. Maybe sooner. Don't let any of your people know where you are coming to.

Lovingly, yours only,

Joe[9]

Davis's desire to have Lula join him in Arizona would prove his undoing. On September 6, 1916, Lula boarded the Fort Worth & Denver City Railroad at Claude and made her way to Douglas on the El Paso & Southwestern, arriving that same evening. Incredible as it may seem, she was on board the exact same train that a gang of outlaws led by her lover held up near a remote desert outpost called Apache Station. Following the unanticipated delay, she arrived in Douglas late that evening and, as directed, checked into the Gadsden Hotel under the name Lula Mayes.[10]

As Lula was boarding the train in Texas, the Oklahoma outlaws left the McGonigle Ranch on horseback early on the morning of September 5. Armed with a .30-caliber Winchester rifle and a pistol, Joe was riding a big sorrel and carrying the sheepskin-wrapped nitroglycerine in a gunnysack tied to his saddle. Following the tracks of the El Paso & Southwestern, the horsemen passed the small, dusty frontier outpost of Rodeo on the Arizona–New Mexico border, camping for the night on the open desert. The next day, September 6, 1916, Bertholf and Carroll left their horses with Joe and Spurlock and began walking back to Rodeo. Local rancher Mary K. Morgan encountered the pair resting their feet in a waterhole about three miles northeast of Apache Station. She asked the men if they had seen a little boy she heard had run away from Douglas. Bertholf and Carroll remained at the waterhole for about fifteen or twenty minutes before continuing northeast toward Rodeo, where they boarded the Golden State Limited at 7:23 in the evening.[11]

### Robbing the Golden State Limited

At dusk that evening, Davis and Spurlock—leading Bertholf's and Carroll's horses—rode to the small hill alongside the railroad southwest of Apache Station. After tying the horses at a cross fence near the track, the two men gathered mesquite to build a large signal fire for their fellow conspirators on the Golden State Limited. Spotting the fire glowing in the desert through the darkness, Bertholf and Carroll climbed over the tinder, pulled out their pistols, and forced the locomotive engineer, fourteen-year railroad veteran Allen Lovett, and the fireman, W. E. Jones, to stop the train. Both men were masked. Carroll had a blue handkerchief covering his face and Bertholf peered out from behind a black handkerchief. Lovett later testified that he turned around at the sound of someone yelling and saw a man in a striped cap holding a revolver pointed at him.

"What do you want?" he asked.

"We want you to stop the train," was the reply. Bertholf assured the frightened engineer that no one would be hurt so long as he cooperated.[12]

As the train screeched to a stop Carroll and Bertholf stepped down one on each side of the locomotive. Carroll quickly emptied four rounds from his revolver in the direction of a pair of inquisitive hoboes who poked their heads out of one of the boxcars.

"Wait a minute, brother, we're nothing but a couple of hoboes," nineteen-year-old Ray "Steamboat" Preston shouted out. "We want to get out of here."

By this time, Davis and Spurlock had arrived on the scene. Joe held aloft the nitroglycerine, threatening to blow up everything and everybody if anyone made a wrong move. Preston, who was on his way home to Oregon after spending the summer with his grandfather in Oklahoma, remembered being so scared he "shook like a leaf." William Hynes, a soldier absent without leave from the border outpost at Hachita, New Mexico, recalled hearing Preston plead with the outlaws, "I am only a poor hobo, if you kill me, you are killing a good man."[13]

From this point, the holdup quickly dissolved into a series of miscalculations and disappointments for the train robbers. First, Bertholf forced fireman Jones and engineer Lovett to uncouple the engine, mail car, and two express cars from the passenger coaches and pull them half a mile down the track toward Douglas. Davis and Bertholf then ordered brakeman John Graham to open the express car.

"You boys have got a pretty hard sheriff to contend with in this county," Jones warned the robbers.

"[We] don't care for that," came the reply. "We will be in Mexico before daylight." The AWOL soldier Hynes, on the other hand, reacted in a completely unexpected manner.

"How's chances of going along?" he asked the holdup men.

"Fine," Davis replied. "If we get anything we'll give you some."[14]

In the meantime, fireman Jones was having difficulty opening the locked

MAP 5. Southeastern Arizona at the time of the
robbery of the Golden State Limited, September 7, 1916
*Map by Carol Zuber-Mallison*

baggage car. Davis grabbed a pick from the engine and ordered one of the hoboes to smash in the door. He then instructed a second hobo to climb through the hole and open the door from the inside. Davis and Bertholf stepped into the car, where Davis soaped the crack around the door of the safe, poured on nitroglycerine, then attached a cap and fuse. Everyone scurried to safety behind the right-of-way fence that paralleled the tracks, and Davis lit the fuse. Six times Joe tried to blow up the safe, while Spurlock and Carroll stood guard over the hoboes and train crew. Each time, Steamboat Preston hoisted the pint bottle of nitroglycerine over his head (to prevent it from spilling on the ground) and carried it to Davis in the baggage car.

"I wish those fellows blowing the safe would hurry," R. M. Collier, one of the postal clerks, impatiently remarked, "so I can get to Los Angeles tomorrow afternoon by 2:30."

"He's taking his time," one of the robbers responded, "so as not to damage the car so badly that it cannot proceed on the trip after we are through."[15]

After an hour Davis finally managed to blow the large outer door on the safe, but he was still unable to remove the smaller inner door. "It is all over," he conceded, "let's go."[16] His inability to make off with thousands of dollars, as he had done before in Oklahoma, was a great disappointment.

Before abandoning the robbery completely, Davis decided to search the mail car. Alerted to the stickup, postal clerks R. M. Collier and R. A. Baker had hidden the registered mail and turned off the lights. Now the outlaws ordered the clerks out of the car and searched them for weapons.

"Show me the registered mail. We are going to get the registered mail," Davis insisted.

"We have no lights on in here. When you cut off the train you disconnected the lights," Collier insisted, adding that the "train was a Sunday run out of New York and a holiday train out of Chicago and all the mail had been taken off at El Paso."

"I will take a look anyway," Davis insisted, as he entered the darkened car with a lantern. Joe found only two registered letters, which he hastily stuffed in his pocket. After ordering everyone into the engine cab, the Oklahoma outlaws climbed the barbed-wire fence along the right-of-way, scurried for their horses, and raced off into the Arizona monsoon night.[17]

### Searchers

The Golden State Limited arrived in Douglas more than an hour and a half late. As soon as he could gather a small posse, Cochise County sheriff Harry C. Wheeler and Constable Sam J. Hayhurst set off by automobile for the scene of the crime.

(Sheriff Wheeler would later become infamous for the mass deportation of striking miners from Bisbee.) This was the first train robbery in the county in many years, and there was considerable agitation in Douglas. Unfortunately, the same rains that Davis encountered on his way to Deming had inundated much of the desert lowlands northeast of Douglas with as much as six inches of water, sending torrents into the normally dry canyons and arroyos that drained the eastern slopes of the Chiricahua Mountains. Unable to proceed further Wheeler and Hayhurst returned to town, where they boarded a special El Paso & Southwestern engine that rolled out of Douglas at roughly half past four in the morning darkness of September 7, just as Lula Cobb was checking into the Gadsden Hotel. Mounted on horses they borrowed from a local rancher, the two lawmen scoured the robbery site for clues. Because of the heavy rainfall they could only locate a few horse tracks. Eventually, the pair separated, with Wheeler making a fifteen-mile circuit of Apache Station, even combing the lower ridges of the Chiricahuas. Wheeler searched the area for another two weeks before finally concluding that the bandits had fled deep into the mountains.[18]

Wheeler later rode out from Tombstone in a buggy to the Guthrie Ranch northeast of Tombstone and arrested Flin "Rusty" Taulk, a red-headed "little box-legged cowboy," and charged him with the crime. Although several cowboys testified that they were with Taulk at the Guthrie Ranch on the day of the robbery, "Steamboat" Preston identified him as one of the robbers. Taulk was indicted and placed under ten-thousand-dollar bond. Taulk was an orphan who came west and allegedly rode with Pancho Villa before returning to Douglas, where he hung out in the bars and pool halls and occasionally found work as a cowboy. Several times Sheriff Wheeler put individuals in the cell with Taulk, hoping to finagle information from him, but the cowboy maintained his innocence and was eventually released. Taulk enlisted in the 158th US Infantry during World War I and died in France.[19]

Local ranchers contributed to the investigation. Mary Webber, who lived five miles west of Apache Station, was passing near the scene of the holdup on the morning of September 7 when she spotted the sheepskin that Davis had used to carry the nitroglycerine. O. E. Patterson, a Cochise County deputy sheriff who lived less than a mile from the robbery site, arrived at the scene on the morning of September 7 and, with Constable Hayhurst, followed the outlaws' trail to a saddle between two barren hills, where their track disappeared. Nevertheless, Patterson recovered the burlap sack that had contained the sheepskin-wrapped explosive.[20]

The Oklahoma outlaws, meanwhile, had spurred their horses northwestward through the darkness and the summer monsoon. Two miles beyond the holdup site, Davis and Spurlock broke off northeast toward the New Mexico border and the Henderson Ranch, while Bertholf and Carroll headed south for a few miles, before turning west into the rugged Chiricahuas. The bandits agreed before parting that they would reunite one day back in Oklahoma.[21]

### Desert Escape

For more than a week Bertholf and Carroll rode west for over ninety miles across the rugged, tree-shrouded Chiricahuas, the Sulphur Springs Valley, and the Dragoon Mountains before arriving at Pink and Emmett Henderson's Interocean ranch near Benson. Pink and Emmett were the sons of their former employer John Henderson. After several days' rest, the bandit pair continued on to Tucson, where they registered at the Orndorf Hotel, Bertholf using the name "Ed Jones" and Carroll signing in as "Bill Brownell." The next day Bertholf boarded the train for El Paso, Fort Worth, and McAlester, Oklahoma. Carroll departed for parts unknown. The two men would never see each other again.[22]

Davis and Spurlock, meanwhile, rode in the darkness and heavy rain through Antelope Pass in the Peloncillo Mountains and on to John Henderson's ranch near Pratt. Davis immediately sent the elderly Henderson to pick up Lula Cobb at the Gadsden Hotel. Hiring a driver and car in Douglas, Henderson returned to the ranch with Lula on Sunday, September 10. Shortly after dinner that evening Joe, Lula, and Spurlock took off for Oklahoma in Davis's Overland automobile. Before departing, Davis asked Hattie Henderson if he could leave behind his saddle, saying she could keep it in the event he failed to return. He and Lula also left behind a trunk containing clothing, a lot of Joe's cowboy gear, and the incriminating letters that Joe had written to Lula from Deming and Douglas. Spurlock asked that Henderson return a saddle he had borrowed from Clay McGonigle.[23]

While the robbers were making their escape, investigators continued to work the case hard, looking for any clues to the train heist. Sheriff Wheeler found it insulting that someone would rob a train in his county, and he was hoping to make an arrest within days. Inspector C. F. Dutton of the San Francisco office of the postal department finally broke the case when he interviewed ranchers near Apache Station and Rodeo. Hattie Henderson was particularly helpful to the investigation. Based on the information Inspector Dutton acquired, it was determined that prime suspects Joe Davis and Buck Bertholf, along with Lula, had departed for Oklahoma.

### Robbing the Santa Fe at Bliss

Within weeks of arriving back in Oklahoma, Joe Davis began to plan another train robbery, this time of the southbound Santa Fe No. 405 on its run from Wichita, Kansas, to Galveston, Texas. Davis chose a site on the famous 101 Ranch, three miles north of the village of Bliss. On Wednesday night, October 18, 1916, two of the Davis Gang boarded the Santa Fe in Ponca City. They climbed over the tinder and pointed revolvers at French Canadian–born locomotive engineer Van C. Secord and forty-one-year-old fireman A. Hamilton. As the train approached Bliss at about nine at night, Secord was ordered to slow the train and look for a signal fire on the east side of the tracks. As the train lurched to a halt, Davis and three other outlaws came out of the night. The conductor, brakeman, and porter were forced at gunpoint to uncouple the engine, mail car, and baggage car from the passenger cars and run the locomotive two hundred yards down the track toward Bliss. Almost all of the passengers on the train were asleep and were unaware of the robbery. Two of the outlaws stood guard over the train crew while two others stood at the end of the baggage car. There was a three-quarter moon as Davis talked freely with the conductor, saying that he and his gang were after the money he knew was for the Otoe-Missouria Indians at the Red Rock Agency in Noble County.[24]

"Come down out of there," Davis shouted to forty-three-year-old Ohio-born Percy A. Norman, as the mail clerk struggled to open the door of the baggage car.[25] Norman may have thought the command was from a member of the train crew to several tramps on the train, and he was slow to react. Impatient, Davis fired at Norman almost point-blank with his Winchester. The bullet ranged upward, ripping through Norman's right hip and coming out his left nipple, and killed him instantly. Two of the bandits then entered the baggage car carrying a vial of nitroglycerin. After three charges they blew the door off the safe. Besides money, the registered mail and several express packages were rifled.

R. J. Huston, who operated an automobile service from Bliss Station to the village of Bliss, saw the headlight of the engine up the track and thought that the train had been derailed. Huston got in his automobile and started toward the train. Nearing the locomotive he heard one of the bandits shout out, "Come on boys they have got us."

But then Huston saw the outlaws disappear into the Oklahoma night. "Come on, Joe, we are leaving," one of the bandits yelled out.

In the eyes of the Oklahoma press, the Bliss holdup, as had been the case with the robberies at Wirth and Onapa, was "among the boldest in the history of Oklahoma."[26] Although the exact amount of money taken in the holdup was never revealed, it was said that the outlaws made off with as much as ten thousand dollars.

### Desperate and on the Run

John J. Clemmer, city marshal in Ponca City twenty miles to the north, was the first on the scene. From Guthrie, sixty miles south, deputies and detectives also hurried to Bliss in a special train composed of a locomotive, boxcar, and caboose. Thirty-two minutes after leaving Guthrie, the train was already at Perry, halfway to Bliss. The train ride was a "wild one," some of the "boys" reported.[27] Countless deputies from at least three counties, with eight Santa Fe and American Express detectives, and citizens from other towns and cities such as Perry and Newkirk, all joined in the search for the outlaws. The "whole country is aroused," the *Tulsa Daily World* reported.[28] People came in automobiles and on horseback. So many people were searching for the outlaws, it was thought it would only be hours before they were captured. There was no way they could get across the Arkansas River without being detected or apprehended, their pursuers believed. Guthrie officers found a fancy lariat near the site of the robbery, causing speculation that the outlaws were from a Wild West show. Automobile tracks found near the railroad indicated that the robbers fled the scene by car, but a set of six horse tracks was also found leading east toward the Arkansas River.

Several saddles, blankets, bedding, camping outfit, together with food wrapped in paper, were all found where the outlaws had camped on Charley Creek in Osage County, ten miles southeast of Kaw City.[29] Three jaded horses were also found tied up near the camp. Some of the paper wrappings revealed that the food had been purchased at a grocery store in Fairfax. However, after three days, all leads had grown cold and the lawmen went home. Joe Davis and his brazen gang of outlaws had gotten away yet again. The famous Miller brothers—George, Zack, and Joseph—were so embarrassed the holdup occurred on their famous 101 Ranch that they offered one hundred dollars for each bandit arrested and convicted.[30]

Norman's body was taken off the train at Bliss and turned over to the local justice of the peace. He took the body north to Arkansas City on a special train, then finally on to Newton, Kansas, where his widow, Anna, waited. When the southbound Santa Fe train reached Oklahoma City, passengers began raising funds for the widow, with the help of the *Daily Oklahoman*.[31]

## Henry F. Grammer

If post office inspector reports are accurate, on October 5 and 6, 1916, Joe Davis drove his Overland touring car from Hugo to a ranch owned by larger-than-life steer roper Henry F. Grammer at Big Hill—on the Arkansas River, just across the river from Kaw City in the Osage country—and stayed there until after the robbery. Grammer and Davis had been close since they competed in steer roping contests in Muskogee and eastern Oklahoma. Grammer was known as a "squaw man" in Osage County.[32] On the streets of Ponca City, Pawhuska, Arkansas City, whether in big cities and small towns, Grammer was remembered as one of the best steer ropers in the West. A picturesque character always wearing cowboy boots and spurs, with a lasso looped around his saddle horn, he performed at Madison Square Garden and before royalty in Europe. Grammer was also one of the quickest draws in the West and was said to have several notches on his pistol. Once in Montana, he had gunned down a sheepshearer and received a three-year sentence for manslaughter at the Montana State Prison at Deer Lodge.[33]

To what extent the thirty-two-year-old Grammer and the outlaw gang he commanded were involved in the Bliss robbery is uncertain. There is little doubt that he provided horses for the holdup, and in the days following the robbery he gave Joe Davis shelter and sustenance. As it turned out, the train robbers had ridden east after the holdup and crossed the Arkansas River before heading for Grammer's ranch. Post office inspectors reported that Davis did not leave the ranch at Big Hill until October 22, four days after the robbery, and Davis did not arrive back in Hugo until four days after that.[34]

If law enforcement officials can be believed, Joe Davis struck again on November 23 when the First National Bank of Boswell was robbed of $11,400.[35] Boswell in Choctaw County, twenty-two miles west of Hugo, was one of the most important settlements in the old Choctaw Nation. Davis had allegedly met with a loose-knit band of robbers in Durant that included Willis "Skinny" Newton of the infamous Newton Boys and a man named Charlie Rankins. It was Newton's first holdup in what would become a life of train and bank robberies. When asked if he wanted in on a daylight bank job "by a guy who lived over at Hugo" who agreed to provide him with a horse, Newton responded, "Hell yeah!" Riding into Boswell and tying their horses to a tree, the gang "told everybody to stay put" or the outlaws "would blow their damn heads off," Newton later confessed. "Then big as you please we untied our horses and slowly trotted off into the brush." The men headed across the South Boggy River and followed the stream to just outside Hugo, where they split up the money. Newton left his horse behind, walked into town with his pockets full of greenbacks, and caught the St. Louis and San Francisco train for Ardmore and then the Santa Fe south to San Antonio, Texas.[36]

Fed up with the epidemic of bank robberies in Oklahoma, 250 bankers met in Oklahoma City three weeks after the Boswell robbery to develop a systematic strategy to stop the holdups. Shotgun squads were organized in many towns and stronger safes were installed, as well as better burglar alarms, and rewards were increased. Ironically, while the bankers were in the midst of their deliberations in Oklahoma City, the Farmers State Bank at Vinita sixty-four miles northeast of Tulsa was held up by four bandits. Fifteen thousand dollars were taken. The president of the bank, Harry F. Bagby, was in Oklahoma City at the time.[37]

## Closing In

Postal inspectors remained hot on the trail of Joe Davis. A reward of as much as twelve thousand dollars was offered for his arrest and conviction by the states of Oklahoma and Arizona, along with Wells Fargo, and the Santa Fe and Southern Pacific Railroads.[38] The Overland touring car he had purchased in Douglas using the name of Joe L. Mayes was located at the family home in Hugo.[39] In early November 1916, although Joe and Lula were nowhere to be found, Bertholf was arrested near Blocker, Oklahoma. Pittsburg County deputy Otto Reed, who was in the countryside collecting delinquent taxes, discovered a "hot trail" and tracked Bertholf to a farm owned by a man named Flem George. Reed telephoned Sheriff T. C. Collier, who jumped in an automobile to join Reed and two deputies. The lawmen drove to the George farm, parked the car in some underbrush, and waited until it grew dark. Then they walked toward the house, where they waited until the lights went out and everyone was in bed. They found Bertholf's horse in a stall in the barn. With two deputies guarding the back door, Collier and Reed approached the front door and knocked. When Mattie George came to the door, they asked for Bertholf. Buck heard the men's request, and without putting on his clothes or grabbing his revolver he dashed out the back door in his underclothes, only to be grabbed by one of the deputies. From Blocker, Bertholf was hustled under guard to the federal jail in Muskogee. Officers from Arizona arrived a few days later with extradition warrants.[40]

For weeks, federal enforcement officers out of Ardmore, postal inspectors from Tulsa and as far away as Brooklyn, New York, special agents for the Santa Fe Railroad from Topeka and Arkansas City, Kansas, and Purcell, Oklahoma, along with two detectives for Wells Fargo from Kansas City were all looking for

Joe Davis and Lula Cobb. They were certain that Davis and his gang of outlaws were responsible for the train robberies at Bliss and Apache Station, Arizona, and were behind a series of bank robberies going all the way back to Stroud and the more recent bank heist at Boswell.[41] By mid-November 1916 the US deputy marshal for the Southern District of Oklahoma J. F. Dillon coordinated efforts out of Chickasha, several of those tracking Davis and Cobb and including US deputy marshals who had been following Davis and Cobb all over Oklahoma and the Southwest. They were ready to make arrests, but they held off, hoping the Davis Gang would come together and they could arrest them all.

### Arrest at Purcell

With federal agents watching Lula arrived in Purcell on a Santa Fe train on Sunday morning, November 26, 1916, and checked in at Emma and W. T. Pollock's boardinghouse on Brule Street, not far from the Santa Fe depot. Located on the west bank of the Canadian River in south central Oklahoma and calling itself the "Queen City of the Chickasaw Nation," Purcell was a proud community that also bragged of being the "Heart of Oklahoma." Newly recruited members of the Davis Gang, John Brogan and John Courtney (said to be men of little intelligence), got off a freight train at the same time. Brogan had recently been run out of Oklahoma City as a vagrant, and both men had served terms in the Purcell city jail for drunkenness. A little later another suspected outlaw, W. E. Wells (the smarter of the trio and close to Davis), also arrived by train. All were known by the police as "yegs," or safecrackers. All three checked into the Pollock boardinghouse. Special agents for the Santa Fe Railroad consulted with J. Q. Newell, US marshal for the Western District of Oklahoma, and he sent Deputy Marshal J. A. Mulkey to Purcell. But where was Joe Davis? Hours later, in typical Davis fashion, he came riding out of the west on horseback.

Late Monday afternoon, as many as eleven men quietly arrived in Purcell to arrest Davis and his gang. Leading the charge was Marshal Mulkey and Dow Brazil, a federal agent from Ardmore; O. C. Pierce, a postal inspector from Tulsa; along with Ed Franks, city marshal in Purcell. Four special agents for the Santa Fe stood by, along with two detectives from Wells Fargo who had arrived from Kansas City.[42]

As dusk set in, while Davis and his gang gathered at the Pollock boardinghouse for dinner, the building was quietly surrounded. Every door and window was covered by one or two lawmen. With pistols drawn Mulkey, Brazil, Pierce, and Franks cautiously entered the dining room just as the gang sat down at the table to eat.

"Put up your hands," one of the officers shouted. Joe, Lula, Courtney, and Brogan quickly complied, but Wells hesitated, slowly raising only one hand while keeping his other hand concealed under the table.

Brazil, who had his revolver pointed at Wells, screamed out, "Stick 'em up or I'll blow your head off." Noticing other guns were also pointed at him, Wells slowly complied. Lula sat "unmoved and smiling."

The Pollocks rushed forth to proclaim their innocence. In the rush and excitement, officers were expecting Davis and Wells to resist.

At the time of his arrest, Davis had in his possession a .45 caliber automatic pistol, $500 wrapped in a bank "sticker," $101 in other bills, and some silver coins; Lula had $62 in her purse; Wells had $41. Brogan and Courtney were penniless. A bag near the table contained eight revolvers and several rounds of pistol and rifle cartridges.[43]

Davis gave his name as "Joe L. Mayes," but when he was shown one of his mug shots at the jail in Purcell, he admitted his real identity. In the evening two days later, because it was feared the Purcell jail was not safe, a special Santa Fe engine was attached to a sleeping car, and the gang were whisked away to Oklahoma City. The speeding train made the thirty-seven-mile run to the capital in less than an hour. On arriving in Oklahoma City the prisoners were taken in special police cars to the county jail.

In Oklahoma City Davis refused once again to give his name, saying only, "Put down anything you like; you've got me."

Arrogant as usual, Lula asked that she be listed in the official records as "Mary Watson." "That's as good as any in a place like this," she said.

Everyone was taken to separate cells, where they were stripped and searched. A long-bladed knife was found in Davis's clothing that had not been detected earlier in Purcell.

Five days later the prisoners were taken, again by train, to the federal jail in Muskogee, where Lula said her name was "Sallie Johnson."[44]

Oklahoma officials were determined to prosecute Davis for the Bliss robbery and for the murder of Percy Norman. But Arizona officials arrived wanting to extradite him to Arizona for the robbery of the Golden State Limited.

### Plain, Ignorant, Little Country Gal

For days on end Oklahoma newspapers played up the arrest of Davis and Cobb, who were reported to be husband and wife. Newspapers charged Joe with killing Norman, Fred Spess, and even Robert Moore, the deputy sheriff who died during the Terlton robbery, even though Davis was nowhere near Terlton at the time. It was the Spess brothers and Inhofe who were arrested for the Terlton robbery and murder. The *Checotah Times* proclaimed Lula, alias "Lula Mayes," "Mary Watson," or "Sallie Johnson," as the "directing genius of an organization which is alleged to have as its purpose the holding up and robbery of mail trains." The *Muskogee County Democrat* said she was a "ring leader of a band that . . . operated in Oklahoma, Arizona and California." Moreover, the press claimed that Lula was the brains behind the train robbery at Apache Station, Arizona.[45]

Joe's dad, Jack Davis, had never liked Lula, thinking she was not good enough for his son, and he was upset that the newspapers were depicting the couple as husband and wife. Lula was "just a plain, ignorant, little country gal, who doesn't know enough to go in out of the rain, let alone to plan robberies as has been intimated by the newspapers," Davis said, "yet they are playing her up and running her picture as a bandit queen."[46]

Arizona officials officially asked for Joe Davis's extradition less than two weeks after his arrest. The US Fidelity and Guaranty Company, bondsmen for Davis in the Wirth robbery, vigorously opposed the extradition in the district federal court of Judge Ralph Campbell in Muskogee. Once again Jack Davis hired Samuel Morton Rutherford, this time to help keep his son in Oklahoma. Rutherford said that the federal government could not try Davis in Arizona until there was a resolution of his case in the Eastern District of Oklahoma. At the federal courthouse a reporter for the *Muskogee Times-Democrat* found Jack Davis pacing the corridor adjacent to Judge Campbell's chambers, denying his son's guilt and worrying that Joe would be sent to Arizona. Without hesitation, without prejudice, Judge Campbell denied the motion of the US Fidelity and Guaranty Company, along with Rutherford's pleas, and Davis was sent to Phoenix. Campbell set bond at twenty-five thousand dollars and gave the Davises two days to come up with the money. At the same time Buck Bertholf, who was also trying to stay in Oklahoma, was also ordered to Arizona.[47] Jack Davis tried one last desperate attempt to keep Joe in Oklahoma by hiring attorney Jean P. Day to file a motion in the Western District of Oklahoma at Guthrie before Judge John Hazelton Cotteral. Deputy Marshals D. P. Miller and J. A. Mulkey—two of the men who had helped arrest him in Purcell—took Davis in chains to the federal lockup at Guthrie. A local newspaper described Davis as "tall and well-built," someone with a "happy disposition." Joe did not "seem to be worrying much over his present predicament," the newspaper went on to say.[48] Judge Cotteral refused to intervene, saying that he had no legal right to keep Davis in Oklahoma. On the night of December 6, 1916, Davis was brought back to Oklahoma City in shackles. Escorted by four armed guards he was put on a train headed west.

With Davis trussed up in "a ton of irons," as the *Bisbee Daily Review* put it, the Katy rambled south through the night to Dallas and on to San Antonio before the long ride across the vast Texas trans-Pecos to El Paso, then through southern New Mexico to Phoenix. When he arrived in the capital Arizona officials were astounded that Davis was so young and did not look much like a "bold, bad bandit." The *Tombstone Daily Prospector* described him as "nothing more than a youngster" who "took his capture in a matter-of-fact way." According to the *Tucson Daily Citizen*, the youthful train robber was "a good looking man, well dressed, and possessed of much self-confidence [who] would not pass for a cowboy in ordinary clothes." The Arizona newspapers quickly dubbed him the "boy bandit."[49]

Back in Oklahoma Lula was taken first to the lockup in Ardmore and then twenty miles south to Marietta, while officials led the press to believe she was being held in Texas. Lula was transferred again, this time to the federal jail in Muskogee. Great caution was taken to keep secret exactly where she was being held for fear that the Davis Gang would attempt to rescue her.[50] In early January 1917 Lula and Bertholf were placed on the Katy bound for San Antonio and Arizona. Unwilling to take any chances senior US marshal E. A. Enole chose four of his more experienced lawmen to accompany the two to Phoenix.[51] After a week of intense interrogation and coercion at the Maricopa County jail, Bertholf agreed to turn state's evidence, and he was transferred to the Tucson immigration quarters. From there he accompanied federal marshals to the Henderson Ranch in New Mexico. With the help of Hattie Henderson, they recovered Davis's trunk, his saddle, horse equipment, clothing, and even the vial of nitroglycerine. Perhaps more incriminating than any of his personal belongings were the letters he had written Lula telling her to come to Arizona, that something "big" was about to happen.[52]

## Prescott Jail

Davis was taken from Phoenix to the Yavapai County jail in Prescott, where he and Spurlock were formally charged with five counts of obstructing the US mail, along with assault and robbery. Bond was set at thirty thousand dollars. It was thought that Jack Davis, a wealthy Oklahoma rancher, would post bond—but the Davises had run out of money. The young and arrogant Oklahoma cowboy was beginning to realize he was unlikely to escape the grasp of federal authorities. Yet he remained optimistic that his father could somehow spring a miracle, as he had done so many times before. With a good attorney and men who would testify to anything for a price, he would again be free. Or so he thought. In jail at Prescott Davis learned that a rodeo friend, C. W. "Doc" Pardee, had a job tearing down an old abandoned barn across the street. With the assistance of a trustee he was able to bribe, Joe got a note smuggled to Pardee asking for a hacksaw and several blades. From conflicting testimony it appears that Pardee procured the items and got them to Davis. That night Joe was able to saw through a couple of bars in his cell window before jail guards confiscated the hacksaw and blades. Pardee was arrested and his "interesting and sensational" trial several months later drew great attention. Despite three witnesses saying that they carried messages back and forth between Davis and Pardee, the rodeo star took the stand to deny everything and was found not guilty. Davis was indicted in Prescott for attempting to escape, but when Pardee was declared innocent those charges were dropped.[53]

On January 28, 1917, shortly after the attempted jail break, Davis was transferred to the Pima County jail in Tucson to await trial. Within days he gained a reputation for his vivacity and jokes. While Bertholf was at the Tucson immigration quarters, federal authorities made sure there was no contact with Davis, for fear that Joe would persuade Bertholf to recant his confession.

## Jeff Spurlock

As much as five thousand dollars were offered for the arrest of Davis Gang member Jeff Spurlock. Twice his trail led across the continent, but all that could be learned was that he had a girlfriend named Millie in Kansas City, Kansas. Secret service men watched her every move, but there were no clues until she was taken ill and went to a hospital. A government detective checked into the hospital as a patient by informing the superintendent of his identity and took the room next to her. Through a nurse he was able to keep track of the mail Millie received. She got letters occasionally from Texas and seemed to write letters back, which puzzled authorities since Spurlock was thought to be a long way from the Lone Star State. As it turned out, the wily Spurlock was writing to a woman he knew in Paris, Texas, enclosing letters that he asked be mailed to his lover in Kansas City. She in turn sent her letters to the Paris woman, who forwarded the letters to Spurlock.

Late one night, one of the nurses took a letter from the girl's bedside while she was asleep. The letter indicated that Spurlock was working for the Armour Packing Company in Sioux Falls, South Dakota. Agents did not know the alias he was using, and no one seemed to have a mug shot. At the post office in Sioux Falls, agents learned that he was getting his mail at a Greek restaurant and was using the alias Tom Miles. Three secret service men and four local detectives finally grabbed him in early January 1917. After several days of interrogation Spurlock admitted his real identity, but he denied any knowledge of the Bliss, Oklahoma, or Apache Station, Arizona, train robberies. He was extradited to Arizona, nevertheless.[54] Spurlock sent a telegram to his mother saying, "Things ain't as bad as they look," and he asked that Millie not be told of his arrest. In Arizona Spurlock retained the former Arizona judge W. L. Barnum for his defense. Well-known El Paso attorney Charles Owen—who was referred to as a "mouthpiece of no mean ability," and who was perhaps best known for having represented Pancho Villa—was retained by both Davis and Spurlock.[55] The able and determined Thomas A. Flynn with his assistants Gerald Jones, William J. Bryan Jr., and John H. Langston would prosecute the case for the government.[56]

### Moman Pruiett to the Rescue

Why Jack Davis did not retain Samuel M. Rutherford to defend his son has not been determined. Rutherford may have sensed that the evidence was too overwhelming, although he had never backed away from a fight before. He had ably represented the Davises with great vigor in the past. Had Jack Davis lost faith in Rutherford's abilities? He turned to the far more famous Moman Pruiett, who was thought by many to be the best criminal lawyer and legal orator in the Southwest. A twenty-year veteran, Pruiett had a reputation throughout the Sooner State for his fiery oratory, quick temper, and heavy drinking. Sometimes called the "dark horse of the Washita," he was a superb criminal lawyer, defending everyone from Klansmen to poor black sharecroppers. With an ego that knew no bounds, Pruiett bragged that out of 343 individuals he had defended for murder he obtained 303 acquittals. None of his clients was executed, he boasted, even when they were found guilty. He had become a legend in the Oklahoma courts for his dramatic psychological appeals to juries, often screaming scripture like a wild evangelist. He was a twice-convicted felon himself, and no one knew the ins and outs of the Oklahoma legal system better than Pruiett.[57]

Pruiett was forty-five at the time and in the prime of his career. But he had at least three serious problems—alcohol, paranoia, and a runaway ego. Calling himself the "Saltiest thing in the West" and a "Black Stud," in an autobiography he later recalled crossing the "Arizona desert" to defend young Joe Davis.[58] With his mother critically ill in Oklahoma, Pruiett arrived in Tucson only days before the trial was to commence. He hurried to the hotel room he had reserved, where fellow attorney Charles Owen and Jack Davis greeted him. Years later Pruiett

FIGURE 16. The egotistical and heavy-drinking Moman Pruiett was retained by Jack Davis to defend his son in the robbery of the Golden State Limited. Although Pruiett was undoubtedly the most successful criminal defense attorney in Oklahoma history, the Davises were dismayed that during the trial he failed to call a single witness for the defense. The Davises would allege that Pruiett was drunk a large part of the time. Men of Affairs and Representative Institutions of Oklahoma, 1916. *Courtesy of the Local History and Genealogy Department of the Muskogee Public Library.*

could recall much of the conversation that followed: "We were getting worried about you," Jack Davis said. "We got a lot of work to do an' just a couple of days to do it in. What was the matter?"

"My Maw's sick," Pruiett answered bluntly. "She's dying. I started once to wire you I wasn't comin', but I decided I might just as well. I figured she'd insist on my comin' if she was in any kind of shape. She always insisted I take care of lawsuits ahead of everything else. I am not going to bother others with my own private troubles. Let's get down to business. Is there any chances of getting severances, an' tryin' these cases one at a time?"

"Not a chance in the world," Owen responded.

"We don't want no continuance," Jack Davis interrupted. "We got a bunch of witnesses here, an' it costs a lot of money. They're high-priced witnesses, an' we want to put 'em on."

### Paranoid and Inebriated

"Shut up," Pruiett hissed in a whisper. "I've had this room reserved ahead in a telegram. It may be tapped."

Pruiett turned over the mattress, examining the bedsprings. He began looking behind mirrors and wall hangings and in the drawers of the writing desk, then even turning over the rug on the floor and examining the light fixtures.

"Check that bathroom, an' be sure you do it good," Pruiett whispered to Owen. "Don't overlook anything. They got a bug in here."

"What the hell you so suspicious about?" Owen asked. "You an' me aren't charged with anything. You think they put a dictograph on us? There isn't anything."

"I can't find a thing, but I can feel it, plain as hell," Pruiett responded. "There isn't anything the government won't do to win this case."

"Everything looks all right to me," Davis pronounced after looking under the bed.

"Now listen," Pruiett interrupted. "Let's put this gabbin' off 'til tomorrow morning," he continued, "an' we'll meet in the café for breakfast. I'm all run down an' I got to get some sleep."

"We ain't got much time," Davis shot back.

"We got plenty of time, 'til we locate that bug or get a place to talk where we won't be talkin' into some dick's ear," Pruiett argued.

"I been up a' hour," Pruiett announced the next morning, as Owen and Davis walked over to his table at the restaurant.

"I didn't think the saloons opened up that early," Davis quipped.

"Joe inherited all the brain you got, an' he's eatin' his breakfast out of a tin tray up in the federal jail," Pruiett shot back.

"That stuff won't get us anywhere," Owen interrupted, stuffing a napkin in his vest. "Let's talk some sense. What're we goin' to announce when the government calls these cases?"

"Not ready, an' have a motion an' a bunch of affidavits for a continuance ready," Pruiett responded.

"I'll be damned if we do," Davis cut in. "I got a perfect alibi right here in town, an' it cost a' plenty. We're goin' to trial."

Obsessed and excessively suspicious, Pruiett was certain that the bartender in the hotel was a federal agent, and that a drunk at the front table was only pretending to be inebriated, that he was really a spy.

"We'll either try it with you or without you," Davis insisted.

"That phony alibi is out," Pruiett said. But Davis continued to demand the witnesses he had brought from Oklahoma be called to the stand.

"One would think I had hired you to give me advice, instead of vice versa," Pruiett retorted. "I won't offer a word of that stuff that's been cooked up."

"We'll try it straight, on what we got, or old Moman don't even go to the courthouse."

"Quittin,' are you?" Davis asked.

"You're damned right I am," Pruiett snapped.[59]

Pruiett claimed that, after the trial was over, he was approached by Thomas Flynn, lead attorney for the prosecution, who told him the government had evidence that Jack Davis was planning a "perjured conspiracy," and it was Pruiett who had prevented it. "I want to commend you, and thank you," Flynn said.[60]

With rare snow flurries in the Tucson sky outside Justice William Sawtelle's district court, Davis and Spurlock's trial began on the morning of February 19, 1917. US marshals holding sawed-off shotguns arrived in a caravan of automobiles with the prisoners chained hand and foot. Other heavily armed federal lawmen lined the steps of the federal courthouse. Standing nearby were "swarthy faced men wearing big brimmed slouch hats" from the Pima County sheriff's office. Rumors had been circulating for days that a band of Oklahoma outlaws would be arriving in town to free Davis and his pals. Reporters from Arizona's leading newspapers huddled impatiently nearby, awaiting the opening of what they perceived to be one of the most sensational trials in the history of the infant state. Curious Tucson citizens lined up for half a block in the cold, anxious to hear the testimony and see the outlaws in person. Davis's "spectacular career [having] drawn much attention from across the country," the young and joyous outlaw seemed to be the center of attention, "his life . . . one of excitement," the *Hugo Husonian* reported.[61]

## A Powerful and Compelling Case

Both Pruiett and Barnum asked Judge Sawtelle for a severance, but they were denied. Because Bertholf had agreed to testify for the prosecution, however, Judge Sawtelle announced that Bertholf would be tried separately. The twelve male jurors—eleven of them Tucsonans—included a Ford Motor Company agent, a life insurance salesman, a Cochise County rancher, and one Native American, Demetrio Gill, all of whom were familiar with the case from articles in the local newspaper but none felt the publicity had prejudiced them. Nonetheless, because of the significance of the case, Judge Sawtelle ordered the jury to be sequestered. Jurors were denied access to newspapers until the "court had read them and cut out the objectionable parts." Jurors could take walks, but they were forbidden to attend a "picture show" or any public gatherings, and they were warned not to "indulge in intoxicating liquors."[62]

From the beginning, federal prosecutors presented a powerful and convincing case. During eight days of grueling testimony, they questioned forty-two witnesses from as far away as Hugo, Oklahoma, and El Paso, Texas. Other witnesses from Deming, Pratt, and Rodeo, New Mexico, and Tucson, Apache Station, Prescott, and Douglas, Arizona, also testified. Eighty-five pieces of evidence in all, including an empty bottle that had held nitroglycerine, Davis's saddle, bridle, boots, saddle blanket, hat, overcoat, chaps, spurs, pocketknife, and even Lula's handbag were introduced. Letters, telegrams, railroad tickets, checks, bank books, post office records, even the hotel register from the Gadsden Hotel and the post office register book from Claude, Texas, were introduced. Some of the most compelling testimony came from the prosecution's first witness, Burk Bertholf, who carefully related how he and Davis had been childhood friends in Oklahoma and how he had come to Arizona; then how the robbery had been planned and executed, and how the outlaws had escaped. As Jack Davis sat in awe, all Pruiett could offer for the defense was a constant stream of ineffectual objections that the testimony was irrelevant and immaterial. Still under arrest, a very pregnant Lula sat quietly in the back of the packed courtroom throughout the trial, frequently appearing in a bright fashionable maroon dress and black veil, intently listening to the testimony. Spurlock's mother and brother followed the courtroom proceedings from afar.[63]

Perhaps the most dramatic moment in the trial came when prosecutors asked Davis to read the letters they found in his trunk on the Henderson Ranch. The letters, they were sure, clearly showed Davis's intentions of robbing the Golden State Limited. He had written Lula from Deming, New Mexico, asking that she join him in Douglas, saying that things were about to get "pretty hot." As the *Muskogee Times-Democrat* observed, "Slowly but surely the government's net of evidence is closing in on Joe Davis."[64]

## Twenty-Five Years in McNeil Island Prison

For some unexplained reason Pruiett did not call a single witness in Davis's defense, although he frequently interrupted the proceedings with endless objections to everything conceivable and offering motions for a dismissal. He would later say the "defense introduced no evidence because they believed that the government had shown nothing against Davis and Spurlock except a mass of suspicions." Jack Davis was shocked by Pruiett's complacency and ineffectiveness. At this point in his career Pruiett was inebriated a large part of the time. He was also paranoid, hearing strange noises in his ears. As it turned out he was no Morton Rutherford. Privately, Jack Davis objected strenuously when Pruiett refused to call any of the witnesses he had gone to great expense to bring from Oklahoma. Pruiett simply argued that there was no "direct testimony to connect the defendants with participation in the holdup, except that of Bertholf, the confessed bandit, and Hynes, the hobo soldier, and . . . they were unworthy of credence."[65]

As his colleague, the attorney Charles Owen, sat quietly Pruiett rested the case for the defense and asked for a directed verdict of innocence, which was denied without comment. It came as no surprise on February 23, 1917, when the jury returned after only forty-five minutes with a verdict of guilty on all counts. As he had done before Joe Davis nervously laughed and joked with Spurlock, as if they were in the justice of the peace office in Texanna. Pruiett asked for a new trial, but Judge Sawtelle denied the motion. Pruiett next asked that the sentencing be delayed, but Judge Sawtelle said that he would sentence the two men four days later. "My heart hasn't broken and I will have hope," Spurlock said.[66] Joe Davis refused to talk to the press. It had been the most sensational trial that many in Arizona could remember.

Davis and Spurlock were both sentenced to twenty-five years in McNeil Island federal prison in the state of Washington. They were given three years for obstructing the mail, three years for assault, five years for taking the registered mail, and twenty-five years for the assault of R. M. Collier and Robert A. Baker, plus twenty-five years for robbing the two men. All sentences were to run concurrently. Davis's term would expire on February 18, 1942, or December 12, 1933, if he were released on good behavior. During the trial and sentencing, Lula Cobb sat quietly in the rear of the courtroom. Realizing that she was seven months pregnant, the district attorney agreed to release her on her own recognizance, and she returned to Oklahoma and was never tried. The night before he was taken to McNeil Island, Davis somehow obtained a hacksaw blade and once again tried—and failed—to saw his way to freedom.[67]

Back in Oklahoma at Dewar, a few miles from Henryetta, on April 25, 1917, Lula gave birth to twins. Only one survived, a girl named Joe Lee Davis after her father.[68]

## → 7 ←

# LONG DARK YEARS

Lula was killed today.

— Phenie Cobb

An hour before sunset on March 3, 1917, Joe Davis, Jeff Spurlock, and thirteen other federal prisoners were shackled and led out of the Pima County jail in Tucson, Arizona, to be escorted to the Southern Pacific Railroad depot. Here they were crowded into a special steel-encased "Prison on Wheels" railroad car bound for the federal lockup at McNeil Island, Washington, sixteen hundred miles away. Isolated in three compartments, the prisoners included an American Indian from White River, Arizona, who was convicted of killing a thirteen-year-old girl, and a man from Miami, Arizona, who was caught with eighteen hundred dollars' worth of cocaine. On board were nine heavily armed special guards plus a cook, all under the guidance of US Marshal Jimmie McDonald.

Into the night across the Sonoran Desert the train rambled westward to the Yuma Crossing on the Colorado River. On the Pacific coast at Los Angeles, a second engine waited to take the prison car north through California's great central valley, past Tulare, Fresno, then to Sacramento, and into the darkness again. In the mountains of northern California, the train rattled on into Oregon, past Medford into the Wilmette Valley, to Eugene, Salem, and finally to Portland and the Columbia River. The train finally screeched to a halt at Tacoma, Washington.

FIGURE 17. Following his conviction in Arizona, Joe Davis entered McNeil Island Federal Penitentiary, Washington, on March 5, 1917. *Courtesy of the National Archives, Seattle, Washington.*

Still in chains, the prisoners were driven to the village of Steilacoom, where they were put on a ferry across a narrow neck of Puget Sound to McNeil Island. The cold and weary journey took three days and four nights. Both the scenery and exhausting journey were unlike anything Joe Davis had ever seen or experienced.[1]

Joe Lynch Davis, inmate no. 2845, walked into McNeil Island federal penitentiary on March 5, 1917. In his mug shot there is still a bit of arrogance, perhaps evidence of one last fleeting hope that his father would somehow intervene to free him. At the time, he had in his possession $159.17, a pair of gold cufflinks with the initial "J," and one green-inlaid scarf pin in the form of an axe. He was a cowboy by profession, he said, literate, had no religion, was of Scots-Irish ancestry, was married with no children, and he was temperate. Somehow his Cherokee blood—of which he had been so proud in Oklahoma—was forgotten. For some unexplained reason, Davis told prison officials he was born in Hugo, Oklahoma. He owned a 320-acre farm, he said, was twenty-six years old,

FIGURE 18. Cell House No. 1 and officers' quarters at McNeil Island Federal Penitentiary a few years before Joe Davis arrived in 1917. *Courtesy of the National Archives, Seattle, Washington.*

five foot nine and one-half inches in height, weighed 159.75 pounds, had brown hair, grey-blue eyes, a thin nose tilted to the right, one false tooth, was of fair complexion and medium build. He had a small scar on the back of one ear and a one-quarter-inch scar on the edge of his left eye. The second toe on his right foot was amputated at the first joint, and he had a vaccination scar on his left arm. On another piece of paper he listed the names and ages of his closest relatives. When Spurlock followed Davis into the prison, all he had in his possession was five cents.[2]

### Inmate No. 2845

Of the 247 prisoners at McNeil Island in 1917, almost all were from Washington, Oregon, or California. The largest number were convicted of violating postal laws, counterfeiting, picking pockets, and smuggling. There were few burglars, and even fewer murderers. Some were convicted of selling liquor to American Indians, and there were a few imprisoned for "white slavery." One inmate was serving time for having lived in a "state of adultery."[3]

In many ways the prison at McNeil Island was a big farm that did much more than sustain the prison. An apple orchard produced over 10,000 pounds of apples annually, and there was also a small pear orchard. Plums from a small orchard were dried into prunes. Fifteen acres were devoted to growing potatoes, carrots, tomatoes, squash, peas, onions, beets, beans, cabbage, pumpkins, blackberries, and even 211 pounds of loganberries annually.[4] Chickens produced thousands of dozens of eggs. There was a rabbit-breeding project, especially of the "Flemish Giant" breed. A Holstein bull was purchased to improve the quality of the dairy herd. There were hundreds of hogs, turkeys, and ducks. There was a tin shop, a machine shop, and a blacksmith shop that assisted in repairs and the upkeep of the prison.

Every Sunday there was a nondenominational religious service, plus Mass for Catholic prisoners. Those prisoners who were in good standing could attend a "moving-picture show" on Sundays, which the warden insisted was "enthusiastically appreciated by all prisoners." Weather permitting, every Friday and on holidays baseball games were held. In the summer, swimming in front of the prison was permitted. A prison library of 2,391 books along with 32 daily or weekly newspapers were available to prisoners on good behavior.

When Jack Davis telephoned Bessie from Arizona with the news that their son had been convicted and sentenced to twenty-five years in prison on McNeil Island, 1,678 miles from Hugo, Bessie had a nervous breakdown. Her life would never be the same. Bessie had always been strong and resolute, but she could not conceive the idea that her son might be imprisoned. If Joe said he was innocent (and Jack assured her that he was), then he must have been framed or somehow failed by his drunken attorney, as Jack claimed. Bessie believed there was no way Joe could be guilty. As her son lingered in federal prison in the decade that followed, she suffered long periods of depression. During the accusations and the trials for bank and train robberies, Joe always professed his innocence, and Bessie never questioned him or her husband.[5]

Only days after Joe arrived at McNeil Island, Bessie wrote the warden saying she had not "heard a word" from her "boy Joe Davis" and that she was worried. "Perhaps they are not allowed to write," she speculated. "Please write me in regards to him. I hope he is getting along all right." A few days later, the warden responded to say that Joe had written a letter on March 14, to Lula Davis in care of Mrs. J. W. Cobb in Dewar, Oklahoma, and that he had also written to his sister Carrie four days later.[6]

From the time Joe stepped ashore on McNeil Island, Jack Davis wrote to his son regularly. He also began working strenuously to obtain a pardon for him. Post office inspectors working out of Muskogee were well aware that the father would use every means possible to "effect the parole or pardon" of his son. On April 7, 1917, the day the United States declared war on Germany, post office inspectors prepared a lengthy report outlining all the crimes and transgressions of Joe and his father over their fifteen years of running roughshod over law enforcement officials and the courts in Oklahoma.[7] At the same time, Jack Davis was busy contacting every individual who he thought could in some way help free his son. Charles D. Carter, a Democrat from Ardmore who represented Oklahoma's Third Congressional District, wrote the warden at McNeil Island to say that Joe Davis was the son of a "constituent and friend," and he urged the warden to "show the prisoner . . . every consideration possible . . . especially to the end that his health may not be impaired." On April 10, 1917, less than two months after arriving at McNeil Island, Davis was abruptly transferred to the newer federal penitentiary at Leavenworth, Kansas.[8]

### A Place Called Leavenworth

Again, there was a long three-day-and-night train trip halfway across the continent. From Seattle, a prison car carried Joe Davis and other prisoners into the snow-capped Rocky Mountains, through northern Idaho, then southeast across the vast wind-swept Big Sky country of Montana, through northeastern Wyoming, along the Missouri River to eastern Kansas, and finally to Leavenworth. On the morning of April 13, 1917, Davis disembarked with the other prisoners and entered the federal prison. He did not know it at the time, but this would be his home for the next fourteen years.

Davis's Leavenworth mug shot reveals a clean-shaven, bewildered young man with fear and trepidation in his eyes. The young Oklahoma Cherokee cowboy who had proudly posed on horseback and roped steers in front of admiring audiences at the fairgrounds in Muskogee and small towns in eastern Oklahoma was now part of a distant, more innocent past. The arrogant young outlaw who laughed at judges and juries, flaunting his wild independence, had at last been caged like a wild animal. McNeil Island had been—psychologically—little more than a testing ground for what lay ahead.

The booking process was similar to the one Davis had experienced at McNeil Island. He was directed into a large room with long wooden benches, not unlike church pews, where he was told to strip. He was vaccinated and given a physical exam. Once again there was the Bertillon and fingerprinting process to make possible his future identification. In a second large room, his head was shaved by the prison barber and he was given a suit of striped clothing.[9] Joe had gained eight

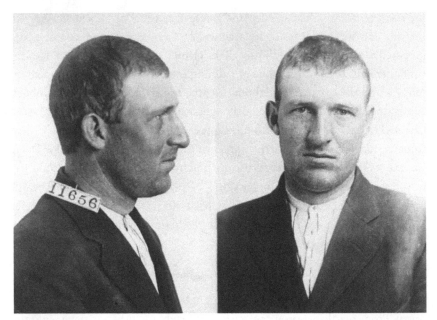

FIGURE 19. Joe Davis's mug shot upon entering Leavenworth Penitentiary, Kansas, on April 13, 1917. He was at Leavenworth for the next fourteen years. *Courtesy of the National Archives, Kansas City, Missouri.*

pounds since arriving at McNeil Island and now weighed 168 pounds. He was using tobacco but said he never drank alcohol or used drugs. The maximum-security federal penitentiary at Leavenworth was an imposing sight, with walls forty feet high and four feet thick that descended twenty feet underground. The prison had a reputation as a "hard joint." The facility was a veritable fortress situated on more than fifteen hundred acres of flat, unobstructed grassland along the west bank of the Missouri River. The prison had first opened in 1903. When Joe Davis arrived fourteen years later, many of the buildings, including several of the cellblocks, were still under construction.

Davis was assigned to the recently completed Cellblock C on the east side of the prison. A large administration building patterned after the US Capitol would eventually be completed with 284,523 bricks. It was under construction and would not be finished for another decade. The building, with its large imposing dome, gave the prison the name of "Big Top." It was bitterly cold in winter and unbearably hot in summer, and prisoners came to call Leavenworth the "Hot House."[10] In

February 1918 Davis was moved to cell no. 438 in Cellblock D at the northwest wing of the prison. He was assigned to the stone-cutting shop. On March 1, 1918, after almost a year in Leavenworth, Joe signed a "Prisoner's Agreement" and was transferred temporarily to the deputy warden's office. While continuing to deny any involvement in the Arizona train robbery, Davis listed his occupation as "rancher."[11] In the long years that followed, he would occupy several different cells and have many different cell mates, but Joe would always remember William J. Creekmore, a Tulsa bootlegger who had grown rich selling liquor in the oilfields of Oklahoma, as his favorite cell mate.[12]

## Inmate No. 11656

Compared to what he had experienced in the county jails in Oklahoma, where he had never stayed for long, the discipline at Leavenworth was excessively harsh and the atmosphere was claustrophobic. No communication was allowed between prisoners, nor were inmates allowed to converse with guards. Guards were not permitted to inform prisoners of any events occurring outside the prison. When a prisoner wished to communicate with a guard, he was forced to take off his cap, stand at attention with his arms folded across his chest, and state his business succinctly and quickly. Prisoners could not look into other cells when moving about the prison, nor make eye contact with any visitor who might be in the prison. All movement of men was in march formation. For many years, prisoners traipsed in lockstep to dinner to the tune of an opera.[13]

Davis had been at Leavenworth for only a few months when the Spanish flu pandemic reached North America and swept across the nation, killing 675,000 Americans, five times the number of American who died in World War I. The particularly virulent virus reached Fort Riley, 126 miles to the west, and then Leavenworth. A total of 169 men came down with the flu and were immediately segregated from the general prison population. Although no effective drugs or vaccines were available at the time, only five of the prisoners died.[14]

No sooner had the flu abated at the prison than on March 12, 1919, a fire believed to be set by a disgruntled prisoner swept the large wooden structure where Davis worked. The building housed the broom shop, stone sawmill, and blacksmith shop. There was only one location where a fire hose could be connected, so prisoners watched as the entire building went up in flames, along with the roof of the power plant.[15] During the fire none of the prisoners attempted to escape, and order was maintained. A note in Davis's inmate file made by acting warden L. J. Fletcher indicated that during the fire Davis acted "heroically . . . in saving other property." For this meritorious service, Fletcher recommended that Davis be given "special consideration should the occasion arise." A little over four months later, on July 19, 1919, a second fire heavily damaged the new west cellblock where Davis was housed. Once again Davis "rendered meritorious service," Warden A. V. Anderson noted.[16]

Leavenworth housed every kind of convict imaginable. There were arsonists, bigamists, rapists, bootleggers, murderers, and even those convicted of violating the Espionage Act, many of whom were notable members of the radical group Industrial Workers of the World, or Wobblies (IWW). Some prisoners had been convicted of bribery and burglary. Several hundred foreign-born convicts—the largest number of them from Germany, Italy, Mexico, and Russia—spoke fifty different languages. In civilian life some convicts had been barbers, cooks, or clerks, but the largest number were simple laborers and farmers. Among them all there were three professional baseball players, two aviators, an author, a German spy, three actors, three former policemen, two undertakers, a jockey, three recently admitted junk dealers, and several Native Americans.[17]

Prisoners had library privileges, and they were permitted to write and receive letters and packages. In Joe's first few years at Leavenworth he received a box of candy, a pair of gloves, twelve lemons, three pairs of socks, and a photo of Lula and their newborn daughter, Joe Lee. Prisoners worked an average of nine and a half hours a day, and from sunrise to sunset during the winter.

Joe's notoriety followed him to Leavenworth. Oklahoma newspapers wrote the warden asking for information on Davis. When the warden put out a physical description of the prisoner, one small town newspaper editor responded, inquiring if Davis was missing the little finger on his left hand. The warden wrote back that Joe had no such amputation. One post office inspector wrote asking for twenty-four photos of Davis.[18]

In December 1919, Joe wrote a letter to Warden A. V. Anderson, with a typed copy to Thomas A. Flynn, the US district attorney who had prosecuted him in Arizona, asking that his personal property taken from the John Henderson ranch near Animas, New Mexico (which was used as evidence against him) be returned. Besides the trunk, there were various clothing and ranching accoutrements including a pair of silver-mounted bridle bits, two pairs of boots, and a Cogshell saddle that he wanted shipped to his father. Davis even wanted Lula's handbag returned.[19]

Meticulously kept prison records indicate every individual that Joe corresponded with while he was at Leavenworth. In 1917 alone, he received ninety-four

FIGURE 20. Lula Davis poses with her daughter, Joe Lee, at Dewar, two miles northeast of Henryetta, Oklahoma, in 1917. Joe Lee later feminized her name to Jo Lee. After her mother's murder in Colorado Springs, Colorado, in 1923, she was raised by Phenie Cobb. *Author's Collection.*

letters, fifty-three of them from Lula. Davis was able to respond every Sunday, and he wrote Lula forty-four letters. Lula wrote Joe almost a hundred letters a year for the following two years. It was obvious that their love endured the most difficult of times. But the letters slacked off in 1921 and lessened further in 1922, totaling only eighteen. Lula was now in Colorado Springs. Abruptly in December 1922, a few days before Christmas, a letter arrived with Lula now using the last name "Nelson." As Davis languished helplessly in Leavenworth, Lula had found a new lover and married twenty-seven-year-old Thomas T. Nelson. Despite her new marriage, however, she continued to write to her former lover several times a year. Undoubtedly, their memories of life and love on the outlaw trail were long and lasting. Beginning in August 1922 and continuing well into 1923, the frequent letters resumed from Lula Davis, as before.[20]

The first year he was at Leavenworth, Joe received a letter from his former partner in crime Henry Starr from the Oklahoma state prison in McAlester. Claude Sawyer, a close friend who had been convicted in the Stroud bank robbery but who was now free, wrote several times from Granite, Oklahoma. During Davis's long dark years at Leavenworth, his sister Carrie corresponded frequently, and his mother wrote several times a month. His brother Sam wrote occasionally from Corrine, and then from Camp Travis outside San Antonio, Texas, when he was in training with the Nineteenth Division; he was one of 88,496 men from Oklahoma who would serve in World War I.[21]

### Murder in Colorado Springs

Only one piece of Davis's correspondence from Leavenworth has survived. On the back of a hand-colored birthday card he sent Lula for their daughter, Joe Lee, Davis wrote:

> Will write you when the investigation is over. I have not heard anything from Washington so far. [W]rite me and tell me all the news [of] yourself and Joe Lee. Guess the 19[th] will be well remembered by you as well as myself. Is Joe Lee going to school? I am sure she must be some big Girl by this time. Have been waiting for the pictures I ask you to send me some time ago. Don't forget it as I am anxious to see how you both look. Well I expect to hear from you soon Joe D[22]

Then on the afternoon of May 26, 1923, dreadful news arrived in a telegram from Phenie Cobb in Colorado Springs: "LULA WAS KILLED TODAY." Shocked and not believing what he was reading, Davis replied immediately: "JUST RECEIVED TELEGRAM STATING LULA WAS KILLED PLEASE GIVE EXPLANATION HOW SHE WAS KILLED IS THERE ANYTHING I CAN DO LETTER FOLLOWING JOE DAVIS."

Grandma Cobb wired back: "NELSON LULAS HUSBAND SHOT HER THEN SHOT HIMSELF BOTH DEAD."[23]

Lula's marriage to Thomas T. Nelson had been a disaster from the beginning. Nelson had worked at odd jobs before finding employment as a delivery man at a local laundry. By 1922, when he and Lula were first acquainted, he was employed as a fireman with the Colorado School for the Deaf and Blind. Only weeks later, he lost his job and was consistently in financial straits.[24] He drank heavily and physically abused Lula. After months of cruelty Lula wrote to a younger sister, Ila Holley, saying that she had decided to seek a divorce and that she was separated from Nelson. Lula had been in a "battle royal" with her husband, she said, and "I got cleaned upon proper, so I packed my old kit bag and Joe Lee and I meandered over to mother's haven of rest." Only six years old at the time, Joe Lee "was never so happy in her life as she is to be close to Grandma's side," Lula concluded.[25]

Nelson was psychologically unable to handle the separation from his wife, and for days he stalked Lula. Moody and despondent, he frequently appeared unannounced in the middle of the night at the Cobb residence on West Kiowa Street, seeking reconciliation with her. Late one evening he showed up at the Cobb household, pleading with Lula to accompany him to a dance in Pueblo. Lula finally conceded, but she said she would do so only if her younger sister Myrtle Montgomery went along. Myrtle said that she would not go unless her older brother Sam also went. But Sam was working in the evenings, so Lula and Myrtle declined the invitation. Nelson apparently took the refusal in "good grace," but then he showed up at ten o'clock the next morning at the Beth-El Hospital laundry room where Lula and Myrtle both worked.[26] For over an hour, Nelson hovered over Lula, talking in low tones, following her around the laundry and never leaving her for an instant, pleading that she return to him and that they go to the dance that evening in Pueblo. With the constant noise of the washing machines and amid the busy activity of the laundry room, no one seemed to pay much attention to his presence. Exasperated and distressed, Nelson turned to Myrtle and demanded to know why Lula was refusing his invitation.

"I told him it was because my big brother could not go along," Myrtle said later.

"Was it because she wanted a protector?" Nelson tersely asked, to which Myrtle replied, "I suppose so."

"Well she will need better protection than that before long," Nelson retorted and rushed out of the laundry.

At precisely 11:30 A.M. on May 26, 1923, Nelson returned to the hospital laundry room and walked up to Lula.

"If I had a wife . . . " he started to say, but before he could finish, Lula interrupted, "But you haven't!"

Nelson promptly pulled out a 7.65 caliber German-made Werke automatic pistol and shot Lula in the head. As she collapsed to the floor in a pool of blood, Nelson fired a second shot that again exploded into her brain, and then a third shot that gashed into her heart. When laundry workers realized what had happened, everyone began screaming and rushing for the exits.

Myrtle shrieked out, "My sister! Oh, my sister!" Nelson calmly put the pistol to his head and pulled the trigger, the bullet entering the temple and blowing off the top of his head. Before he collapsed, he was able to pull the trigger again, but the revolver jammed. Nelson never regained consciousness and died six hours later.

As the Cobb family gathered on West Kiowa Street that evening, Myrtle, "dim-eyed and tearful," sobbed out the awfulness of what she had seen that day. "What a horrible thing!" she told a reporter for the *Gazette and Telegraph*, "what a horrible thing to have happen!" Six-year-old Joe Lee seemed dazed, unable to comprehend the tragedy, refusing to believe that her mother was dead.

"I'm glad he shot himself," she told the reporter through her tears and sobs. Grandma Cobb, her "eyes brimming with tears, vainly tried to comfort the little girl."

On Monday, May 28, 1923, Lula's body was taken from Swan and Sons Funeral Home and buried in an unmarked grave in Evergreen Cemetery. She was thirty years old.[27] That same day, Thomas T. Nelson, also thirty, was laid to rest in a separate grave.

At Leavenworth Joe Davis was beset with sorrow. He worried about his young daughter. What would happen to her without her mother? He pleaded with the warden for permission to send another telegram, this time to Lula's sister Myrtle. In Colorado Springs, Myrtle promised she would write Davis a full account of the tragedy, and she also promised that she and her mother would care for Joe Lee.

During Davis's early years at Leavenworth, family legend holds that when Sam Davis, Joe's younger brother, visited the prison, Joe tried to enlist Sam in helping him to escape, but Sam was scared and refused to see his older brother at the prison anymore.[28]

### Life in the Hard Joint

During Davis's first few years at Leavenworth, the prison was controlled by the deputy warden L. J. Fletcher, who ran the daily activities of the fortress from the inside. After 1920 Davis watched as the prison became congested and overcrowded as a consequence of the Volstead Act. Every year more and more bootleggers, rum runners, and big city gangsters arrived at the prison, and conditions grew worse.

No fewer than forty men were said to have found religion while at Leavenworth during Davis's first few years. The largest number of inmates were Catholics, Baptists, and then Methodists. But there were a few Mormons, some Spiritualists, Theosophists, Universalists, one Vendentist, and one "Holy Roller." Over 350 inmates said that they were "nonbelievers." Protestant Sunday services and a Catholic Mass were popular. If Davis did have a conversion to Catholicism following Lula's death, as he indicated in a form he filled out (assuming he was

FIGURE 21. A hand-colored Christmas card Joe Davis sent his daughter from Leavenworth.
*Author's Collection.*

sincere), he was certain to have fallen under the influence of Father A. J. Phelan or his assistant, Father Henry Courtney, who were assigned to Leavenworth. The priests were normally accompanied by two sisters from St. Mary's Academy in the nearby town. Fathers Pheland and Courtney conducted a Sunday Mass, heard confession, attended the sick, provided Holy Communion, and offered a special Christmas service.[29]

There was a day school for illiterates at Leavenworth, as well as an elementary school with curriculum for grades one through eight. Classes were taught by fellow inmates, who were sometimes given an extra meal as compensation. As many as 610 men took classes in auto mechanics, agriculture, poultry, history, typewriting, and shorthand. Some of the classes were taught by inmates, many of whom were college educated. It seems evident from the hand-colored birthday and Christmas cards that Davis sent his daughter that he took advantage of drawing classes. At the prison there were also language classes in Spanish, French, and Russian.[30]

Leavenworth was a Jim Crow prison. Black inmates lived in segregated cells, ate at segregated tables, and bathed in segregated showers. They sat in segregated bleachers at baseball games and boxing matches, and racial tensions were often inflamed during competitive sporting events.

Athletics, especially baseball, were always popular at Leavenworth, and there was no better team than the Booker Ts, a black prison team, four of whom would go on to compete in the Negro League. The Booker Ts often competed with a white prison team called the White Sox, and both teams frequently competed with military and town teams from as far away as Kansas City. All the games were inside the prison yard. On most Saturday afternoons and holidays beginning in April, the bleachers were packed with "men of good standing" who were allowed to attend and "forget their troubles for the time being."[31] Needless to say, there were no road games.

When Davis first arrived at Leavenworth, Congressman Charles D. Carter wrote on behalf of his friend Jack Davis, urging Warden A. V. Anderson to use "every consideration possible" to assure that Joe Davis was being treated fairly. A few days later Anderson responded, saying that Davis was "apparently getting along all right." He had transferred from the stone-cutting warehouse to the prison steel shop, where he was working seven hours a day and seemed content. The food at the prison was excellent and the prisoners' sleeping places sanitary and comfortable, the warden insisted.[32]

Joe learned from Thomas A. Flynn, the US attorney in Phoenix who was one of the men who had prosecuted him in Tucson, that his petition had been received at the Pardon Attorney's Office at the Department of Justice. Joe wrote to Pardon Attorney James A. Finch directly in January 1920, hoping that Finch might appreciate the "keen and tense anxiety in which I am." In Ardmore, Jack Davis hired local attorney J. H. Mathers to assist with the petition.[33] In fact, Jack Davis contacted every politician he thought might help obtain a pardon for his son. After the family moved to Ardmore in 1920, Jack Davis continued to press for Joe's release, spending a large portion of the money he received from the sale of the McCurtain County ranch and the family's Hugo home.

### Hopes for a Pardon

Congressman Charles D. Carter assured Jack Davis that he would do everything in his power to assist Joe. He wrote to Attorney General A. Mitchell Palmer asking that the Justice Department consider a commutation of sentence for Joe, offering to meet with Palmer in person in Washington if necessary. Palmer was too busy chasing Communists, Socialists, anarchists, and anyone he perceived as radical, however, and he paid Carter little heed.[34]

In May 1919 Jack and Bessie made their way to Leavenworth by train to visit their son. On their way back to Hugo they stopped in Muskogee, hoping to see US Senator Robert Latham Owen Jr. They wanted to persuade him to press the issue of obtaining a commutation or pardon with the Justice Department. Owen was the first senator from Oklahoma after the granting of statehood, and he was one of the most influential men in the country. In Oklahoma and in the Senate, Owen frequently represented Cherokee and other American Indian interests. The son of a Cherokee woman and a Virginia planter, Owen had worked as head teacher at the Cherokee Male Seminary in Tahlequah, and he had gone on to help organize the First National Bank in Muskogee. As senator he helped push Wilson's Federal Reserve Act and was influential in the passage of the Women's Suffrage Amendment.

Jack found Owen to be out of his office at the time, so he wrote to the senator pleading Joe's case for a pardon, emphasizing his Native American heritage, his young age, and the fact that he had been "arrested and tried away from home." Moreover, "Mrs. Davis is very anxious about this matter," Jack continued.[35] Owen sent Jack's letter on to James A. Finch, the pardon attorney in the Department of Justice, but all Finch did was to refer the request to the US attorney and asked for a report on the facts of the case.[36]

At the same time Jack Davis spent months and thousands of dollars lining up support in an effort to obtain executive clemency for his son. Those supporting the application included the governor of the state, the state representative from Stillwater, prominent bankers, oil and gas magnates, plus the county judge and county attorney from Pittsburg County. Jack even persuaded the pastor of the First Presbyterian Church in Hugo to write to Senator Owen on his behalf. Joe, who was from a good family, had the misfortune of having fallen in with the "wrong crowd of men & became one of them and into trouble," the pastor wrote.[37]

### A First-Class Fighting Man

The clemency request was also endorsed by several prominent citizens of Ardmore, including bankers, physicians, cattlemen, oilmen, a former sheriff, and prominent Oklahomans, even including policemen from McAlester. The principal chief of the Cherokee Nation, Victor M. Locke Jr., wrote President Wilson saying that Joe had been "unfortunate . . . at an early period in life," and that he "would make a first class fighting man." A livery stable groom in McAlester said that he heard

Bertholf confess he had "swore against Joe Davis to clear himself." Mayor of Muskogee J. E. Wyand signed an affidavit that Bertholf confessed to having lied at the Arizona bank robbery trial, as did the owner of a confectionary who related how Bertholf had bragged "how he came to get out of it" by "sticking Joe Davis."[38]

Jack Davis was able to enlist eighty-seven prominent citizens in Hugo, including the mayor, lawyers, bankers, salesmen, merchants, physicians, real estate agents, the chief of police, the county clerk, the county attorney, the county assessor, the superintendent of schools, along with farmers, clerks, barbers, grocers, and a Catholic priest, who all petitioned President Woodrow Wilson for clemency, saying that Joe Davis would make an excellent soldier.[39]

Jack Davis made sure that the Oklahoma press picked up on the story of how Joe Davis was hoping President Wilson would grant him clemency to give him an opportunity to go fight the Germans. "If Joe goes, he'll let the Germans know he's among the present," Jack Davis told the *Daily Oklahoman*. "All he wants is a chance to fight Germany." But Joe was only one of 1,246 young men at Leavenworth who had registered for the draft. Most said they were also eager to go to France.[40]

A justice of the peace in Muskogee wrote directly to President Wilson, saying that Joe was of "good blood and good family" who had fallen "in bad company." Joe was "absolutely honest . . . and as truly patriotic as any American boy." Moreover, Joe wanted to be "permitted to shoulder arms and go to the front in the defense of this, his country." President of the First National Bank in Muskogee H. H. Ogden encouraged the president to pardon Davis and "permit him to join the army." A cashier at the Commercial National Bank in Muskogee, G. T. Thompson, told the president that Joe was "a fearless young man" who had "always been sober," and if given a chance, he would "make a most excellent soldier." The president of the Exchange National Bank in Muskogee, N. M. Board, and his vice president W. T. Wisdom wrote Wilson to say that Davis was a "man of undoubted courage" and that there was "no more fearless young man in this country." Joe would make an excellent soldier and help "carry the American flag right to Berlin." Jack Davis also enlisted the support of the sheriff of Carter County, Buck Garrett, who wrote to President Wilson from Ardmore saying he was acquainted with Joe Davis and his family, and that he was convinced from what Jack Davis told him that Joe had been wrongly convicted in Arizona.[41]

Even veteran Oklahoma barrister Samuel Morton Rutherford, who had defended the Davises for almost a decade and knew as much about their transgressions as anyone in Oklahoma, joined the crusade to get Joe Davis out of prison. Rutherford told Senator Owen that he had a confidential talk with Jack Davis and was assured that Joe was innocent of the Arizona holdup, that Joe knew it was going to happen and he refused to join the party since he already had a charge against him. "I know of no finer specimen of manhood than Joe," Rutherford wrote. "He is strictly temperate, and I doubt if he knows the taste of whiskey. He does not use tobacco or gambles, and his conversation, as it has come under my observations, has always been clean." Moreover, Joe was "truthful and I believe I can safely say as loyal as any boy I ever knew." If Senator Owen could help secure a pardon, Joe could "go to the front."[42] Senator Owen immediately sent Rutherford's letter to Attorney General Thomas W. Gregory, who replied that "persons convicted of [a] felony cannot legally be enlisted into the army and will not be, even though pardoned." Bluntly put, the army wanted nothing to do with criminals.[43] All of Jack Davis's efforts seemed to be in vain.

When word got around eastern Oklahoma that Jack Davis was working day and night to get his son out of Leavenworth, there was an immediate reaction among peace officers and railroad workers. They did not want Davis in the army; they wanted him in prison. Postal clerks, in particular, objected strenuously. If Davis was released, there was little doubt he would "kill some innocent unarmed railroad postal clerk, or anyone else for that matter who might get in his way." Any petition to obtain Joe Davis's release should be "construed in the light of a camouflage." Counter-petitions with the names of 254 railroad workers—from track foremen and pipe fitters to firemen and conductors, from Kansas to Texas and beyond—all reminded President Wilson that Joe Davis was head of the gang that had held up the Santa Fe near Bliss on the night of October 18, 1916, and murdered Percy Norman. If paroled, Davis would undoubtedly "prey upon the good citizens of Oklahoma" once again. In the end, the pardon attorney for the Department of Justice responded that Davis's application would not be considered for another six years.[44]

### Never Giving Up Hope

Although guilt-ridden, in bad health, and running out of money, Jack Davis never gave up hope of somehow freeing his son. With the end of World War I in November 1918, he undertook new efforts to obtain a pardon for Joe. In doing so he enlisted James H. Mathers, county attorney in Ardmore, who wrote to Warden Anderson in November 1920 saying that he anticipated having Joe Davis pardoned in the near future. "We feel that Joe did not have a fair deal in his trial," Mathers wrote, "for he said he was not anywhere near when this unfortunate affair happened." Mathers knew the Davis family personally and said that they were "all very straight forward and law abiding people." In the meantime, perhaps Joe could become a trusty, Mathers suggested. Joe came from a "good family" and he would never violate the rules of being a trusty. Anderson would say only that Davis had "maintained a most excellent record since his incarceration." By late 1919, Joe was working as chief clerk in the package department, a position, Anderson insisted, that necessitated a large amount of trust and confidence. Joe was doing admirably well, the warden went on to say, and he was willing to provide a letter of good conduct should Mathers request it. Mathers responded that he would appreciate any favor shown Davis.[45]

Rutherford Brett, another attorney from Ardmore, also wrote Warden Anderson in an attempt to have Davis made a trusty. Brett did not know Joe Davis personally, but he knew the father and was familiar with the history of the "boy." Joe Davis would never "betray your confidence," Brett wrote. Anderson responded that Davis was being considered for outside work and that he had "maintained a most splendid record" while at Leavenworth. At the same time, Congressman C. D. Carter wrote again, pointing out that Davis was from a "good family" and that the "boy was highly recommended."[46]

Jack Davis continued to press for Joe's release. There were "no better people anywhere" than the Davis family, County Attorney Mathers insisted. Mathers was hoping that Congressman Ferris would go in person to see President Wilson, although the president was deathly ill and restricted to the upstairs of the White House. Ferris did write to A. Mitchell Palmer, the attorney general of "Red Scare" fame, only to be told there was little that could be done. Although disappointed, Jack persisted, again enlisting the support of Congressman Carter, his "friend," saying that he was going to make another effort "to get the boy out."[47]

Jack also turned to Senator Owen, saying that Joe had "made good in every respect." Davis was hoping that the senator could somehow get "Joe's sentence cut down." Jack wrote, "Please help me out a little if you can." In the Arizona train robbery, no money was taken, and all the harm done was that the mail was slightly delayed, Jack insisted. Moman Pruiett was drunk during most of the trial and never put a single defense witness on the stand, he argued. Pruiett had promised to appeal Joe's Arizona conviction and sent a telegram on April 14, 1917, saying he would arrive in Leavenworth in three days, but there was never any appeal and Pruiett, who was all bluster, never arrived at the prison. There was a major discrepancy between state and federal law, Jack pointed out. Punishment for obstructing the mail in Arizona was twenty-five years, while in Oklahoma it was only two years.[48] What Jack forgot to point out was that his son and Spurlock had been convicted in federal court, not state court, and they were found guilty of much more than just obstructing the mail.

Jack Davis also had some of his prominent friends contact Senator Owen. One individual wrote the senator to say that Bessie Davis was in ill health and "sinking fast." Her son's confinement had driven her almost mad. Bessie's personal physician in Ardmore confirmed that she had "chronic ulcers" that were caused by long periods of "brooding over her son's being in the prison." Bessie was a "good Christian mother" and could not survive much longer "unless she gets relief." Her bad health was aggravated by her "grief and anxiety" over her son's imprisonment, the physician pointed out.[49]

Jack Davis also enlisted the support of John William Harreld, the newly elected first Republican senator from Oklahoma. In 1920 Harreld had won election in the GOP landslide that swept Warren G. Harding into the White House. The senator contacted the federal pardon attorney, only to receive a rather terse response that repeated the often-heard refrain that Joe Davis was the equivalent of Jesse James.[50]

### Trusty

Joe Davis first wrote to Warden A. V. Anderson in August 1920, requesting that he be made a "trusty." Anderson did little more than scribble on the request, "matter under consideration," and place it in Davis's prison file. Five months later, on January 17, 1921, a new warden, William I. Biddle, perhaps acceding to Congressman Charlie Carter's consistent prodding agreed to make Davis a trusty and gave him outside privileges. Davis's new status was more the result of his heroism during a raging fire at the prison than from the deluge of letters on his behalf. Regardless, the Davis family were greatly relieved that Joe had "made good."[51]

Edward L. Halsell, the influential Muskogee entrepreneur, wrote Warden Biddle on January 8, 1922, disclosing that he was related to Davis but arguing nonetheless that Joe was of "good blood" and that he had simply got in "bad company." After quoting several lines of scripture, Halsell asked Biddle if he had a date when Joe might be paroled. Biddle responded immediately, relating how Davis had escaped and that his term would not expire until early 1942.[52]

### Escape and Capture

As a trusty Davis was assigned to one of the outside prison gates. Here, or somewhere in the prison, he fell in with Roy D. Sherrill, another trusty who was the chauffeur for the prison physician, Dr. A. F. Yohe. Sherrill was a notorious Kansas train robber who ran with Dale Jones and his gang of thugs who terrorized

Colorado Springs and Denver in 1918.[53] Davis would later say that the reason for his escape was that he needed to see his critically ill mother. Regardless, on the afternoon of June 22, 1921, the two men, with Sherrill at the wheel, sped away from the prison in Dr. Yohe's black Ford sedan, racing west across the Kansas grasslands, through Okaloosa, past corn and barley fields, and across the vast Kansas landscape.[54]

As soon as the car and the two convicts were reported missing, prison officials sounded the alarm. Warden Biddle found the escape embarrassing and a challenge to him personally, and he assured the attorney general that "every effort" was being made to catch Davis and Sherrill, that the two convicts would be "apprehended in a short time." A reward poster was prepared giving Davis's description as 30 years of age, 5 feet, 9.75 inches in his bare feet, weighing 159 pounds, with chestnut hair, light blue eyes, ruddy complexion, and of medium build. Davis was declared a "bad one," although the warden had made him a trusty only five months earlier. A one-hundred-dollar reward was offered for the apprehension of either of the escapees.[55] Telegrams describing the two as "notorious characters" who were expected to resist arrest were sent to police chiefs and post office inspectors in every town and city where Davis had relatives or associates or communities where there were individuals he had communicated with while in prison. These included the chiefs of police in Ardmore, Muskogee, Pawhuska, Broken Bow, Batesville, Tahlequah, Hugo, and Tulsa, Oklahoma, as well as Topeka, Kansas, Kansas City, Missouri, Tucson, Arizona, Birmingham, Alabama, Colorado Springs, Colorado, even Brooklyn, New York, and Los Angeles and San Francisco, California. Hearing that Davis had escaped, chiefs of police and post office inspectors in other cities and towns wrote for information. George E. Lewis, who had been the post office inspector in Muskogee at the time of the Wirth robbery, warned that Davis was a "bad man," who would not "hesitate to take human life, if it suited his convenience."[56]

Davis had "run away," Warden Biddle admitted, and he was sure he would try to reach his family back in Oklahoma, or perhaps friends in Sand Springs. But it was a photograph sent to G. A. Swallow, police chief in Topeka, sixty miles southwest of Leavenworth that paid off. The Topeka police were sweeping the city looking for a conman who swindled some migrant workers at the Rock Island depot. By accident, Davis happened to be walking by the police station and the police thought he resembled the description of the swindler. When they attempted to question him, Davis fled down an alley with the cops in close pursuit. Apprehended, he was taken to the police station for questioning. It was not until Davis's photo arrived from Leavenworth that the police realized they had captured a prison escapee. When shown his mug shot, Davis had no choice but to admit his identity.[57]

"Am very glad that we had the good fortune to capture one of your men," Swallow wired Warden Biddle. The stolen Ford was found two weeks later in Kansas City, Kansas. Sherrill, who was also serving a twenty-five-year sentence, was gone. Two years later Sherrill, who was going under the name of Homer Johnson, was caught in a "high powered" Cadillac along with two other gang members, while stranded in high water near Scipio in Pittsburg County, Oklahoma.[58]

### The Loneliness of Solitary Confinement

Handcuffed and shackled, Joe Davis was taken back to Leavenworth on the morning after his capture in Topeka. He was thrown into solitary confinement on the second floor of the isolation building, given only a tin cup and a sanitary bucket. Davis would remember the days and months that followed as his darkest times at Leavenworth. A twenty-five-pound iron ball was chained to one leg. Prisoners in solitary confinement were frequently handcuffed to the cell door during the day, except at noon when they were allowed to eat their ration of bread and drink water. If those in isolation misbehaved, they were forced to carry the ball and walk around a perimeter fence.[59] This was known as "carrying the baby." Most depressing of all was the fact that any hope of early release for good behavior was gone. With his escape Davis lost three thousand days of good time, amounting to eight years and four months. Moreover, forced to serve his full sentence, he could not appear before the parole board and would not be eligible for release until February 28, 1942.[60]

Prisoners in solitary confinement had it the hardest. As punishment, they slept on a board, and they were sometimes given a hammer and a pile of stones. If they broke the stones, they received rations for twenty-four hours; if they broke half of the stones, they received half the food. Bad behavior resulted in bread and water only once a day, and their letter writing and receiving privileges were restricted.[61]

Able to communicate with the warden several months later, Davis wrote to Biddle asking for an interview, saying that his parents and friends knew nothing of his "present affairs," and that they were preparing to start for Washington, DC, to ask that the Justice Department intervene in his case. When the news that Joe was in solitary confinement reached the Davis family, Bessie again sank into depression. She wrote Biddle inquiring as to the welfare of her son. Biddle responded two weeks before Christmas in 1921, saying that Davis had been involved in yet another escape, and that a revolver, bombs, and hand grenades were confiscated.

Davis had been released from solitary confinement, but because he was implicated in the escape plans, he ended up back in confinement again, although he strongly denied being involved in any plans to escape. "I have had a number of interviews with your son," Biddle told Bessie, and "he assures me that he intends to conduct himself in a proper manner from now on." He was in "good health and getting along about as usual." In all, Joe Davis would serve three years and six months in solitary confinement.[62]

### A Loving and Troubled Mother

Three weeks later Bessie wrote Biddle again, assuring the warden that she was positive her son was innocent. Jack had assured her Joe was innocent, Bessie said. Moreover, her son had also written to her professing his innocence. Joe was a kind boy, Bessie said, and the warden should call him into his office and talk to him. On March 1, 1922, she wrote to Biddle again, asking that the warden give Joe a "chance to be an ideal prisoner." She had no doubt that he was innocent and she was praying that he would have a chance to make good. Joe was "broken hearted" and was "innocent and did not know why they put the blame on him."[63]

The second week of January 1922, Biddle wrote back to Bessie, warning that the "men accused of being in the conspiracy to use dynamite and revolvers to force their way out" of the prison were "acting in a stubborn manner" and would be held in "segregation until the facts about this are fully known." Bessie responded two weeks later, inquiring how her "dear boy" was "getting along." "I pray you will help a mother," Bessie concluded.[64]

Every month Bessie wrote the warden, pleading for any news relating to her son and asking that he be treated humanely. Biddle finally grew impatient and would say only that Davis was in solitary confinement.[65] In early December 1922, Bessie wrote again, this time asking if she could send her son a Christmas box. She knew that Joe had been "accused of doing wrong and I have hoped and prayed that he might be able to clear up everything to show his innocence," she continued. Although she was "not for this world very much longer," she always "remembered my boy on Christmas . . . so please let me send him a box." Biddle responded saying a Christmas gift would be appropriate as long as prison guidelines were followed.[66]

Three months later, with the help of a Leavenworth attorney, Joe Davis filed for executive clemency. Davis was an "Indian man" and only twenty-four at the time of his conviction, it was argued. He had been twenty-five miles from the scene of the robbery in the Arizona desert. Moreover, Buck Bertholf had admitted that he lied in the Tucson trial, Joe pointed out, and the word of the army deserter was worthless. Moreover, "owing to the condition of his counsel he was not able to properly present his case." There were numerous credible witnesses with "good and valid evidence" that would prove his innocence. Pruiett, who was drunk a large part of the time, refused to call a single defense witness. There was no doubt he was denied the "services and advice of a competent counsel." Moreover, Pruiett had promised to appeal the case but he had never done so. "I was a stranger in Arizona," Joe went on to say.[67]

L. J. Fletcher, who had been deputy warden at Leavenworth before being transferred to the federal prison in Atlanta, Georgia, wrote Senator Owen in March 1923 relating how Joe had worked under his supervision in the package room at Leavenworth. Fletcher said that he found Joe to be trustworthy and honest, and his behavior excellent. He was a "nervy, dangerous man, but not a petty thief." Joe enjoyed the "confidence of the toughest element in the prison, and the respect of the better element." On one occasion he "prevented the most spectacular escape that was ever planned at the institution in which several lives no doubt would have been lost. From information furnished by him the firearms, ammunition, and other weapons to be used in the tragedy were found and confiscated." Davis was no "snitch," but he had been compelled to reveal the details of the planned escape.[68]

Joe's cousin in San Antonio, J. W. Barnes, even appealed to the assistant secretary of the Navy, Theodore Roosevelt Jr., who forwarded the appeal to Attorney General Harry M. Daugherty. In response, Daugherty repeated the catchphrase that had long been heard in the Justice Department, that Davis was equal to Jesse James.[69]

"Anything you can do to help get this boy out will be dearly appreciated," E. L. Halsell wrote Senator Owen in March 1923. A railroad agent also wrote to Owen, saying that he had always found Davis to be "truthful, sober and honest and a mannerly young man." On the other hand, the agent said, Buck Bertholf was "a low down thief and drunkard." With a flood of mail, Owen wrote Attorney General Daugherty, asking that "executive clemency be extended to Joe Davis."[70] Congressman Charlie Carter pressed the issue with the government pardon attorney, and again Davis was compared to Jesse James. Davis had no "equal as a cool, deliberate and rather nervy bank and train robber," and he had lost all his good time because of his escape attempt.[71]

## Getting Along All Right

In January 1926 Biddle wrote Jack Davis to say that Joe was "getting along all right" and that he was "obeying the prison rules." He had recently been released from solitary confinement and now had the privileges of a first-grade, well-behaved prisoner. Biddle was peeved, however, that Davis kept reminding him how lawyers and prominent family friends were in contact with the Department of Justice in Washington. Biddle said he would be happy to inform anyone in the capital that Davis was "getting along all right with us."[72]

In 1926 Thomas A. Flynn, who helped prosecute Davis in 1917, wrote to President Calvin Coolidge from Phoenix, saying that Joe had "been sufficiently punished for his crime." Eleven years and six months is a long period, Flynn wrote. "The deprivation of liberty for so long, coupled with all the discipline and mental anguish that such imprisonment entails, could in my judgment satisfy the demands of justice in his case." Joe Davis's ill health and the desire of his aged parents to have him returned to them "before death closes their eyes" was a compelling factor in asking for Davis's release, Flynn argued.[73]

He was imprisoned during the entire decade of the 1920s—known as the Roaring Twenties or Jazz Age, a decade of great prosperity—and it was as if history had passed Davis by. While at Leavenworth, Joe learned that Henry Starr had been paroled, and at the urging of friends Starr had entered the motion picture industry. He played himself in *Debtor to the Law*, a film about the double bank robbery in Stroud. The movie was an immediate success, and Starr went on to play major parts in two other movies. Starr made as much as fifteen thousand dollars from his acting. It was better than robbing banks. But the lawless side of Starr again took possession of him. On February 18, 1921, Starr and three other gangsters drove into Harrison, Arkansas, in a high-powered touring car to rob the People's State Bank of six thousand dollars. As Starr was fleeing, a former president of the bank shot him in the back, much as Paul Curry had done six years earlier. He was carried to the jail and the bullet was removed, but this time the wound was fatal. Starr died four days later. He died as he had lived. True to the code of the outlaw, just as he had done following the Stroud robberies, Starr refused to name his accomplices. In his final hours Starr boasted that he robbed more banks than any man in history. He was probably right. Starr's family took his body back to Oklahoma, where he was buried in the small cemetery at Dewey in Washington County, five miles northeast of Bartlesville.

Back in Oklahoma, Ethan Allen "Al" Spencer, whom Joe had ridden with for a while, continued the tradition of robbing banks and escaping on horseback. After pleading guilty of cattle theft, Spencer was sentenced to between three and ten years in the Oklahoma state penitentiary in McAlester. But in January 1922, Spencer escaped, robbed a bank in Pawhuska, and then another in the lumber town of Broken Bow in the far southeastern part of the state. Again, Spencer escaped. This time he hid in the Osage Hills, where friends and family brought him food. Spencer robbed several more banks, not only in Oklahoma but also in Kansas and Arkansas. Unlike Joe Davis six years earlier, he was successful in making the transition from escaping on horseback to fleeing in an automobile. Early in the morning of August 21, 1923, Spencer and several outlaws held up the Katy Limited near Okesa, eleven miles west of Bartlesville. They made off with fifty thousand dollars before fleeing into the Osage Hills. It was one of the largest train holdups in Oklahoma history—and it would be the last. Less than a month later, on September 15, 1923, US Marshal Alva McDonald, veteran lawman and personal friend of Teddy Roosevelt, at the head of a posse caught up with Al Spencer on a cold, drizzly night just north of Coffeyville, Kansas. There they shot him dead.[74] Two days later, his bullet-riddled body was put on display at a funeral parlor in Bartlesville. As many as five thousand people crushed in to get a look, among them Spencer's widow and his twelve-year-old daughter. In many ways, Spencer's death was the end of an era.

### Robert Franklin Stroud

A year before Davis arrived at Leavenworth, a sociopath named Robert Franklin Stroud, who had spent time at McNeil Island (as had Davis), killed a guard in front of twelve hundred inmates during the noon meal in the main dining room. Stroud was tried and sentenced to be hanged at the prison. A gallows was under construction behind the isolation ward when President Wilson commuted Stroud's sentence to life in prison. Considered too dangerous to be mixed with the general population, Stroud was placed in segregated quarters, where he remained most of his adult life. While at Leavenworth, Stroud found a broken nest of sparrows in an exercise yard near his cell. He not only nursed the sparrows back to health but also aided one sparrow with a broken leg by making a splint from a matchstick and a bit of thread. Wardens welcomed any form of rehabilitation that would keep prisoners from going "stir crazy," and Stroud was allowed to breed and accumulate as many as three hundred canaries. He was given an adjacent cell for his aviary where he operated a canary-breeding business and sold birds to the general public, accumulating half a ton of equipment and corresponding with two thousand bird owners and breeders. During World War II, Stroud was transferred to Alcatraz, where he gained a worldwide reputation as the "Birdman of Alcatraz."[75]

One of the most distinguished prisoners to arrive at Leavenworth while Davis was imprisoned there was the one-eyed William D. "Big Bill" Haywood, along with fourteen other members of the IWW or "Wobblies," who were convicted of violating the Red Scare–inspired 1917 Espionage Act. The group arrived in a special train under heavy guard on September 7, 1918. Released on bail Haywood fled to Russia and remained there until his death from diabetes and alcoholism in 1928. Half his ashes were buried in the Kremlin Wall, and the other half were sent to Chicago and buried near the Haymarket Martyrs' Monument.[76]

Another radical who was imprisoned at Leavenworth while Joe Davis was there was Cipriano Ricardo Flores Magón. Mexican anarchist, social reform activist, and leader of the Partido Liberal Mexicano, Magón was convicted of sedition under the Espionage Act for publishing an antiwar manifesto. Magón died at the prison on November 21, 1922. It has been speculated that prison guards beat him to death, although at the time of his death he was already suffering from diabetes and going blind. Although the Mexican Chamber of Deputies requested the repatriation of his body, Magón was buried in Los Angeles. In 1945 his remains were removed and entombed in the Rotunda de las Hombres Ilustres in the Panteón Civil de Dolores in Mexico City.[77]

In the fall of 1920 Jack "Lil' Arthur" Johnson, the former world heavyweight boxing champion who was convicted of taking a white woman across state lines for immoral purposes, arrived at the prison. Born the son of a slave, Johnson had knocked out James J. Jeffries for the heavyweight title in 1910. At the prison Johnson was assigned to the baseball yard as the caretaker, and he umpired a baseball game on his first day at the prison. On Thanksgiving Day 1920, Johnson entertained fifteen hundred fellow prisoners and five hundred visitors when he boxed ten rounds—six rounds with one boxer, and four with another.[78]

### Hanging at Leavenworth

While Joe Davis was in his last few years at Leavenworth, there was a rare hanging at the prison. Carl Panzram—a six-foot-tall, tattooed man with cold grey eyes—was one of America's most sadistic serial killers. He was hanged for beating a prison laundry foreman to death with an iron bar. An alcoholic by the time he was fourteen, Panzram said he "had no conscience, never believed in man, God, or the devil." Upon arriving at Leavenworth in 1928 he warned the warden, "I will kill the first man that bothers me." After being sentenced to death for the murder of the laundry foreman, the thirty-six-year-old convict refused any appeals. He was hanged on September 5, 1930. As guards attempted to place a black hood over his head, it was said that he spat in the executioner's face. When asked if he had any last words, Panzram blurted out, "Yes, hurry it up, you Hoosier bastard! I could kill a dozen men while you're screwing around."[79]

### Hopes for Clemency

On September 15, 1928, Joe Davis again completed an application for executive clemency that would amount to a commutation of his sentence. He tried hard to say the things that might evoke some degree of compassion, including the fact that he was part Cherokee. Joe claimed that, before Buck Bertholf died, he had filed an affidavit recanting everything he had said at the 1917 Tucson trial. Joe continued to insist he had nothing to do with the Arizona holdup. He was made a trusty in January 1920, he pointed out, but admitted he had "walked away" in June 1921, although he returned two days later. "For this act that occurred on the spur of the moment on account of my mother [being] low from a bad spell of fever and expected to die, and on account of not being allowed to go to see her," Davis confessed, "I tried to see her before it was to[o] late, and on account of my great love for my mother, as all loyal boys should be, I took the liberty to leave." He was "very sorry that it occurred."[80]

Both his parents were old and "in exceedingly bad health and both need my support," Davis went on to say. Should he be paroled, he would "go immediately to them to give the necessary support to make them comfortable as they are in destitute circumstances." Even his own health was "very much impaired," Davis pointed out, and he was "compelled to be checked in for treatment every two weeks." Moreover, he was "growing worse." Dr. C. A. Bennett, the prison physician, had diagnosed Joe with a "Recurrent Appendicitis," and his appendix was removed. But then Joe began suffering from chronic cholecystitis, an inflammation of the gallbladder because of gallstones that was causing severe upper abdominal pains.[81] "I do not believe I will live much longer," Davis wrote in his application. After his operation, he "layed [sic] at death's door for seventy two days and have never recovered and never will." His solitary confinement proved to be a "severe penalty" for "walking away to see my mother," Joe continued. Should he be granted executive clemency, he pledged to "always live an honorable life and as a law abiding citizen."[82]

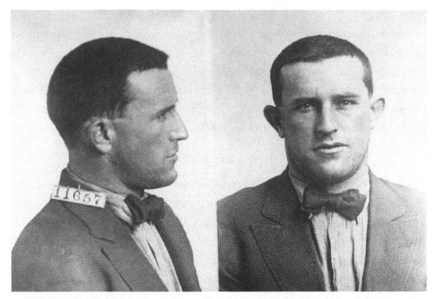

FIGURE 22. Mug shot of Thomas Jefferson Spurlock on entering Leavenworth Penitentiary, Kansas, in April 1917. Spurlock was released in July 1925. Spurlock worked for a while in Sioux City, Iowa, and then drifted west where he spent several years in the copper mines at Butte, Montana. Because of an escape in 1921, Davis was not released until 1931. *Courtesy of the National Archives, Kansas City, Missouri.*

In his hopes for clemency, Joe sent the application to Judge William H. Sawtelle in Tucson, asking the judge to endorse the application on the back and forward it to the attorney general in Washington. His application came from "the depths of my heart," Joe told the judge. "You have my solemn promise that I shall lead an honorable life and that you will never have cause to regret the performance of this Christian Deed."[83]

As the decade dragged on, the letters Joe received became fewer. His mother and father wrote regularly from Hugo and then from the small village of Berwyn, eight miles east of Springer, where the family had moved once again. They were now living on a small farm on the west bank of the Washita River.[84] Bad news arrived that Jack had suffered a stroke and was partially paralyzed. For the rest of his life, Jack would walk around dragging a leg.

In April 1930 Bessie, who was in constant anguish over the welfare of her son, wrote to the new warden, Thomas B. White, who had made a name for himself uncovering and helping to prosecute the Osage Reign of Terror murderers, complaining that she had not heard from her son in over a month. An assistant to the warden, N. R. Timmons, replied that he would tell Davis to communicate with his mother. Joe was now working as a hospital attendant, Timmons pointed out, and he was "getting along well."[85]

As Davis languished at Leavenworth, Jeff Spurlock was released on July 3, 1925. It was the day that Joe was originally scheduled to be released. After his release Spurlock traded in cowboying and train robbing for a more prosaic job working for the Sioux City, Iowa, water department. He eventually drifted west and took up a miner's pick in Butte, Montana. Davis never heard from him again.[86]

Less than two weeks after Davis filed his latest request for clemency, he was again in trouble, however. On September 15, 1928, guards were searching the electrical shop on the fourth floor of the shoe factory when they found various "contraband articles." An electric lock was attached to the door, which had to be forced open. Suspected articles included parts of a radio, a small knife, a razor blade with an attached handle, a belt made from leather belonging to the shoe factory, and a rope with pulleys and hooks attached. Since Joe worked in the shoe shop, he was immediately suspected. Once again, he was thrown into solitary confinement.[87]

Receiving the news of the latest incident, Bessie wrote Warden White, saying that Joe was "hurt and broken because he had been banished wrongfully." She assured the warden that Joe knew nothing about any escape plans and that he "would not want to hurt any of your people." Concerned that her "boy was under investigation," she was forced to conclude that White was mistaken because he was "a new warden" and did not know Joe "very well."[88]

### Decade Drags On

On October 1, 1928, Bessie again wrote to Warden White from Berwyn, wanting to know why she had not heard from her son. Joe had previously written that he was in bad health, and she was fearful that he was unable to write. Two days later White wrote to explain that Joe had been reduced to third-grade status and the rules allowed him to write only once a month. He assured her that Joe was not sick and was "getting along very well" and "everything is being done for his welfare consistent with our rules." At Bessie's request, the warden enclosed a photo of her son.[89] She responded immediately, thanking White for his letter but complaining that the image did not "look like the same dear boy" who had arrived at Leavenworth eleven years earlier. "You don't know how I regret his misfortune," she continued. Joe's father was in bad health, Bessie said, and the family worried when they did not hear from their son. Signing the letter a "loving mother," Bessie wanted to know what Joe had done to deserve being relegated to third class, also arguing that whatever he had done, she was certain it was "unintentional." White patiently responded that Joe had been caught with a number of contraband articles, "such as one would have in an attempt to escape."[90]

The warden reminded Bessie that Joe had escaped in June 1921, and had he not done so he would have been paroled in 1925. "I am indeed sorry of your and his father's condition," White wrote, and "I also regret his indiscretions which make it impossible for me to do anything for him." Davis had sent a note to the warden asking for an interview to explain his innocence and that of two other inmates regarding the contraband items. He said he was being punished for an offense that did not warrant such action. "I have violated no prison rule that would call for such drastic action," Joe pointed out. The warden agreed to hear Joe out, and on October 23, 1928, Joe presented his case to White. After a thorough examination, it was determined that Davis had nothing to do with the contraband articles, and he was released from solitary confinement.[91]

The country was now in the depths of the Great Depression, and the Davis family had lost most of their land and money. Thousands of dollars were paid to lawyer after lawyer who tried in vain to get Joe out of prison. Realizing that his family was suffering, Joe felt a great sense of loss and guilt. The Davis family had always been near the top of the Oklahoma economic ladder, and now they were close to the bottom.

Warden T. B. White was far more sympathetic to Davis's plea for parole or clemency than previous wardens had been. White became convinced that Davis would make a useful citizen, and he wrote Pardon Attorney James A. Finch to recommend that Davis be paroled. Finally, at a parole board meeting on October 31, 1930, Davis was granted a parole effective December 12, 1930. Because of a recent ruling of the attorney general that prisoners who had lost good time were not eligible for parole, the actions of the board were effectively abrogated. But prisoners could be paroled, providing their good time was restored.[92] Out of desperation Jack Davis turned to a prominent Muskogee County attorney and former Rough Rider, Loren G. Disney, who wrote the director of prisons asking for a restoration of Davis's good time. Both the prosecuting attorney and the judge who had sentenced Davis in Arizona agreed that Joe should be granted clemency. Edward Halsell, one of the wealthiest entrepreneurs in Muskogee, agreed to employ Davis as his personal chauffeur and to "take care and look after him upon his release," Disney pointed out.[93] Surely Davis had been punished enough.

## Bureaucracy beyond Imagination

In late November 1930, however, despite his previous recommendations for a parole, Warden White surprisingly wrote the Bureau of Prisons in Washington, DC, to say that he was not inclined to recommend the restoration of Davis's good time. "To make his way back" into civilian society, Joe would need some kind of "restraining hand . . . and the longer that we have that guiding and correcting hand, the better off this prisoner is and society," White argued.[94] In Washington, Pardon Attorney James A. Finch, under constant pressure to grant Davis parole, wrote to White recommending that the case be submitted to the attorney general, who could grant the restoration of the good time. Davis could not be released otherwise. But White would not agree unless specific conditions were met. "I do not want to make a recommendation for restoration of this man's good time," White bluntly told the attorney.[95]

Disney even went to Washington to appeal directly to the Department of Justice and to make application for Joe's release under the conditions that White was demanding. No sooner had Disney made application to the Bureau of Prisons than the bureau referred the matter back to Warden White at Leavenworth. White then took the matter up with the pardon attorney in the Department of Justice, only to have Finch refuse to submit the matter to President Herbert Clark Hoover.

Davis was caught in a never-ending cycle of Washington bureaucracy. He was in an almost impossible situation. But Disney was persistent and continued to pressure Warden White, pointing out that Davis was the youngest of the Arizona train robbers. Spurlock had been released on parole six years earlier, Disney argued, and few denied that Davis had been "sufficiently punished for the mistakes of his youth." If he was to ever have the "opportunity to make good in this life, he should be released as soon as possible."[96] But White refused to budge, telling Disney in a curt note that he could no longer be of any assistance.

Finally, in January 1931, Attorney General William DeWitt Mitchell sent President Hoover a six-page summation in the "matter of the application for commutation of sentence of Joe Davis." Mitchell summarized Davis's fourteen years at Leavenworth. He pointed out that after his escape Davis's conduct had been "exemplary" and highly "commendable." He had also "heroically assisted in saving property" after the disastrous fire in March 1919. Despite his own escape, he had "prevented the most spectacular escape that was ever planned in the Leavenworth Penitentiary." Although he had a "bad prior record" before arriving at the prison, his attitude as a prisoner "indicates reformation and he has the confidence and good will of the prison officials," it was concluded.[97]

## Commutation at Last

Three days later President Hoover agreed to a conditional commutation. On February 6, 1931, Joe Davis walked out of Leavenworth a free man. He gave his home address as Box 7, Springer, Oklahoma. Davis pledged to abstain from the possession and use of any intoxicating beverages; not to commit any crime; not to associate with persons of evil character; to lead an orderly, industrious life; to work where the superintendent of prisons directed; to report his residence the first week of every month; and to help support his family. The prisoner's personal items included $96.12, one gold ring, one watch, one watch chain, a compass, a knife, collar buttons, and a diary. Only hours after his release, Davis was on the Santa Fe train bound for Ardmore.[98] On the long road south, he is certain to have taken more than just a glance at the lonely spot on the prairie near Bliss where he and his gang had robbed the Santa Fe train on the night of October 18, 1916, and where Percy Norman had died such a senseless death.

→ ←

# EPILOGUE

## BACK HOME IN OKLAHOMA

Joe Davis was one of the last of [the]
really western men of the "gun man" variety.

— Newspaper clipping

**M**any in Oklahoma never forgot or forgave Joe Davis. His release from prison set off a firestorm among law enforcement officials across the state. The superintendent of special services of the Santa Fe Railroad wrote the warden at Leavenworth, incredulous that Davis was released. The chiefs of police in Oklahoma City and Tulsa also wrote, as did officials in Ardmore. Some asked for fingerprints and a photograph in case Davis again turned to crime.[1]

The Oklahoma that Joe Davis saw from a train window in 1931 was radically different from what he had known before the war. The desperate conditions of the people were evident everywhere. Along the railroad tracks and roads across the heartland of the country, through Topeka, Wichita, and Oklahoma City, there was devastation everywhere. Filthy children and men with hollow eyes and gaunt bodies huddled around bonfires and makeshift tents. Davis was horrified at what he saw. In the industrial heartland of America, 25 percent of the workforce was unemployed. In a few cities, unemployment ran as high as 80–90 percent.

The wind swept down the Oklahoma plains in great black blizzards that covered the sun and blew the topsoil away. Nature and the banks pushed the farmers off their land, and the great migration of Okies had begun. In McIntosh and Pittsburg

Counties, as many as a third of the population fled west to California.[2] In Berwyn, where the Davises lived, half the population headed west. Banks had seized many of the farms while other farms lay abandoned. Fields and farmhouses were in ruins. In the Dust Bowl that engulfed a large part of western Oklahoma, some farmers and their families died of dust pneumonia. It was a terrible time to be alive.

Four days after getting off the train at Springer and visiting his family, Joe wrote his parole supervisor that he was going on to Muskogee where the influential entrepreneur and politician Edward L. Halsell had promised him employment as a chauffeur or ranch hand.[3] Davis was sure that he could find employment somewhere, despite his criminal record. The Davises still had friends in high places. Well-to-do local cattleman Clem Vann said he could even get Joe a job as a deputy sheriff. After all, no one in the county was better with a gun than Joe Davis. Vann was the father of Virginia Vann Perry, who sixty-nine years later recalled seeing Joe when he first got out of prison. He was anxious to find a job, she remembered, and he refused to talk about his troubled past.[4]

Carlile Vowell remembered seeing Joe at Vann's house when Davis first arrived in Muskogee. "Last time I saw you, [you] were a busy man," Vowell remarked. Joe politely inquired as to when that might have been. "I told him it was when he was standing on the southeast corner of Pony Starr's house giving the bunch the devil," Vowell responded in an obvious reference to the deadly 1911 Porum gun battle.[5]

When Joe first arrived at Muskogee, several of his old friends came up to hug him and shake his hand. Many scarcely recognized him. He professed to have "no animosity against anyone." Yet memories of the bloody Porum Range War were still fresh in the minds of many in Muskogee County, especially the families in the southern part of the county who had lost loved ones in the violence. At Porum, moods were still intense, and Joe Davis was feared and hated.[6] Joe finally wound up in Sand Springs, just west of Tulsa on the north bank of the Arkansas River, where he went to work at the Sand Springs Home as a security guard—carrying a gun and wearing a badge.

### Sand Springs Home

The Sand Springs Home was the creation of the philanthropist Charles Page, who had once worked as a bellhop for a Wisconsin railroad. Page then made his way up the economic and political ladder of the Gilded Age to become a police chief, a Pinkerton detective, and a colonization agent for the Great Northern Railroad. He invested in mining, logging, and real estate but lost it all in the Panic of 1893. In Colorado he was successful in gold mining. In 1903 Page arrived in Tulsa, where he joined the feverish rush for black gold.[7] Four years later he began to realize his dream when he launched a diversified industrial community that would provide employment for laborers, as well as a place where orphans and widows with children could find peace and security. Page turned his eyes to a piece of land north of the Arkansas River where there were several clear sandy springs. In the years that followed, the Sand Springs Home and the town of Sand Springs took shape. The home became reality when Page rescued twenty-one pitiful orphans from a dilapidated orphanage in Tulsa. Three years after Charles Page died, Sand Springs was hit hard by the collapse of the stock market in October 1929. When Davis arrived in 1931, 20 percent of the Sand Springs workforce was unemployed.

The Sand Springs Home where Davis found employment was said to be the "most wonderful charitable institution hereabouts." Davis's employment was verified in a letter from James A. Harris at Sand Springs to James A. Finch, the pardon attorney at the Department of Justice. Harris wanted President Hoover and Attorney General Mitchell to know that Joe had "kept the faith" and that he would "carry on and continue to be an upright useful citizen." The sheriff of Tulsa County told Mitchell that Joe had become a "useful citizen and that his conduct has been above reproach." Davis was a "law 'biding man in every way." The general counsel for the Sand Springs Home, C. B. Stuart, also wrote to Mitchell, probably at Davis's request, saying that Joe was leading "an upright, law-abiding life" and had "developed into a fine citizen."[8]

While Davis was working for the Sand Springs Home, the community was hit hard by labor unrest when the National Textile Workers' Union tried to unionize the Commander Mills, one of the largest cotton mills west of the Mississippi. Beginning on Labor Day 1934 and lasting through the following year, strikes, shutdowns, bombings, and shootings were common in Sand Springs. The labor unrest did not ease until the National Guard arrived.

During his first few years at Sand Springs, Joe drove a company car. When time permitted, he made the long drive south to visit his parents at Berwyn. He also drove west through Osage County to Fairfax to see his teenage daughter. Joe Lee was living with her grandmother and attending Fairfax High School. Like so many other American families, the Cobbs were struggling to survive the Great Depression. After Lula's tragic death in Colorado Springs a decade earlier, Grandma Cobb and her son Johnny moved to the Osage country, where Johnny got a job as a chauffeur for Mollie Burkhart. It was in nearby Gray Horse a few years later that Johnny and Mollie married and lived happily for several years, until Mollie's unexpected death at the age of fifty in 1937.

### A Daughter Lost

Davis family legend holds that Grandma Phenie Cobb was "mean as hell" and a real "hell cat." Phenie told Joe not to come back unless he had money to help support the family. A few weeks later, Joe returned with money from his Sand Springs salary. Despite his efforts the two of them never got along. Once Joe asked for a photograph of his daughter, Joe Lee, but Phenie refused, saying he was a criminal and "not fit," and that he had "caused enough trouble already." Another time when Joe arrived in Fairfax, Phenie threatened to call the police. Joe later told his mother that he intended to use every effort possible to "get that girl away from that woman." But with a criminal record, there was little Davis could do. Joe tried to correspond with his daughter, but the letters came back "return to sender." Davis remembered his daughter as a shy young lady who was "scared to death" during the times he visited her.[9] When the Cobbs moved west to New Mexico in 1939, Joe gave up trying to see Joe Lee. In fact, he would never see her again.

Besides his job as a special agent at the Sand Springs Home, Davis was also in charge of a large cattle herd. Working with cattle seemed to be a natural instinct, and he loved the challenge. At the same time he took great pride in carrying a gun and wearing a badge. It was certainly strange for Davis to be on the other side of the law. He frequently roamed over both Tulsa and Osage Counties, where he held a deputy sheriff's commission. At times, it became necessary to "check, pursue and arrest law violators." Although peace officers in both counties held him in respect and a few of the older lawmen even admired him, he still found it embarrassing that many people knew he was a convicted criminal on parole. Because of this Davis was uncomfortable and complained that he did not have a "free hand." This "condition is not only embarrassing but in a measure [is] a handicap," he wrote. "I surely appreciate . . . that none other than the major officers ever may know of my past troubles," he went on to say.[10] For the rest of his life, Davis would struggle to keep his criminal record confidential.

Joe sought the support of Tulsa County sheriff Charles Price, who wrote to the attorney general, asking that Davis not be required to make his monthly reports. Davis had become a "useful citizen," Price pointed out, and had gained the "confidence of everyone who knows him." Harry T. Pratt, Joe's boss in charge of the Sand Springs Home, wrote the attorney general, also asking that Davis be relieved from having to make the monthly report of his whereabouts. Pratt pointed out that Davis was also helping to police the Sand Springs Railway, which operated a thirty-two-mile passenger and freight line to Tulsa. Joe has "made them a very good officer," Pratt went on to say.[11]

Besides the peace officers he befriended, Davis's only friends seemed to be some of the elderly cowboys in the area whom he had known before he went to prison. Perhaps his crowning moment came at an "Old Cowboy" reunion in Pawkuska, when he was given an appreciation award and a standing ovation.[12]

Joe's mother passed on to him eighty acres of rich Arkansas River bottomland near Webbers Falls that she had inherited from her family. It was in Webbers Falls that she and his father, Jack, first courted and married in 1888. From his Sand Springs salary, Joe was able to buy a few shares in the local bank in Webbers Falls, and he would often hang out in the town at the local drugstore, where a few old cowboys and settlers came by to talk and shake his hand. Remembering the violence of the Porum Range War, others shied away, and a few were "scared to death of him," one oldtimer remembered.[13] At times, his enduring reputation as a gunman and outlaw seemed to haunt him.

Not having time to work the farm in Webbers Falls, Joe leased the land to a man named Harley Cude, who farmed much of the property for the next fifty years. He grew corn, soybeans, and cotton. A tall, proud dirt farmer, Cude remembered Davis as a "very good fellow," an "awful good man . . . straight as he could be," and someone that "everyone respected." On his frequent visits to the "Falls," as Joe called the small community, Cude said that Joe was always dressed in khaki pants, and in winter he wore a long sheepskin-lined coat, under which he carried a big pistol. Joe would drive around the property and frequently lay the pistol on the seat of the car, which always made Cude nervous. Davis sold forty acres on a hill to Cude, where the farmer built a small house, a barn, and a small shed. For five thousand dollars Joe also sold ten acres to a "man who sold dope," and Cude remembered the man paying for the land in fifty- and one-hundred-dollar bills.[14]

The family that Davis found at the small village of Berwyn near Ardmore was very different from the family he had known before his incarceration. The Davises had sold their spacious home in Hugo and the large ranch in McCurtain County to help pay the legal bills incurred in their attempts to get Joe out of prison and to appeal Joe's and his father's convictions in the Wirth train robbery case. While he was in prison Joe also lost his 320 acres near Featherston that he had been so proud of. "The lawyers got it all," one family member recalled many years later.[15]

When Joe first got out of prison, Jack was sixty-six years old and fading fast. Bessie, now sixty-three, tall and white-haired, was also in ill health. Neither was able to do much of the work that the farm required. Seriously handicapped and only able to utter a few words, Joe's younger brother Jacy, twenty-six, stayed close to his father. His other brother, Sam, the war veteran, lived with the family for a while and did much of the work.[16]

## Marriage

Living comfortably in a white house in Sand Springs on North Main Street, Joe Davis married late in life. His bride was a widow, part Cherokee, and a distant cousin—Beulah, or as everyone called her, "Toots." Bessie for some strange reason had never wanted her son to marry, so for a while Joe kept his marriage a secret. For some reason Bessie even threatened to take back the land near Webbers Falls if her son ever married. His new wife, Beulah, kept her distance from the Davis family. One of Joe's nieces remembered her as being overly possessive and very protective of her new husband.

Less than two years after Joe was released from Leavenworth, Jack Davis, the indefatigable warrior who never quit fighting, either with a gun or in a courtroom, died quietly on January 5, 1933, at the age of sixty-seven. He was buried in Rose Hill Cemetery in Ardmore.[17] For several years he had spent a large part of his life conspiring with his son to rob banks and trains. He had then spent over a decade struggling to get his son out of prison. With the patriarch gone, the Davis family again sold their land and moved to twelve sunbaked acres near Springer, where they farmed and raised some livestock. In two decades the family had gone from being one of the wealthiest and most influential families in eastern Oklahoma to struggling to survive the worst economic downturn in American history.

Despite the death of her husband and her advanced age, Bessie was still the boss, and she clung to life with admirable vigor. Joe adored his mother, and she had never doubted his innocence. He always took the time to make the three-hour trip south to visit her during the Christmas holidays and always sent a card on Mother's Day. Bessie had almost gone mad with grief during her son's long incarceration at Leavenworth. Now in her old age, she developed cancer, suffered a series of strokes, and finally went blind. Bessie Satterwhite Davis died on February 22, 1953, at the age of eighty-five. Once more, Joe made the long drive south and watched with great sorrow as his mother was laid to rest beside his father in the family plot in Rose Hill Cemetery in Ardmore.[18]

Joe was given a gold watch when he retired from the Sand Springs Home in 1952. In the years that followed, he lived comfortably on the rent from the Webbers Falls property, his small pension, and his social security. One of his greatest joys was his little black bulldog who always slept at the foot of his bed. Several times a year Joe drove south to the "Falls" to check on Harley Cude and to make sure that the irrigation ditches on the property were cleaned. He worried about his younger brother, Jacy, and his other brother, Sam, who was trying to make a living on a few sparse acres near Springer.

## Growing Old

During his retirement Joe carried on a lively correspondence with his favorite sister, Caroline. Carrie was a real cowgirl, and she could ride as well as anyone he had ever seen. The two of them had ridden together as teenagers on the ranch near Texanna. At roping contests throughout eastern Oklahoma, Carrie was always Joe's biggest fan. In March 1959 he wrote her to say that it had snowed recently in Sand Springs, and that he had been down to Webbers Falls again. "I have no use of my left arm & hand at all and my eyes are bad," he confessed.[19] A stroke had left his arm hanging limp by his side, and he was now walking with a pronounced limp, using a cane. Joe could still see well enough to read and write, but he eventually lost the sight in one of his eyes and began wearing a black patch and using thick glasses. In late November of 1968, he wrote Carrie of having a good Thanksgiving in Sand Springs, although the weather was bitterly cold. Despite his age, he said that he had been down to the Falls where everything was "awfully muddy." But age was taking a toll on the old bandit. "I haven't felt very good this fall at all," he told his sister a few days before Christmas 1971.[20] The slender young man who had weighed 160 pounds when he entered McNeil Island Federal Penitentiary in 1917 had put on weight over the years and now weighed well over 200 pounds. In the end, he was confined to a wheelchair.

Joe Lynch Davis, one of the last of the Oklahoma outlaws, died at the age of eighty-six on July 15, 1979. He was buried on a green hillside in Woodland Memorial Park in Sand Springs. Few attended his funeral, and a Tulsa newspaper dismissed him in a few lines with no mention of his outlaw past. In other Oklahoma towns and villages, where he had wreaked so much havoc as a young man, no one seemed to notice his passing. To the end he refused to talk about his outlaw years, all the banks and trains he had robbed, and the dark and difficult days he had spent at Leavenworth. In the mountains of New Mexico, in the high country of the far Southwest, his only daughter, Jo Lee, who had feminized her first name, received the news of her father's death with considerable sorrow and sadness. A few years later she placed a shoebox full of family letters in the bottom drawer of an old dresser.

→ ←

# NOTES

### Prologue

1. David Grann, *Killers of the Flower Moon: The Osage Murders and the Birth of the FBI* (New York: Doubleday, 2017), 6–7. For a more scholarly study of the Osage murders, see Dennis McAuliffe Jr., *The Deaths of Sybil Bolton: An American History* (New York: Times Books, 1994). The McAuliffe study was republished as *Bloodlands: A Family History of Oil, Greed and Murder on the Osage Reservation* (San Francisco: Council Oak Books, 1999). For two of the more detailed newspaper articles on the subject, see Marilyn Mullins, "Oil Riches Brought Only Tragedy to Many Members of Osage Tribe," *West Texas Livestock Weekly*, December 10, 1970, 8–19; Mullins, "Bigheart Family Might Have Been Really Happy except for Oil Money," *West Texas Livestock Weekly*, January 14, 1971, 8–9.
2. Mollie's tombstone proclaims her to have been "a kind and affectionate wife and a fond mother and a friend to all." Anyone with any knowledge of the Osage murders is likely to sense great sorrow when visiting the well-kept cemetery at Gray Horse.
3. For a fictionalized version of Phenie Cobb's life, see M. J. Cobb Young, *Phenie's World* (West Conshohocken, PA: Infinity, 2005).
4. "Woody Guthrie" at http://woodyguthrie.rog/Lyrics/Oklahoma_Hills.htm [accessed March 16, 2015].

5. Ila Holley to Jerry, Don and Folks, September 19, 1952, author's collection.

6. Grandma Cobb to Dear Jo, September 19, 1952, author's collection.

7. Betty Ann Rushing to Jo Thompson, October 6, 1952, author's collection.

8. Rushing to Jo Lee, November 1952, author's collection.

9. Rushing to Jo Lee, 1952, author's collection.

10. Aunt Ila and Grandmother to Joe Lee, November 19, 1952, author's collection.

11. Bet[ty] to Jo Lee, December 11, 1952, author's collection.

12. Bet[ty] to Hi Folks, October 4, 1963, Bet[ty] to Jo Lee, July 19, 1979; both in author's collection.

13. Christmas card, n.d., author's collection.

14. Jo Lee to Bet and All, July 23, 1982, author's collection.

15. Lula to H. Holley, April 5, 1923, author's collection.

16. Lula to Hello Kids, May 6, 1923, author's collection.

17. Telegram, May 26, 1923, author's collection.

18. Twauna Scoggin, interview by author, December 24, 2003.

19. Olivia E. Myers, "The Porum Range War," *True West* 19 (July–August 1971): 48.

20. Virginia Vann Perry, interview with author, July 14, 2000.

21. Virginia Vann Perry, interview with author, July 14, 2000; Theda Perdue, "The Conflict Within: The Cherokee Power Structure and Removal, 1838–1839," *Georgia Historical Quarterly* 73 (Fall 1989): 478–79, 488.

22. The only meaningful studies of the Porum Range War remain Myers's article "The Porum Range War," in *True West* 19 (July–August 1971): 6–14, 42–48, and Frankie Sue Gilliam, "Hell's Half Section: The Porum Range War Feud," *Twin Territories* (Muskogee) 7 (2000): 6, 16.

23. Jerry Thompson, "'That's Just What Kids Did Back Then': Joe Lynch Davis, the Oklahoma Gang, and the Robbery of the Golden State Limited," *Journal of Arizona History* 42, no. 4 (Winter 2001): 409–28.

24. Attorney General to Theodore Roosevelt Jr., October 16, 1923, Joe Davis Pardon File, Records of the Bureau of Prisons, Department of Justice, Record Group 129, National Archives, Washington, DC (hereafter Davis Pardon File, RG 129, NA). The quote seems to have originated with Thomas A. Flynn in a parole report dated May 3, 1917, and was repeated in Pardon Attorney to Senator J. W. Harrold, March 7, 1922; all in Joe Davis Pardon File, RG 129, NA.

25. Thomas A. Flynn, parole report, May 3, 1917, Joe Davis Pardon File, RG 129, NA; Miscellaneous newspaper clipping, Joe Davis Inmate File (11656), Leavenworth Penitentiary, Bureau of Prisons, Record Group 129, National Archives, Kansas City, Missouri (hereafter Davis Inmate File, Leavenworth, RG 129, NAKC).

26. *Journal of the American Bankers' Association: Bulletin of the American Institute of Banking, Sections Two, Protective Department* 10 (July 1917): 8. Copy courtesy of the University of Minnesota, Minneapolis.

## 1. Death at a Gate by a Cornfield

*Epigraph. Muskogee Times-Democrat*, May 3, 1907.

1. For the Davis family, see Don L. Shadburn, *Upon Our Ruins: A Study in Cherokee History and Genealogy* (Cummings, GA: Cottonpatch Press, 2012).

2. Some of the better scholarly studies of the Cherokee include Robert Conley, *The Cherokee Nation: A History* (Albuquerque: University of New Mexico Press, 2007); Rose Stremlau, *Sustaining the Cherokee Family: Kinship and the Allotment of an Indigenous Nation* (Chapel Hill: University of North Carolina Press, 2011); Thomas E. Mails, *The Cherokee People: The Story of the Cherokees from Earliest Origins to Contemporary Times* (Tulsa: Council Oak Books, 1992); John Ehle, *Trail of Tears: The Rise and Fall of the Cherokee Nation* (New York: Doubleday, 1988); John R. Finger, *The Eastern Band of Cherokee, 1819–1900* (Knoxville: University of Tennessee Press, 1984); Finger, *Cherokee Americans: The Eastern Band of Cherokees in the 20th Century* (Knoxville: University of Tennessee Press, 1991); William G. McLoughlin, *Cherokee Renascence in the New Republic* (Princeton, NJ: Princeton University Press, 1992); Julie L. Reed, *Serving the Nation: Cherokee Sovereignty and Social Welfare, 1800–1907* (Norman: University of Oklahoma Press, 2016); Gregory D. Smithers, *The Cherokee Diaspora: An Indigenous History of Migration, Resettlement, and Identity* (New Haven, CT: Yale University Press, 2015); Circe Sturm, *Blood Politics: Race, Culture, and Identity in the Cherokee Nation of Oklahoma* (Berkeley: University of California Press, 2002); Fay A. Yarbrough, *Race and the Cherokee Nation: Sovereignty in the Nineteenth Century* (Philadelphia: University of Pennsylvania Press, 2008); William G. McLoughlin, *After the Trail of Tears: The Cherokees' Struggle for Sovereignty, 1839–1880* (Chapel Hill: University of North Carolina Press, 1993); Andrew Denson, *Demanding the Cherokee Nation: Indian Autonomy and American Culture, 1830–1900* (Lincoln: University of Nebraska Press, 2004).

3. Members of the Davis family are enumerated on rolls of the Eastern Cherokee compiled after the removal period. See, for example, Mullay, Siler, and Chapman rolls, Records of the Bureau of Indian Affairs (BIA), RG 75, NA.

4. Gary E. Moulton, *John Ross: Cherokee Chief* (Athens: University of Georgia Press, 1982), 8–33.

5. Shadburn, *Upon Our Ruins*, 55. In addition to his children with Saphronia Tate, John had children by at least two other women, both before and during his marriage.

6. For Davis Crossroads, see www.chickamaugacampaign.org/pdfs/daviscrossroads .htm [accessed December 24, 2016].

7. Seventh Census (1850), Slave Schedules, Walker County, Georgia, Bureau of the Census, RG 29, NA.

8. Eighth Census (1860), Walker County, Georgia, RG 29, NA.

9. Shadburn, *Upon Our Ruins*, 51. Children included George A., Samuel, Susanna, Daniel, Cicero, Jane S., and Robert.

10. Jeremiah C. Donahower Papers at the Minnesota Historical Society library, St. Paul, Minnesota, at http://www.chickamaugacampaign.org/pdfs/daviscrossroads.htm [accessed December 24, 2016].

11. Mary Davis to Susan Davis, March 6, 1864, in Jeremiah C. Donahower Papers, http://www .chickamaugacampaign.org/pdfs/daviscrossroads.htm [accessed December 24, 2016].

12. Smithers, *Cherokee Diaspora*, 177.

13. Ninth Census (1870), Walker County, Georgia, RG 29, NA.

14. Smithers, *Cherokee Diaspora*, 182, 188, 195.

15. Smithers, *Cherokee Diaspora*, 196.

16. Shadburn, *Upon Our Ruins*, 54–55, quoting Cherokee Citizenship Records, BIA, RG 75, NA.

17. Tenth Census (1880), Walker County, Georgia, RG 29, NA.

18. Mrs. Cicero Davis, Dawes Case No. 9829, RG 48, NA.

19. Gary L. Thompson, "Changing Transportation Systems of Oklahoma," in John W. Morris, ed., *Geography of Oklahoma* (Oklahoma City: Oklahoma Historical Society, 1977), 116–17.

20. Dawes Packet Case No. 10133, at www.footnote.com/image/143852162 [accessed December 24, 2016]. A distant relative living near Texanna was Stand Watie Davis and his son Jeff Davis.

21. Looking for Native American trading partners, the French explorer Jean Baptiste Bernard, Sieur de la Harpe, passed through the area in 1719. Charles Robert Goins and Danney Goble, *Historical Atlas of Oklahoma* (Norman: University of Oklahoma Press, 2006), 38–38.

22. *Porum Press*, March 3, 1911.

23. Several towns in Oklahoma acquired their names by combining part of the word "Texas" with other syllables, but how the "anna" was added to "Tex" remains a mystery.

24. Susan Toney, interview, *Indian Pioneer Papers*, 112:344–45, and Richard Wilkerson, interview, *Indian Pioneer Papers*, 104:63; both in Western History Collection, University of Oklahoma, Norman.

25. *Polk's Indian Territory Gazetteer, 1902–03* (Chicago: R. L. Polk, 1903), 613; Elijah Cooper, interview, *Indian Pioneer Papers*, 2:196–99; H. A. Scott to Carolyn Thomas Foreman, March 22, 1951, Grant Foreman File, Oklahoma Historical Society, Oklahoma City; Carolyn Thomas Foreman, "Texanna," *Chronicles of Oklahoma* 31, no. 2 (Summer 1953): 179.

26. Lattie David Ogden, interview, *Indian Pioneer Papers*, 107: 261.

27. Lattie David Ogden, interview, *Indian Pioneer Papers*, 107:261–63. Checotah was named after Samuel Checote, a Creek chief who had been a lieutenant colonel with the Creek Mounted Volunteers in the Confederate Army during the Civil War, and who was elected principal chief of the tribe after the war.

28. Dawes Packet Case No. 10133, RG 75, NA. A relative, J. J. Vann, testified that he presided over the marriage.

29. Mattie Lorraine Adams, *Family Tree of Daniel and Rachel Davis* (Duluth, GA: Claxton Printing, 1973).

30. Records of the Bureau of the Census: US Population Schedules for 1850, 1860, 1870, 1880, Walker County, Georgia, RG 29, NA. See also http://person.ancestry.com /tree/157156/person/1206245773/facts [accessed December 22, 2016].

31. Miscellaneous newspaper clipping (probably a Muskogee newspaper), June 22, [1912], in Fred S. Barde Papers, Oklahoma Historical Society, Oklahoma City, Oklahoma (hereafter cited as Barde Papers, OHS).

32. Goins and Goble, *Historical Atlas*, 139.

33. Dawes Packet, CD 1127, Department of the Interior, Commission to the Five Civilized Tribes, March 20, 1902, RG 75, NA (hereafter Dawes Packet, CD 1127); Thirteenth Census (1910), Muskogee County, Oklahoma, RG 29, NA.

34. Dawes Packet, CD 1127. This particular packet can be viewed at www.footnote.com /image/143852162 [accessed December 23, 2016].

35. Dawes Packet, CD 1127. www.footnote.com/image/143852162 [accessed December 23, 2016]. See also Mrs. Cicero Davis, Dawes Case No. 9829 (testimony taken February 21, 1901), RG 48, Records of the Secretary of the Interior, NA.

36. *Index and Final Rolls of Citizens and Freedmen of the Cherokee Tribe in Indian Territory* (Washington, DC: Secretary of the Interior, 1907), 45. See also Dawes packet at www .footnote.com/image/205320670 [accessed December 24, 2016]. The family's listing on rolls of the "Eastern Cherokee Residing West of Mississippi River" can be seen at www.footnote.com/image/143852162 [accessed December 24, 2016].

37. Dawes Packet, CD 1127, Department of Interior, RG 75, NA; Thirteenth Census (1910), Muskogee County, Oklahoma, RG 29, NA. In 1878 Bessie's mother, Susan C. Vance, died when she was only eleven. Her father, Richard, died in 1886, when she was eighteen, shortly before the family moved to Indian Territory.

38. Twelfth Census (1900), Muskogee County, Oklahoma, RG 29, NA; Dawes Packet at www.footnote.com/image/143852162 [accessed December 24, 2016].

39. Under the terms of the Reconstruction Treaty of July 16, 1866, the government sold a tract of land about two and a half miles wide and lying along the Thirty-Seventh parallel in Kansas and opened it to would-be wheat farmers. In 1892 the government purchased the Cherokee Outlet for eight and a half million dollars, which led to the opening by run of the Cherokee Outlet on September 16, 1893. Goins and Goble, *Historical Atlas*, 60–61, 98.

40. Jack Davis, Application (9684), June 7, 1907, Eastern Cherokee Applications of US Court of Claims, 1908–1909, BIA, RG 75, NA. See also Shadburn, *Upon Our Ruins*, 46–49, 659–62.

41. Guion Miller to Jack Davis, June 19, 1909, in Jack Davis Eastern Cherokee Application, RG 75, NA.

42. "Township Maps of the Cherokee Nation," Township 10 North, Range 17 East, Muskogee Public Library, Muskogee, Oklahoma.

43. "Township Maps of the Cherokee Nation," Township 11 North, Range 19 East, and Township 10 North, Range 19 East.

44. Twelfth Census (1900), Muskogee County, Oklahoma, RG 29, NA.

45. Ellen Collins Johnson, "Porum," *The Encyclopedia of Oklahoma History and Culture*, www.okhistory.org [accessed October 17, 2017]. See also Thomas E. Shugart to Dear Sirs, June 2, 1994, "Porum File," Oklahoma Historical Society, Oklahoma City, Oklahoma.

46. *Porum Press*, February 2, 1907. See also *Muskogee Phoenix*, July 1, 1904; *R. L. Polk & Co's Oklahoma State Gazeteer* (Chicago: R. L. Polk, 1909), 677; Thomas E. Shugart to Dear Sirs, June 2, 1994, in Porum file, Grant Foreman Collection, Oklahoma Historical Society, Oklahoma City, Oklahoma.

47. Victoria Sheffler, archivist at the John Vaughan Library at Northeastern State University in Tahlequah, must be acknowledged for her detective work in identifying the building in the background of the photograph. V. Sheffler to author, June 29, 2005, author's files.

48. *Hartshorne Sun*, April 1, 1909. In one game, Jones Academy beat Bacone Indian University by a score of seven to two. For a history of Jones Academy, see J. N. Kagey, "Jones Academy," *Chronicles of Oklahoma* 4, no. 10 (December 1926): 338–39. No records of Jones Academy or the Baptist Cherokee Mission at Tahlequah survive for the time when Joe Davis was enrolled.

49. Sixteenth Census (1940), Tulsa County, Oklahoma, RG 29, NA.

50. *Muskogee Times-Democrat*, July 26, 1907. In 1885, not long after he first came to the Indian Territory, Cicero lived with a Cherokee woman named Annie Wilson, and they had a daughter and a son. Shortly after the birth of his son, however, Cicero deserted his Cherokee lover and married Sidney Whisenhunt. After her husband's death, Sidney Whisenhunt married a lawyer named M. T. Sharp. When his first family learned they were not included in Davis's will, Annie (Wilson) Eschback and her children sued in Fort Smith, Arkansas, seeking their share of the Davis estate valued at almost one hundred thousand dollars. Annie Eschback argued that she and Cicero had agreed to live as man and wife. Moreover, Cicero had seen to the education of their daughter, Willie, at the Cherokee Female Seminary in Tahlequah; Willie later married Thomas Bruce "Spy" Starr. *Checotah Times*, January 28, 1901, September 19, 1906; *Ardmore Daily Ardmoreite*, January 27, 1910.

51. *Checotah Enquirer*, August 11, 1905.

52. Elijah Cooper, interview, *Indian Pioneer Papers*, 2:196–99.

53. *Muskogee Phoenix*, August 3, 1894.

54. Lucinda Starr died unexpectedly on April 26, 1908, and was buried in the Starr Cemetery in the woods just west of Briartown.

55. Thirteenth Census (1910), Muskogee County, Oklahoma, RG 29, NA. See also Wally Watts, "Cassie Starr, Heroine," *Muskogee Phoenix*, October 18, 2007, http://muskogeephoenixonline.com/blogs/WallyWatts/2007/10,carrie-star-heroine.html [accessed March 15, 2016].

56. W. A. Arnold, interview, *Goingsnake Messenger* (Colcord, OK) 19, no. 3 (2002): 67–68.

57. All quotes from O. C. Pierce, T. J. Butler, and Geo. F. Lewis to Inspector in Charge, April 7, 1917, Davis Inmate File, Leavenworth, RG 129, NAKC. See also Fort Smith Criminal Case Files, 1866–1900, Cicero Davis, 1884, US District Court, Western District of Arkansas, Fort Smith Division, Case file 12236, National Archives Fort Worth (NAFW); George Weaver, interview, *Indian Pioneer Papers*, vol. 96, 35–36; "Township Maps of the Cherokee Nation," Township 10 North, Range 17 East, Muskogee Public Library, Muskogee, Oklahoma; "Township Maps of the Cherokee Nation," Township 11 North, Range 19 East, and Township 10 North, Range 19 East.

58. Zoe Agnes Tilghman, *Outlaw Days: A True History of Early-Day Oklahoma Characters* (Oklahoma City: Harlow, 1926), 1.

59. Glenn Shirley, *Marauders of the Indian Nation: The Bill Cook Gang and Cherokee Bill* (Stillwater: Barbed Wire Press, 1994), 16, 32–33, 44, 67–71, 106–11, 146.

60. Elijah Conger, interview, *Indian Pioneer Papers*, Vol. 11.

61. *Muskogee Phoenix*, June 24, December 23, 1897.

62. Twelfth Census (1900), Muskogee County, Oklahoma, RG 29, NA.

63. *Muskogee Daily Phoenix*, June 4, 1911.

64. Neither Hufman nor Seehorn appears on the Indian Territory census for 1880 or 1900. Only a James Cewborn, eighty-eight, who does not appear to be one of the victims, was living at Sulphur Springs in the Chickasaw Nation in 1880. Tenth Census (1880), Chickasaw Nation, Indian Territory, NA.

65. *Muskogee Daily Phoenix*, June 4, 1911.

66. *Checotah Enquirer*, October 12, 1906. Many of the ads appeared after Cicero Davis's murder, perhaps in an attempt to influence jurymen and public opinion.

67. The 1900 Indian Territory census shows a George W. Spivey, an Alabama-born tenant farmer and boarder with Mac Alford. Most Oklahoma newspapers list the victim as J. M. Spivey, however. Twelfth Census (1900), Township 11 north, 18 east, Cherokee Nation, Indian Territory, RG 29, NA.

68. Frank W. Jones, interview, *Indian Pioneer Papers*, Vol. 31:481; F. W. Jones, *The Experiences of a Deputy U.S. Marshal in the Indian Territory* (Muskogee: Starr-Hill Association, 1937), 14.

69. *Muskogee Times-Democrat*, September 13, 1906.

70. *Checotah Times*, February 22, 1907; *Muskogee Times-Democrat*, September 26, 1906, May 2, 1907.

71. *Muskogee Times-Democrat*, July 26, 1907.

72. *Muskogee Times-Democrat*, September 26, 1906.

73. *Checotah Enquirer*, September 19, 1906.

74. *Muskogee Times-Democrat*, May 1, 2, 1907; *Council Hill Eagle*, September 27, 1906.

75. *Muskogee Times-Democrat*, September 26, 1906.

76. *Muskogee Times-Democrat*, September 18, 1906.

77. *Muskogee Times-Democrat*, September 12, 1906. See also *Checotah Enquirer*, September 19, 1906.

78. *Checotah Times*, February 22, 1907. See also *New State Tribune* (Muskogee), January 31, 1907.

79. *Muskogee Times-Democrat*, September 28, 1906.

80. *Checotah Times*, February 22, 1907.

81. *Checotah Times*, February 22, 1907; *Muskogee Times-Democrat*, September 28, 1906.

82. *Checotah Times*, September 28, 1906.

83. *Muskogee Times-Democrat*, September 13, 1906.

84. *Muskogee Times-Democrat*, September 13, 1906.

85. *Muskogee Times-Democrat*, September 13, 1906.

86. *Muskogee Times-Democrat*, September 13, 1906. Much of King's testimony is repeated in the second trial in Muskogee and reported in the *Checotah Times*, May 10, 1907.

87. *Muskogee Times-Democrat*, September 13, 1906.

88. *Checotah Times*, March 1, 1907.
89. *Checotah Times*, March 1, 1907.
90. *New State Tribune* (Muskogee), March 7, 1907.
91. *Muskogee Times-Democrat*, May 2, 1907.
92. *Muskogee Times-Democrat*, May 2, 1907.
93. *Muskogee Times-Democrat*, May 3, 1907; *Checotah Times*, May 10, 1907.
94. *Muskogee Times-Democrat*, May 4, 1907.
95. *Muskogee Times-Democrat*, May 6, 1907.
96. *Muskogee Times-Democrat*, May 6, 1907; *Checotah Times*, May 10, 1907.
97. *Muskogee Times-Democrat*, May 7, 1907. For Dunlap, see *Muskogee Daily Phoenix*, April 26, July 10, 1904, September 7, 1905.
98. *New State Tribune*, June 18, 1907.
99. *New State Tribune*, May 16, 1907.
100. *New State Tribune*, June 18, 1907.
101. *New State Tribune*, July 4, 1907.
102. *New State Tribune*, July 4, 1907.
103. *Muskogee Times-Democrat*, July 5, 1907.
104. *Porum Press*, July 27, 1907.
105. *Muskogee Times-Democrat*, July 5, 1907. See also *Muskogee Times-Democrat*, July 11, 1907; *Muskogee Tri-State Tribune*, July 25, 1907; *Council Hill Eagle*, July 25, 1907; *Ardmore Daily Ardmoreite*, July 27, 1907; *Porum Press*, July 27, 1907.
106. *Porum Press*, July 27, 1907.
107. *Porum Press*, July 27, 1907.
108. *Porum Press*, October 16, 1907.
109. For a biographical sketch of Starr, see http://www.findagrave.com/cgi-bin /fg.cgi?page=gr&GRid=42327271. See also *Shawnee Daily Herald*, July 30, 1910; *Ralston New Era*, November 10, 1910; *Muskogee Times-Democrat*, May 5, 1911.
110. *Enid Events*, November 13, 1908.
111. *Muskogee Times-Democrat*, November 5, 1908.
112. *Muskogee Times-Democrat*, November 4, 1908.
113. *Muskogee Times-Democrat*, November 6, 1908; *Daily Admoreite*, November 8, 1908; *Edmond Enterprise*, November 12, 1909; *Davis News*, November 12, 1908. Newspapers throughout Oklahoma ran stories on the trial. See *Talala Gazette*, November 12, 1908; *Luther Register*, November 13, 1908; *Enid Events*, November 13, 1908; *Foss Enterprise*, November 13, 1908; *Weekly Examiner* (Bartlesville, OK), November 13, 1908; *Gatebo Gazette*, November 13, 1908; *Canute Leader*, November 16, 1908.
114. *Muskogee Times-Democrat*, November 6, 1908.
115. *Muskogee Evening News*, February 17, 1909.
116. *Muskogee Daily Phoenix*, August 8, 9, 1954. Hester died at the age of eighty-three on August 7, 1954. His tombstone has his birth date as January 16, 1871. Hester was married to Lillie Bell Reynolds. At the time of his death the Hesters had two daughters, seven grandchildren, and ten great-grandchildren. See also Hester Tombstone, Memorial

Park Cemetery, Muskogee, Oklahoma; Fifteenth Census (1930), Muskogee County, Oklahoma, NA.

117. *Twin Territories* (Muskogee) 7 (2000): 7.

## 2. The Bloody Porum Range War

*Epigraph. McAlester News Capital*, May 30, 1911.

1. *R. L. Polk and Co.'s Oklahoma Gazeteer*, 787–88.

2. Ninth Census (1870), Fannin County, Texas; Billie Louise Gilbert Edlin, *Cobb Cousins* (Odessa: N.p., n.d.), 144.

3. Edlin, *Cobb Cousins*, 145.

4. W. R. Mulkey, interview, *Indian Pioneer Papers*, 65:365–66.

5. Ninth Census (1870), Robertson County, Tennessee, NA; Twelfth Census (1900), Johnson County, Arkansas, NA; Thirteenth Census (1910), McIntosh County, Oklahoma, NA; Fourteenth Census (1920), Okmulgee County, Oklahoma; Young, *Phenie's World*, 200–210.

6. Betty Rushing, interview with author, July 15, 2000.

7. Norman Arthur Graebner, "History of Cattle Ranching in Eastern Oklahoma," *Chronicles of Oklahoma* 21 (September 1943): 300–311.

8. *Anti–Horse Thief Association (AHTA) Weekly News* (St. Paul, KS), May 23, 1912.

9. *AHTA Weekly News*, May 11, 1911.

10. *Muskogee Times-Democrat*, May 6, 1911.

11. Jerry Rand, "Samuel Morton Rutherford," *Chronicles of Oklahoma* 30, no. 2 (1952): 150 (quotes), also 155.

12. Rand, "Samuel Morton Rutherford," 151.

13. Rand, "Samuel Morton Rutherford," 152.

14. John D. Benedict, *Muskogee and Northeastern Oklahoma, Including the Counties of Muskogee, McIntosh, Wagoner, Cherokee, Sequoyah, Adair, Delaware, Mayes, Rogers, Washington, Nowata, Craig, and Ottawa* (Chicago: S. J. Clarke, 1922), 2:369–71. For biographical sketches of Rutherford, see Paul W. H. Dewitz, *Notable Men of Indian Territory at the Beginning of the Twentieth Century, 1904–1905* (Muskogee: Southwestern Historical Company, 1905), 105; D. C. Gideon, *Indian Territory: Descriptive Biographical and Genealogical, Including the Landed Estates, County Seats, etc. with a General History of the Territory* (New York: Lewis, 1904), 610–11; Joseph B. Thoburn, *A Standard History of Oklahoma* (Chicago: American Historical Society, 1916), 1:278.

15. *Ada Evening News*, March 29, 1911.

16. *AHTA Weekly News*, May 23, 1912.

17. Cindy Higgins, "Frontier Protective and Social Network: The Anti–Horse Thief Association in Kansas," *Journal of the West* 42, no. 4 (Fall 2003): 63–64.

18. Higgins, "Frontier Protective and Social Network," 67.

19. Patrick Keen, "The Anti-Horsethief Association in Old Oklahoma," *Oklahombres* (Summer 1997): 23–24.

20. *AHTA Weekly News*, February 18, 1909.

21. *Muskogee Times-Democrat*, September 5, 1911; *AHTA Weekly News*, July 13, 27, 1911.

22. *AHTA Weekly News*, November 2, 1911.

23. *State Sentinel* (Stigler), August 4, 1911.

24. Keen, "Anti-Horse-Thief Association," 23–24; Higgins, "Frontier Protective and Social Network," 67. Thousands of AHTA members flocked to the KKK during World War I, but by the time of the onset of the Great Depression fewer than five thousand remained.

25. *AHTA Weekly News*, November 14, 1912.

26. *Ada Evening News*, March 29, 1911; *Canadian Valley Record* (Canton), November 10, 1910.

27. *Ralston New Era*, November 10, 1910.

28. *Checotah Times*, February 10, 1911.

29. *Muskogee Daily Phoenix*, February 25, 1911; *Checotah Times*, March 3, 1911. Two associates of the mayor, Ben Call and Dave Spears, were also found guilty of forgery. The three men had forged a deed to eighty acres of farmland near Porum.

30. Bill Wade testimony, Muskogee County Criminal Court Bond Records (Muskogee Public Library, Muskogee, Oklahoma), vol. 4 (July 1910–October 1912), 126.

31. *Davis v. State*, 1912, OK, CR 174, 123 P. 560, 7 Okl. Cr. 322, Oklahoma Court of Criminal Appeals, Case No. A-1183 at http://www/pscm/met/applications/oscn/deliverdocument .asp?id=16864&hits= [accessed January 31, 2008] (hereafter *Davis v. State [1912]*).

32. *Davis v. State (1912)*.

33. *Davis v. State (1912)*.

34. *Porum Press*, March 3, 1911.

35. *Davis v. State (1912)*.

36. *Davis v. State*, 1913, OK CR 14, 128 P 1097, 8 Okl. Cr. 515, Case No. A-1223, Oklahoma Court of Criminal Appeals at http://www.oscn.net/applications/oscn/DeliverDocument .asp?CiteID=17181 [accessed January 27, 2008] (hereafter *Davis v. State [1913]*).

37. *Davis v. State (1913)*.

38. *Davis v. State (1913)*.

39. *McAlester News Capital*, May 5, 1911; *Checotah Times*, May 5, 1911.

40. *Muskogee Times-Democrat*, May 5, 1911.

41. *Eufaula Indian Journal*, May 5, 1911. Dialogue and details in the following description are from *Muskogee Times-Democrat*, September 27, 1911.

42. *Muskogee Times-Democrat*, September 27, 1911. See also Fourteenth Census (1920), Cherokee County, Oklahoma, NA.

43. *Muskogee Times-Democrat*, May 5, 1911.

44. *Checotah Times*, May 5, 1911.

45. *Muskogee Daily Phoenix*, May 6, 1911.

46. *Checotah Times*, May 12, 1911; *Muskogee Daily Phoenix*, May 10, June 3, 1911.

47. *Muskogee Daily Phoenix*, May 10, 1911.

48. *Muskogee Daily Phoenix*, June 3, 1911; Thirteenth Census (1910), Muskogee County, Oklahoma, NA.

49. *Checotah Times*, June 23, 1911.

50. *Muskogee Daily Phoenix*, May 16, 1911. Viewed as the founder of anthropometry and the inventor of the mug shot, Alphonse Bertillon had devised the system. Bertillon was hailed by Arthur Conan Doyle in his *Hound of the Baskervilles* as having inspired the character of Sherlock Holmes. https://www.nlm.nih.gov/visibleproofs/galleries/biographies /bertillon.html and http://jimfisher.edinboro.edu/forensics/bertill [accessed November 5, 2017].

51. *McAlester News Capital*, May 5, 1911.

52. *Muskogee Times-Democrat*, May 6, 1911.

53. *Muskogee Daily Phoenix*, May 10, 1911.

54. *Muskogee Times-Democrat*, May 9, 1911.

55. *Muskogee Daily Phoenix*, May 10, 1911.

56. *Muskogee Daily Phoenix*, September 28, 1911.

57. *Muskogee Daily Phoenix*, September 28, 1911.

58. *Twin Territories* 7 (2000): 7.

59. *Muskogee Daily Phoenix*, May 14, 15, 16, 1911; *Oklahoma Leader* (Guthrie), May 18, 1911; *AHTA Weekly News*, May 11, 1911; *Eufaula Indian Journal*, May 19, 1911. Dialogue and details in the following description are from *Muskogee Daily Phoenix*, May 16, 1911.

60. *Muskogee Daily Phoenix*, May 16, 1911.

61. *Muskogee Daily Phoenix*, October 5, 1911.

62. *Ardmore Daily Ardmoreite*, October 16, 1911; *Daily Oklahoman* (Oklahoma City), October 16, 1911; *Muskogee Daily Phoenix*, October 15, 1911.

63. *Daily Oklahoman*, October 11, 1911; *Muskogee Daily Phoenix*, October 12, 1911, 9–14.

64. *Muskogee Daily Phoenix*, March 3, 1911.

65. *State Sentinel*, June 2, 1911.

66. *Muskogee Daily Phoenix*, May 30, 1911.

67. *McAlester News Capital* May 31, 1911.

68. *Daily Oklahoman*, May 31, June 1, 1911; *Muskogee Daily Phoenix*, May 31, 1911.

69. Details and dialogue in the following description are from *Muskogee Daily Phoenix*, May 31, 1911.

70. *Muskogee Daily Phoenix*, May 31, 1911. See also *Webbers Falls Record*, June 2, 1911.

71. *Tulsa Daily World*, May 31, 1911. Following details again from *Muskogee Daily Phoenix*, May 31, 1911.

72. *Muskogee Daily Phoenix*, May 31, 1911.

73. *Muskogee Daily Phoenix*, June 2, 1911; Thirteenth Census (1910), Muskogee and McIntosh Counties, Oklahoma, NA.

74. *Checotah Times*, June 2, 1911.

75. *Muskogee Daily Phoenix*, May 30, 1911. See also *Muskogee Times-Democrat*, May 29, 1911. See also Thirteenth Census (1910), Muskogee County, Oklahoma, NA.

76. *Muskogee Daily Phoenix*, May 30, 1911.

77. *Ada Evening News*, May 31, 1911; *Muskogee Times-Democrat*, January 16, 1912.

78. *Daily Oklahoman*, May 31, 1911.

79. *Muskogee Times-Democrat*, May 31, 1911.

80. Carl Ray Sherwood, "Biography of Self," November 22, 1927, in *Indian Pioneer Papers*, 109:444–45, no. 12312 (WHC),

81. Young woman quoted in Carlile Vowell, "Recollections: Eyewitness Account of the Porum Riot," *Twin Territories* 7 (2000): 6.

82. *Muskogee Daily Phoenix*, May 31, 1911.

83. *Daily Oklahoman*, May 31, 1911.

84. *Daily Oklahoman*, May 31, 1911. See also *Tulsa Daily World*, May 30, 1911; *Muskogee Times-Democrat*, May 29, 30, 1911; *Muskogee Daily Phoenix*, May 30, June 2, 1911; *Oklahoma Leader*, June 8, 1911.

85. *Tulsa Daily World*, May 30, 1911; *Claremore Messenger*, June 2, 1911; *Oklahoma State Register* (Guthrie), June 1, 1911; *Checotah Times*, June 2, 1911; *El Reno American*, June 2, 1911; *Webbers Falls Record*, June 2, 1911.

86. *Ada Evening News*, May 30, 1911.

87. *Muskogee Times-Democrat*, May 31, 1911.

88. Wally Watts, "Cassie Starr, Heroine," *Muskogee Phoenix*, October 18, 2007, at http://muskogeephoenixonline.com/blogs/WallyWatts/2007/10,carrie-star-heroine.html [accessed March 15, 2016]; *Muskogee Daily Phoenix*, May 30, 1911. See also https://www.amazon.com/ap/signin1911 [accessed December 24, 2016]. The *Daily Phoenix* misidentifies Nina Starr as an adopted daughter who was born to Minnie Berry. Nina Lois Starr Hodgkins was born to Pony and Cassie Starr on April 14, 1903, and died in Fort Worth, Texas, on August 14, 1989. The Pony Starr "Find a Grave" website identifies her correctly, as does https://www.findagrave.com/memorial/141604769/Nina-Lois-Hodgkins [accessed December 24, 2016].

89. *Muskogee Daily Phoenix*, May 31, 1911.

90. *Muskogee Daily Phoenix*, May 31, 1911. See also *Twin Territories* 7 (2000): 8.

91. *Daily Oklahoman*, May 31, 1911.

92. *Daily Oklahoman*, May 31, 1911.

93. *Ada Evening News*, May 30, 1911.

94. *Muskogee Daily Phoenix*, May 31, 1911.

95. Carlile Vowell, "Recollections," *Twin Territories* 7 (2000): 8.

96. *Tulsa Daily World*, May 30, 1911; *Eufaula Indian Journal*, June 1, 1911.

97. *State Sentinel*, September 15, 1911.

98. *Muskogee Daily Phoenix*, May 31, 1911.

99. Newspaper quoted from Carlile Vowell, "Recollections," *Twin Territories* 7 (2000): 8.

100. *Oklahoma State Register*, June 1, 1911.

101. *Muskogee Times-Democrat*, May 30, 1911; *McAlester News Capital*, May 31, 1911; *Ada Evening News*, May 31, 1911; *Daily Oklahoman*, May 31, 1911.

102. *AHTA Weekly News*, August 24, 1911.

103. *Tulsa Daily World*, May 30, 31, June 1, 1911; *Evening Free Press* (Oklahoma City), May 30, 1911; *Ada Evening News*, June 1, 1911; *Oklahoma Leader*, June 1, 8, 1911; *Muskogee Daily Phoenix*, June 3, 1911; *Muskogee Times-Democrat*, May 30, June 3, 1911.

104. *Tulsa Daily World*, May 31, 1911; *Eufaula Indian Journal*, June 1, 1911.

105. One Oklahoma newspaper falsely reported that Little was employed by Joe Davis. *Tulsa Daily World*, June 2, 1911.

106. *Muskogee Times-Democrat*, May 31, 1911. Seven men would be charged with "knowingly, unlawfully, willingly and feloniously, by use of force and violence, act together and without authority of law, and being masked and disguised, did then there beat, bruise and assault one Steve Little on the morning of May 31." The men who were charged included Charles Terrell, J. M. McClure, Jack Rigon, Dan Coody, Fred Oliver, and Toll Reddin. *Tulsa Daily World*, June 2, 1911. Little does not appear on the Oklahoma census from either 1900, 1910, or 1920.

107. *Bartlesville Enterprise*, June 2, 1911. See also *Muskogee Daily Phoenix*, June 3, 1911.

108. *Ada Evening News*, May 31, 1911; *Eufaula Indian Journal*, June 1, 1911; *Shawnee News*, June 1, 1911.

109. *Daily Oklahoman*, June 1, 1911.

110. *Checotah Times*, June 2, 1911.

111. *Muskogee Times-Democrat*, May 31, 1911.

112. *Tulsa Daily World*, June 1, 1911. For the grand jury, see *Muskogee Times-Democrat*, June 2, 1911. For an example of the extent of the publicity, see *Herald Democrat* (Leadville, CO), June 1, 1911.

113. *Muskogee Times-Democrat*, June 3, 19, 1911; *Checotah Times*, June 23, 1911; *Tulsa Daily World*, June 20, 1911. Those charged with rioting included Lon Baker, T. T. and E. V. Brashears, Charles Brooks, Barney Call, Jim Childers, Dan Coody, Jack Counts, C. S. Dunnigan, Webb Easton, Claude Eichling, Charles Evans, Pete Graham, T. L. Hester, Jesse Maxwell, John McMillan, Ben Morgan, Dan Morgan, A. M. Mullins, Gilbert Nicholson, Fred Oliver, Jack Reagan, Bill Reddin, George Stout, and Charlie Terrell.

114. *Porum Journal*, June 23, 1911; *Muskogee Times-Democrat*, June 16, 19, 1911; *Checotah Times*, June 23, 1911; *Canadian Valley Record*, June 29, 1911.

115. *AHTA Weekly News*, July 27, 1911.

116. *State Sentinel*, August 4, 1911.

117. *AHTA Weekly News*, June 8, 1911.

118. *Muskogee Daily Phoenix*, June 2, 1911.

119. *Ada Evening News*, June 2, 1911.

120. *El Reno American*, June 2, 1911. See also *Tulsa Daily World*, June 1, 1911; *Muskogee Times-Democrat*, June 1, 1911; *Claremore Messenger*, June 2, 1911; *Ada Evening News*, May 30, 1911.

### 3. Arson, Murder, and Mayhem

*Epigraph. Muskogee Daily Phoenix*, June 12, 1942.

1. Dialogue and details in the following description are from *Muskogee Daily Phoenix*, June 7, 1911.

2. *Muskogee Daily Phoenix*, June 7, 1911. See also *Muskogee Daily Phoenix*, June 8, 1911; *Muskogee Times-Democrat*, June 7, 1911; *Checotah Times*, June 11, 1911.

3. *Muskogee Times-Democrat*, June 8, 1911.

4. *Muskogee Times-Democrat*, June 9, 1911.

5. *Checotah Times*, June 16, 1911.

6. Rutherford quoted from *Ada Evening News*, June 13, 1911; *Muskogee Times-Democrat*, June 12, 1911; *Checotah Times*, June 16, 1911. See also *Muskogee Daily Phoenix*, June 14, 1911.

7. *Muskogee Times-Democrat*, June 14, 1911; *Muskogee Daily Phoenix*, June 15, 1911.

8. *Davenport New Era*, December 8, 1911; *Weleetka American*, December 15, 1911; *Canadian Valley Record*, December 21, 1911; *Hennessey Clipper*, December 21, 1911; *Texhoma Argus*, December 21, 1911; *Eufaula Indian Journal*, December 22, 1911.

9. *Muskogee Daily Phoenix*, July 16, 1911. Courtesy of John Baxter.

10. *Muskogee Daily Phoenix*, July 18, 1911. McGonigle's son (also named Clay) was killed on October 24, 1921, near Sacaton, Arizona, when he stopped to clear the road of a fallen electrical line and was electrocuted.

11. *Indianola Herald*, July 21, 1911; Bill Modisett, "Clay McGonagill: The Wildest Cowboy, the Greatest Steer Roper," in *Cowboys Who Rode Proudly: Carrying Cattle . . . and the Methods of Handling Them*, comp. and ed., J. Evetts Haley (Midland: Nita Steward Haley Memorial Library, 1992), 89–90.

12. *Muskogee Daily Phoenix*, June 14, 1911; *Checotah Times*, June 16, 1911.

13. *Muskogee Daily Phoenix*, June 18, 1911.

14. *Muskogee Daily Phoenix*, June 20, 1911.

15. *Hennessey Clipper*, July 6, 1911.

16. *Muskogee Daily Phoenix*, June 15, 17, 20, 1911; *Ada Evening News*, June 17, 1911.

17. *Porum Journal*, August 18, 1911.

18. *Muskogee Times-Democrat*, September 16, 1911.

19. *Muskogee Daily Phoenix*, September 26, 1911.

20. *Porum Journal*, September 29, 1911.

21. *Muskogee Times-Democrat*, December 5, 1911.

22. Details and dialogue in the following description are from *Muskogee Times-Democrat*, September 27, 1911.

23. *Muskogee Times-Democrat*, September 27, 1911.

24. *Muskogee Daily Phoenix*, September 17, 27, 1911.

25. *Muskogee Times-Democrat*, October 2, 1911.

26. *Muskogee Times-Democrat*, October 2, 1911.

27. *Muskogee Daily Phoenix*, September 18, 27, 28, 1911.

28. *Muskogee Daily Phoenix*, September 28, 1911; *Muskogee Times-Democrat*, October 2, 1911.

29. *Muskogee Times-Democrat*, September 27, 1911.

30. *Muskogee Daily Phoenix*, September 30, October 2, 1911.

31. *Muskogee Daily Phoenix*, September 30, October 2, 1911 (quote).

32. *Muskogee Daily* Phoenix, October 4, 1911; *Checotah Times*, October 6, 1911.

33. *Muskogee Times-Democrat*, October 3, 1911.

34. *Muskogee Daily Phoenix*, October 4, 1911; *Muskogee Times-Democrat*, October 4, 1911.

35. *Eufaula Indian Journal*, October 6, 1911; *Checotah Times*, October 6, 1911.

36. *Muskogee Daily Phoenix*, October 5, 1911.

37. *Eufaula Indian Journal*, October 6, 1911.

38. *Muskogee Times-Democrat*, October 4, 1911.

39. *Muskogee Daily Phoenix*, June 3, 1911.

40. *AHTA Weekly News*, August 10, 1911, quoting the *Muskogee Democrat*, n.d.

41. *AHTA Weekly News*, July 27, 1911.

42. *State Sentinel*, August 4, 1911. See also *Daily Oklahoman*, August 4, 1911; *Ada Evening News*, August 4, 1911; *Shawnee Daily Herald*, August 5, 1911; *AHTA Weekly News*, August 10, 1911.

43. *Ada Evening News*, August 4, 1911.

44. *AHTA Weekly News*, August 10, 1911, quoting the *Muskogee Democrat*, n.d.

45. *Hugo Husonian*, December 28, 1911.

46. *Ada Evening News*, August 30, 1911; *Checotah Times*, September 1, 1911; *Porum Journal*, September 1, 1911.

47. *Porum Journal*, September 1, 1911. See also Thirteenth Census (1910), Muskogee County, Oklahoma, NA. Reddin's name is frequently spelled in the newspapers as Redding and Redden.

48. Carlile Vowell, "Recollections," *Twin Territories* 7 (2000): 8.

49. *Muskogee Times-Democrat*, August 28, 1911; *Tulsa Daily World*, August 27, 1911; *Daily Oklahoman*, August 27, 1911.

50. *Ada Evening News*, August 30, 1911; *Porum Journal*, September 8, 1911. See also *Garfield County Press* and *Enid Wave-Democrat*, September 7, 1911.

51. *Muskogee Times-Democrat*, September 5, 1911; *Muskogee Daily Phoenix*, September 13, 1911, December 10, 1912.

52. *Porum Journal*, December 13, 1912; *Muskogee Daily Phoenix*, December 15, 1912; *Tulsa Democrat*, October 11, 1914.

53. *Muskogee Daily Phoenix*, December 27, 1912.

54. *McAlester News Capital*, September 7, 1911. See also *Muskogee Times-Democrat*, September 7, 1911; *Daily Oklahoman*, September 8, 1911.

55. *Muskogee Times-Democrat*, September 7, 1911.

56. *Muskogee Daily Phoenix*, September 9, 1911; *Ada Evening* News, September 13, 1911; *Muskogee Times-Democrat*, September 10, 12, 1911; *Eufaula Republican*, September 15, 1911; *Porum Journal*, September 15, 1911; *Eufaula Indian Journal*, September 15, 1911.

57. *Muskogee Times-Democrat*, September 12, 1911; *Ada Evening News*, September 13, 1911.

58. *Muskogee Times-Democrat*, September 14, 1911.

59. Edlin, *Cobb Cousins*, 147; *Muskogee Times-Democrat*, September 21, 1911.

60. "Yankee Robinson's Circus, 1911 Season Route" at http://www.karlking.us/1911_route.htm [accessed December 20, 2016].

61. *Eufaula Indian Journal*, September 22, 1911, quoting the *McIntosh County Democrat*, n.d.

62. *Muskogee Times-Democrat*, September 21, 1911; *Eufaula Republican*, September 22, 1911; *Checotah Times*, September 22, 1911.

63. For Tom Cobb's wounding in 1911, see *Muskogee Times-Democrat*, September 21, 1911; *Eufaula Indian Journal*, September 22, 1911; *Checotah Times*, September 22, 1911; *Eufaula Republican*, September 22, 1911. For rumors of his death, see *Checotah Times*, September 10, 17, 1915. For his actual death, see *Checotah Times*, December 10, 1915. For Tom's and his father's deaths, see Edlin, *Cobb Cousins*, 146–47; Young, *Phenie's World*, 206–207; M. J. Cobb Young, interview by author, September 16, 2016 (notes in author's possession).

64. *Muskogee Daily Phoenix*, October 5, 1911.

65. *Muskogee Daily Phoenix*, October 16, 1911.

66. *Checotah Times*, October 18, 1911; *Eufaula Republican*, October 20, 1911; *Crowder City Guardian*, October 21, 1911.

67. *Eufaula Indian Journal*, October 20, 1911; *Checotah Times*, October 18, 1911.

68. *Crowder City Guardian*, October 21, 1911, quoting the *McAlester Capital*, n.d.

69. *Porum Journal*, November 17, 1911; *State Sentinel*, November 17, 1911.

70. *Muskogee Times-Democrat*, November 16, 1911.

71. *Tahlequah Arrow*, November 23, 1911; *Porum Journal*, November 24, 1911.

72. *Muskogee Daily Phoenix*, January 16, 1912.

73. *Checotah Times*, January 19, 1912; *State Sentinel*, January 19, 1912; *Daily Oklahoman*, January 19, 1912; *Muskogee Daily Phoenix*, January 20, 1912.

74. *Wagoner County Courier*, January 18, 1912. See also *Muskogee Times-Democrat*, January 18, 1912; *Oklahoma Leader*, January 25, 1912.

75. *Muskogee Daily Phoenix*, January 20, 1912.

76. *Wagoner County Courier*, January 25, 1912.

77. *Porum Journal*, January 26, 1912.

78. *Muskogee Times-Democrat*, January 25, 1912; *Porum Journal*, February 2, 1912.

79. Ammon Davis, Find a Grave, at http://www.findagrave.com/cgi-bin /fg.cgi?gr&GRid=14720437 and http://genealogytrails.com/wagoner/obits.html [accessed November 21, 2017]. Donnie Daniel in his *Murder in Muskogee* (Forsyth, GA: Private, 2016) has Ammon Davis as nineteen at the time of his death, although his tombstone in the Davis Cemetery has his birth as 1889.

80. *Muskogee Times-Democrat*, March 23, 1912.

81. *Muskogee Times-Democrat*, April 9, 1912; *Muskogee Daily Phoenix*, April 9, 1912; *Eufaula Republican*, April 12, 1912; *Checotah Times*, April 12, 1912; *Eufaula Indian Journal*, April 12, 1912.

82. *Eufaula Indian Journal*, April 12, 1912.

83. *Muskogee Daily Phoenix*, April 9, 1912.

84. *Muskogee Times-Democrat*, May 10, 1912; *Hennessey Clipper*, May 2, 1912.

85. *Eufaula Republican*, April 19, 1912.

86. *Muskogee Daily Phoenix*, May 11, 1912.

87. *Muskogee Daily Phoenix*, April 16, 1912; *Muskogee Times-Democrat*, April 26, 1912.

88. *State Sentinel*, April 19, 1912. See also Daniel, *Murder in Muskogee*, 5–6.

89. *Muskogee Daily Phoenix*, May 11, 1912.

90. *Muskogee Times-Democrat*, April 16, 1912.

91. *Muskogee Times-Democrat*, April 17, 1912; *Guthrie Daily Star*, April 17, 1912; *Porum Journal*, April 19, 1912.

92. *Porum Journal*, April 19, 26, 1912; *Dover* News, April 25, 1912; *Ada Evening News*, April 19, 1912.

93. *Eufaula Republican*, April 19, 1912.

94. *Muskogee Daily Phoenix*, April 21, 1912.

95. *Muskogee Daily* Phoenix, April 30, 1912; *Muskogee Times-Democrat*, May 4, 1912.

96. *Hugo Husonian*, May 2, 1912.

97. *Muskogee Times-Democrat*, May 4, 1912.

98. *Muskogee Daily Phoenix*, May 1, 1912.

99. *Muskogee Daily Phoenix*, May 3, 1912.

100. *Muskogee Times-Democrat*, May 9, 10, 1912; *Muskogee Daily Phoenix*, May 10, 1912.

101. *Muskogee Times-Democrat*, May 10, 1912.

102. *Muskogee Times-Democrat*, May 11, 1912.

103. *Muskogee Times-Democrat*, May 13, 1912.

104. *Porum Journal*, May 14, 1912.

105. *Muskogee Times-Democrat*, May 15, 1912.

106. *Muskogee Times-Democrat*, May 20, 1912.

107. *Muskogee Daily Phoenix*, May 11, 1912.

108. *Muskogee Daily Phoenix*, May 11, 12, 1912. Details and dialogue for the following description are from *Muskogee Daily Phoenix*, May 12, 1912.

109. *Muskogee Daily Phoenix*, May 12, 1912.

110. *Muskogee Times-Democrat*, May 13, 1912.

111. *Muskogee Times-Democrat*, May 13, 1912.

112. *Muskogee Times-Democrat*, May 16, 1912.

113. *Muskogee Times-Democrat*, May 16, 1912; *Eufaula Republican*, May 17, 1912. See also Daniel, *Murder in Muskogee*, 5–6.

114. *Eufaula Indian Journal*, May 17, 1912; *Eufaula Republican*, May 17, 1912.

115. *Muskogee Daily Phoenix*, May 17, 1912.

116. *Muskogee Times-Democrat*, May 14, 1912; *Muskogee Daily Phoenix*, May 14, 1912.

117. *Muskogee Times-Democrat*, May 15, 1912. Born at Briartown, Jeff Davis was the son of Earl Davis.

118. *Ardmore Daily Ardmoreite*, June 17, 1913; *Checotah Times*, June 20, 1913.

119. *Hugo Husonian*, May 23, 1912. See also *Muskogee Daily Phoenix*, May 18, 19, 1912; *Shawnee Daily News-Herald*, May 21, 1912; *Eufaula Indian Journal*, May 24, 1912.

120. *Muskogee Times-Democrat*, June 5, 1912.

121. Details and dialogue in the following description are from *Muskogee Daily Phoenix*, June 12, 1912.

122. *Muskogee Daily Phoenix*, June 12, 1912.

123. *Muskogee Times-Democrat*, June 15, 1912.

124. *Muskogee Daily Phoenix*, June 7, 1912.

125. *Muskogee Times-Democrat*, June 15, 1912. See also *Muskogee Daily Phoenix*, June 7, 1912.

126. *Daily Oklahoman*, June 16, 1912.

127. *Muskogee Times-Democrat*, June 15, 1912. See also *Porum Journal*, June 21, 1912; *Eufaula Indian Journal*, June 21, 1912.

128. *Porum Journal*, June 28, 1912.

129. *Muskogee Times-Democrat*, June 15, 1912.

130. *Muskogee Times-Democrat*, June 15, 1912. See also *Daily Oklahoman*, June 16, 1912.

131. *Muskogee Times-Democrat*, June 15, 1912.

132. *Muskogee Times-Democrat*, June 15, 1912.

133. *Muskogee Times-Democrat*, August 15, 1912; *State Sentinel*, August 12, 16, 1912; *Eufaula Republican*, August 16, 1912; *Taloga Times*, August 29, 1912.

134. *Muskogee Times-Democrat*, August 9, 1912.

135. *Porum Journal*, August 16, 1912.

136. *Muskogee Times-Democrat*, August 15, 1912.

137. Details and dialogue in the following description are from *Globe Democrat* (St. Louis), n.d., miscellaneous newspaper clipping, in Barde Papers, OHS.

138. *Globe Democrat*, n.d., Barde Papers, OHS. See also *Guthrie Daily Star*, August 10, 1912; *Dover News*, August 15, 1912; *Daily Oklahoman*, August 10, 1912.

139. *Muskogee Times-Democrat*, August 15, 1912.

140. *Muskogee Daily Phoenix*, December 20, 1912.

141. *Muskogee Daily Phoenix*, December 20, 21, 22, 25, 1912.

142. *Muskogee Daily Phoenix*, January 10, 1913. Near Sadler Elementary School in North Muskogee, Standpipe Hill should not be confused with the more famous Standpipe Hill in Tulsa that was closely associated with the 1921 Tulsa Race Riot. See http://www.newson6.com/story/25761541/historical-marker-dedicated-on-standpipe-hill [accessed December 20, 2016].

143. *Muskogee Daily Phoenix*, December 21, 1912.

144. *Muskogee Daily Phoenix*, December 21, 22, 24, 25, 27, 1912. A search of the census indicated that the only "young farmer" in the Porum area was twenty-one-year-old Texas-born Ben Baker. Thirteenth Census (1910), Muskogee County, Oklahoma, NA.

145. *Porum Journal*, December 27, 1912; *Muskogee Daily Phoenix*, December 27, 1912.

146. *Muskogee Times-Democrat*, August 15, 1912. Jack Davis and his family appear in the *Muskogee City Directory* at 705 South Third Street from 1910 to 1912; the family is not listed in the 1913 directory.

147. *Muskogee Daily Phoenix*, August 17, 1912.

148. *Muskogee Times-Democrat*, August 17, 1912. See also *Eufaula Indian Journal*, August 23, 1912; *Eufaula Republican*, August 23, 1912.

149. *Muskogee Times-Democrat*, August 17, 1912.

150. *Carney Enterprise*, October 2, 1914; *Porum Journal*, October 9, 1914; *Tulsa Democrat*, October 11, 1914; also *Hugo Husonian*, April 24, June 12, 1913.

151. *Crowder City Guardian*, March 21, 1913.

152. *Oklahoma Clipper* (Indianola), March 21, 1913.

153. *Hugo Husonian*, September 19, 1912. See also *Dover News*, September 19, 1912; *Hennessey Clipper*, September 26, 1912; *Taloga Times*, September 26, 1912.

154. *Hugo Husonian*, January 16, 1913.

155. Joe Davis and Bob Worthman testimony in *United States of America vs. Joe Davis, et al.*, Case No. 1786, District Court, Eastern District of Oklahoma, Records of the District Courts of the United States, June Term, 1914, RG 21, National Archives, Fort Worth (NAFW), Texas (hereafter *US vs. Davis, et al. [1915]*).

156. *Muskogee Daily Phoenix*, January 23, 1913.

157. *Muskogee Daily Phoenix*, January 23, 1913.

158. *Porum Journal*, January 13, 1913.

159. *Muskogee Times-Democrat*, July 14, 1913.

## 4. "Alibi Joe" in the Land of the Six-Shooter

*Epigraph. Muskogee Daily Phoenix*, February 21, 1915.

1. *Muskogee Times-Democrat*, February 17, 1915. The moon was 88.76 full at the time of the robbery. See http://www.moonpage.com/index.html?go=T&auto dst=T&tzone=et&m=10&d=29&y=1912&hour=1&min=55&sec=0 [accessed May 14, 2014].

2. Details and dialogue in the following description are from William Kelm testimony in *US vs. Joe Davis, et al. (1915)*.

3. Kelm testimony in *US vs. Joe Davis, et al. (1915)*.

4. *Dover News*, September 12, 1912. See also *Hennessey Clipper*, September 26, 1912.

5. Robert Worthman testimony in *US vs. Joe Davis, et al. (1915)*. His name is sometimes spelled as "Wortham" in the Oklahoma press, although the young outlaw clearly spelled it as "Worthman," as in court documents.

6. Buck Bertholf testimony in *US vs. Joe Davis, et al. (1915)*. His name is frequently spelled as "Burdolf" or "Burdolff" in newspapers and court documents, but the young cowboy spelled it as "Bertholf."

7. E. L. Halsell to Owen, March 2, 1923, Davis Pardon File, RG 129, NA.

8. *Hugo Husonian*, March 20, 1913. *Yeggeman* was a commonly used term at the time.

9. *Muskogee Daily Phoenix*, October 30, 1912.

10. M. R. Crosby testimony in *US vs. Joe Davis, et al. (1915)*.

11. Roy Van Brunt testimony in *US vs. Joe Davis, et al. (1915)*.

12. *Muskogee County Democrat*, February 18, 1915.

13. Van Brunt testimony in *US vs. Joe Davis, et al. (1915)*.

14. *Daily Oklahoman*, October 6, 1912; *Tulsa Daily World*, October 12, 1912; *Muskogee Daily Phoenix*, October 5, 12, 1912.

15. *Muskogee Times-Democrat*, October 31, 1912.

16. Kelm testimony in *US vs. Joe Davis, et al. (1915)*.

17. Kelm and Jim Blevins testimony in *US vs. Joe Davis, et al. (1915)*.

18. Kelm and Blevins testimony in *US vs. Joe Davis, et al. (1915)*.

19. Kelm and Blevins testimony in *US vs. Joe Davis, et al. (1915)*.

20. Blevins testimony in *US vs. Joe Davis, et al. (1915)*.

21. John M. Dolan testimony in *US vs. Joe Davis, et al. (1915)*.

22. Kelm testimony in *US vs. Joe Davis, et al. (1915)*.

23. *Eufaula Republican*, October 25, 1912; *Eufaula Indian Journal*, November 1, 1912.

24. *Muskogee Daily Phoenix*, October 30, 1912.

25. *Eufaula Republican*, October 25, 1912.

26. *Eufaula Indian Journal*, November 1, 1912.

27. *Eufaula Indian Journal*, October 25, 1912.

28. W. J. Irwin testimony in *US vs. Joe Davis, et al. (1915)*.

29. *Muskogee Daily Phoenix*, October 30, 1912.

30. *Muskogee Times-Democrat*, October 30, 1912. See also *Muskogee Daily Phoenix*, October 30, 1912.

31. *Muskogee Times-Democrat*, October 31, 1912.

32. *Muskogee Daily Phoenix*, November 1, 1912; *Tulsa Weekly Democrat*, November 7, 1912; *Maramec News*, November 7, 1912; *Porum Journal*, November 8, 1912.

33. *Muskogee Times-Democrat*, October 31, 1912.

34. *Muskogee Daily Phoenix*, November 1, 1912.

35. Dolan testimony in *US vs. Joe Davis, et al. (1915)*.

36. *Muskogee Times-Democrat*, October 31, 1912.

37. *Crowder City Guardian*, November 8, 1912, quoting the *McAlester Capital*, n.d.; *Eufaula Indian Journal*, December 2, 1912; *Muskogee Daily Phoenix*, December 3, 1912.

38. Blevins testimony in *US vs. Joe Davis, et al. (1915)*.

39. *Checotah Times*, April 4, 1913. See also Thirteenth Census (1910), McIntosh County, Oklahoma, NA.

40. Walter Spess testimony in *US vs. Joe Davis, et al. (1915)*.

41. Blevins testimony in *US vs. Joe Davis, et al. (1915)*.

42. *Checotah Times*, April 4, 1913. See also *Ada Evening News*, April 3, 1913; *Hugo Husonian*, April 10, 1913.

43. *Eufaula Indian Journal*, March 21, 1913. See also *Hawthorne Sun*, March 20, 1913.

44. M. Blackenship, R. Y. Snow, and Welch Evans testimony in *US vs. Joe Davis, et al. (1915)*.

45. *Crowder City Guardian*, March 21, 1913.

46. *Checotah Times*, March 21, 1913.

47. Dan Holman and R. W. Cornell testimony in *U.S. vs. Joe Davis, et al. (1915)*.

48. Holman and Cornell testimony in *U.S. vs. Joe Davis, et al. (1915)*; *Rogers County Leader and Rogers County News*, March 21, 1913.

49. *Hugo Husonian*, April 10, 1913.

50. *Checotah Times*, April 4, 1913. The Blevins testimony was also reported in the *Ada Evening News*, April 3, 1914.

51. *Hugo Husonian*, April 10, 1913.

52. *Choctaw Herald* (Hugo), September 3, 1913.

53. *Eufaula Indian Journal*, October 3, 1913.

54. *Muskogee Daily Phoenix*, October 8, 1913.

55. Thirteenth Census (1910), Pawnee County, Oklahoma, NA.

56. *Eufaula Democrat*, October 10, 1913.

57. *Daily Oklahoman*, October 11, 1913.

58. *Muskogee Times-Democrat*, October 30, 1913.

59. *Eufaula Democrat*, October 17, 1913.

60. *Eufaula Democrat*, October 17, 1913; *Daily Oklahoman*, October 15, 1913.

61. *Muskogee Times-Democrat*, October 18, 1913.

62. *Daily Oklahoman*, October 15, 1913; *Muskogee Times-Democrat*, October 18, 1913; *Osage Journal* (Pawhuska, OK), October 16, 1913.

63. Grann, *Killers of the Flower Moon*, 28.

64. *Eufaula Democrat*, October 17, 1913; *Eufaula Indian Journal*, October 17, 1913.

65. *Muskogee Daily Phoenix*, November 11, 1913.

66. *Hugo Husonian*, November 13, 1913.

67. *Muskogee Times-Democrat*, November 11, 1913. See also *Osage Journal* (Pawhuska, OK), November 13, 1913; *Hugo Husonian*, November 13, 1913; *Checotah Times*, November 14, 1913; *Texhoma Times*, November 14, 1913; *Eufaula Indian Journal*, November 14, 1913.

68. *Oklahoma Leader*, January 21, 1914.

69. *Norman Democrat-Topic*, June 12, 1914.

70. *Muskogee Daily Phoenix*, February 17, 1914.

71. *Hugo Husonian*, May 28, 1914; *Hartshorne Sun*, May 28, 1914.

72. *Hugo Husonian*, May 28, 1914.

73. *Pawnee Courier Dispatch*, September 10, 1914. When the Keystone dam was completed in 1968 the village of Keystone was submerged beneath Keystone Lake.

74. *Choctaw Herald*, November 26, 1914; *Eufaula Democrat*, November 27, 1914.

75. *Muskogee Times-Democrat*, September 23, 1914.

76. "Baxter Springs, a Most Robbed Town," at http://www.theroadwanderer.net/66Kansas /baxter.htm [accessed January 9, 2018].

77. *Oklahoma Farmer and Laborer* (Sapulpa), September 25, 1914.

78. *Ada Weekly News*, September 23, 1914; *Daylight* (Cuba, KS), September 23, 1914; *Tulsa Daily World*, September 23, 1914.

79. *Tulsa Democrat*, October 1, 1914.

80. *Daily Oklahoman*, November 15, 1914.

81. *Ada Evening News*, November 5, 1914.

82. *Tulsa Daily World*, November 15, 2014.

83. *Tulsa Daily World*, November 19, 1914. See also *Daily Oklahoman*, November 15, 1914.

84. *Choctaw Herald*, November 26, 1914.

85. *Tulsa Daily World*, November 22, 1914.

86. *Eufaula Democrat*, November 27, 1914.

87. *Baxter Springs News*, November 26, 1914.

88. *Baxter Springs News*, December 10, 1914, January 14, 1915; *Pawnee Courier Dispatch*, January 14, 1915; *Tulsa Daily World*, January 10, 1915.

89. *Eufaula Indian Journal*, November 27, 1914; *Pawnee Courier Dispatch*, December 17, 1914.

90. *Hugo Husonian*, December 24, 1914.

91. Zoe A. Tilghman, *Marshal of the Last Frontier: Life and Services of William Matthew (Bill) Tilghman* (Glendale: Arthur H. Clark, 1964), 317–18.

92. *Pawnee Courier-Dispatch*, January 14, 1915.

93. The concept of the social bandit originated with the Marxist historian Eric Hobsbawm in his *Primitive Rebels: Studies in Archaic Forms of Social Movements in the 19th and 20th Centuries* (New York: Frederick A. Praeger, 1959), and *Bandits* (New York: Penguin, 1985).

94. O. C. Pierce, T. J. Butler, and Geo. F. Lewis to Inspector in Charge, April 7, 1917, in Davis Inmate File, Leavenworth, RG 129, NAKC.

95. *Muskogee County Democrat*, January 14, 1915; *Terlton Enterprise*, January 14, 1915.

96. *Muskogee Daily Phoenix*, January 14, 1915.

97. "Henry Starr—The Cherokee Bad Boy," at https://www.legendsofamerica.com /we-henrystarr/ and https://www.legendsofamerica.com/we-henrystarr/2 [accessed January 9, 2018]. See also *Muskogee Daily Phoenix*, January 15, 1915; *Fort Gibson Daily Era*, January 21, 1915; *Checotah Times*, January 22, 1915; *Oklahoma Leader*, January 28, 1915.

98. *US vs. Joe Davis, et al. (1915)*.

99. Thoburn, *A Standard History*, 6:1481–82. See also *Who's Who in America* (Chicago: A. N. Marquis, 1920), 11:1731; *Muskogee County Democrat*, February 25, 1915.

100. *Muskogee Daily Phoenix*, January 14, 1915; *Muskogee County Democrat*, January 21, 1915. See also Ralph E. Campbell, Court Order, March 21, 1915, in *US vs. Joe Davis, et al. (1915)*. Otto Reed went on to become Pittsburg County sheriff and chief of police in McAlester. Seventeen years after Worthman's arrest, on June 17, 1933, however, FBI agents asked him to help escort a small-town Oklahoma gangster, Frank "Jelly" Nash, to Leavenworth. Reed was ambushed and killed in a hail of machine-gun fire by "Pretty Boy" Floyd and his gang at Union Station in Kansas City.

101. *Daily Ardmoreite*, February 3, 1915.

102. *Tulsa Daily World*, February 13, 1915.

103. W. J. Irwin, W. R. Robinson, and William B. Webb testimony in *US vs. Joe Davis, et al. (1915)*.

104. *Muskogee Times-Democrat*, February 17, 1915. See also *Muskogee County Democrat*, February 18, 1915.

105. *Muskogee Times-Democrat*, February 17, 1915.

106. Dolan testimony in *US vs. Joe Davis, et al. (1915)*.

107. Kelm testimony in *US vs. Joe Davis, et al. (1915)*. See also *Muskogee Daily Phoenix*, February 18, 1915.

108. Charles C. Cissna testimony in *US vs. Joe Davis, et al. (1915)*; *Muskogee County Democrat*, February 11, 1915.

109. James M. Green testimony in *US vs. Joe Davis, et al. (1915)*.

110. Jack Lane testimony in *US vs. Joe Davis, et al. (1915)*; *Muskogee County Democrat*, February 19, 1915.

111. *Muskogee Times-Democrat*, February 17, 1915.

112. Van Brunt testimony in *US vs. Joe Davis, et al. (1915)*.

113. Spess testimony in *US vs. Joe Davis, et al. (1915)*. See also *Muskogee Times-Democrat*, February 17, 1915.

114. Spess testimony in *US vs. Joe Davis, et al. (1915)*.
115. Blevins testimony in *US vs. Joe Davis, et al. (1915)*. Some of the Blevins testimony was reported in the *Muskogee Daily Phoenix*, February 18, 1915.
116. M. F. Cosby, W. F. Logan, J. C. Hubert testimony in *US vs. Joe Davis, et al. (1915)*. See also *Muskogee Daily Phoenix*, February 18, 1915.
117. *Muskogee Daily Phoenix*, February 18, 1915. See also Tom McGuire testimony in *US vs. Joe Davis, et al. (1915)*.
118. Y. R. Davenport testimony in *US vs. Joe Davis, et al. (1915)*.
119. Blakenship, R. Y. Snow, Welch Evans testimony, all in *US vs. Joe Davis, et al. (1915)*. See also *Muskogee Daily Phoenix*, February 18, 1915.
120. W. C. Grayson and Holman testimony in *US vs. Joe Davis, et al. (1915)*.
121. Bessie Boatright testimony in *US vs. Joe Davis, et al. (1915)*.
122. *Muskogee Daily Phoenix*, February 18, 1915.
123. A. Neal, Howard Ross, Emma Ogden, William Ogden testimony, all in *US vs. Joe Davis, et al. (1915)*. See also *Muskogee Times-Democrat*, February 18, 1915.
124. William Hall and T. Matlock testimony in *US vs. Joe Davis, et al. (1915)*. See also *Muskogee Times-Democrat*, February 18, 1915.
125. *Muskogee Times-Democrat*, February 18, 1915. See also Simeon W. Lewis testimony in *US vs. Joe Davis, et al. (1915)*.
126. A. C. Dusenbury testimony in *US vs. Joe Davis, et al. (1915)*.
127. E. S. Norton testimony in *US vs. Joe Davis, et al. (1915)*. See also *Muskogee Times-Democrat*, February 18, 1915.
128. Bob Baldwin, Pat Robinson, and John Culver testimony in *US vs. Joe Davis, et al. (1915)*.
129. T. D. Taylor testimony in *US vs. Joe Davis, et al. (1915)*.
130. Sig T. Wilkerson testimony in *US vs. Joe Davis, et al. (1915)*.
131. Worthman testimony in *US vs. Joe Davis, et al. (1915)*.
132. *Muskogee Daily Phoenix*, February 19, 1915; Bertholf testimony in *US vs. Joe Davis, et al. (1915)*.
133. Joe Davis testimony in *US vs. Joe Davis, et al. (1915)*. See also *Muskogee Times-Democrat*, February 18, 1915.
134. *Muskogee Times-Democrat*, February 18, 1915.
135. Joe Davis to Mrs. Fred Spess, July 27, 1914, in *US vs. Joe Davis, et al. (1915)*.
136. Jack Davis testimony in *US vs. Joe Davis, et al. (1915)*.
137. H. B. Garrison, George McKee, and Cornell rebuttal testimony in *US vs. Joe Davis, et al. (1915)*.
138. *Muskogee Daily Phoenix*, February 19, 1915.
139. S. M. Rutherford, Motion in Arrest of Judgment, February 25, 1915, in *US vs. Joe Davis, et al. (1915)*.
140. *Muskogee Times-Democrat*, February 18, 1915.
141. *Muskogee Times-Democrat*, February 18, 1915.
142. *Muskogee Daily Phoenix*, February 20, 1915. This may well have been the Eagle Film Company's six-reel *Passing of the Oklahoma Outlaws* directed by famed lawman

Bill Tilghman, which depicted the end of the outlaw gangs in Oklahoma. Tilghman organized the company in response to several movies that glamorized outlaws and depicted lawmen as fools. Hoping to make a movie that depicted the closing days of the Twin Territories more objectively, Tilghman recruited several cowboys from the 101 Ranch. He even played himself and also enlisted Deputy Marshal Bud Ledbetter. See http://www.imdb.com/title/tt0005861 [accessed December 24, 2017].

143. *Muskogee Daily Phoenix*, February 21, 1915.

144. Ralph E. Campbell, Order Overruling Motion for a New Trial, February 27, 1915, in *US vs. Joe Davis, et al. (1915)*.

145. Details and dialogue for the following description are from *Muskogee Daily Phoenix*, February 21, 1915.

146. *Muskogee Daily Phoenix*, February 21, 1915.

147. R. L. Rushing, interview by author, August 15, 2018.

148. Details and dialogue for the following description are from either the *Muskogee Daily Phoenix*, February 22, 1915, or the *Daily Ardmoreite*, February 22, 1915.

149. *Muskogee Daily Phoenix*, February 22, 1915, or the *Daily Ardmoreite*, February 22, 1915.

150. *Daily Ardmoreite*, February 22, 1915.

151. *Muskogee Daily Phoenix*, February 22, 1915.

152. *Muskogee County Democrat*, February 25, 1915.

153. *Muskogee Daily Phoenix*, February 25, 1915. See also *Oklahoma Leader*, March 4, 5, 1915.

154. *Muskogee Daily Phoenix*, February 25, 28, 1915. See also *Porum Journal*, March 5, 1915; *Oklahoma Leader*, March 4, 1915; *Hollis Post-Herald*, March 4, 1915; *Inola Register*, March 4, 1915.

155. *Checotah Times*, March 5, 1915.

156. *Muskogee Daily Phoenix*, February 28, 1915.

157. *Muskogee Daily Phoenix*, February 28, 1915; *Checotah Times*, March 5, 1915; *Eufaula Indian Journal*, March 5, 1915.

158. *Checotah Times*, March 5, 1915.

159. S. M. Rutherford and DeRoose Bailey, Exhibit A, Assignment of Errors, in *US vs. Joe Davis, et al. (1915)*.

160. James Clark, affidavit, February 23, 1915, in *US vs. Joe Davis, et al. (1915)*.

161. F. L. Farley, affidavit, February 23, 1915; J. W. Price, affidavit, February 24, 1915; both in *US vs. Joe Davis, et al. (1915)*.

162. John R. Harris, affidavit, February 24, 1915; Caleb Starr, affidavit, February 24, 1915; both in *US vs. Joe Davis, et al. (1915)*. See also *Muskogee Daily Phoenix*, February 28, 1915.

163. Morton Rutherford, affidavit, February 25, 1915, in *US vs. Joe Davis, et al. (1915)*.

164. Rutherford and Bailey, Assignment of Errors, in *US vs. Joe Davis, et al. (1915)*.

165. Carrie Davis, affidavit, February 25, 1915, in *US vs. Joe Davis, et al. (1915)*.

166. Crayen T. Flanigan, affidavit, February 25, 1915; H. H. Horton, affidavit, February 24,

1915; Claude Sawyer, affidavit, February 25, 1915; O. Leroy, affidavit, February 24, 1915; A. B. Taylor, affidavit, February 24, 1915; all in *US vs. Joe Davis, et al. (1915)*.

167. Mrs. Peal E. Medland, affidavit, February 1915, in *US vs. Joe Davis, et al. (1915)*.

168. *Oklahoma Leader*, March 4, 1915. See also S. M. Rutherford, affidavit, February 25, 1915; Charles B. Daw, affidavit, February 23, 1915; Charles Kimsey, affidavit, February 23, 1915; R. Mattox, February 23, 1915; W. W. Asquith, affidavit, February 23, 1915; all in *US vs. Joe Davis, et al. (1915)*.

169. *Muskogee Daily Phoenix*, March 5, 1915. See also *Muskogee Times-Democrat*, March 6, 1915; *Liberal Democrat* (Liberal, KS), March 19, 1915.

### 5. Fearless to a Reckless Degree

*Epigraph. Tulsa Daily World*, March 28, 1915.

1. *Tacoma Times* (Tacoma, WA), April 8, 1915. Henry Starr was born in a log cabin near Fort Gibson in 1873. His father, George Miflin Dallas "Hop" Starr, was a half-blood Cherokee. His mother, Mary Ellen Scot, was a woman of Irish descent and one-quarter Cherokee. Henry's grandfather was the notorious Tom Starr, a well-known outlaw Henry called the "Devil's own." His uncle Sam Starr was the husband of the "Outlaw Queen" Belle Starr, who spent a large part of her life in Younger's Bend. Henry never liked Belle. He found her crude and reprehensible, and he made sure everyone knew she was his aunt by marriage only. Pony Starr denied knowing Henry, but the two were first cousins, and it may have been through Pony that Joe Davis first came to know Henry. As a young man Henry once worked on a ranch with a humorous and soon-to-be famous cowboy named Will Rogers. Blaming many of his youthful indiscretions on his cruel stepfather, Henry was only one in a long line of Starr family criminals who left their mark on the history of eastern Oklahoma.

2. *Daily Oklahoman*, November 15, 1914; *Hugo Husonian*, December 24, 1914; *Muskogee County Democrat*, April 1, 1915; "Henry Starr—The Cherokee Bad Boy," at https://www.legendsofamerica.com/we-henrystarr [accessed January 1, 2018]; Glenn Shirley, *Henry Starr: Last of the Real Badmen* (New York: David McKay, 1965), 1–2. Shirley's biography of Starr remains the best scholarly study of the outlaw. For Starr in fiction, see Richard Slotkin, *The Return of Henry Starr* (New York: Atheneum, 1988).

3. Shirley, *Henry Starr*, 112–31. See also "Last of the Romantic Outlaws," typescript, Barde Papers, OHS; *Tulsa Daily World*, August 8, 1915.

4. Henry Starr, *Thrilling Events: Life of Henry Starr by Himself* (College Station: Creative Publishing, 1982), 68.

5. Starr, *Thrilling Events*, 68.

6. *Lawton Constitution*, November 19, 1914.

7. "Last of the Romantic Outlaws," Barde Papers, OHS.

8. Shirley, *Henry Starr*, 166–67; *Daily Oklahoman*, April 18, 1915; *Tulsa Daily World*, April 18, 1915.

9. *Tulsa Daily World*, April 18, 1915.

10. *Tulsa Daily World*, April 11, 1915; *Tulsa Weekly Democrat*, April 15, 1915.

11. *Chandler News-Publicist*, April 16, 1915. See also Fourteenth Census (1920), Pittsburg County, Oklahoma, NA; *Daily Oklahoman*, April 10, 1915.

12. *Prague Record*, April 1, 1915; *Stroud Messenger*, April 2, 1915; *Tulsa Weekly Democrat*, April 15, 1915; *Tulsa Daily World*, August 4, 1915; *Muskogee Daily Phoenix*, August 4, 1915; *Santa Fe Magazine* 10 (January 1916): 80.

13. *Chandler News-Publicist*, August 6, 1915.

14. *Oklahoma Leader*, April 1, 1915.

15. *Stroud Messenger*, April 2, 1915.

16. *Daily Oklahoman*, August 4, 1915.

17. *Oklahoma Leader*, April 1, 1915.

18. Details and dialogue for the following description are from *Stroud Messenger*, April 2, 1915.

19. *Stroud Messenger*, April 2, 1915.

20. *Daily Oklahoman*, March 28, 1915.

21. Details and dialogue are from *Stroud Messenger*, April 2, 1915.

22. *Stroud Messenger*, April 2, 1915.

23. *Chandler News-Publicist*, August 6, 1915.

24. *Stroud Messenger*, April 2, 1915.

25. Details and dialogue from *Prague Record*, April 1, 1915. The *Daily Oklahoman*, March 28, 1915, has Davis saying, "You men stand still a few minutes and you will not be hurt. We are waiting because another bank is being robbed up the street."

26. *Stroud Messenger*, April 2, 1915.

27. *Tulsa Daily World*, March 28, 1915. Parks is also quoted in the *Davenport New Era* (Davenport, OK), April 1, 1915.

28. Details and dialogue are from *Stroud Messenger*, April 2, 1915.

29. As Starr was being carried to Dr. Evans's office, someone cried out, "Look out, they're coming back." Starr was dropped heavily to the sidewalk while everyone scurried for cover, only to learn that the rumor was false. *Stroud Messenger*, April 2, 1915.

30. *Stroud Messenger*, April 2, 1915.

31. *Bismarck* (ND) *Daily Tribune*, August 3, 1915; *Muskogee Daily Phoenix*, August 4, 2005.

32. *Oklahoma Leader*, April 1, 1915.

33. *Chandler News-Publicist*, April 2, 1915.

34. *Ardmore Daily Ardmoreite*, March 29, 1915.

35. *Daily Oklahoman*, June 12, 1915.

36. *Muskogee Daily Phoenix*, March 31, 1915.

37. *Oklahoma Leader*, April 1, 1915.

38. Robber's Cave, http://www.exploresouthernhistory.com/okrobberscave.html [accessed January 28, 2018].

39. *Muskogee Times-Democrat*, March 30, 1915; *Tulsa Daily World*, March 30, 1915.

40. *Oklahoma Leader*, April 1, 1915.

41. *Oklahoma Leader*, April 1, 1915.

42. *Daily Oklahoman*, March 30, 1915.

43. *Chandler News-Publicist*, April 2, 1915.

44. *Muskogee Daily Phoenix*, March 30, 1915.

45. Details and dialogue in the following description are from *Stroud Messenger*, April 2, 1915.

46. *Stroud Messenger*, April 2, 1915.

47. *Muskogee Times-Democrat*, March 29, 1915.

48. *Stroud Messenger*, April 2, 1915.

49. *Muskogee Daily Phoenix*, March 28, 1915.

50. *Muskogee Daily Phoenix*, April 2, 1915.

51. *Tulsa Daily World*, April 7, 1915.

52. *Pawnee News-Publicist*, April 9, 1915. Some of the outlaws were misidentified. The gang was said to be composed of not only Starr, Estes, Davis, and Johnson, but also Vann, Morgan, and Ward. Sawyer and Liege were not mentioned.

53. *Pawnee News-Publicist*, April 9, 1915.

54. *Prague Record*, April 1, 1915.

55. *Oklahoma Leader*, April 8, 1915; *Tulsa Daily World*, April 15, 1915. Curry enrolled at Central State Normal School in Edmond, or what became the University of Central Oklahoma, where he obtained both a bachelor of arts and a master's degree. He was drafted into the army during World War I. After the war he served as school principal and coach at Oilton, Talala, and Pittsburg, Oklahoma. He also taught at Shady Glenn School, Prairie View, Oak Grove, and Deer Creek, all near Stroud. During World War II, Curry worked at a war plant in Oakland, California. He and his wife, Lula Shaw, raised four sons, who all served in World War II. After the war Curry returned to the family farm southwest of Stroud. Although the census consistently has Curry's birth date as 1895, he was actually born in Stillwater on December 31, 1894. He died in Oklahoma City at the age of fifty-eight on October 7, 1952. He was buried at the Stroud Cemetery. Thirteenth, Fourteenth, Fifteenth, Sixteenth Census, Lincoln County, Oklahoma, NA; Headstone Applications for Military Veterans, 1925–1963, RG 92, NA; World War I Draft Registration Cards, 1917–1918; *Stroud Democrat*, October 9, 1952; Equala Brothers to author, February 3, 2018; M. Morgan to author, January 24, 25, 2018.

56. *Tulsa Daily World*, April 18, 1915; *Daily Oklahoman*, April 18, 1915. A graphophone was an improved version of the phonograph.

57. *Oklahoma Leader*, May 27, 1915.

58. *Tulsa Daily World*, July 18, 1915.

59. *Tulsa Daily World*, April 11, 1915.

60. *Oklahoma Leader*, April 15, 1915.

61. *Chandler News-Publicist*, July 23, 1915; *Daily Oklahoman*, July 12, 1915; *Tulsa Daily World*, July 18, 1915, quoting the *Cushing Independent*, n.d.

62. *Daily Oklahoman*, July 12, 1915.

63. *Tulsa Daily World*, May 7, 1915. In early May, Sheriff Woolley heard that two of the outlaws had been seen in Tulsa. Woolley feared that the two were meeting with other members of the gang to arrange another robbery.

64. *Muskogee Times-Democrat*, April 8, 1915; *Tulsa Daily World*, April 8, 1915.

65. *Daily Oklahoman*, April 11, 1915; *Ardmore Daily Ardmoreite*, April 11, 1915.

66. *Chandler News-Publicist*, April 16, 1915.

67. *Chandler News-Publicist*, July 16, August 13, 1915. See also, *Ardmore Daily Ardmoreite*, July 13, 1915; *Checotah Times*, July 23, 1915. Speakman died in Sapulpa at the age of fifty-nine on July 31, 1948. *Lawton Constitution*, August 16, 1948.

68. *Tulsa Daily World*, August 4, 1915; *Muskogee Daily Phoenix*, August 4, 1915; *Hugo Husonian*, August 5, 1915.

69. *Daily Oklahoman*, August 5, 1915.

70. *Chandler News-Publicist*, August 6, 1915.

71. *Oklahoma Leader*, August 5, 1915; *Chandler News-Publicist*, August 6, 1915; *Ardmore Daily Admoreite*, August 2, 4, 1915; *Muskogee County Democrat*, August 5, 1915.

72. *Chandler News-Publicist*, August 13, 1915.

73. Wells rode with Joe Davis, Al Spencer, and Frank Nash for a time. Spencer once showed Wells the hideout he used in the Osage Hills, a rock ledge surrounded by thick brush not far from the tiny community of Okesa. Michael Wallis, *Oil Man: The Story of Frank Phillips and the Birth of Phillips Petroleum* (New York: St. Martin's Press, 1995), 81.

74. *Tulsa Daily World*, August 11, 1915.

75. *Tulsa Daily World*, August 12, 13, 1915.

76. *Chandler News-Publicist*, August 20, 1915.

77. *Tulsa Daily World*, April 7, 1915.

78. *Tulsa Daily World*, April 7, 1915. See also *Muskogee Daily Phoenix*, April 7, 1915; *Oklahoma Leader*, April 8, 1915; *Tulsa Weekly Democrat*, April 8, 1915.

79. *Muskogee County Democrat*, May 27, 1915.

80. *Tulsa Daily World*, August 24, 1915; *Muskogee Daily Phoenix*, August 14, 1915.

81. *Muskogee Daily Phoenix*, August 25, 1915.

82. *Tulsa Daily World*, August 26, 1915.

83. *Tulsa Daily World*, September 9, 1915; *Muskogee Daily Phoenix*, September 9, 1915; *Enid Events*, September 9, 1915.

84. *Choctaw Herald*, September 9, 1915.

85. *Muskogee Daily Phoenix*, October 6, 1915.

86. *Tulsa Daily World*, October 19, 1915.

87. *Muskogee Daily Phoenix*, October 28, 1915. The train was en route to San Antonio, Texas, from Chicago, Illinois.

88. Details and dialogue in the following description are from *Eufaula Democrat*, November 5, 1915.

89. *Eufaula Democrat*, November 5, 1915.

90. *Muskogee Times-Democrat*, October 28, 1915.

91. *Muskogee Times-Democrat*, October 27, 1915; *Muskogee Daily Phoenix*, October 29, 1915.

92. *Muskogee Times-Democrat*, October 27, 1915.

93. *Eufaula Democrat*, October 29, 1915.

94. *Checotah Times*, October 29, 1915.

95. *Muskogee Daily Phoenix*, October 29, 1915.

96. *Muskogee Times-Democrat*, October 27, 1915.

97. *Oklahoma Leader*, November 11, 1915.

98. *Muskogee Daily Phoenix*, November 5, 1915.

99. *Muskogee Daily Phoenix*, November 15, 1915. Surprisingly, the weekly *Fort Gibson Gazette*, November 18, 1915, makes no mention of the robbery.

100. *Muskogee Daily Phoenix*, November 15, 1915.

101. *Fort Gibson New Era*, December 3, 1915.

102. *Muskogee Times-Democrat*, November 30, 1915.

103. O. C. Pierce, T. J. Butler, and Geo. F. Lewis to Inspector in Charge in Kansas City, April 7, 1917, Davis Inmate File, Leavenworth, RG 129, NAKC.

104. Pierce et al., to Inspector in Charge, April 7, 1917, Davis Inmate File, Leavenworth, RG 129, NAKC.

## 6. Boy Bandit in the Land of Endless Sunshine

Part of this chapter originally appeared as Thompson, "'That's Just What Kids Did Back Then': Joe Lynch Davis, the Oklahoma Gang, and the Robbery of the Golden State Limited," *Journal of Arizona History* 42 (Winter 2001): 409–28.

*Epigraph. United States of America vs. Joe Davis, otherwise called Joe L. Mayes, W. T. Bertholf, Jeff Spurlock and John Carroll,* Tucson District Court, District Court Records, RG 21, NA, Laguna Niguel, California (NALN); hereafter cited as *US vs. Joe Davis, et al. (1917).*

1. *Prescott Journal-Miner*, July 2, 1916. Copy courtesy of John O. Baxter. See also Baxter to author, February 10, 2005, author's files; Parole Report, May 3, 1917, Joe Davis Pardon File, Bureau of Prisons, RG 21, NA. The alias may have come from Samuel Houston Mayes, principal chief of the Cherokee Nation from 1895 to 1899. Mayes, the name of an Oklahoma county today, was also the name of an area of the Cooweescoowee Recording District in the Cherokee Nation north and east of Wagoner. See also John O. Baxter, "Ropers and Rangers: Cowboy Tournaments and Steer Roping Contests in Territorial Arizona," *Journal of Arizona History* 46 (Winter 2005): 315–46).

2. Jeff Spurlock (Prisoner No. 2855) Inmate File, McNeil Island Penitentiary, Federal Bureau of Prisons, RG 129, National Archives, Seattle, Washington (NAS). Born in Kansas City, Kansas, of German stock on January 8, 1891, Spurlock was two days younger than Joe Davis. Local oral history holds that Clay McGonigle had earlier rustled cattle near Paradise. Alden Hayes, *A Portal to Paradise* (Tucson: Arizona University Press, 1999), 350. For several years, the Henderson and McGonigle ranches had become havens for bandits and rustlers. Neither McGonigle nor Henderson appears in the 1910 Grant County, New Mexico, census as residing at Pratt or other neighboring communities. Nor do they appear in the 1910 Cochise County, Arizona, census. Large parts of the 1910 New Mexico census, however, are indecipherable.

3. Ervin Bond, *Douglas, Arizona: Its First Seventy-Five Years "and a Few Before"* (Douglas: N.p., 1975), 5.

4. W. T. Bertholf grand jury and trial testimony, *US vs. Joe Davis, et al. (1917)*. See also *Tucson Daily Citizen*, February 22, 1917.

5. Henry Levran grand jury and trial testimony, *US vs. Joe Davis, et al. (1917)*. The Golden State Limited was rumored to be carrying two hundred thousand dollars. Most of the money on the train had been taken off at Columbus, New Mexico, however, to pay the soldiers of General John J. Pershing's Punitive Expedition, who were pursuing Pancho Villa in Mexico. *Douglas Daily International*, September 7, 1916. The *Tombstone Daily Prospector*, September 7, 1916, reported that the safe Davis attempted to blow up contained between three and four hundred thousand dollars. For an overview of the chaotic situation in Mexico, see John P. Wilson, *Islands in the Desert: A History of the Uplands of Southeastern Arizona* (Albuquerque: University of New Mexico Press, 1995), 225–32. Trial testimony, especially that of Buck Bertholf, indicates that the robbery site was three miles from Apache. A reconnaissance of the area and an examination of various maps place the hill and the robbery site closer to five miles from Apache. The El Paso & Southwestern station was across the valley from Skeleton Canyon in the Peloncillo Mountains, where Lieutenant Charles B. Gatewood persuaded Geronimo to surrender in September 1886. In 1916 Apache Station consisted of a depot, stock pens, a small store, a schoolhouse, and a few other structures. Little remains today.

6. Edlin, *Cobb Cousins*, 147; Joe Lee Davis, birth certificate, author's files.

7. [Joe Davis] to Lula Davis, July 23, 1916, Government Exhibit A-22, *US vs. Joe Davis, et al. (1917)*. An edited version of the letter appeared in the *Tucson Daily Citizen*, February 23, 1917.

8. Ella Taylor testimony; [Joe Davis] to Lula Davis, August 30, 1916, Government Exhibit A-30; both in *US vs. Joe Davis, et al. (1917)*. Taylor was the Deming, New Mexico, telephone operator.

9. [Joe Davis] to Lula Davis, August 31, 1916, Government Exhibit A-25, *US vs. Joe Davis, et al. (1917)*. See also *Tucson Daily Citizen*, February 23, 1917.

10. Joe R. Davey and C. C. O'Neil grand jury testimony, *US vs. Joe Davis, et al. (1917)*. O'Neil was the manager of the Gadsden Hotel.

11. Bertholf and Mary K. Morgan trial testimony, *US vs. Joe Davis, et al. (1917)*.

12. *Douglas Daily International*, September 7, 1916; *Tombstone Daily Prospector*, September 7, 1916; Allen Lovett grand jury and trial testimony, *US vs. Joe Davis, et al. (1917)*. Bertholf and Carroll evidently boarded the Golden State Limited at Rodeo rather than Apache, since the latter was strictly a cattle shipping point. Ervin Bond, *Cochise County, Arizona, Past and Present* (Douglas: N.p., 1982), 37.

13. R. M. Collier grand jury testimony; William Hynes grand jury and trial testimony, *US vs. Joe Davis, et al. (1917)*. See also *Douglas Daily International*, September 7, 1916. See also *Tucson Daily Citizen*, February 21, 1917.

14. Hynes and Lovett trial testimony, *US vs. Joe Davis, et al. (1917)*. Although one woman was close to hysterics and a "Mexican girl" was in tears during the robbery, passengers—once they had hidden their valuables—were reported to have calmly sipped lemonade. *Douglas Daily International*, September 7, 1916.

15. *Yuma Morning Sun*, February 23, 1917.

16. John Graham and R. A. Baker grand jury testimony; Bertholf trial testimony (quote); *US vs. Joe Davis, et al. (1917)*.

17. Bertholf trial testimony, *US vs. Joe Davis, et al. (1917)*; *Tombstone Daily Prospector*, September 7, 1916.

18. Harry C. Wheeler grand jury testimony, *US vs. Joe Davis, et al. (1917)*; *Douglas Daily International*, September 8, 28, 1916; *Tucson Daily Citizen*, September 7, 1916. For Douglas at the time of the robbery, see Robert S. Jeffrey, "The History of Douglas, Arizona" (M.A. thesis, University of Arizona, 1951); Bond, *Douglas, Arizona*. Anxious to make an arrest in the case, Sheriff Wheeler was "wearing a week's crop of beard and tired from a long and eventful chase through the Chiricahua Mountains." *Douglas Daily Citizen*, February 21, 1917.

19. Bruce Short to author, May 5, 2005, quoting "The Tom Short Family' (1993; privately published for the Short Family); Tom Short to Era Keith, February 3, 1918, copy courtesy of Bruce Short, author's files.

20. Mary Webber and O. E. Patterson grand jury testimony, *US vs. Joe Davis, et al. (1917)*.

21. Bertholf grand jury testimony, *US vs. Joe Davis, et al. (1917)*; *Tucson Daily Citizen*, February 21, 1917.

22. Bertholf grand jury and trial testimony; Pink Henderson grand jury testimony; both in *US vs. Joe Davis, et al. (1917)*.

23. Hattie Henderson grand jury testimony, *US vs. Joe Davis, et al. (1917)*. See also Thirteenth Census (1910), Grant County, New Mexico, NA.

24. *Oklahoma Leader*, October 26, 1916; *Evening Kansas & Republican* (Newton, KS), October 19, 1916; *Arkansas City Daily Traveler*, October 23, 1916; *Wellington Daily News* (KS), October 19, 1916; *Railway Review*, October 21, 1916, 541. Only Hamilton's first name of "A." appears in both newspapers and census records. Thirteenth Census (1910), Cowley County, Kansas, NA.

25. Details and dialogue for the following description are from *Daily Oklahoman*, October 19, 1916. See also *Oklahoma Leader*, October 26, 1916.

26. *Tulsa Daily World*, October 19, 1916.

27. *Oklahoma Leader*, October 26, 1916.

28. *Tulsa Daily World*, October 24, 1916.

29. *Tulsa Daily World*, October 24, 1916; *Daily Oklahoman*, October 24, 1916.

30. *Daily Oklahoman*, October 20, 1916.

31. *Daily Oklahoman*, October 20, 1916; Thirteenth Census (1910), Harvey County, Kansas, RG 29, NA.

32. Henry F. Grammer (Prisoner No. 1680) Inmate File, Montana State Prison, Montana Historical Society, Helena, Montana. For Grammer's complicity in the murder of a prominent Osage named Henry Roan, see *Hale v. United States*, 25 F 2d 430 (8th Cir. 1928) at https://law.justia.com/cases/federal/appellate-courts/F2/25/430/1548629/ [accessed February 26, 2018].

33. Grann, *Killers of the Flower Moon*, 86–87. Grammer came to command a bootlegging empire in Osage and adjacent counties and held sway over an army of bandits. He was implicated in the Osage "Reign of Terror" in and around Fairfax and died in

an automobile accident west of the boomtown of Whizbang on June 14, 1923, from a broken neck when the automobile he was riding in overturned while being driven at a high speed. *Ponca City News*, June 16, 1923; Arthur Shoemaker, *The Road to Marble Halls: The Henry Grammer Saga* (2000), 36–43, 131–40. For a short sketch of Grammer's life, including photographs of the rodeo star, see http://theharryrowellfamily.org /unclehenrygrammer.htm [accessed February 26, 2018].

34. Pierce, Butler, and Lewis to Inspector in Charge, April 7, 1917, Davis Inmate File, Leavenworth, RG 129, NAKC; *Oklahoma Leader*, December 7, 1916.

35. *Daily Oklahoman*, November 28, 1916; *Norman Transcript*, November 30, 1916.

36. Claude Stanush and David Middleton, *The Newton Boys: Portrait of an Outlaw Gang by Willis and Joe Newton* (Austin, TX: State House Press, 1994), 148–50; G. R. Williamson, "Willis Newton's First Bank Hold-up-1916," at http://ezinearticles .com/?Willis-Newton-Interview—-1979&id=8366088 [accessed February 12, 2018].

37. *Daily Oklahoman*, December 12, 1916.

38. *Hugo Husonian*, February 1, 1917.

39. Thomas J. Butler trial testimony, *US vs. Joe Davis, et al. (1917)*; Davis Inmate File, Leavenworth, RG 129, NAKC. Fifty-six-year-old John Henderson was seriously injured in an automobile accident on September 16, 1916, while traveling from his ranch in New Mexico to the Henderson Ranch in Pima County, and he died a few days later at Mammoth, Arizona.

40. *Hartshorne Sun* (OK), November 9, 1916. See also Fourteenth Census (1920), McIntosh County, Oklahoma, NA.

41. *Norman Transcript*, November 28, 1916; *Tulsa Daily World*, November 28, 1916; *Purcell Register*, November 30, 1916; *Muskogee County Democrat*, November 24, 1916; *Oklahoma Leader*, November 30, 1916.

42. Details and dialogue for the following description are from *Purcell Register*, November 30, 1916.

43. *Purcell Register*, November 30, 1916.

44. Details and dialogue from *Muskogee County Democrat*, November 30, 1916, and the *Ardmore Daily Ardmoreite*, December 19, 1916.

45. *Muskogee County Democrat*, December 7, 1916. See also *Checotah Times*, December 1, 1916.

46. The quote is from both *Muskogee Times-Democrat*, December 5, 1916, and *Muskogee County Democrat*, December 7, 1916.

47. *Muskogee Times-Democrat*, December 5, 1916; *Hallett Herald* (OK), December 14, 1916; *Willow Times* (OK), December 15, 1916; *Daily Oklahoman*, December 6, 7, 1916.

48. *Oklahoma Leader*, December 7, 1916.

49. *Bisbee Daily Review*, December 12, 1916; *Tombstone Daily Prospector*, December 12, 1916; *Tucson Daily Citizen*, March 1, 1917.

50. *Chickasha Daily Express*, January 9, 1917.

51. *Daily Oklahoman*, January 5, 1917.

52. Bertholf testimony, *US vs. Joe Davis, et al. (1917)*.

53. *Prescott Weekly Journal-Miner*, March 21, 28, 1917; *Tombstone Epitaph*, March 25, 1917; *Nogales Border Vidette*, March 31, 1917; *Coconino Sun* (Flagstaff), March 30, 1917; Thomas A. Flynn to Joe Davis, November 30, 1916, Davis Inmate File, Leavenworth, RG 129, NAKC.

54. *Tombstone Epitaph*, March 4, 1917; *Copper Era and Morenci Leader* (Clifton), March 4, 1917; *Daily Oklahoman*, January 31, 1917; *Hugo Husonian*, February 1, 1917.

55. Howard K. Berry, *He Made It Safe to Murder: The Life of Moman Pruiett* (Oklahoma City: Oklahoma Heritage Foundation, 2001), 507.

56. *Tucson Daily Citizen*, February 20, 1917; *Daily Oklahoman*, February 20, 1917.

57. Larry O'Dell, "Pruiett, Moman H. (1872–1945)," at http://www.okhistory.org/publications /enc/entry.php?entry=PR022 [accessed January 21, 2018]. Novelist Jim Thompson used Pruiett as the model for many of the lawyers in his books. Walter Harrison proclaimed Pruiett "the greatest master of backwoods psychology, actor, hypocrite, fakir, lawyer, showman, and publicity expert the courts of Oklahoma ever will look upon." Walter Harrison, *Me and My Big Mouth* (Oklahoma City: Britton Printing, 1954).

58. Details and dialogue of the following description are from Berry, *Safe to Murder*, 507–8. The book by Moman Pruiett and Howard Berry, *Moman Pruiett: Criminal Lawyer* (Oklahoma City: Harlow, 1944), was built from text extracted from the much larger work by Berry, a young attorney who first met Pruiett in the 1930s and began collecting stories, newspaper accounts, and court records and interviewing individuals who had come to know Pruiett's "win at all costs" defense strategy and his legendary career.

59. Berry, *Safe to Murder*, 506–8. See also Pruiett and Berry, *Criminal Lawyer*, 434–47.

60. Pruiett and Berry, *Criminal Lawyer*, 438.

61. *Hugo Husonian*, February 22, 1917. See also *Tucson Daily Citizen*, February 19, 1917; *Daily Oklahoman*, February 20, 21, 22, 1917; *Muskogee Times-Democrat*, February 22. 1917.

62. Trial transcript, *US vs. Joe Davis, et al. (1917)*.

63. Bertholf trial reexamination, *US vs. Joe Davis, et al. (1917)*; *Tucson Daily Citizen*, February 20, 23, 26, 1917.

64. *Muskogee Times-Democrat*, February 23 (quote), 24, 1917.

65. Pruiett and Berry, *Criminal Lawyer*, 434. See also Index of witnesses and exhibits of plaintiffs, *US vs. Joe Davis, et al. (1917)*.

66. *Daily Oklahoman*, February 27, 1917. See also *Bisbee Daily Review*, March 1, 1917; *Daily Oklahoman*, March 2, 1917; *Nogales Border Vidette*, March 4, 1917; *Tombstone Epitaph*, March 4, 1917.

67. *Tucson Daily Citizen*, February 26, March 1, 1917; Judgement and Commitment, *US vs. Joe Davis, et al. (1917)*; Memorandum A, List of Charges, Joe Davis (Prisoner No. 2845) Inmate File, RG 129, NALN; Flynn parole report, Davis Inmate File, McNeil Island, RG 129, NAS.

68. Joe Lee Davis birth certificate, author's collection; Edlin, *Cobb Cousins*, 147.

### 7. Long Dark Years

*Epigraph.* Phenie Cobb, telegram to Joe Davis, May 27, 1923.

1. *Yuma Morning Sun*, March 4, 1917; *Tombstone Epitaph*, March 4, 1917.
2. Joe Davis and Jeff Spurlock Inmate Files, McNeil Island, RG 129, NAS. See also *McNeil Island Penitentiary Records of Prisoners Received, 1887–1951*, Records of the Bureau of Prisons, RG 129, NA.
3. Table No. 8, Crimes of Prisoners Received during Fiscal Year, *Report of the Warden of the United States Penitentiary, McNeil Island, Washington State* (Leavenworth, KS: US Penitentiary Press, 1917), 11.
4. "Farm Department," in *Report of the Warden of the United States Penitentiary, McNeil Island, Washington State*, 12–14.
5. Betty Rushing, interview with author, July 7, 2005.
6. Mrs. Jack Davis to Warden, March 10, 1917; Warden to Mrs. Jack Davis, March 17, 1917; both in Davis Inmate File, McNeil Island, RG 129, NAS. While at McNeil Island, Davis received two letters from Lula Davis, three from his father, and one from his brother Sam. Carrie Davis also wrote, and there was a letter from Sears Roebuck and Co.
7. O. C. Pierce, T. J. Butler, and Geo. F. Lewis to Inspector in Charge, April 7, 1917, Davis Inmate File, Leavenworth, RG 129, NAKC.
8. C. D. Carter to Warden, April 11, 1917; Warden to Carter, April 16, 1917; both in Davis Inmate File, McNeil Island, RG 129, NAS.
9. J. H. Johnston III, *Leavenworth Penitentiary: A History of America's Oldest Federal Prison* (Leavenworth, KS: J. H. Johnston III, 2005), 52–53.
10. Pete Earley, *The Hot House: Life inside Leavenworth Prison* (New York: Bantam Books, 1992), 30–31.
11. Trusty Prisoner's Agreement, March 1, 1918, in Davis Inmate File, Leavenworth, RG 129, NAKC.
12. Individual Daily Labor Record, Davis Inmate File, Leavenworth, RG 129, NAKC; Rushing interview, July 14, 2000. For Creekmore, see *Leavenworth Times*, August 29, 1917; *Los Angeles Herald*, July 18, 1917. The third month he was at Leavenworth, Joe received the sad news that his supportive uncle, Samuel Tate Davis, had died at Tahlequah on June 23, 1917, at the age of sixty-six.
13. *AHTA Weekly News*, June 5, 1913.
14. Exhibit No. 24, "Report of the Warden and Special Disbursing Agent," United States Penitentiary, Leavenworth, Kansas, in *Annual Report of the Attorney General of the United States* at https://books.google.com/books?id=DOhOLW_IPlwC&pg =PA535&lpg=PA535&dq=fire+at+leavenworth+prison+broom+shop&source=bl&ot s=OWQZ3J-gZm&sig=S8ZWH6KINlFs7cMoEGQo9Imohnc&hl=en&sa=X&ved= 0ahUKEwiqpMKrp7XZAhVSG6wKHSJjC4cQ6AEIPTAD#v=onepage&q=fire%20at %20leavenworth%20prison%20broom%20shop&f=false [accessed February 20, 2018].
15. Exhibit No. 24, "Report of the Warden and Special Disbursing Agent," United States Penitentiary, Leavenworth, Kansas. See also Johnston, *Leavenworth Penitentiary*, 161.

16. L. J. Fletcher, notation, n.d.; A. V. Anderson, notation, August 25, 1919; both in Davis Inmate File, Leavenworth, RG 129, NAKC. The cellblock was not completely rebuilt for another five years.

17. *United States Penitentiary, Leavenworth, Kansas: Annual Report, 1921* (Leavenworth: US Press of United States Penitentiary, 1921), 27–29.

18. Mary Davis to Warden, April 25, 28, 1917; Warden to Mary Davis, April 30, 1917; C. F. Dutton to Warden, April 28, 1917; all in Davis Inmate File, Leavenworth, RG 129, NAKC.

19. Joe Davis to A. V. Anderson, December 2, 1919; Davis to Thomas A. Flynn, n.d.; both in Davis Inmate File, Leavenworth, RG 129, NAKC.

20. Letters Received, Davis Inmate File, Leavenworth, RG 129, NAKC. In November 1921 Lula Cobb and a woman named Mrs. Ernest Ford were charged with assaulting a Mrs. George W. Casey at a garage in Ardmore. Mrs. Casey was "struck, beaten, scratched, stamped, kicked and otherwise mistreated." A handful of her hair was even pulled from her head. Mrs. Casey claimed that she miscarried the following day as a result. Moman Pruiett arrived on the scene to defend Lula. Pruiett called the altercation a "cat fight" and a "hen fight." Pruiett called to the stand four local physicians who had examined Casey, and they all testified that there was no evidence she had given birth prematurely or had undergone an abortion. Thanks to Pruiett, instead of being convicted of manslaughter Lula would only have to pay a one-hundred-dollar fine. *Ardmore Daily Ardmoreite*, November 8, 11, 18, 22, 1921; *Oklahoma Leader*, November 16, 1921; *State Sentinel*, November 24, 1921.

21. Letters Received, Davis Inmate File, Leavenworth, RG 129, NAKC.

22. [Joe Davis] to [Lula Cobb], n.d., back of hand-colored birthday card, author's possession.

23. P[henie] C. Cobb, telegram to Davis, May 26, 1923; Davis, telegram to Mr[s.] P. C. Cobb, May 26, 1923; Mrs. P. C. Cobb, telegram to Davis, May 27, 1923; all in Davis Inmate File, Leavenworth, RG 129, NAKC.

24. One of seven children, six boys and one girl, Nelson appears to have lived with his mother and father for much of his life. In 1920, a younger brother was also working for a laundry as a "wringer." Thirteenth Census (1910) and Fourteenth Census (1920), El Paso County, Colorado, NA. In 1922, when the two were living together at 21 South Limit Street, Nelson was employed as a "sanitary wet washer." *Colorado Springs City Directory* (1922) at https://www.ancestryheritagequest.com/interactive/2469/132478 18?pid=793770403&backurl=https://search.ancestryheritagequest.com/cgi-bin/sse .dll?_phsrc%3Dliw66%26_phstart%3 [accessed March 4, 2018].

25. Lula Davis to I. Holley, April 4, 1923, author's collection.

26. Details and dialogue in the following description are from *Gazette and Telegraph* (Colorado Springs), May 28, 1923.

27. See *McIntosh County Democrat*, May 31, 1923; *Checotah Times*, June 1, 1923.

28. Betty Rushing interview with author, November 26, 2000.

29. *Annual Report, 1921*, 81–82. Davis, miscellaneous information form, Davis Inmate File, Leavenworth, RG 129, NAKC.

30. *Annual Report, 1921*, 78–79.

31. *Annual Report, 1921*, 80–81.

32. Carter to Warden, April 24, 1917, Warden to Carter, April 26, 1917, both in Davis Inmate File, Leavenworth, RG 129, NAKC.

33. Joe Davis to James A. Finch, January 22, 1920; J. H. Mathers to Ferris, December 2, 1920; both in Davis Pardon File, Records of the Office of the Pardon Attorney, DOJ, RG 204, NA.

34. C. D. Carter to Attorney General, February 26, 1919, Davis Pardon File, RG 204, NA.

35. Jack Davis to Robert L. Owen, May 26, 1919, Davis Pardon File, RG 204, NA.

36. Owen to John A. Finch, May 29, 1919, Davis Pardon File, RG 204, NA.

37. C. C. Anderson to R. L. Owen, December 28, 1917, Davis Pardon File, RG 204, NA.

38. Bud Groom, affidavit, April 10, 1918; J. E. Wyand, affidavit, April 27, 1918; Victor M. Locke Jr. to President, December 27, 1917; R. D. Minter, affidavit, April 11, 1918; all in Davis Pardon File, RG 204, NA.

39. T. H. Hunter et al., to President, n.d., Davis Pardon File, RG 204, NA.

40. *Daily Oklahoman*, January 11, 1918. See also Johnston, *Leavenworth Penitentiary*, 155.

41. W. G. Miller to Woodrow Wilson, January 12, 1918; H. H. Ogden to President of the United States, January 14, 1918; G. T. Thompson to the President, January 10, 1918; N. M. Board and W. T. Wisdom to the President, January 9, 1918; Buck Garrett to Woodrow Wilson, February 4, 1919; all in Davis Pardon File, RG 204, NA.

42. Samuel M. Rutherford to Robert L. Owen, December 15, 1917, Davis Pardon File, RG 204, NA.

43. Robert L. Owen to Thomas W. Gregory, January 7, 1918; Gregory to Owen, January 10, 1918; both in Davis Pardon File, RG 204, NA.

44. Superintendent Special Service to Edward Butcher and Mr. Van Secord, February 28, 1918; E. H. Kitching et al., to Woodrow Wilson, n.d.; Pardon Attorney to Charles D. Carter, May 23, 1919; all in Davis Pardon File, RG 204, NA.

45. James H. Mathers to Warden, November 16, 1920; Warden to Mathers, November 11, 1920; Mathers to A. V. Anderson, November 22, 1920; all in Davis Inmate File, Leavenworth, RG 129, NAKC.

46. Rutherford Brett to A. V. Anderson, November 24, 1920; Warden to Brett, November 26, 1920; C. D. Carter to Anderson, November 24, 1920; Anderson to Carter, December 4, 1920; all in Davis Inmate File, Leavenworth, RG 129, NAKC.

47. Mathers to Ferris, December 2, 1920; Jack Davis to Carter, April 18, 1920; also Attorney General to Ferris, December 11, 1920; all in Davis Pardon File, RG 204, NA.

48. Jack Davis to Owen, January 30, 1921, Davis Pardon File, RG 204, NA.

49. G. E. Johnson to DOJ, February 23, 1923. See also L. R. Stacy to Owen, February 7, 1923, and H. Hesslaite to DOJ, February 25, 1923. All in Davis Pardon File, RG 204, NA.

50. Pardon Attorney to J. W. Harreld, March 7, 1922, Davis Pardon File, RG 204, NA.

51. Wm. H. Sawtelle to John A. Finch, April 3, 1929, Davis Pardon File, RG 204, NA.

52. E. L. Halsell to W. I. Biddle, January 8, 1922; Biddle to Halsell, January 9, 1922; both in Davis Pardon File, RG 204, NA.

53. *Beatrice Daily Sun*, May 29, 1923; *Dubuque Telegraph Herald*, September 15, 1918;

*McAlester News Capital*, May 29, 1923. See also Jeffery S. King, *Kill-Crazy Gang: The Crimes of the Lewis-Jones Gang* (Washington, DC: Frank Manley, 2012), 63–66, 114–48.

54. Joe Davis Reward Poster, June 22, 1921; Warden to Attorney General, June 23, 24, 1921; G. A. Swallow to Bill [William I. Biddle], June 24, 1921; Warden to George E. Lewis, June 22, 1921; all in Davis Inmate File, Leavenworth, RG 129, NAKC.

55. Warden to Attorney General, June 23, 1921; Davis Reward Poster, June 22, 1921; both in Davis Inmate File, Leavenworth, RG 129, NAKC.

56. Geo. E. Lewis to Biddle, July 30, 1921. See also Warden to various police chiefs and post office inspectors, June 23–25, 1921; all in Davis Inmate File, Leavenworth, RG 129, NAKC.

57. *Topeka State Journal*, June 24, 27, 1921.

58. G. A. Swallow to Bill [William I. Biddle], June 24, 1921, in Davis Inmate File, Leavenworth, RG 129, NAKC. For Sherrill's capture, see *Beatrice Daily Sun*, May 29, 1923; *McAlester News Capital*, May 29, 1923; *Dubuque Telegraph Herald*, September 15, 1918.

59. Johnston, *Leavenworth Penitentiary*, 173.

60. Biddle to E. L. Halsell, January 9, 1922, Davis Inmate File, Leavenworth, RG 129, NAKC.

61. *AHTA Weekly News*, June 5, 1913.

62. Joe Davis to Biddle, November 3, 1921; Warden to Mrs. Jack Davis, December 13, 1921; both in Davis Inmate File, Leavenworth, RG 129.

63. Mrs. Jack Davis to Biddle, January 22, [1922]; Mrs. Jack Davis to Warden, March 1, 1922; both in Davis Inmate File, Leavenworth, RG 129.

64. Mrs. Jack Davis to Warden, January 28, 1922, Davis Inmate File, Leavenworth, RG 129, NAKC.

65. Biddle to Mrs. Jack Davis, March 8, 1922, Davis Pardon File, RG 204, NA.

66. Mrs. Jack Davis to Biddle, December 3, 1922; Biddle to Mrs. Jack Davis, December 6, 1922; both in Davis Pardon File, RG 204, NA.

67. Application for Executive Clemency, February 21, 1923, Davis Inmate File, Leavenworth, RG 129, NA.

68. L. J. Fletcher to Robert L. Owen, March 14, 1923; Davis Pardon File, RG 204, NA.

69. Theodore Roosevelt to Attorney General, October 10, 1923; Attorney General to Roosevelt, October 16, 1923; both in Davis Pardon File, RG 204, NA.

70. Halsell to Owen, March 2, 1923; J. M. Chancellor to Owen, February 7, 1923; Owen to Harry M. Daugherty, March 20, 1923; all in Davis Pardon File, RG 204, NA.

71. Pardon attorney to Carter, December 24, 1924; Davis Pardon File, RG 204, NA.

72. Biddle to Jack Davis, January 8, 1926; Davis Pardon File, RG 204, NA.

73. Thomas A. Flynn to the President, September 26, 1926, Davis Pardon File, RG 204, NA.

74. *Pawhuska Daily Capital*, September 17, 1923, May 9, 1924. It was thought that Spencer was killed just south of Caney, Kansas.

75. "Birdman of Alcatraz," excerpt from the *Congressional Record*, Senate, July 25, 1962, in Jack Cope, *1300 Metropolitan Avenue: A History of the United States Penitentiary at Leavenworth, Kansas* (Leavenworth: N.p., n.d.), 48–56.

76. Johnston, *Leavenworth Penitentiary*, 158–59.

77. Ward S. Albro, *Always a Rebel: Ricardo Flores Magón and the Mexican Revolution* (Fort Worth: Texas Christian University 1992); John M. Hart, *Anarchism and the Mexican Working Class, 1860–1931* (Austin: University of Texas Press, 1978).

78. Johnston, *Leavenworth Penitentiary,* 165–66.

79. Henry Lesser, "Panzram Papers" at http://www-rohan.sdsu.edu/nas/streaming/dept/scuastaf/collections/Panzram/Panzram-Box01Folder03.pdf [accessed February 27, 2018].

   See also https://en.wikipedia.org/wiki/Carl_Panzram; *Carl Panzram: The Spirit of Hatred and Vengeance* at http://www.panzram.com; *Killer: A Journal of Murder* (1996) at http://www.imdb.com/title/tt0113542 [accessed February 27, 2018].

   The son of East Prussian immigrants, he was first confined in the Minnesota State Training School, where he was repeatedly beaten, tortured, and raped. Panzram enlisted in the US Army, but he was convicted of larceny and sentenced to the US Disciplinary Barracks at Fort Leavenworth. He suffered numerous beatings, tried to escape, set fire to one of the prison workshops, and was once chained to a fifty-pound metal ball. After his release Panzram went on to become a burglar, arsonist, rapist, and serial killer. An imposing man with great physical strength, he bragged of committing twenty-one murders and over one thousand sodomies of boys and men. In 1920 he burglarized the New Haven, Connecticut, home of former president William Howard Taft. In addition to jewelry and bonds taken from the Taft home, Panzram took a Colt .45 caliber handgun, with which he committed several murders.

80. Joe Davis, Application for Executive Clemency, September 15, 1928, Davis Pardon File, RG 204, NA. In his pending appearance before the board of parole, Davis listed his closest living relatives as his mother, father, and brother Sam living at Springer, a small town ten miles north of Ardmore; F. J. Clark, an uncle in Webbers Falls; Robert Davis, another uncle living in Tahlequah; Mrs. J. Reeves, his sister in Ardmore; and another sister, Mrs. R. B. Miller, in Tulsa. List of nearest living relatives, n.d., Davis Pardon File, RG 204, NA.

81. C. A. Bennett to T. B. White, December 16, 1928. See also C. A. Bennett to T. B. White, October 22, 1930; K. E. Conklin to T. B. White, October 22, 1930. All in Davis Pardon File, RG 204, NA.

82. Davis, Application for Executive Clemency, Davis Pardon File, RG 204, NA.

83. Joe Davis to William H. Sawtelle, September 16, 1928, Davis Pardon File, RG 204, NA.

84. The name of the village was changed in 1941 to Gene Autry, two years after the Hollywood cowboy singing star bought a ranch nearby.

85. Mrs. Jack Davis to Warden, April 20, 1930; N. R. Timmons to Mrs. Jack Davis, April 23, 1930; both in Davis Inmate File, RG 204, NA.

86. N. R. Timmons to Parole Board, April 13, 1926; Milton Perry Smith to M. W. Wade, July 13, 1925; both in Jeff Spurlock Inmate File (11657), RG 129, NAKC.

87. John M. Conlough, Joe Davis Conduct Report, December 10, 1928, Davis Pardon File, RG 204, NA.

88. Mrs. Jack Davis to Warden, n.d.; Mrs. Jack Davis to Warden, December 10, [1928],

Davis Pardon File, RG 204, NA.

89. Mrs. Jack Davis to Warden, October 1, 1928, Warden to Mrs. Jack Davis, October 3, 1928, Davis Pardon File, RG 204, NA.

90. Mrs. Jack Davis to Warden, October 5, 1928, Warden to Mrs. Jack Davis, October 9, 1928, both in Davis Pardon File, RG 204, NA.

91. Warden to Mrs. Jack Davis, October 9, 1928, and Joe Davis Conduct Report, December 10, 1928, both in Davis Pardon File, RG 204, NA.

92. T. B. White to James A. Finch, October 21, 1930, Davis Pardon File, RG 204, NA.

93. L. G. Disney to Director of Prisons, November 21, 1930, Davis Pardon File, RG 204, NA.

94. White to Director of the Bureau of Prisons, November 26, 1930, Davis Pardon File, RG 204, NA.

95. James A. Finch to White, January 3, 1931; Warden to Finch, January 8, 1931; both in Davis Pardon File, RG 204, NA.

96. Disney to White, January 10, 1931; Warden to Disney, January 13, 1931; Disney to White, January 14, 1931; White to Disney, January 14, 1931; all in Davis Pardon File, RG 204, NA.

97. [William DeWitt Mitchell] to President Hoover, January 30, 1931, Davis Pardon File, RG 204, NA.

98. Herbert Hoover, Conditional Commutation, January 13, 1931; AG to President, January 30, 1931; Finch to Warden, January 31, 1931; White to Finch, February 6, 1931; Receipt, February 3, 1931; Carl F. Carter to Chief of Police in Oklahoma City, June 13, 1931; all in Davis Pardon File, RG 204, NA. Unfortunately, Davis's diary did not survive.

## Epilogue

*Epigraph*. Miscellaneous newspaper clipping, Davis Inmate File, Leavenworth, RG 129, NAKC.

1. H. B. Baker to Warden, June 16, 1931; F. E. Carson to Warden, February 20, 1931; Carl F. Carter to Superintendent of Special Services (AT&SF), June 16, 1931; Carl F. Carter to Chief of Police, June 13, 1931; all in Davis Pardon File, RG 204, NA.

2. Goins and Goble, *Historical Atlas,* 2006.

3. Finch to Frank Loveland, February 10, 1931; Davis Pardon File, RG 204, NA.

4. Virginia Vann Perry, interview with author, November 24, 2000. See also Finch to Loveland, February 10, 1931, Davis Pardon File, RG 204, NA.

5. Carlile Vowell, "Eyewitness Account of the Porum Riot," *Twin Territories* 7 (2000): 4.

6. Virginia Vann Perry, interview with author, November 24, 2000.

7. Opal Bennefield Clark, *A Fool's Enterprise: The Life of Charles Page* (Sand Springs, OK: Dexter, 1988), 19–22.

8. James A. Harris to Finch, April 27, 1932; Chas. Price to AG, April 26, 1932; C. B. Stuart to AG, April 25, 1932; all in Davis Pardon File, RG 204, NA.

9. Betty Rushing interview with author, July 15, 2000.

10. Joe Davis to AG, March 6, 1933; Davis Pardon File, RG 204, NA.

11. Charles Price to AG, March 10, 1933; Harry T. Pratt to AG, March 10, 1933; both in Davis Pardon File, RG 204, NA.
12. Betty Rushing interview with author, July 15, 2000.
13. Betty Rushing interview with author, July 15, 2000.
14. Harley Cude, interview with author, November 26, 2000.
15. Betty Rushing, interview with author, July 10, 2005.
16. Fifteenth Census (1930), Carter County, Oklahoma, NA.
17. Robert Lee Davis, Joe's uncle, died at Tahlequah in September 1942 at the age of seventy-two.
18. Rushing to Jo Thompson, October 6, 1952, author's collection; Bessie Davis, Last Will and Testament, July 24, 1937, courtesy of R. L. Rushing. Joe Davis's older sister, Sue Jane Reeves, died on April 5, 1972, and his invalid brother, Jacy (Jack Davis Jr.), passed away at the age of sixty-nine on April 5, 1967. His World War I veteran brother, Sam Tate Davis, died at the age of eighty-one on March 5, 1975. Both Sam and Jacy were buried in the Davis plot in the Rose Hill Cemetery in Ardmore. Only Joe's favorite sister, Caroline Miller, outlived him, dying on July 23, 1986. Adams, *Family Tree*, 25. For Sam Tate Davis, see https://www.findagrave.com/memorial/19343369 [accessed March 2, 2018].
19. Joe to Carrie, March 17, 1959, courtesy of Betty Rushing.
20. Joe to Carrie, November 29, 1968, December 19, 1971, also November 29, 1960; letters courtesy of Betty Rushing.

# BIBLIOGRAPHY

### Archival Materials

Barde, Fred S., Papers. Oklahoma Historical Society, Research Center, Oklahoma City, Oklahoma.

Davis, Bessie. Last Will and Testament. R. L. Rushing, Mandill, Oklahoma.

Davis, Joe. Social Security Death Index No. 444-01-6747. Social Security Administration. http://search.ancestry.com/cgi-bin/sse.dll?rank=1&new=1&MSAV=/ (The Social Security Administration incorrectly lists his birth date as 1893 instead of 1891.)

Davis, Joe Lynch. World War I Draft Registration Cards. http://interactive.ancestry.com /6482/005152327_00343?pid=33935/.

Dawes Packets. Department of the Interior, RG 48, National Archives, Washington, DC.

Dawes Rolls. "Application for Enrollment of the Commission of the Five Civilized Tribes, 1898–1914." Dawes Commission, Dawes Packets (Cicero, Jack, Samuel, and Robert Davis), RG 75, National Archives, Washington, DC.

Eastern Cherokee Applications of the US Court of Claims. 1906–1909. Department of the Interior, RG 123, National Archives, Washington, DC.

*Final Rolls of Citizens and Freedmen of the Five Civilized Tribes in Indian Territory, with Supplements Dated September 25, 1914.* Microfilm T529, 3 rolls. Records of the Office of the Secretary of the Interior, RG 48, National Archives, Washington, DC.

Foreman, Grant, Papers. Oklahoma Historical Society, Oklahoma City, Oklahoma.

Grammer, Henry F. (Prisoner No. 1680). Inmate File, Montana State Prison, Montana Historical Society, Helena, Montana.

Guion Miller Enrollment Applications. 1908–1910. Bureau of Indian Affairs, RG 75, National Archives, Washington, DC.

*Indian Pioneer Papers.* Vols. 2, 11, 31, 67, 104, 107, 112. Western History Collections, University of Oklahoma, Norman, Oklahoma.

Jennings, Al, Papers. Oklahoma Historical Society, Oklahoma City, Oklahoma.

Leavenworth Penitentiary, Leavenworth, Kansas. Joe Lynch Davis Inmate Case File. Bureau of Prisons, Record Group 129, National Archives, Kansas City, Missouri (NAKC).

McNeil Island Penitentiary. Inmate Case Files, 1899–1920. Bureau of Prisons, Record Group 129, National Archives, Seattle, Washington (NAS).

McNeil Island Penitentiary. Prisoner Identification Photographs, 1875–1923. Bureau of Prisons, Record Group 129, National Archives, Seattle, Washington (NAS).

McNeil Island Penitentiary. Record of Prisoners Received, 1867–1939. Bureau of Prisons, Record Group 129, National Archives, Seattle, Washington (NAS).

McNeil Island Penitentiary. Record of Prisoners Received, 1887–1951. Bureau of Prisons, Record Group 129, National Archives, Washington, DC (NA).

Muskogee County Clerk's Office, Muskogee, Oklahoma. Muskogee County Records. Court Records, vols. 1–61; *Index to Civil Cases*, vols. 1–11; *Index to Judgement Records*, vol. 1; Probate Records; Superior Court Cases.

Oklahoma Court of Criminal Appeals Records. https://law.justice.com/cases/oklahoma court-of-appeals-criminal/.

Oklahoma Court of Criminal Appeals Records. *Davis vs. State.* May 14, 1912. In *Pacific Reporter*, 560–64. *Davis v. State*, 1912 OK CR 174, 123 P. 560, 7 Okl. Cr. 322, Case No. A-1183. Oklahoma State Courts Network. http://www/pscm/met/applications/oscn /deliverdocument.asp?id=16864&hits=/.

Oklahoma Court of Criminal Appeals Records. *Davis v. State*, 1913 OK CR 14, 128 P 1097, 8 Okl. Cr. 515, Case No. A-1223. Wyoming State Law Library. http://www.oscn.net /applications/oscn/DeliverDocument.asp?CiteID=17181/.

Oklahoma Court of Criminal Appeals Records. *Starr v. State*, 1912 OK CR 221, Case No. A-1355. Oklahoma State Courts Network. http://www.oscn.net/applications/oscn /DeliverDocument.asp?CiteId/.

Oklahoma Superior Court Records. Joe Lynch Davis Pardon Case File No. 47–780.

Oklahoma Superior Court Records. *Poney Starr, et al. vs. State of Oklahoma*, Ex. Rel. Att., May 12, 1911.

"Porum File." Oklahoma Historical Society, Oklahoma City, Oklahoma.

Porum 1916 City Directory. http://www.usgennet.org/usa,ok/county/muskogee/city directories/1916porumdirectory.htm.

Shirley, Glenn, Papers. Cowboy Hall of Fame. Oklahoma City, Oklahoma.

Short, Maggie, Papers. Western History Collections, University of Oklahoma, Norman, Oklahoma.

Sporteder, Don, Papers. Western History Collections, University of Oklahoma, Norman, Oklahoma.

Tilghman, William Matthew, and Zoe A. Tilgham, Papers. Western History Collections, University of Oklahoma, Norman, Oklahoma.

"Tom Short Family History." Manuscript, 1993. Courtesy of Bruce Short.

US District Courts, Eastern District of Oklahoma, Muskogee. Index to Criminal Proceedings; Index to Defendants. RG 21, National Archives, Fort Worth, Texas (NAFW).

US District Courts, Eastern District of Oklahoma, Muskogee. *United States of America vs. Joe Davis, et al.* Case No. 1786, Records of the District Courts of the United States, June Term, 1915. RG 21, National Archives, Fort Worth, Texas (NAFW).

US District Courts, Indian Territory, Central District, McAlester Division. Case Files, 1898–1905; Index to Criminal Proceedings, 1890–1907; Record of Jail Sentences, 1897–1907; Record of Sentences and Fines, 1890–1897. RG 21, National Archives, Fort Worth, Texas (NAFW).

US District Courts, Indian Territory, Northern and Western Districts, Muskogee. Criminal Bench Docket, 1889–1907. RG 21, National Archives, Fort Worth, Texas (NAFW).

US District Courts, Tucson District Court. Criminal Case File (C 435–437). District Court Records, RG 21, National Archives, Laguna Niguel, California (NALN).

US District Courts, Tucson District Court. *United States of America vs. Joe Davis, otherwise called Joe L. Mayes, W. T. Bertholf, Jeff Spurlock and John Carroll.* District Court Records, RG 21, National Archives, Laguna Niguel, California (NALN).

US Population Schedules. Sixth (1840), Seventh (1850), Seventh Slave Census (1850), Eighth (1860), Eighth Slave Census (1860), Ninth (1870), Tenth (1880), Twelfth (1900), Thirteenth (1910), Fourteenth (1920), Fifteenth (1930), Sixteenth (1940). Records of the Bureau of the Census, RG 29, National Archives, Washington, DC.

US Population Schedules. For Arkansas: Johnson County, 1900. For Colorado: El Paso County, 1910, 1920. For Georgia: Lumpkin County, 1840, 1850; Walker County, 1850, 1860, 1870, 1880. For Kansas: Leavenworth County, 1920, 1930. For Montana: Silver Bow County, 1930. For New Mexico: Catron County, 1940. For Oklahoma: Carter County, 1930, 1940; Choctaw County, 1920; McIntosh County, 1900, 1910, 1920; Muskogee County, 1900, 1910, 1920; Okmulgee County, 1920; Osage County, 1930; Tulsa County, 1940. For Tennessee: Robertson County, 1870. For Texas: Fannin County, 1870. Records of the Bureau of the Census, RG 29, National Archives, Washington, DC.

Works Progress Administration (WPA) Indian-Pioneer History Collection of Oral Interviews, Archives and Manuscripts Division, Oklahoma Historical Society, Oklahoma City, Oklahoma. Frank W. Jones.

## Books and Articles

Adams, David Wallace, and Crista DeLuzio, eds. *On the Borders of Love and Power: Families and Kinship in the Intercultural American Southwest.* Berkeley: University of California Press, 2012.

Adams, Mattie Lorraine. *Family Tree of Daniel and Rachel Davis.* Duluth, GA: Claxton Printing, 1973.

Adams, Ramon F. *Burs under the Saddle.* Norman: University of Oklahoma Press, 1964.

Agnew, Brad. *Fort Gibson: Terminal on the Trail of Tears.* Norman: University of Oklahoma Press, 1980.

Allen, F. M. "Henry Starr—Gentleman Outlaw." *True West* 18 (December 1956): 46–47.

Anderson, Dan, and Laurence Yadon. *100 Oklahoma Outlaws, Gangsters, and Lawmen, 1839–1939.* Gretna, LA: Pelican, 2017.

Babyak, Jolene. *Bird Man: The Many Faces of Robert Stroud.* Berkeley: Ariel Vamp Press, 1994.

Baird, W. David, and Danney Goble. *The Story of Oklahoma.* Norman: University of Oklahoma Press, 1994.

Baker, Jack D., and David Keith Hampton, eds. *Old Cherokee Families: Notes of Dr. Emmet Starr, Volume One: Letter Books A–F.* Oklahoma City: Baker, 1988.

Ball, Eve. "Clay McGonagill: A Colorful Cowboy." *Persimmon Hill* 9 (Winter 1979): 63–69.

Barron, Lynn Sr. "Henry Starr: Oklahoma Outlaw." *Quarterly of the National Outlaw Lawman Association* (April 1981): 9–17.

Baxter, John O. "Ropers and Rangers: Cowboy Tournaments and Steer Roping Contests in Territorial Arizona." *Journal of Arizona History* 46 (Winter 2005): 315–46.

Bell, Roger, and Jerry Hoffman. *Muskogee.* Charleston, SC: Arcadia, 2014.

Bend, Erwin. *Cochise County, Arizona: Past and Present.* Douglas: Privately published, 1975.

Benedict, John D. *Muskogee and Northeastern Oklahoma, Including the Counties of Muskogee, McIntosh, Wagoner, Cherokee, Sequoyah, Adair, Delaware, Mayes, Rogers, Washington, Nowata, Craig, and Ottawa.* 2 vols. Chicago: S. J. Clarke, 1922.

Berry, Howard K. *He Made It Safe to Murder: The Life of Moman Pruiett.* Oklahoma City: Oklahoma Heritage Association, 2001.

Black, J. Dickson. "The Day Starr Robbed Our Bank." *Frontier Times* 19 (Summer 1962): 20–21, 34.

Bond, Ervin. *Douglas, Arizona: Its Final Seventy-Five Years "and a Few Before."* Douglas: N.p., 1975.

Breihan. Carl W. "Bank Robber Extraordinary." *The West* (January 1968): 10–13, 63–66.

Breihan. Carl W. "Close the Banks—Starr's Coming." *Westerner* (June 1971): 36–39, 58, 60–61.

Breihan. Carl W. "Guns of the Badmen." *Western Round-Up* (August 1970): 38–45.

Breihan. Carl W. "Incredible Career of Henry Starr." *Oldtimes Wild West* (December 1977): 23–31.

Breihan, Carl W. "King of Bank Robbers." *Frontier Times* 29 (May 1964): 24–25, 42, 44, 56.

Brown, Loren N. "The Establishment of the Dawes Commission for Indian Territory." *Chronicles of Oklahoma* 18 (June 1940): 171–81.

Burton, Art. *Black, Red, and Deadly: Black and Indian Gunfighters of the Indian Territory, 1870–1907.* Austin: Eakin Press, 2001.

Burton, Art T. "Frontier Gunfights of the Muscogee Region." *Oklahombres* (Spring 1994): 25–27.

Butler, Ken. *More Oklahoma Renegades.* Gretna, LA: Pelican, 2007.

Butler, Ken. *Oklahoma Renegades: Their Deeds and Misdeeds.* Gretna, LA: Pelican, 1997.

Butler, Kenneth A. "Outlaw Joe Davis: Charged with Many Crimes, But Seldom Convicted." *Oklahombres* (Spring 1999): 7–10.

Butler, Kenneth A. "The Passing of the Oklahoma Outlaws." *Oklahombres* (Spring 1996): 26–31.

Campbell, O. B. *Tales They Told: A Collection of Anecdotes and Stories of the Early Days of Vinita, I.T. and the Cherokee Nation.* Oklahoma City: Metro Press, 1977.

Campbell, O. B. *Vinita, I.T.: The Story of a Frontier Town of the Cherokee Nation, 1871–1907.* Oklahoma City: Oklahoma, 1969.

Casey, Orban J. *And Justice for All: The Legal Profession in Oklahoma, 1821–1989.* Oklahoma City: Western Heritage Books, 1989.

Clark, Ira G. *Then Came the Railroads: The Century from Steam to Diesel in the Southwest.* Norman: University of Oklahoma Press, 1958.

Clark, Opal Bennefield. *A Fool's Enterprise: The Life of Charles Page.* Sand Springs, OK: Dexter, 1988.

Collings, Ellsworth, and Alma Miller England. *The 101 Ranch.* Norman: University of Oklahoma Press, 1937.

Conley, Robert. *The Cherokee Nation: A History.* Albuquerque: University of New Mexico Press, 2007.

Conley, Robert J. *The Saga of Henry Starr.* New York: Doubleday, 1989.

Cope, Jack. *1300 Metropolitan Avenue: A History of the United States Penitentiary at Leavenworth, Kansas.* Leavenworth: N.p., n.d.

Cordry, Dee. "Outlaws and Lawmen of the Cherokee Nation." http://209.35.75.65/cochran.htm.

Daniel, Donnie. *Murder in Muskogee.* Forsyth, GA: Privately published, 2016.

Davis, John B. "The Life and Work of Sequoyah." *Chronicles of Oklahoma* 8, no. 2 (June 1930): 149–50.

Decker, Frank G. "Letter from Los Angeles." *Chronicles of Oklahoma* 7, no. 4 (December 1929): 458–60.

DeNevi, Don. *Western Train Robberies.* Millbrae, CA: Celestial Arts, 1976.

Denson, Andrew. *Demanding the Cherokee Nation: Indian Autonomy and American Culture, 1830–1900.* Lincoln: University of Nebraska Press, 2004.

*Development of the Federal Prison System.* Washington, DC: US Bureau of Prisons, Federal Prison System, 1977.

Dewitz, Paul W. H. *Notable Men of Indian Territory at the Beginning of the Twentieth Century, 1904–1905.* Muskogee: Southwestern Historical Company, 1905.

Drago, Harry Sinclair. *Outlaws on Horseback: The History of the Organized Bands of Bank and Train Robbers Who Terrorized the Prairie Towns of Missouri, Kansas, Indian Territory, and Oklahoma for Half a Century.* Lincoln: University of Nebraska Press, 1964.

Drago, Harry Sinclair. *Road Agents and Train Robbers: Half a Century of Western Banditry.* New York: Dodd, Mead, 1973.

Duvall, Deborah L. *An Oral History of Tahlequah, the Cherokee Nation.* Charleston, SC: Arcadia, 2000.

Earley, Pete. *The Hot House: Life inside Leavenworth Prison.* New York: Bantam Books, 1992.

Edlin, Billie Louise Gilbert. *Cobb Cousins.* Odessa: N.p., n.d.

Ehle, John. *Trail of Tears: The Rise and Fall of the Cherokee Nation.* New York: Doubleday, 1988.

Ernst, Bob. "Prohibition Enforcement in Oklahoma." *Oklahombres* (Spring 1994): 1–3.

Faulk, Odie B. *Muskogee City and County.* Muskogee: Five Civilized Tribes Museum, 1982.

Feeling, Durgin, William Pulte, and Gregory Pulte. *Cherokee Narratives: A Linguistic Study.* Norman: University of Oklahoma Press, 2018.

Finger, John R. *Cherokee Americans: The Eastern Band of Cherokee in the 20th Century.* Knoxville: University of Tennessee Press, 1991.

Foreman, Carolyn Thomas. "Journal of a Tour in the Indian Territory." *Chronicles of Oklahoma* 10 (June 1931): 219–56.

Foreman, Carolyn Thomas. "Texanna." *Chronicles of Oklahoma* 31, no. 2 (Summer 1953): 179.

Foreman, Grant. *The Biography of an Oklahoma Town.* Norman: University of Oklahoma Press, 1943.

Foreman, Grant. "Early Trails through Oklahoma." *Chronicles of Oklahoma* 3 (June 1925): 99–119.

Foreman, Grant. *Muskogee and Eastern Oklahoma.* Muskogee: Star, n.d.

Foreman, Grant, ed. *A Traveler in Indian Territory: The Journal of Ethan Allen Hitchcock, late Major-General in the United States Army.* Cedar Rapids: Torch Press, 1930.

Gard, Wayne. *Frontier Justice.* Norman: University of Oklahoma Press, 1982.

Gibson, Wayne D. "More like Comets than Starrs: The Story of Tom Starr." *Oklahombres: The Journal of Lawman and Outlaw History of Oklahoma* 10, no. 1, 1–3.

Gideon, D. C. *Indian Territory: Descriptive Biographical and Genealogical, Including the Landed Estates, County Seats, etc., with a General History of the Territory.* New York: Lewis, 1904.

Gilliam, Frankie Sue. "Hell's Half Section: The Porum Range War Feud." *Twin Territories* (Muskogee) 7 (2000): 6, 16.

Glasscock, C. B. *Bandits and the Southern Pacific.* New York: Frederick A. Stokes, 1929.

Goins, Charles Robert, and Danney Goble. *Historical Atlas of Oklahoma.* Norman: University of Oklahoma Press, 2006.

Graebner, Norman Arthur. "History of Cattle Ranching in Eastern Oklahoma." *Chronicles of Oklahoma* 21 (September 1943): 300–311.

Grann, David. *Killers of the Flower Moon: The Osage Murders and the Birth of the FBI.* New York: Doubleday, 2017.

Graves, Richard S. *Oklahoma Outlaws: A Graphic History of the Early Days in Oklahoma: The Bandits Who Terrorized the First Settlers and the Marshals Who Fought Them to Extinction.* Oklahoma City: State Printing, 1915.

Green, Donald E., ed. *Rural Oklahoma.* Oklahoma City: Oklahoma Historical Society, 1977.

Hall, Ted Byron. *Oklahoma Indian Territory.* Fort Worth: American Reference, 1971.

Harris, Phil. *This Is Three Forks Country.* Muskogee: Hoffman Printing, 1963.

Harrison, Walter. *Me and My Big Mouth.* Oklahoma City: Britton Printing, 1954.

Haynes, Bailey C. *Bill Doolin, Outlaw O. T.* Norman: University of Oklahoma Press, 1968.

Henry, O. "Holding Up a Train." In *Complete Works of O. Henry,* 818–19. Garden City, NY: Garden City, 1937.

Herring, Edward. *Malice, Murder and Mayhem in the Oklahoma and Indian Territories.* N.p., 1999.

Higgins, Cindy. "Frontier Protective and Social Network: The Anti–Horse Thief Association in Kansas." *Journal of the West* 42, no. 4 (Fall 2003): 63–73.

Hinkle, Milt. "Henry Starr and the Rough Ones." *The West* (February 1968): 12–15, 62.

Hobsbawm, Eric. *Bandits.* New York: Penguin, 1985.

Hobsbawm, Eric. *Primitive Rebels: Studies in Archaic Forms of Social Movements in the 19th and 20th Centuries.* New York: Frederick A. Praeger, 1959.

Hofsommer, Donovan L. *Katy Northwest: The Story of a Branch Line Railroad.* Bloomington: Indiana University Press, 1999.

Hofsommer, Donovan L. *Railroads in Oklahoma.* Oklahoma City: Oklahoma Historical Society, 1977.

Hollon, W. Eugene. *Frontier Violence: Another Look.* New York: Oxford University Press, 1974.

Holzbauer, Dorothy E. "Robbers Cave." *True West* 48 (December 1961): 36–37, 68–69.

Hurst, Irvin. "Robbingest Robber." *Frontier Times* 10 (Spring 1960): 16–17, 52, 54.

*Index and Final Rolls of Citizens and Freedmen of the Cherokee Tribe in Indian Territory.* Washington, D. C.: Secretary of the Interior, 1907.

Jennings, Al. *Beating Back.* New York: D. Appleton and Co., 1914.

Johnston, J. H. III. *Leavenworth Penitentiary: A History of America's Oldest Federal Prison.* Leavenworth, KS: J. H. Johnston III, 2005.

Jones, W. F. *The Experiences of a Deputy U.S. Marshal of the Indian Territory.* Muskogee: Starr-Hill Association, 1937.

Jordan, Philip D. *Frontier Law and Order: Ten Essays.* Lincoln: University of Nebraska Press, 1970.

Kagey, J. N. "Jones Academy." *Chronicles of Oklahoma* 4, no. 1 (December 1926): 338–39.

Kazanjian, Howard, and Chris Enss. *Sam Sixkiller: Cherokee Frontier Lawman.* Guilford, CT: Globe Pequot Press, 2012.

Keen, Patrick. "The Anti-Horsethief Association in Old Oklahoma." *Oklahombres* (Summer 1997): 23–26.

Keve, Paul W. *The McNeil Century: The Life and Times of an Island Prison.* Chicago: Nelson-Hall, 1984.

Keve, Paul W. *Prisons and the American Conscience: A History of U.S. Federal Corrections.* Carbondale: Southern Illinois University Press, 1991.

King, Jeffery S. *Kill-Crazy Gang: The Crimes of the Lewis-Jones Gang.* Washington, DC: Frank Manley, 2012.

Koch, Mike. "The Life and Times of Henry Starr." *Oklahombres* 14 (Fall 2002): 1–8.

LaMaster, Kenneth M. *U.S. Penitentiary, Leavenworth.* Charleston, SC: Arcadia, 2008.

Lamb, Arthur H. *Tragedies of the Osage Hills*. Pawhuska, OK: Raymond Red Corn, n.d.

Linderman, Gerald. "Outlaw Henry Starr Relishes 'The Spice of Danger' and Indulged in It Right to the End." *Wild West* (June 1997): 28, 30, 75.

Litton, Gaston L. *History of Oklahoma at the Golden Anniversary of Statehood*. 4 vols. New York: Lewis Historical, 1957.

Mails, Thomas E. *The Cherokee People: The Story of the Cherokees from Earliest Origins to Contemporary Times*. Tulsa: Council Oak Books, 1992.

Mason, John. "The Miracle Bank Robber." *Real West* (February 1959): 34–37, 75–76, 79.

Masterson, V. V. *The Katy Railroad and the Last Frontier*. Norman: University of Oklahoma Press, 1952.

McKennon, C. H. *Iron Men: A Saga of the Deputy United States Marshals Who Rode the Indian Territory*. Garden City, New York: Doubleday, 1967.

McKennon, C. H. "The Last Marshal." *True West* 50 (April 1962): 6–10, 62–65.

McLoughlin, William G. *After the Trail of Tears: The Cherokees' Struggle for Sovereignty, 1839–1880*. Chapel Hill: University of North Carolina Press, 1993.

McLoughlin, William G. *Cherokee Renascence in the New Republic*. Princeton, NJ: Princeton University Press, 1992.

*Men of Affairs and Representative Institutions of Oklahoma, 1916*. Tulsa: World, 1916.

Meserve, John B. "The Mayes." *Chronicles of Oklahoma* 15 (March 1937): 58–62.

Mihesuah, Devon A. *Ned Christie: The Creation of an Outlaw and Cherokee Hero*. Norman: University of Oklahoma Press, 2018.

Miller, Floyd. *Bill Tilghman: Marshal of the Last Frontier*. Garden City, NY: Doubleday, 1968.

Modisett, Bill. "Clay McGonagill: The Wildest Cowboy, the Greatest Steer Roper." In *Cowboys Who Rode Proudly: Carrying Cattle . . . And the Methods of Handling Them*, compiled and edited by J. Evetts Haley. Midland, TX: Nita Steward Haley Memorial Library, 1992.

Moore, Gerald E. *Outlaw's End*. N.p., n.d. [recollections of Henry Wells].

Morgan, Anne Hodges, ed. *Oklahoma Image Materials Guide*. Oklahoma City: University Printing Services, 1981.

Morgan, R. D. *Bad Boys of the Cookson Hills*. Stillwater, OK: New Forums Press, 2002.

Morgan, R. D. *Bandit Kings of the Cookson Hills*. Stillwater, OK: New Forums Press, 2005.

Morgan, R. D. *Desperadoes: The Rise and Fall of the Poe-Hart Gang*. Stillwater, OK: New Forums Press, 2003.

Morris, Connie, ed. *Eufaula: A Pictorial History, 1833–1993*. Marceline, MO: Heritage House, 1993.

Moulton, Gary E. *John Ross: Cherokee Chief*. Athens: University of Georgia Press, 1978.

Mullins, Marilyn. "Bigheart Family Might Have Been Really Happy except for Oil Money." *West Texas Livestock Weekly*, January 14, 1971, 8–9.

Mullins, Marilyn. "Oil Riches Brought Only Tragedy to Many Members of Osage Tribe." *West Texas Livestock Weekly*, December 10, 1970, 8–9.

*Muskogee County Cemetery Index*. Cushing, OK: Thunder Publications, 2007.

*Muskogee City Directory, 1910.* http://interactive.ancestry.com/2469/15262417?pid=974
   185760&ba/.

*Muskogee City Directory, 1911.* Muskogee: Model, 1911.

*Muskogee City Directory, 1912.* http://interactive.ancestry.com/2469/13721252?pid=8367
   00684&ba/.

*Muskogee City Directory, 1913.* Muskogee: Muskogee County Gazeteer, 1913.

Myrick, David F. *Railroads of Arizona, Volume I, the Southern Roads.* San Diego: Howell-
   North Books, 1975.

Nash, Jay Robert. *Bloodletters and Badmen: An Encyclopedia of American Criminals.*
   New York: M. Evans, 1973.

Nix, Evett Dumas. *Oklahombres: Particularly the Bad Ones.* Lincoln: University of
   Nebraska Pres, 1929.

O'Neal, Bill. *Encyclopedia of Western Gun-Fighters.* Norman: University of Oklahoma
   Press, 1979.

Patterson, Richard. *Historical Atlas of the Outlaw West.* Boulder: Johnson, 1985.

Patterson, Richard. *The Train Robbery Era: An Encyclopedic History.* Boulder, CO: Pruett,
   1991.

Perdue, Theda. "The Conflict Within: The Cherokee Power Structure and Removal,
   1838–1839." *Georgia Historical Quarterly* 73 (Fall 1989): 467–91.

Perry, Virginia Vann. "Porum Range War." *Goingsnake Messenger* 19, no. 3 (2002): 66.

Perry, Virginia Vann. "Porum Range War." *Muskogee County Genealogical Society
   Quarterly* (2009): 1–2.

*Polk's Indian Territory Gazetteer, 1902–03.* Chicago: R. L. Polk, 1903.

Porter, Williard H. *Who's Who in Rodeo.* Oklahoma City: Powder River, 1982.

*Porum Primer.* Porum, OK: Porum Townsite, June 1904.

Prassel, Frank Richard. *The Great American Outlaw: A Legacy of Fact and Fiction.* Norman: University of Oklahoma Press, 1993.

Proctor, Charles. "Memories of Henry Starr." *True West* 163 (February 1981): 6.

*A Proud Past: A Pictorial History of Muskogee, Oklahoma.* Marceline, MO: D. Books, 1998.

Pruiett, Moman, and Howard Berry. *Moman Pruiett: Criminal Lawyer.* Oklahoma City:
   Harlow, 1945.

*R. L. Polk & Co's Oklahoma State Gazeteer, 1909–10.* Chicago, R. L. Polk, 1909.

Rand, Jerry. "Samuel Morton Rutherford." *Chronicles of Oklahoma* 30, no. 2 (1952): 149–59.

Rascoe, Burton. *Belle Starr: "The Bandit Queen."* New York: Random House, 1941.

Raymond, Jack. "Henry Starr—The Articulate Bandit." *Great West* (May 1968): 24–29, 46.

Reed, Julie L. *Serving the Nation: Cherokee Sovereignty and Social Welfare, 1800–1907.*
   Norman: University of Oklahoma Press, 2016.

*Report of the Warden of the United States Penitentiary, McNeil Island, Washington State.*
   Leavenworth, KS: US Penitentiary Press, 1917.

Robinson, Ella. "Indian International Fair." *Chronicles of Oklahoma* 17, no. 4 (December
   1939): 413–16.

Rosa, Joseph G. *The Gunfighter: Man or Myth?* Norman: University of Oklahoma Press,
   1969.

*Sand Springs, Oklahoma: A Community History, Volume I.* Sand Springs: Sand Springs
Cultural and Historical Museum Trust, 1994.

Savage, William W. Jr. "Rural Images, Rural Values and American Culture: A Comment."
In *Rural Oklahoma*, edited by Donald E. Green, 113–27. Oklahoma City: Oklahoma
Historical Society, 1977.

Scots, O. C. "Marvelous, Magnificent Muskogee." *Wild West* (January 1911): 5–7.

Shadburn, Don L. *Upon Our Ruins: A Study in Cherokee History and Genealogy.* Cummings, GA: Cottonpatch Press, 2012.

Shirk, George H. *Oklahoma Place Names.* Norman: University of Oklahoma Press, 1965.

Shirley, Glenn. *Belle Star and Her Times: The Literature, the Facts, and the Legends.*
Norman: University of Oklahoma Press, 1982.

Shirley, Glenn. *The Fourth Guardsman: James Franklin "Bud" Ledbetter (1852–1937).*
Austin: Eakin Press, 1997.

Shirley, Glenn. *Guardian of the Law: The Life and Times of William Matthew Tilghman
(1954–1924).* Austin: Eakin Press, 1988.

Shirley, Glenn. *Heck Thomas: Frontier Marshal.* Norman: University of Oklahoma Press,
1981.

Shirley, Glenn. *Henry Starr: Last of the Real Badmen.* New York: David McKay, 1965.

Shirley, Glenn. "He Out Robbed Them All." *True West* 12 (December 1955): 16–18, 32–35.

Shirley, Glenn. *Law West of Fort Smith: A History of Frontier Justice in the Indian Territory,
1834–1896.* New York: Henry Holt, 1957.

Shirley, Glenn. *Marauders of the Indian Nation: The Bill Cook Gang and Cherokee Bill.*
Stillwater, OK: Barbed Wire Press, 1994.

Shirley, Glenn. "No God West of Ft. Smith." *True West* 19 (February 1959): 14–17, 35–36.

Shirley, Glenn. *Shotgun for Hire.* Norman: University of Oklahoma Press, 1980.

Shirley, Glenn. *Six-Gun and Silver Star.* Albuquerque: University of New Mexico Press,
1955.

Shirley, Glenn. "Train Robbery That Fizzled." *Old West* 90 (Winter 1986): 12–17.

Shirley, Glenn. *West of Hell's Fringe: Crime, Criminals, and the Federal Peace Officers
in Oklahoma Territory, 1889–1907.* Norman: University of Oklahoma Press, 1978.

Shoemaker, Arthur. *The Road to Marble Halls: The Henry Grammer Saga.* N.p., 2002.

Skaggs, Jimmy M. *Ranch and Range in Oklahoma.* Oklahoma City: Oklahoma Historical
Society, 1978.

Slotkin, Richard. *Gunfighter Nation: The Myth of the Frontier in Twentieth Century
America.* Norman: University of Oklahoma Press, 1998.

Slotkin, Richard. *The Return of Henry Starr.* New York: Atheneum. 1988.

Smith, James F. *Cherokee Land Lottery, 1832.* Baltimore: Genealogical, 1969.

Smith, Robert Barr. *Oklahoma Scoundrels: History's Most Notorious Outlaws, Bandits
& Gangsters.* Charleston, SC: History Press, 1916.

Smith, Robert Barr. *Outlaw Tales of Oklahoma: True Stories of the Sooner State's Most
Infamous Crooks, Culprits, and Cutthroats.* Guilford, CT: Globe Pequot Press, 2008.

Smithers, Gregory D. *The Cherokee Diaspora: An Indigenous History of Migration, Resettlement, and Identity.* New Haven, CT: Yale University Press, 2015.

Speer, Bonnie Stahlman. *The Killing of Ned Christie*. Norman, OK: Reliance Press, 1990.

Stagner, Lloyd E. *Midland Valley: Rails for Coal, Cattle and Crude*. David City, NE: South Platte Press, 1996.

Starr, Emmet. *Old Cherokee Families*. Norman: University of Oklahoma Foundation, 1972.

*State of Oklahoma, Session Laws of 1916, Passed at the Extraordinary Session of the Fifth Legislature*. Guthrie, OK: Co-operative Publishing, 1916.

Stemlau, Rosa. *Sustaining the Cherokee Family: Kinship and the Allotment of an Indigenous Nation*. Chapel Hill: University of North Carolina Press, 2011.

Stout, Linda. "The Anti–Horse Thief Association: 'Protect the Innocent; Bring the Guilty to Justice.'" *Journal of the Muskogee Genealogical Association*, 56–57.

Sturm, Circe. *Blood Politics: Race, Culture, and Identity in the Cherokee Nation of Oklahoma*. Berkeley: University of California Press, 2002.

Thoburn, Joseph B. *A Standard History of Oklahoma*. 5 vols. Chicago: American Historical Society, 1916.

Thoburn, Joseph B., and Muriel H. Wright. *Oklahoma: A History of the State and Its People*. 4 vols. New York: Lewis Historical, 1929.

Thompson, Jerry. "'That's Just What Kids Did Back Then': Joe Lynch Davis, the Oklahoma Gang, and the Robbery of the Golden State Limited." *Journal of Arizona History* 42, no. 4 (Winter 2001): 409–28.

Tilghman, Zoe Agnes. *Marshal of the Last Frontier: Life and Services of William Matthew (Bill) Tilghman*. Glendale: Arthur H. Clark, 1964.

Tilghman, Zoe Agnes. *Outlaw Days: A True History of Early-Day Oklahoma Characters*. Oklahoma City: Harlow, 1926.

Truman, Phil. *Red Lands Outlaw: The Ballad of Henry Starr*. Denton, TX: Roots and Branches, 2012.

*United States Penitentiary, Leavenworth, Kansas: Annual Report for Fiscal Year Ending June 30, 1907*. Leavenworth: U.S. Penitentiary Press, 1907.

*United States Penitentiary, Leavenworth, Kansas: Annual Report for Fiscal Year Ending June 30, 1911*. Leavenworth: U.S. Penitentiary Press, 1911.

*United States Penitentiary, Leavenworth, Kansas: Annual Report for Fiscal Year Ending June 30, 1916*. Leavenworth: U.S. Penitentiary Press, 1916.

*United States Penitentiary, Leavenworth, Kansas: Annual Report, 1921*. Leavenworth: U.S. Press of United States Penitentiary, 1921.

Van Develder, Paul. *Savages and Scoundrels: The Untold Story of America's Road to Empire through Indian Territory*. New Haven, CT: Yale University Press, 2009.

Waits, Wally. "Carrie Starr, Heroine." http://www.muskogeehistorian.com/2007/10/carrie-starr-heroine.html.

Walker, Wayne T. "King of Bank Robbers." *True Frontier* (Fall 1975): 32–37, 52–53, 55–56.

Wallis, Michael. *Oil Man: The Story of Frank Phillips and the Birth of Phillips Petroleum*. New York: St. Martin's Press, 1988.

Wallis, Michael. *The Real West: The 101 Ranch and the Creation of the American West*. New York: St. Martin's Press, 1999.

Watkins, Thurman. *Cherokee Tragedy: The Story of the Ridge Family and the Decimation of a People*. New York: Macmillan, 1970.

Weadick, Guy. *Clay McGonagil: A Fast Man with a Rope*. Clarendon, TX: Clarendon Press, 1962.

Wellman, Paul I. *A Dynasty of Western Outlaws*. Garden City, NY: Doubleday, 1962.

West, C. W. "Dub." *Muskogee, Indian Territory: The Queen City of the Southwest*. Muskogee: Muskogee Publishing, 1972.

West, C. W. *Muskogee: From Statehood to Pearl Harbor*. Muskogee: Muskogee Publishing, 1976.

West, C. W. *Muskogee: The Biography of an Oklahoma Town*. Norman: University of Oklahoma Press, 1976.

West, C. W. *Outlaws and Peace Officers of Indian Territory*. Muskogee: Muskogee Publishing, 1987.

West, C. W. *Persons and Places in Indian Territory*. Muskogee: Muskogee Publishing, 1974.

Wilson, Donald Powell. *My Six Convicts: A Psychologist's Three Years in Fort Leavenworth*. New York: Rinehart, 1951.

Woodward, Grace Steele. *The Cherokee*. Norman: University of Oklahoma Press, 1993.

Woodworth, Steven F. *The Chickamauga Campaign*. Carbondale: Southern Illinois University Press, 2010.

Wright, George Bert. *Two Years' Experience as a Prisoner in the United States Penitentiary at Leavenworth, Kansas*. Leavenworth: Leavenworth Bag, 1915.

Yarbrough, Fay A. *Race and the Cherokee Nation: Sovereignty in the Nineteenth Century*. Philadelphia: University of Pennsylvania Press, 2008.

Young, M. J. Cobb. *Phenie's World*. West Conshohocken, PA.: Infinity, 2005.

## Interviews with the Author

Cude, Harley: May 16, 2000.

Perry, Virginia Vann: November 24, 25, 2000; January 10, 2001.

Rushing, Betty: numerous, 1999–2006.

Scoggin, Twauna: December 24, 2003.

Young, Mary Jane: July 14, 15, 2017.

## Correspondence with the Author

Ball, Larry: May 11, 2000.

Baxter, John: October 18, November 16, 2003.

Berg, Erik: May 1, 1901.

Brothers, Equala: February 3, 2018.

Butler, Ken: February 5, 13, 2005.

Calhoun, Nancy: February 1, 5, 9, 12, 14, 2018.

Daniel, Donnie: April 5, 7, 2017.

Diestel, Anne: July 31, 2000; February 2, 26, 2001.

Doty, Bill: March 9, 2000.

Drew, Patricia: March 9, 2017.

Fitzgerald, John: March 6, 7, 8, 2001.

Martin, Laura: February 13, 14, 23, 28; March 2, 2018.

Mooney, Wayne: December 13, 2004.

Moore, Sharon: December 15, 2004.

Morgan, M.: January 24, 25, 2018.

Morgan, R. D.: December 11, 14, 15, 2004; January 2, 2005; February 1, 2, 4, 5, 2005; May 21, 2005.

Perry, Virginia Van: November 24, 2000; January 10, March 13, April 3, 16, 2001.

Rives, Timothy: January 30, February 28, 2001.

Romanski, Fred: February 2, 2001.

Rushing, Betty: numerous, 1901–1906.

Rushing, R. L., August 13, 14, 17, 2018.

Scheffler, Victoria: June 13, 18; July 8, 13, 1905.

Short, Bruce: May 5, 2005.

Smolovik, Cindy C.: February 6, 2001.

Stege, Harry W.: August 23, 2001.

Tolbert, Sue: December 13, 2004.

Waits, Wally: December 4, 2004.

Young, Mary Jane: March 13, 2006.

## Newspapers

*Ada (OK) Evening News*
*Anti–Horse Thief Association (AHTA) Weekly News* (St. Paul, KS)
*Ardmore Daily Ardmoreite*
*Arkansas City Daily Traveler*
*Bartlesville (OK) Enterprise*
*Baxter Springs (KS) News*
*Beatrice (NE) Daily Sun*
*Bisbee (AZ) Daily Review*
*Bismarck (ND) Daily Tribune*
*Canadian Valley Record* (Canton, OK)
*Canute (OK) Leader*
*Carney (OK) Enterprise*
*Chandler (OK) News-Publicist*
*Checotah Enquirer*
*Checotah Times*
*Chickasha Daily Express*
*Choctaw Herald* (Hugo, OK)
*Claremore (OK) Messenger*
*Coconino Sun* (Flagstaff, AZ)
*Copper Era and Morenci Leader* (Clifton, AZ)
*Council Hill (OK) Eagle*
*Crowder City (OK) Guardian*

*Cushing (OK) Independent*
*Daily Oklahoman* (Oklahoma City)
*Davenport New Era*
*Davis (OK) News*
*Daylight* (Cuba, KS)
*Dewar (OK) Telegram*
*Douglas (AZ) Daily International*
*Dover (OK) News*
*Dubuque Telegraph Herald*
*Edmond (OK) Enterprise*
*El Reno (OK) American*
*Enid (OK) Events*
*Enid (OK) Wave-Democrat*
*Eufaula (OK) Indian Journal*
*Eufaula (OK) Republican*
*Evening Free Press* (Oklahoma City)
*Evening Kansas & Republican* (Newton, KS)
*Fort Gibson (OK) Gazette*
*Fort Gibson (OK) New Era*
*Foss (OK) Enterprise*
*Garfield County (OK) Press*
*Gatebo (OK) Gazette*
*Gazette and Telegraph* (Colorado Springs)
*Globe Democrat* (St. Louis)
*Goingsnake Messenger* (Colcord, OK)
*Guthrie Daily Star*
*Hallett (OK) Herald*
*Hartshorne (OK) Sun*
*Haskell (OK) News*
*Hennessey Clipper*
*Herald Democrat* (Leadville, CO)
*Hollis (OK) Post-Herald*
*Hugo (OK) Husonian*
*Indianola (OK) Herald*
*Inola (OK) Register*
*Kansas City Times*
*Lawton (OK) Constitution*
*Leavenworth Times*
*Liberal (KS) Democrat*
*Luther (OK) Register*
*McAlester Capital*
*McAlester News Capital*
*Muskogee County Democrat*

*Muskogee Daily Phoenix*
*Muskogee Democrat*
*Muskogee Evening News*
*Muskogee Phoenix*
*Muskogee Times-Democrat*
*Muskogee Tri-State Tribune*
*New State Tribune* (Muskogee)
*Nogales (AZ) Border Vidette*
*Norman Democrat-Topic*
*Norman Transcript*
*North Dakota Bismarck*
*Oklahoma Farmer and Laborer* (Sapulpa)
*Oklahoma Leader* (Guthrie)
*Oklahoma State Register* (Guthrie)
*Okmulgee (OK) Chieftain*
*Osage Journal* (Pawhuska)
*Pawhuska Daily Capital*
*Pawnee Courier Dispatch*
*Ponca City (OK) News*
*Porum Journal*
*Porum Press*
*Prague (OK) Record*
*Prescott (AZ) Journal-Miner*
*Prescott (AZ) Weekly Journal-Miner*
*Purcell (OK) Register*
*Railway Review*
*Ralston New Era*
*Rogers County Leader and Rogers County News*
*Santa Fe Magazine*
*Shawnee (OK) Daily Herald*
*Shawnee (OK) News*
*State Sentinel* (Stigler, OK)
*Stroud (OK) Messenger*
*Tacoma Times*
*Tahlequah Arrow*
*Talala Gazette*
*Taloga (OK) Times*
*Texhoma (OK) Argus*
*Tombstone (AZ) Daily Prospector*
*Tombstone (AZ) Epitaph*
*Topeka Daily State Journal*
*Topeka State Journal*
*Tucson Daily Citizen*

*Tulsa Daily World*
*Tulsa Democrat*
*Tulsa Weekly Democrat*
*Twin Territories* (Muskogee)
*Wagoner County (OK) Courier*
*Webbers Falls (OK) Record*
*Weekly Examiner* (Bartlesville, OK)
*Weleetka (OK) American*
*Wellington (KS) Daily News*
*Willow (OK) Times*
*Yuma (AZ) Morning Sun*

✦ ✧

# INDEX

Page numbers in *italic* refer to illustrations.

brothers and, 149–50; Tulsa home, 168, 169, 182
Starr, Joe, 76
Starr, Lucinda (Lucy). See Davis, Lucinda Starr
Starr, Nina Lois, 30, 48, 80, 85, 87, 89, 270n88
Starr, Sally, 111
Starr, Sam (1859–86), 23, 283n1
Starr, Samuel Saguila (Pony), 30, 31, 48–49, 61, 65, 69–70, 72, 77; arrests, 60; at Bob Davis trial, 92; cattle rustling, 54, 56, 60–63, 89–90, 91, 101; daughter Nina's birth, 270n88; Dobson and, 73; envisioned movie actor, 126; Henry Starr relationship, 283n1; Hugo, Oklahoma, 112; at Jack Davis murder trial, 118, 120; at Joe Davis trial, 104; May 29, 1911, shootout and aftermath, 72–87, 114; Muscogee job, 98; nonfatal shooting of, 118; parole, 124–25; ranch house, 79; Robbers Cave, 178; Spess brothers and, 150; steer roping, 73, 90, 102; threat from "Black Hand," 94; trials, 61–63, 89–90, 101–2
Starr, Theodore Roosevelt, 168, 183
Starr, Thomas (Tom), 30, 283n1
Starr, Thomas, Jr., 30
Starr, Willie Davis, 264n50
Starr ranch shootout (May 29, 1911) and aftermath, 72–86, 97, 105–7, 114
Stegall, Oscar, 63, 93
Stephens, Russell, 174
Stout, George, 271n113
Stroud, Oklahoma, 15; bank robberies, 169–85
Stroud, Robert Franklin, 243–44
Stuart, C. B., 253
Sugar Mountains, 192
Swallow, G. A., 238–39

Tahlequah, Oklahoma, 61, 84; bank casing, 187; Bob Davis, 150; Joe Davis,

29; John M. Davis, 21; Sam Davis, 124; Worthman arrest, 135
Tate, Julia Ann. See Davis, Julia Ann Tate
Tate, Saphronia. See Davis, Jane Saphronia Tate
Tatum, Dave J., 104, 132–33, 136, 144, 191
Taulk, Flin (Rusty), 202
Taylor, T. D., 157
Terlton, Oklahoma: bank robbery, 141, 147, 148, 209–10
Terrell, Charles, 100, 271n106, 271n113
Texanna, Oklahoma, 13–14, 23–24, 108, 158; AHTA, 59, 86; Cobb family, 51, 52, 54, 102; Davis family, 23, 24, 28, 33, 51, 54, 108, 112, 120; Jesse Maxwell, 109, 110, 111; May 29, 1911, shootout and aftermath, 86
Texas: Cobb family, 51, 196, 198; Spurlock, 212
Thomas, Ed, 127, 131, 189
Thompson, Charles, 21
Thompson, Claude, 81, 108, 110, 112–13, 114, 115
Thompson, G. T., 234
Thompson, Jerry Winfield, Jr., 5–6, 11–12
Thompson, Jim, 291n57
Thompson, Joe ("Jo") Lee Davis, 5, 6–7, 10, 11–12, 15, 228, 229, 253; baby picture, 227; father's cards to, 231, 231; father's death and, 257
Thornberry, Tuck, 35, 36, 37, 41, 49
Tilghman, Bill, 146, 181, 183–84, 186, 281–82n142
Tilley, H. T., 81
Topeka, 238–39
train robberies, 9, 15, 32, 38; Arizona, 195–96, 198–99, 200, 201–3, 208, 288n5; "Hominy case" (abandoned attempt, 1913), 139–40; Kansas Southern (1912), 129; Katy Limited (1912) ("Wirth robbery"), 127–39, 148–66, 210; Katy Limited (1915), 188–91; Katy Limited (1923), 243; Santa Fe (1916), 204–5, 208

9 780806 164366